GREEK HISTORY

GREEK HISTORY

Advisory Editor:

W. R. CONNOR

CHAIRMAN, DEPARTMENT OF CLASSICS
PROFESSOR OF GREEK
PRINCETON UNIVERSITY

AN ECONOMIC HISTORY OF ATHENS UNDER ROMAN DOMINATION

By JOHN DAY

ARNO PRESS

A New York Times Company

New York / 1973

Library of Congress Cataloging in Publication Data

Day, John, 1902-
    An economic history of Athens under Roman domination.

    (Greek history)
    Bibliography: p.
    1. Athens--Economic conditions. I. Title.
HC37.D3 1973   330.9'38'509   72-7887
ISBN 0-405-04781-9

AN ECONOMIC
HISTORY OF ATHENS
UNDER ROMAN
DOMINATION

AN ECONOMIC HISTORY OF ATHENS UNDER ROMAN DOMINATION

By JOHN DAY

ASSISTANT PROFESSOR OF
GREEK AND LATIN IN BARNARD COLLEGE
COLUMBIA UNIVERSITY

1942

COLUMBIA UNIVERSITY PRESS

NEW YORK

TO

WILLIAM LINN WESTERMANN

AND

MICHAEL IVANOVICH ROSTOVTZEFF

PREFACE

THE SUGGESTION which led to the writing of this book came from Professor Michael I. Rostovtzeff's *Social and Economic History of the Roman Empire*, where the need for an economic history of Greece during the imperial period was pointed out. A beginning of the work was made possible by the generous award, and subsequent renewal, of a Sterling Fellowship by Yale University. The pressure of other duties forced me to lay aside the work for some years, and when I took it up again it seemed best that the scope be restricted to a treatment of the economic history of Athens. The suspension of the work was, however, not without compensation, for I have been able to include the valuable material which has been discovered in the meantime in the Agora at Athens.

The book is dedicated to two eminent scholars, each of whom it has been my privilege to call teacher. Without their active aid, encouragement, and inspiration it could not have been undertaken or completed. Professor William L. Westermann has helped me not only with suggestions, but also on various occasions with invaluable advice, for which I am deeply grateful. To Professor Rostovtzeff I am greatly indebted for his kindness in making valuable suggestions at various times during the preparation of the manuscript and in allowing me to consult in page proof his *Social and Economic History of the Hellenistic World*, shortly to appear, published by the Oxford University Press. Naturally, the proof to which I refer in my text did not represent exactly the final form of the book. I should also like to record my gratitude to Professor W. B. Dinsmoor for his kindness in turning over to me, before his book was published, the dates of the Athenian archons that he had arrived at in his *The Athenian Archon List in the Light of Recent Discoveries* and for the interest which he has shown in my work. My indebtedness to my predecessors in the field with which this book deals—of which no one is more conscious than I—has, I hope, been adequately acknowledged in the notes which accompany the text. However, I regret that I have been unable to use the Russian work of S. Shebeleff, 'Αχαϊκά (a history of Athens from 229 to 31 B.C.; St. Petersburg, 1898).

I would also make grateful acknowledgement to Dean Virginia C. Gildersleeve, of Barnard College, for her generosity in providing, during two years, some relief from unavoidably heavy academic duties and for the interest she has shown in my work. To my colleague, Professor Gertrude M. Hirst, of Barnard College, I am deeply grateful for encouragement at times when it meant much. I should like also to remember Professor David M. Robinson, of The Johns Hopkins University, for whose continued interest his former students are happy to express thanks. My former student, Miss Isabelle R. Kelly (now Mrs. Anton Raubitschek), verified, with her customary efficiency, a number of my citations. Thanks are due my wife for help in ways too numerous to mention.

To the authorities of the Columbia University Press I would express my gratitude for their generous support, without which this book could not have been published. To the staff of the Press I would express my thanks for their most efficient aid throughout the entire process of publication.

The passages quoted from the Loeb Classical Library are reprinted by permission of the President and Fellows of Harvard College, for whose courtesy I express sincere thanks. I am also grateful to the Johns Hopkins Press for permission to quote from Frank's *An Economic Survey of Ancient Rome*, to the Macmillan Company for permission to quote from Ferguson's *Hellenistic Athens* and Frazer's *Pausanias's Description of Greece*, and to The Clarendon Press, Oxford, for permission to reprint the translations from FitzGerald's *Letters of Synesius*.

Finally, certain associations called to mind by the title of the book have detracted from the otherwise pleasant task of writing. May the tribulations of the Athenians and their fellow Greeks be of short duration!

JOHN DAY

New York
November 15, 1941

ABBREVIATIONS

ΑΔ: Ἀρχαιολογικὸν Δελτίον.

ΑΕ: Ἀρχαιολογικὴ Ἐφημερίς.

AJA: *American Journal of Archaeology.*

AJP: *American Journal of Philology.*

AM: *Mitteilungen des deutschen archäologischen Instituts, athenische Abteilung.*

BCH: *Bulletin de correspondance hellénique.*

BSA: *Annual of the British School at Athens.*

CAH: *Cambridge Ancient History.*

CIG: *Corpus inscriptionum Graecarum.*

CIL: *Corpus inscriptionum Latinarum.*

CRAI: *Comptes-rendus de séances de l'Académie des Inscriptions et Beles-Lettres.*

Daremberg-Saglio: C. Daremberg, E. Saglio, and others, *Dictionnaire des antiquités grecques et romaines.*

FDD: *Fouilles de Delphes.*

FHG: C. Müller, *Fragmenta historicorum Graecarum* (Paris, 1841–73).

Hesperia: Hesperia; Journal of the American School of Classical Studies at Athens.

IDD: *Inscriptions de Délos.*

IG: *Inscriptiones Graecae.*

IGRR: *Inscriptiones Graecae ad res Romanas pertinentes*, edited by R. Cagnat and others (Paris, 1906–).

ILS: H. Dessau, *Inscriptiones Latinae selectae* (Berlin, 1892–1916).

JAOS: *Journal of the American Oriental Society.*

JDAI: *Jahrbuch des deutschen archäologischen Instituts.*

JDS: *Journal des savants.*

JHS: *Journal of Hellenic Studies.*

JOAI: *Jahreshefte des österreichischen archäologischen Instituts.*

JRS: *Journal of Roman Studies.*

NPA: J. Sundwall, *Nachträge zur Prosopographia Attica* (Helsingfors, 1909–10; Öfversigt af Finska Vetenskaps-Societetens Förhandlingar, LII, Afd. B., No. 1).

OGIS: W. Dittenberger, *Orientis Graeci inscriptiones selectae* (Leipzig, 1903–5).

PA: J. Kirchner, *Prosopographia Attica* (Berlin, 1901–3).

P. Cairo Zen.: C. C. Edgar, *Zenon Papyri* (Cairo, 1925–28; Catalogue général des antiquités égyptiennes du Musée du Caire).

P. Grenf. I.: B. P. Grenfell, *An Alexandrian Erotic Fragment and Other Greek Papyri Chiefly Ptolemaic* (Oxford, 1896).

PIR: *Prosopographia Imperii Romani* (First edition, by E. Klebs and others, Berlin, 1897–98; second edition, by E. Groag and A. Stein, Berlin, 1933–).

P. Lond.: F. G. Kenyon and H. I. Bell, *Greek Papyri in the British Museum* (London, 1893–1917).

P. Mich. Zen.: C. C. Edgar, *Zenon Papyri in the University of Michigan Collection* (Ann Arbor, 1931).

P. Ox.: B. P. Grenfell, A. S. Hunt, and H. I. Bell, *The Oxyrhynchus Papyri* (London, 1898–1927).

P. Strassburg: F. Preisigke, *Griechische Papyrus der kaiserlichen Universitäts- und Landesbibliothek zu Strassburg* (Leipzig, 1912).

QDAP: *Quarterly of the Department of Antiquities in Palestine.*

RA: *Revue archéologique.*

RE: *Paulys Real-Encylopädie der classischen Altertumswissenschaft,* edited by G. Wissowa and others.

REA: *Revue des études anciennes.*

REG: *Revue des études grecques.*

RM: *Mitteilungen des deutschen archäologischen Instituts, römische Abteilung.*

SEG: *Supplementum epigraphicum Graecum.*

SIG: W. Dittenberger, *Sylloge inscriptionum Graecarum* (Third edition by F. Hiller von Gaertringen, Leipzig, 1915–24).

ZFN: *Zeitschrift für Numismatik.*

CONTENTS

CHAPTER I

ATHENS BEFORE THE ROMANS:

THIRD CENTURY B.C.

I N THE fifth century B.C. Athens had attained to a position of
great power and prestige. It was the center of a maritime empire of importance and the leading sea power of the Mediterranean world. With political power and prestige came a very
high degree of prosperity. The seaport of Athens, the Piraeus, was,
as an ancient writer aptly asserted,[1] the common market of all
Greece. In the Deigma of the port town goods from all parts of the
eastern Mediterranean, as well as from the West, were placed on
display.[2] Athens was, as it were, the most important clearinghouse
of the Mediterranean world. But the hardships of the long-drawn-
out Peloponnesian War and the loss of empire brought about by
the adverse outcome of that war contributed to bringing this period
of great prosperity to an end. With the formation of the Second
Athenian Confederacy in the early part of the fourth century B.C.
the economic condition of Athens improved considerably, but not
to the extent of attaining the prosperity of the fifth century.[3]
While the maritime trade of the city throve exceedingly in the first
part of the century, unfavorable factors had crept into the situation. Athenian commerce in the West failed to regain its former
volume in the face of competition with the growing power of
Syracuse.[4] At the same time important markets for industrial
products were lost. From the middle of the sixth century B.C. to
the end of the Peloponnesian War Athens had held a practical

[1] Sopater, *De div. quaest.* xlvii, 3–4, in C. Walz, *Rhetores Graecae*, VIII (Stuttgart and Tübingen, 1835).
[2] Ps.–Xen., *De re publ. Athen.* ii, 7.
[3] M. Cary, in CAH, VI, 70–72; Beloch, *Griechische Geschichte*, III, i, 313–50.
[4] M. Cary, in CAH, VI, 71.

monopoly in the field of the finer ceramic wares. Athenian black-and red-figure wares were exported in large amounts to southern Italy and Etruria, to South Russia, Palestine, Phoenicia, Syria, and much of the Persian Empire.[5] But by the end of the fifth century B.C., and increasingly during the fourth, local schools of pottery were established (possibly in part by expatriated Athenian potters) in southern Italy, in Etruria, and in the Crimea at Panticapaeum (modern Kertch), with the result that the Athenian ceramic industry no longer possessed the extensive outlets for its products that it had formerly enjoyed, and markets in the Persian Empire, in Syria, and in the East were lost.[6] Moreover, painted vases lost their vogue. It is possible—although uncertain—that the Athenian metalworker, also, lost his foreign markets.[7]

The loss of foreign markets was a matter of great importance to Athenians, for they had great need of imported products, such as grain and other foodstuffs, and payment for these products had to be made by means of exported products. The situation was, therefore, not at all favorable at the middle of the fourth century B.C.; it was, however, temporarily ameliorated by the opening up of new markets. Greece had for a long time enjoyed some trade with the Orient, but in the latter part of the fourth century Alexander's conquests and the ensuing colonization of the Orient by the Greeks provided new outlets for Greek products.[8] Trade was benefited by

[5] Pfuhl, *Malerei*, I, 232–33. For the most recent literature on the subject, see Rostovtzeff's *Social and Economic History of the Hellenistic World*, which, through the generosity of the author, I have been able to consult in page proof.

[6] Pfuhl, *Malerei*, II, 707. See the most recent literature in Rostovtzeff's *Social and Economic History of the Hellenistic World*.

[7] Objects of art made of gold and silver were exported to South Russia throughout the fourth century B.C., but it is generally assumed that the workshops in which they were produced were located in Ionia. See Minns, *Scythians and Greeks*, pp. 386–410, cf. pp. 283–87; Rostovtzeff, *Iranians and Greeks*, pp. 69, 74, cf. pp. 3, 53. However, the precious metals were widely employed in works of art at Athens in the latter part of the fifth century B.C. (cf. D. B. Thompson, in *Hesperia*, VIII [1939], 313–15; Courby, *Vases grecs*, p. 158), and it would be occasion for surprise if the works of Athenian artists did not, at that time, find outlets in foreign markets.

[8] M. Rostovtzeff, "The Hellenistic World and Its Economic Development," *American Historical Review*, XLI (1936), 231–52, especially 233–36; Beloch, *Griechische Geschichte*, IV, i, 270–328; U. Wilcken, *Alexander the Great*, pp. 283–98, and "Alexander der Grosse und die hellenistische Wirtschaft," in Schmoller's *Jahrbuch für Gesetzgebung, Verwaltung, und Volkswirtschaft*, XLV (1921), 349–420.

the establishment of peace and by the undertaking of various measures, such as the establishment of a uniform currency throughout the East, the opening of new trade routes, and the founding of new cities on the old trade routes.[9] Athenian business received an added stimulus from the development of new types of pottery, the so-called West Slope ware and relief vases which imitated vases made of metal;[10] these new wares, we learn from archaeological evidence, were imported into South Russia, Alexandria, Palestine, and Syria.[11] Consequently, Athens enjoyed or ؛ of the most prosperous periods of its history at the time of Demetrius of Phalerum.[12]

A few years later, in the opening years of the third century B.C., we find the city sufficiently prosperous to undertake the reconstruction of various public buildings as well as the construction of some new ones. At this time a reconstruction of the Tholus was undertaken.[13] A porch and propylaea were added to the new Bouleuterion,[14] and a large basilica-like structure was erected on the northern slope of the Colonus Agoraeus.[15] Other work undertaken at this time included the construction of the peribolus of the Temple of Hephaestus[16] and the original planting of the so-called Garden of Hephaestus,[17] a temple garden which consisted of rows of flower pots embedded in the surface of the Colonus Agoraeus. The prosperity of these years was, however, to a certain extent illusory; for it had been undermined almost at its beginning by the loss of Athenian sea power after the battle of Amorgus, by the aristocratic reforms of Demetrius of Phalerum whereby many poor citizens lost the franchise and consequently their source of income, and by the

[9] Wilcken, *Alexander the Great*, pp. 254–55.

[10] H. A. Thompson, "Two Centuries of Hellenistic Pottery," *Hesperia*, III (1934), 311–480; Courby, *Vases grecs*, pp. 268–73, 359–61, 428; C. Watzinger, in AM, XXVI (1901), 67–102; M. Z. Pease, in *Hesperia*, IV (1935), 293–96; W. Schwabacher, "Hellenistische Reliefkeramik im Kerameikos," A JA, XLV (1941), 182–228.

[11] Courby, *Vases grecs*, pp. 271–72, 357–59, 413. The more recent literature is assembled by Rostovtzeff in his *Social and Economic History of the Hellenistic World*.

[12] Beloch, *Griechische Geschichte*, IV, i, 271; Ferguson, *Athens*, pp. 58–59.

[13] H. A. Thompson, in *Hesperia*, VI (1937), 167. H. A. Thompson, *The Tholos of Athens and Its Predecessors*, p. 135.

[14] H. A. Thompson, in *Hesperia*, VI (1937), 167.

[15] D. B. Thompson, in *Hesperia*, VI (1937), 400.

[16] *Ibid.*, pp. 398–400.   [17] *Ibid.*, pp. 410–11.

abandonment of imperialism by the same politician.[18] Moreover, the distribution in Greece of the hoarded Persian treasure which Alexander had seized induced an inflation with rapidly rising prices between about 310 B.C. and 270 B.C.[19] The rising spiral of prices gained further impetus from the inability of Greek producers to meet the greatly increased demand for their products.[20] Most disastrous consequences of this inflation were avoided only because Alexander abandoned the Persian practice of hoarding the precious metals and introduced a money economy into the eastern kingdoms.[21] In the meantime, upon the opening of the East by Alexander's conquests and the immigration of Greeks into those parts, the demand for Greek goods rose, with the consequent expansion of Greek productive capacity.[22] But soon the Hellenistic kings organized the productive capacity of their cities, and the industries of the homeland were left without foreign outlets.[23] Thereupon industry and trade shifted eastward to centers such as Rhodes, Antioch, Seleucia, and Alexandria, with the latter becoming the foremost center of trade in the Mediterranean.[24] Moreover, various factors that were operative within Attica hastened the decline of Athenian prosperity. The Macedonian domination in Attica, which had begun in 322 B.C. and was to continue with only slight interruption to 229 B.C., brought about a decentralization of Attic life—political, social, and economic—which could only be harmful to the material welfare of the city.[25] But there were other forces working to the detriment of business. Between 290 B.C. and 269 B.C. the price of lead rose very rapidly at Delos,[26] and, inasmuch as lead

[18] Ferguson, *Athens*, pp. 65–67.

[19] Heichelheim, *Schwankungen*, pp. 40–41, 55–56; "New Light on Currency and Inflation in Hellenistic-Roman Times from Inscriptions and Papyri," *Economic History: a Supplement to the Economic Journal*, III (1935), 1–11, especially 1–3; *Wirtschaftsgeschichte*, I, 440–42. See also G. Glotz, in JDS, XI (1913), 16–29. For the hardships occasioned at Athens by the high prices see Ferguson, *Athens*, p. 66.

[20] Rostovtzeff stresses this point in his *Social and Economic History of the Hellenistic World*.

[21] U. Wilcken, in Schmoller's *Jahrbuch für Gesetzgebung, Verwaltung, und Volkswirtschaft*, XLV (1921), 51–57.

[22] M. Rostovtzeff, in *American Historical Review*, XLI (1936), 235.

[23] *Ibid.*, p. 239.

[24] Beloch, *Griechische Geschichte*, IV, i, 278–79; W. W. Tarn, in CAH, VII, 212.

[25] Ferguson, *Athens*, pp. 230–31.

[26] The price of lead at Delos rose from 5 drachmas per talent at c.290 B.C. (IG,

was an important by-product at Laurium[27] (which seems to have been the main source of lead among the Greeks),[28] it is very reasonable to suppose that lead from Laurium was no longer available and that production of silver had been abandoned for the time being.[29] Consequently, there is some reason to believe that the inflation induced by the dispersion of the Persian treasure so lowered the price of silver that it was no longer profitable to continue operations in the mines at Laurium.[30] Both the state and its citizens lost thereby a prolific source of wealth. It may well be that it was a shortage of silver, rather than the prohibition of the Macedonians, that was responsible for the abandonment of silver coinage at the end of the Chremonidean War, in 261 B.C.[31] Whatever the cause of this diminution of its coinage, Athens lost much of the prestige and

---

XI, ii, 153, l. 13) to 7 drachmas and 3 obols per talent in 269 B.C. (IG, XI, ii, 203A, l. 52); cf. Larsen, "Roman Greece," pp. 398–99.

[27] Davies, *Roman Mines*, pp. 246–47. Argentiferous galena, from which silver was extracted at Laurium, contains 65 percent lead.

[28] *Ibid.*, pp. 246–47.

[29] M. Cary, "The Sources of Silver for the Greek World," *Mélanges Gustave Glotz*, I, 133–42, especially 139–40. The mines were still being actively worked at the time of Demetrius of Phalerum (Strabo, III, 147).

[30] M. Cary, in *Mélanges Gustave Glotz*, I, 139–40.

[31] At that time Antigonus Gonatas seems to have forbidden the Athenians to coin silver for a few years. See Seltman, *Greek Coins*, p. 259 and note 3; J. P. Shear, in *Hesperia*, II (1933), 254; cf. W. W. Tarn, in CAH, VII, 220, who disagrees with this contention. In the inventories of the priests of Asclepius (IG, II–III,[2] 1534B, ll. 230–79; between c.262/1 B.C. and 255/4 B.C. [Ferguson, *Cycles*, pp. 37–38], or between 257/6 B.C. and 250/49 B.C. [Dinsmoor, *Archon List*, pp. 96, 97, 106; cf. *Archons*, p. 159, where years between 259/8 B.C. and 252/1 B.C. are favored; Pritchett and Meritt, *Chronology*, p. 77, adhere to this date]), there are listed certain coins which are called τέτραχμα 'Αντιγόνεια. These coins are interpreted as issues of a mint established at Athens by Antigonus at this time. See Ferguson, "Priests," p. 148; Head, *Hist. Num.*, p. 378; U. Köhler, in *Sitzungsberichte der preussischen Akademie der Wissenschaften*, 1896, pp. 1089–97; J. Kirchner, in *Berliner philologische Wochenschrift*, XXVI (1906), p. 986; and, with reservations, Seltman, *Greek Coins*, p. 260 and note 1. On the other hand, W. Kolbe, in *Göttingische gelehrte Anzeigen*, CLXXVIII (1916), 447–48, maintains that this attribution of the coins rests on insufficient evidence. Ferguson, "Priests," p. 148, holds that the last of the Athenian old style coinage was issued before the first appearance of the τέτραχμα 'Αντιγόνεια. It seems likely, however, that the city resumed the issuance of the old style coinage in a slightly modified form, in 255 B.C., but only in small amounts between that date and 229 B.C. For this coinage see Seltman, *Greek Coins*, p. 260; Svoronos, *Les Monnaies d'Athènes*, Pls. XXIII, XXIV; J. P. Shear, in *Hesperia*, II (1933), 254.

prosperity which it had enjoyed through the integrity and high reputation of its "owls." The decline in business that took place at Athens during the first forty years of the third century was certainly very great.

Recently Heichelheim, building upon the very valuable work of Glotz,[32] has developed an interesting thesis concerning prices in the Mediterranean world.[33] With the opening up of the East and the development of new cities, he maintains, trade and commerce grew rapidly and the interconnections among the economies of the various cities became so close that what might be called an "international market" was developed; on this "market" prices in the individual cities were determined by supply and demand at the leading centers of commerce. Prices were, of course, not the same in all cities—transportation costs and distances from the sources of supply affected the price of individual commodities in each city —but the price curve followed approximately the same course in all cities. Most of our evidence for prices in the eastern Mediterranean during the Hellenistic period, it is to be observed, is derived from the Temple accounts at Delos. Moreover, we must bear in mind two additional facts. First, owing to the great influx of foreigners into the island, conditions approximating those of a boom town may have prevailed. Certainly we must assume that rents were high. On the other hand it is most likely that so many workers were attracted there by the famed prosperity of the island that wages were actually lower than elsewhere.[34] Second, commodities may have sold at a higher price there because most of them had to be imported.[35] But the variation from levels prevalent elsewhere could not have been too great—otherwise Delos would not have developed as a center of transit trade. It would seem, therefore, injudicious to use the Delian evidence to draw conclusions about prices elsewhere in the Aegean area unless there is confirmatory evidence from the district in question. But if proper allowance be made, similar price trends may be assumed elsewhere,[36] except in

[32] G. Glotz, "Les Prix des denrées à Délos," JDS, XI (1913), 16–29.

[33] Heichelheim, Schwankungen, pp. 2–4. For an excellent critical treatment of Heichelheim's work, see Larsen, "Roman Greece," pp. 379–414.

[34] Tarn, Hellenistic Civilization, p. 111.

[35] Rostovtzeff stresses this point in his Social and Economic History of the Hellenistic World.   [36] Cf. Larsen, "Roman Greece," pp. 379–80.

the instance of wages and house rents. As we saw above, the distribution of the Persian treasure seized by Alexander induced inflation with rapidly rising prices up to approximately the end of the first quarter of the third century B.C. This period of inflation was followed by a severe decline in prices which continued to about the middle of the century.[37] The complex nature of our evidence does not permit any conclusion about the general trend of prices, even at Delos, during the latter half of the third century B.C.[38] However, we are able to determine the trend, at Delos, of four commodities which played the most important parts in Athenian economy, and we may assume a similar trend at Athens. Wheat, which sold for an average of 6 drachmas and 5 obols per medimnus over a period of seven months in 282 B.C.,[39] fell to a low of possibly 4 drachmas at about the middle of the century[40] and thereafter rose to a price of 8 to 10 drachmas at the beginning of the second century B.C.[41] Barley followed a trend similar to that of wheat.[42] Oil sold for as much as 55 drachmas per metretes in 305/3 B.C.;[43] by 250 B.C. the price ranged between 16 and 18 drachmas,[44] and after that time remained fairly stable, the lowest price, 11 to 13 drachmas, being reached in 190–180 B.C.[45] Our evidence concerning the price of wine during this period is rather difficult to interpret, but it will suffice to state that it seems to have fallen after 250 B.C. and to have remained low during the early years of the second century.[46] From these statistics we learn that during the latter

[37] G. Glotz, "Les Prix des denrées à Délos," JDS, XI (1913), 16–29; Heichelheim, Schwankungen, pp. 55–56.

[38] Larsen, "Roman Greece," p. 380. Convenient tables of prices, with citations, may be found in L. Spaventa-de Novellis, I prezzi in Grecia e a Roma nell' antichità (Istituto di Statistica della Reale Università di Roma, II, 1934).

[39] IG, XI, ii, 158A, ll. 38, 40, 41, 43, 44, 45, 47.

[40] The price in the text is the result of a deduction from the price of barley. Cf. Larsen, "Roman Greece," p. 386. See also note 42, below.

[41] Heichelheim, Schwankungen, pp. 51–52; cf. Larsen, "Roman Greece," p. 385.

[42] Heichelheim, Schwankungen, pp. 51–52; cf. Larsen, "Roman Greece," pp. 384–85. Wheat generally sold for twice the price of barley. See G. Glotz, in JDS, XI (1913), 20; Jardé, Céréales, pp. 182–83; cf. Larsen, "Roman Greece," p. 384.

[43] IG, XI, ii, 144A, l. 30; cf. ll. 31, 33, 37, and IG, XI, ii, 144B, ll. 21, 24. The average price for the year was 44½ drachmas.

[44] IG, XI, ii, 287A, ll. 43, 47, 54, 58, 63, 65, 68, 74, 76, 79, 82. Cf. the critique of Heichelheim, Schwankungen, p. 53, by Larsen, "Roman Greece," pp. 388–90.

[45] IDD, 440, ll. 18, 22.   [46] Larsen, "Roman Greece," pp. 391–92.

half of the third century the price of Athens' main export product (oil) had fallen, whereas the price of the one commodity (grain) which it was most necessary to import had risen. Here, as with other commodities, the Athenians suffered from an adverse balance of trade.

At the prices which he received the producer of oil could have earned only a small margin of profit, while vineyard owners probably did not fare at all well. On the other hand, those farmers who could cultivate a sufficiently large crop of wheat or barley found their businesses relatively profitable.[47] But these were comparatively few in number, for the amount of land suitable for the growth of grain was relatively small, not more than one fifth of the total area being of such a sort as to produce cereals, and of this one half was left to lie fallow each year.[48] Moreover, of these lands the greater part was unsuited to the production of wheat, the actual proportion of wheat to barley raised being approximately 1:9.3, as is shown by the inscription which records the tithes paid to the Eleusinian divinities in 329/8 B.C.[49] The lands adapted to the cultivation of grain were distributed among the four Attic plains, none of which was of large extent and none of which was particularly fertile, especially as compared with the lands of such districts as Boeotia or Laconia.[50] The sizes of the four plains were ap-

[47] *Ibid.*, pp. 380–81, 406. Glotz (*Ancient Greece At Work*, pp. 347–48, and in JDS, XI [1913], 19–20), Heichelheim (*Schwankungen*, pp. 82–83), and others have assumed that the decline in land rents at Delos after c.280 B.C. proves that agriculture throughout Greece was distinctly an unprofitable, even a ruinous, pursuit. On the other hand, Tarn (*Hellenistic Civilization*, p. 110) contends that the decline in these rents was the result of a special circumstance, namely, the tendency on the part of farmers at Delos to seek the higher rewards that were to be gained from transit trade, and should not be taken as proof of the decline of agriculture throughout Greece, especially since the cry, raised in many places, for redistribution of land suggests that agriculture was still a pursuit that fared moderately well. The concluding portion of this argument is decisive. However, to Larsen ("Roman Greece," pp. 403–7, and in *Classical Philology*, XXXVI [1941], 165, note 21) goes the credit for showing clearly that the decline in land rents at Delos was not general, but was limited to those estates that were devoted almost entirely to the production of wine. Larsen's conclusion, which has been adopted here, is eminently reasonable.

[48] For the treatment of the land referred to in the text, see Jardé, *Céréales*, pp. 83–87.

[49] IG, II–III², 1672; cf. Jardé, *Céréales*, p. 48.

[50] Jardé, *Céréales*, pp. 71–72, 74–75.

proximately as follows: Thriasian, 36.6 square miles; Athenian, 50.2 square miles; the Mesogeia, 27.8 square miles; Marathonian, 5.8 square miles. Not all of these lands, however, were consistently productive during the third century. Large sections of the Athenian countryside were subjected to hostile raids and the crops were destroyed, the Thriasian and Athenian plains being most affected, whereas the Mesogeia and the plain of Marathon were comparatively immune, owing to their location.[51] Accordingly, some of the farmers in the two latter regions, especially those farmers who were able to cultivate a relatively substantial amount of grain, found agriculture a remunerative occupation. Many landowners from other parts of Attica—some from the districts where the soil was not suited to grain culture, others from the districts subject to raids—must have found it necessary to give up ownership of land. Possibly these individuals undertook, as has been suggested,[52] leasehold farming, at least for a time. Ultimately, a number of them must have been tempted away to the cities and to lands in the East which were being opened, by the Hellenistic kings, to exploitation. In any event, the third century B.C. witnessed the quickening of a movement which had begun in Greece centuries before—the movement toward increasing concentration of land in the hands of fewer and fewer individuals.

If the lot of the farmer was poor, did the wage earner in the city fare better? The only direct evidence at our disposal concerning wages is that from the Temple accounts at Delos. It is true, as we have already observed, that wages at Delos were affected to a great extent by local conditions, such as, for example, an influx of workers which glutted the labor market.[53] But we are probably safe in concluding that a similar trend in wages prevailed at Athens, for there are numerous signs that throughout the Hellenistic period there existed at Athens a large population of urban workers whose low wages must have been brought about by intense competition. Stated briefly, the evidence from Delos indicates that wages remained stationary for a short time after the beginning of the inflation at the end of the fourth century B.C., that soon thereafter

[51] Ferguson, *Athens*, p. 231; "Priests," pp. 160–61.
[52] Glotz, *Ancient Greece at Work*, pp. 347–48.
[53] Tarn, *Hellenistic Civilization*, p. 111.

they fell and continued to fall until about the middle of the third century B.C., and that thenceforward, when the cost of living was again rising wages, remained low.[54] The lot of the worker was desperate; his standard of living was declining steadily.[55] Even at the depth of depressed prices, at the middle of the third century B.C., he fared very badly. When the standard of living of an Egyptian fellah is compared with that of a specialized Delian worker, such as an architect, it is shown that the former (unskilled) was, in terms of real wages, better paid than the latter (skilled).[56] However we interpret the Delian evidence, it seems probable that the laborer at Athens, as elsewhere in the Hellenistic world, could by no means be said to have shared in the prosperity of the age.

We have seen that only a limited number of country dwellers fared well in Attica during the third century, that the lot of the city laborer was desperate, and that the lot of many Athenians was aggravated by rising prices at the beginning and end of the century. Under such circumstances men are strongly tempted to migrate to other environments in search of better fortunes. However, it is quite likely that the change of abode of Athenians was not one of transference from city to country or country to city—at least not in sufficient numbers to constitute a definite trend—but rather one of migration to eastern lands which were now offering more op-

[54] G. Glotz, "Les Salaires à Délos," JDS, XI (1913), 206–15, 251–60; Heichelheim, *Schwankungen*, pp. 97–98; Larsen, "Roman Greece," pp. 408–12. Caution must, however, be exercised in drawing deductions from these wage statistics. It is not certain that they represent the sole income of the workers; in some cases the workers were employed at other tasks, while the stated wages were for seasonal work. See M. Rostovtzeff's review of Heichelheim, *Schwankungen*, in *Zeitschrift für die gesamte Staatswissenschaft*, LXXXIX (1930), 577–82, especially 581.

[55] For discussions of the cost of living at various times between the latter part of the fourth and the opening of the second centuries, see G. Glotz, in JDS, XI (1913), 209–10; Heichelheim, *Schwankungen*, pp. 98–101; Larsen, "Roman Greece," pp. 412–14. Cf. the discussion of rations by Jardé, *Céréales*, pp. 128–36. These studies would indicate that when prices were high and employment was seasonal, wages of ordinary workers barely attained a subsistence minimum, and that maintenance of a family was difficult, both for the trained and untrained worker, even when prices were low and employment was continuous. However, the extent to which members of the family other than the father contributed to the family income is uncertain, as Larsen, "Roman Greece," p. 414, points out. See also the preceding note.

[56] Heichelheim, *Schwankungen*, pp. 102–3.

portunities than the Greek homeland. At the end of the fourth century a large number of poor Athenians joined the expedition of Ophelas of Cyrene against the Carthaginians.[57] A number of Athenians also migrated to Egypt, where the Greeks became the dominant force in the economic exploitation of the country.[58] We have explicit evidence from Egyptian papyri that Athenians were serving in the army of the Ptolemies before 200 B.C.[59] However, the Athenian immigrants to Egypt came more from the upper classes; there were among these immigrants comparatively few soldiers, farmers, and other persons of the lower economic status.[60] It is likely, too, that Athenians migrated to still other lands of the East which were prosperous. However, it is quite certain that migration did not progress to the extent of such actual depopulation as Polybius asserts[61] for certain sections of Greece during the second century; there are too many indications of a dissident political group of unemployed and impoverished workmen in the city during the third and second centuries to allow us to subscribe to any such belief.

During the first forty years of the third century B.C. the prosperity of the city had diminished greatly, and near the end of that period, in 263 B.C., control of the government was taken over by a new group of men, individuals registered in demes located in or near the Mesogeia.[62] The identity of the class from which the leading men in the new government were drawn has been deduced from an inscription of the year of the archon Diomedon, not long after 250 B.C.,[63] in which a record is found of the contributions made by

[57] Diodorus, XX, xl, 5–6.

[58] P. Jouguet, *L'Impérialism macédonien et l'hellénisation de l'Orient* (Paris, 1926), pp. 373–86. An English translation (by M. R. Dobie) of this work has appeared (London, 1928) as *Macedonian Imperialism*. W. L. Westermann, "The Greek Exploitation of Egypt," *Political Science Quarterly*, XL (1925), 517–39; Heichelheim, *Wirtschaftsgeschichte*, I, 443–44.

[59] Heichelheim, *Auswärtige Bevölkerung*, pp. 84–85, lists the names of seven Athenians.

[60] *Ibid.*, pp. 46–48; cf. Ferguson, *Athens*, p. 188, note 1, and p. 197; Edgar, P. Cairo Zen. VII, 91, note 1.

[61] XXXVI, 17.

[62] Ferguson, *Cycles*, pp. 93–94; *Athens*, pp. 231–32, cf. 204–7; Dinsmoor, *Archons*, p. 95.

[63] The archonship of Diomedon is dated in 246/5 B.C. by Dinsmoor, *Archon List*, pp. 77–82, 85–96; in 241/0 B.C. by Ferguson, *Cycles*, p. 26; in 247/6 B.C. by Prit-

more than 133 individuals—the entire list has not been preserved—toward a fund to be administered by the military treasurer, Eurycleides of Cephisia, in defense of the state and for the safeguarding of the harvest of that year.[64] At least twenty thousand drachmas were contributed for this purpose, the individual contributions ranging from a minimum of fifty to a maximum of two hundred drachmas, the amounts specified in the decree which authorized the *epidosis*. The contributors came, in conformity with the practice customarily followed in this type of subscription, from among the wealthiest inhabitants of Attica, foreigners included.[65] Among the deme names of contributors to the fund those from the Mesogeia or near by were prominent, Erchia being represented by nine, Paeania by five, Sphettus by five, and Halae, Phlya, and Cephisia by three each. City demes and demes from other sections of Attica are represented by smaller contingents.[66] From the facts that Eurycleides, the leader of the movement, was registered in Cephisia, and that the largest number of contributors —as well as the subscriptions largest in amount—were made by individuals registered in the Mesogeia, Ferguson drew the conclusion that a party of landholders from that part of Attica had

---

chett and Meritt, *Chronology*, p. xxii. J. Kirchner, "Archon Diomedon," *Athenian Studies*, pp. 503–7, argues that there were two archons of that name, Diomedon (I) in 241/0 B.C. and Diomedon (II) in 232/1 B.C.

[64] IG, II–III², 791. A new fragment of the inscription has been found very recently in the Agora at Athens; T. L. Shear, in *Hesperia*, VIII (1939), 245.

[65] Kuenzi, p. 31. The foreign contributors were Lycon of Alexandria Troas (the head of the Peripatetic School at Athens), Diogenes (the commander of the Macedonian garrison in the Piraeus), Philocles of Corinth, Hecataeus of Mesembria, and Zopyrus of Syracuse; also Apollas (?) the Lacedaemonian (?). For the last named see note 92, below. For the restoration of the name of Diogenes in the inscription (IG, II–III², 791d, I, l. 6), see Wilhelm, *Beiträge*, p. 81; Dinsmoor, *Archons*, pp. 109, 507–8. The term ἐπίδοσις is applied to contributions, supposedly voluntary, solicited by the state in accordance with the terms of a decree which specifically stated the purpose for which the funds thus collected were to be employed. Foreigners and citizens alike were eligible to contribute. Rostovtzeff maintains, in his *Social and Economic History of the Hellenistic World*, that these contributions were "voluntary" only in name.

[66] Ferguson, "Priests," pp. 160–61. While the inscription is fragmentary, it is likely that the proportional representation would be the same were the list complete, for no logical system of classification was followed and the names of individuals registered in the same deme are not listed together.

taken over control of the government.[67] Recent investigations, however, have shown conclusively that a deme name is a very unsatisfactory indication of residence; that by the third century B.C. a citizen might well have been living outside his deme of registry.[68] Nevertheless, there is at hand evidence which justifies the belief that in the present instance the deme names are largely correct indicators of the source of income, at least, of the individuals to whose names they were attached. We have already seen that the most prosperous landholders in Attica were those who raised a considerable amount of grain, and that grain could be grown only in the four Attic plains; also that, owing to intermittent raids throughout the third century, crops did not prosper in the Athenian and Thriasian plains, and that, therefore, the farmers of the Mesogeia and the plain of Marathon were the most prosperous landholders in Attica. Moreover, that the greatest wealth in Attica at this time came from the lands in these plains is indicated by the fact that the Marathonian Tetrapolis began, in the latter third of the third century, to send its own Pythais to Delphi and continued to do so until the latter part of the second century, while on the other hand Athens had omitted the dispatch of a Pythais at the end of the fourth century and did not undertake it again until 138/7 B.C.[69] Such a state of affairs should not be at all surprising, since Athens had been severely affected by the great decline in its industry and commerce.

The initiative of the prosperous landholders who derived their income from the Mesogeia led finally to the negotiations with Diogenes, the commander of the Macedonian garrison in the

[67] Ferguson, *Athens*, pp. 204, 231–32; Jardé, *Céréales*, p. 163.

[68] Gomme, *Population*, p. 40, note 4.

[69] Boethius, *Die Pythaïs*, pp. 38–51; Daux, *Delphes*, pp. 531–40. Other indications of the presence of wealth in this district during the third century may be cited. First, there is the endowment established by a wealthy patron for Dionysus and the other gods of the Tetrapolis (IG, II–III², 1243; cf. Laum, *Stiftungen*, Vol. II, No. 19a). Second, in an inscription of the end of the century, in which provision is made for the repair of a sanctuary where an association of *Amphiaraistae* met at Rhamnus, reference is made to the original endowment of the association by a wealthy patron (IG, II–III², 1322; cf. Laum, *Stiftungen*, Vol. II, No. 20a). The neglect indicated by the necessity of repairing the roof, wall, and table of the god need not necessarily—especially in view of other indications of prosperity in this district—be attributed to straitened finances.

Piraeus, for the withdrawal of his troops and the liberation of Athens in 229 B.C.[70] But their release from foreign domination was secured only at the cost of one hundred and fifty talents, which Diogenes needed to pay off his troops.[71] Thereupon Aratus contributed the sum of twenty talents[72] in the hope, apparently, of securing the adherence of Athens to the Achaean League. The remaining one hundred and thirty talents constituted a huge sum for the Athenians, in their poor circumstances, to meet. But it was raised with the aid of a gift from the Thebans[73] (made, apparently, in return for the aid extended to them in 316 B.C. toward the rebuilding of their walls) and with the aid of a loan from the city of Thespiae.[74] Where the remaining funds came from we are not informed, but it has been suggested, with some plausibility, that the state raised a large loan and called upon foreigners as well as citizens to contribute toward the liquidation of it.[75]

Upon their release from Macedonian domination in 229 B.C. the Athenians set about restoring normal conditions within the city. What with the Macedonian control of the city, a foreign garrison in the Piraeus, and the attendant uncertainties in the political situation, the Athenians had been discouraged from undertaking any but the most cautious business ventures and public expenditures. But now that freedom had been restored the wealthy—those who had retained their fortunes through the straitened years between 263/2 B.C. and 229/8 B.C.—were less chary in the employment of their funds; with prospects more favorable money came out of hiding.[76] The most prominent man of wealth at Athens at this time was Eurycleides of Cephisia, who gave huge sums to the state for public purposes.[77] Thus, as *agonothetes* of the Dionysia, he incurred an expenditure of seven talents,[78] and in the following year he pro-

---

[70] Ferguson, *Athens*, pp. 206–7.

[71] Plutarch, *Aratus*, 34; Pausanias, II, viii, 6.

[72] Plutarch, *Aratus*, 34; cf. Aymard, *Premiers Rapports*, p. 22.

[73] IG, VII, 2405–6.   [74] IG, VII, 1737–38.

[75] IG, II–III², 786, 835; cf. Kuenzi, pp. 17–19, 50.

[76] The decline of interest rates from 12 percent to 10–6⅔ percent (cf. Billeter, *Geschichte des Zinsfusses*, pp. 58–70; Heichelheim, *Schwankungen*, pp. 108–10 and Table XII, and *Wirtschaftsgeschichte*, I, 429; Larsen, "Roman Greece," p. 374) makes it evident that there was no shortage of money in Greece between 300 B.C. and 150 B.C.

[77] Ferguson, *Athens*, p. 205.   [78] IG, II–III², 834, ll. 4–5.

vided his son with the funds needed for the *agonothesia* of the Panathenaea.[79] Immediately after the liberation of the city very necessary repairs were undertaken on the fortifications of the city[80] and of the Piraeus and its harbors;[81] and it is probable that here again resort was made to citizens and foreigners alike for contributions toward the requisite expenditures.[82] A number of citizens seems now to have returned to the Piraeus for purposes of trade.[83] Operations in the mines at Laurium had been discontinued in the first quarter of the third century B.C., or soon thereafter, but were resumed again c.229 B.C.,[84] whereupon the state began to issue large amounts of a new currency, the so-called New Style coinage.[85] The renewal of activity in the Laurium district was reflected not only in the construction of a temple and temenos of Asclepius at Sunium in 220/19 B.C.,[86] but also in expanded activity throughout Attica. The revenues from the mines redounded to the benefit of the city, and the prestige of the new coinage, which was soon used in large amounts both in domestic and in foreign trade, contributed in no small way to the upward movement which was to lead ultimately to the renewed prosperity of Athens in the second century B.C. Within the city itself the precinct of the Demos and the Graces[87]

[79] *Ibid.*, 834, ll. 5–7.   [80] *Ibid.*, 834, ll. 14–15.

[81] *Ibid.*, 786, l. 6; 834, l. 14; 835, ll. 9–10.   [82] Kuenzi, pp. 17–19, 50.

[83] The evidence adduced by Ferguson (*Athens*, p. 247, cf. 222, note 1) is not conclusive, but one may assume, on a priori grounds, that the cessation of restrictions incidental to the presence of a foreign garrison in the Piraeus would have encouraged immigration of business-minded individuals from other demes to the port town. Ferguson's argument depends upon the invalid assumption that the deme name is an indication of place of residence in the third century. See Gomme, *Population*, p. 40, note 4.

[84] The issuance of the New Style coinage, beginning in 229 B.C., is sufficient indication of the resumption of operations at Laurium at this time. With reviving prosperity the working of the mines would be more profitable. M. Cary, in *Mélanges Gustave Glotz*, I, 142, advances the contention that the mines were not reopened until 150 B.C.

[85] Head, *Hist. Num.*, p. 378; Seltman, *Greek Coins*, p. 260. The first class of this coinage was issued between 229 B.C. and 196 B.C. For the importance of the New Style coinage, see my account in chap. ii. A new system of chronological classification of these coins is being worked out by M. L. Kambanis, "Notes sur le classement chronologique des monnaies d'Athènes," *Aréthuse*, XXI (1928), 121–35; BCH, LVI (1932), 37–59, LVIII (1934), 101–37, LIX (1935), 101–20, LX (1936), 101–17, LXII (1938), 60–84.

[86] IG, II–III², 2857; AE, 1900, pp. 141–44.

[87] Judeich, *Topographie*, pp. 92, 379.

and the Diogeneum[88] were erected, the latter a gymnasium which was named for the Macedonian commander who had freed Athens and which was employed as a center of instruction for the ephebes. Other building activity at Athens at this time is to be attributed to two foreign potentates whose dynasties maintained friendly relations with the city in the succeeding century. The gymnasium known as the Ptolemaeum was bestowed upon the city by Ptolemy III Euergetes,[89] while the Lacydeum, a garden plot named after the head of the Academic school, was laid out in the enclosure of the Academy, the gift of Attalus I of Pergamum.[90] The practice of granting subsidies to the Academy, which was continued in the next century by the Attalids, began with this ruler.[91]

We have very explicit evidence to show that a number of foreigners, who were largely merchants, resided at Athens throughout the third century B.C. First, names of foreigners appear in the lists of subscribers to funds raised at several different times during the century to meet various public needs.[92] Second, a large number of foreign cults, representing many districts of the eastern Mediterranean, enjoyed a prosperous existence both in the city and in the Piraeus.[93] Third, a large number of foreign names appears on Attic tombstones of the period between the archonship of Eucleides (403/2 B.C.) and the accession of the emperor Augustus at Rome. At least some of these names must be assigned to the third century. However, by no means all of them were merchants or even semipermanent residents; some may have been, for example, mercenaries and students. Fourth, in the course of a revision of the laws

[88] *Ibid.*, pp. 92, 379.

[89] Pausanias, I, xvii, 2; Judeich, *Topographie*, p. 92; Ferguson, *Athens*, pp. 239–40.

[90] Diogenes Laertius, IV, viii, 4; Judeich, *Topographie*, pp. 94, 414.

[91] Ferguson, *Athens*, p. 234.

[92] For the foreigners who participated in the *epidosis* during the archonship of Diomedon, see note 65, above. Proxeny was conferred upon Apollas (?) the Lacedaemonian (?), possibly in recognition of his contributions toward the defense of the land during the archonship of Diomedon, toward the loan taken up by the state in 229 B.C., and toward the fortification of the harbors (IG, II–III², 835, ll. 1–16; cf. Kuenzi, pp. 17–19, 50). Aristocreon of Seleucia Pieria also made contributions, possibly toward the liquidation of the loan of 229 B.C. and toward the fortification of the harbors (IG, II–III², 786; cf. Kuenzi, pp. 17–19, 50). Aristocreon's uncle Chrysippus became head of the Stoic school in Athens in 232/1 B.C.

[93] Ferguson, *Athens*, pp. 216–29; Clerc, *Les Métèques athéniens*, pp. 140–46.

that was undertaken soon after the city's release from the overlord-ship of Macedon, the provisions of an old law were revised in such a way as to limit drastically the rights of foreigners in the holding of property within Attica; not only was the amount of property which they might own limited, but also its location was carefully specified with respect to the frontiers.[94] Apparently, wealthy im-migrants had bought up substantial amounts of choice land at depression prices. Fifth, in the course of the same revision of the laws, provision was made that individuals upon whom it was pro-posed that proxeny rights be bestowed were to be subjected to judicial scrutiny.[95] This provision would indicate that numerous aliens were coming to Athens for purposes of trade over short periods of time. Our evidence from the third century, therefore, indicates that credence may well be placed in a statement in a work of the middle of the second century B.C. which has come down to us under the name of Heracleides the Critic,[96] to the effect that for-eigners found Athens a very pleasant place in which to live. It is very likely that a goodly number of foreigners remained at Athens through the years of declining prosperity during the first forty years of the century, but many must have left the city during the lean years between about 263 B.C. and 229 B.C. After the latter date, however, the foreign population of the city probably increased again.

The directions of the city's trade, and, to a certain extent, even the articles of trade, are reflected by the ethnics of foreigners whose names appear on tombstones found in Attica.[97] Comparatively few names of inhabitants of the Peloponnesus appear, and of these, the inhabitants of the Argolid and Messenia seem to have been most closely connected with Athens. The contingents from northern Greece, especially from Thessaly, Aetolia, and Boeotia, are rela-.tively large, and evidence is forthcoming from other sources to sup-plement the testimony of the stones. A fair number of Thessalians

---

[94] IG, II–III², 834; cf. Ferguson, *Athens*, p. 245.

[95] J. G. Schubert, *De proxenia Attica* (Leipzig, 1881), pp. 40–41; A. Wilhelm, in *Hermes*, XXIV (1889), 330–31; Ferguson, *Athens*, p. 246.

[96] Fragment 1, section 2 (ed. W. H. Duke, "Three Fragments of the περὶ τῶν ἐν τῇ Ἑλλάδι πόλεων of Heracleides the Critic," *Essays and Studies Presented to William Ridgeway* [Cambridge, 1913], pp. 228–48). For the date and authorship of the tract, see Duke, p. 248; Daebritz, in RE, VIII, 484–86.

[97] These names are treated in greater detail in chap. ii.

received proxeny rights from Athens during the third century B.C.,[98] and numerous Athenians were granted similar rights at Oropus in the decades immediately following 229 B.C.[99] Proximity naturally favored trade with Athens' neighbor to the north, but there was also a good road, free from bandits, which ran from Attica through Oropus into the heart of Boeotia.[100] As regards the Aetolians, the political relations of Athens with this sturdy people were very close at times throughout the third century, especially after 229 B.C.[101] The stelae also indicate that a fairly large number of inhabitants of the Chalcidice, excluding Olynthus, were interested in trade at Athens. The names of inhabitants of cities in the region of the Propontis, such as Cyzicus, Cius, and Byzantium, and of cities on the southern shore of the Black Sea, such as Heraclea and Sinope, are frequently encountered on the tombstones. Numerous names appear from the islands of the Aegean and from Crete and Cyprus. Curiously, there are comparatively few names of Rhodians. But that there was considerable Rhodian trade with Athens is beyond doubt, for the finding of large numbers of Rhodian amphorae in the Agora at Athens demonstrates conclusively the close relations that obtained between the two cities.[102] Inland and coastal cities of western and southern, even of central, Asia Minor are substantially represented. Very significant are the names from Syria, Phoenicia, and Palestine, especially those from the thriving city of Antioch,

[98] AE, 1914, pp. 167–72, No. 232. For the bestowal of Athenian proxeny upon citizens of Priene in the early part of the third century B.C., see IG, II–III², 693, cf. 566. The *proxenia* had lost much of its former significance by the third century B.C. (G. Glotz, *The Greek City* [London, 1929], p. 269) and had almost been abandoned by 200 B.C. (P. Monceaux, in Daremberg-Saglio, IV, i, 740).

[99] IG, VII, 301, 302, 304, 308, 310, 312, 314, 317, 319, 325, 329, 335, 339, 345–47, 353–54, 358, 371; cf. Ferguson, *Athens*, p. 247.

[100] Fragment 1, section 8 (ed. Duke; see note 96, above). Polybius, XX, vi, refers to the prosperity of Boeotia. Cf. Tarn, *Hellenistic Civilization*, pp. 107–8. At this time Plataea enjoyed closer relations with Athens than with Thebes. See Heracleides Criticus, fragment 1, section 11 (ed. Duke); cf. Ferguson, *Athens*, p. 247.

[101] R. Flacelière, "Les Rapports d'Athènes et de l'Aitolie au IIIᵉ siècle avant J.-C.," *Athenian Studies*, pp. 471–81; and *Les Aitoliens à Delphes* (1937; Bibliothèque des Écoles françaises d'Athènes et de Rome, CXLIII), p. 190; H. Benecke, *Die Seepolitik der Aitoler* (Dissertation, Hamburg, 1934), p. 24. For the prosperity of the Aetolians in the third century, see Polybius, XXI, xxvi, 9.

[102] See note 108, below.

which was the starting point of important caravan routes leading to the Orient.[103] Equally significant are the names from Alexandria, which was the very important center of transit trade from the Red Sea, Ethiopia, Arabia, and India.[104] Only a few names appear from the West, from Italy and Sicily; the great period of Italian traders in the East was to begin during the following century.[105] It is clear, therefore, that traders from the more important commercial centers of the eastern Mediterranean were active at Athens, perhaps not in large numbers, but at least in numbers not to be ignored. The presence, side by side, of Greeks from cities of the mainland other than Athens and of foreigners from other regions of the eastern Mediterranean suggests that Athens probably served as a mainland center for trade, particularly with northern Greece. The presence at Athens of the Pontic merchants noted above affords a clue to the nature of some of this trade: It is very likely that during the first third of the century and, again, after 229 B.C. the city was a distributing center for the merchants who brought grain from the Pontus.[106] Indeed, in the early part of the century Athens and Rhodes were the leading commerical cities of the Aegean area. It seems, therefore, that Athens benefited to some extent from transit trade, a type of trade enjoyed by the most prosperous commercial centers of the Hellenistic world, such as Alexandria, Delos, Rhodes, and Antioch.[107]

Further corroboration of these conclusions may be obtained from a consideration of the various articles imported and exported by

[103] For these routes, see Charlesworth, *Trade Routes*, pp. 46–48; Rostovtzeff, *Caravan Cities*, pp. 1–36; Schaal, *Vom Tauschhandel zum Welthandel*, pp. 157–63; Heichelheim, "Roman Syria," pp. 198–200; Grant, *The Syrian Desert*, pp. 33–78.

[104] Schaal, *Vom Tauschhandel zum Welthandel*, pp. 138–57; Kortenbeutel, *Ägyptischer Süd- und Osthandel;* Leider, *Der Handel von Alexandria*, pp. 45–65; M. Rostovtzeff, "Foreign Commerce of Ptolemaic Egypt," *Journal of Economic and Business History*, IV (1932), 728–69, especially 737–47; Heichelheim, *Wirtschaftsgeschichte*, II, 1084–87.

[105] Although Roman traders appeared in the East before 200 B.C. (Ferguson, *Athens*, p. 264), the great period of the *negotiatores* did not begin until the middle of the second century B.C. (Hatzfeld, *Trafiquants*, pp. 17–20).

[106] An inscription of the end of the third century B.C. records honors bestowed by the city of Oropus upon two Phoenician merchants in recognition of their generosity in selling grain to the city at a low price; IG, VII, 4262. It has been assumed—and with considerable probability—that these traders were metics residing in the Piraeus. Ziebarth, *Beiträge*, p. 71.

[107] Cf. Tarn, *Hellenistic Civilization*, p. 220.

Athens during the third century. Let us first consider the articles imported by the city. Wine was imported from the islands of the Aegean and from Asia Minor, especially in the period following 225 B.C., as is shown by the large number of amphora handles recently found in the Agora at Athens. The amphorae came from Rhodes[108] and Cnidus[109] in large numbers, and from Thasus[110] and Paros[111] in smaller numbers. From the Aegean area, also, a plain type of pottery such as was used for cooking vessels was imported.[112] From Syria came fusiform unguentaria bearing eastern perfumes.[113] From the Pontus grain, hemp, hides, fish, and wood were probably imported.[114] Egypt supplied Athens with grain and probably some papyrus, trade with that country probably being encouraged by the favorable attitude of the Ptolemies and by the institution of the Ptolemaea at Athens.[115] The imported commodity which was most essential to Athens and which was bought in large amounts was, of

[108] V. Grace, in *Hesperia*, III (1934), 201 and note 2, and 214–20. Of 1,545 stamps classified by Miss Grace, 565 were Rhodian, 437 Cnidian, 75 Thasian, and 5 Parian. Cordella, *Le Laurium*, p. 33, records the finding of Rhodian, Cnidian, and Cyprian (!) amphorae at Laurium.

[109] V. Grace, in *Hesperia*, III (1934), 201 and note 2, and 241.

[110] *Ibid.*, p. 201 and note 2, and p. 209. It is rather surprising that none of the Thasian stamps seems to be of a date later than 200 B.C., for soon after that time Thasus regained the prosperity it had had in the sixth century and again enjoyed an extensive foreign trade—which it finally lost at the beginning of the imperial period. See F. von Hiller, "Thasos," RE, Zweite Reihe, V, 1310–27, especially 1320–21.

[111] V. Grace, in *Hesperia*, III (1934), 276.

[112] H. A. Thompson, "Two Centuries of Hellenistic Pottery," *Hesperia*, III (1934), 311–480, especially 465, 467–68.

[113] *Ibid.*, pp. 472–74.

[114] Polybius, IV, xxxviii, 4–5; cf. Ziebarth, *Beiträge*, p. 60. For the uncertainties attendant upon the grain supply from southern Russia, as indicated by Polybius, see Minns, *Scythians and Greeks*, pp. 442–43; Rostovtzeff, *Iranians and Greeks*, p. 147. For the salt-fish industry, see the elaborate monograph of M. Köhler, ΤΑΡΙΧΟΣ; *ou Recherches sur l'histoire et les antiquités des pêcheries de la Russie meridionale* (1832; Mémoires de l'Académie impériale des sciences de Saint-Pétersbourg, 6me série, I), pp. 347–490; D. Bohlen, *Die Bedeutung der Fischerei für die antike Wirtschaft* (Dissertation, Hamburg, 1937). For the importance of Sinope and Amisus in the trade in wood, see Strabo, XII, 546; Ziebarth, *Beiträge*, p. 79; Robinson, *Ancient Sinope*, pp. 140–41. For hides from the Pontus, see Demosthenes, *Phorm.* 10; *Lacr.* 34; Polybius, IV, xxxviii, 4.

[115] Leider, *Der Handel von Alexandria*, p. 23; Lewis, *Industrie du papyrus*, pp. 18, 19; M. Rostovtzeff, in *Journal of Economic and Business History*, IV (1932),

course, grain. Attica had not, since very early times, produced grain in sufficient amounts to feed more than half its population. Its predicament was more serious still during the third century B.C., when intermittent wars and disturbances of trade hindered the importation of grain to such an extent that the Greek cities generally resorted to the institution of the *sitonae*, which had been established in the classical period at Athens. The *sitonae* were appointed only when it became necessary for the state to intervene and take special measures in connection with the grain supply,[116] but they are attested at Athens on numerous occasions between the closing years of the fourth century and the beginning of the second century.[117] It is certainly not without significance that Heracleides the Critic stated that Athens was the most pleasant place in the world to visit—provided one took his food with him—and offered the consolation that the shows and entertainments open to the public might divert the visitor's mind from thought of food.[118]

To pay for the products imported from foreign districts Attica exported pottery and agricultural products, olive oil, honey, and figs in the main. The product exported in largest quantity was probably olive oil. The Pontus exported grain to the Aegean and took oil in return, Polybius informs us.[119] Attic honey, that is, honey produced on Hymettus, was widely prized. Epinicus, as

---

748; Heichelheim, *Wirtschaftsgeschichte*, I, 461–62. For the Ptolemaea, see Ferguson, *Athens*, pp. 242–43; *Klio*, VIII (1908), 338–45.

[116] H. Francotte, "Le Pain à bon marché et le pain gratuit dans les cités grecques," *Mélanges Nicole* (Geneva, 1905), pp. 135–46, 148–50; F. Heichelheim, "Σιτωνία." RE, Supplementband III, 397–98, and "Sitos," RE, Supplementband VI, 819–92, especially 876–79; Thalheim, "Σιτῶναι," RE, Supplementband III, 396–97; K. Köster, *Die Lebensmittelversorgung der altgriechischen Polis* (1939; Neue deutsche Forschungen, Band 245, Abteilung alte Geschichte, Band 7), pp. 73–76. For honors conferred, during the third century, upon individual foreigners in recognition of their services in connection with the food supply at times of stress at Athens, see *ibid.*, p. 56.

[117] Cf. IG, II–III², 479; 480; 584, l. 4; 670, l. 11; 744, l. 8; 792; 906; 1272.

[118] Fragment 1, section 2 (ed. Duke; see note 96, above).

[119] Polybius, IV, xxxviii, 5; cf. IG. II–III², 903, where, in the first half of the second century B.C., a metic is honored for selling to the city grain brought from the Pontus and, apparently in the following year, for turning over to the city—at a time of extraordinary scarcity—a supply of oil which he had collected from various Aegean ports for transport to the Pontus.

quoted by Athenaeus, attests its exportation to Antioch;[120] and there is evidence, derived from Egyptian papyri, to show that it was imported into Egypt in the time of Ptolemy Philadelphus.[121] Attic trade in agricultural products during the third century B.C., however, was not so remunerative as in other periods. The one product which was exported in large quantities, namely oil, declined steadily in price between 305 B.C. and 246 B.C., and after the latter date fluctuated slightly until the end of the third century B.C.[122] The Attic pottery industry of the third century enjoyed a moderate degree of prosperity. After 275 B.C. Megarian bowls were produced in numbers sufficiently large not only to supply the home market, but also to meet a moderately large foreign demand.[123] These bowls were exported to South Russia, among other places, and were imitated by various foreign schools of pottery.[124]

When their exports of agricultural and manufactured products declined in the third century the Greek cities generally found it difficult to pay for grain and for the imported raw materials necessary to their industries. This factor would have occasioned even greater distress had it not been for the fact that up to c.250 B.C. freight rates declined and thereafter did not rise during the succeeding century.[125] The situation at Athens, however, was more favorable than in some Greek cities, for it still possessed in abundance most of the materials which its industries had utilized during the fifth and fourth centuries. Excellent clay and marble, the two chief materials employed in its industries, were readily accessible within Attica, and in the latter third of the third century excellent

[120] Athenaeus, X, 432. For the date of Epinicus, in the latter part of the third century B.C., see Kaibel, in RE, VI, 185.

[121] P. Cairo Zen. 59012, ll. 28–30; 59426, l. 6; P. Mich. Zen. iii, l. 3. It is to be observed that the Attic honey imported into Egypt in the third century B.C. was brought there by way of Syria. See V. Tscherikower, in *Mizraim*, IV–V (1937), 25–27.

[122] Larsen, "Roman Greece," p. 390; cf. Heichelheim, *Schwankungen*, p. 53.

[123] H. A. Thompson, in *Hesperia*, III (1934), 459.

[124] *Ibid.*, p. 459. Attic influence is apparent not only in South Russia—aside from the vases actually exported to that region—but also at Myrina, in Asia Minor (*ibid.*, p. 459; cf. Courby, *Vases grecs*, pp. 402–3). The very popular type of decoration which Courby, p. 333, calls "à godrons" was probably developed at Athens; H. A. Thompson, in *Hesperia*, III (1934), 459.

[125] Larsen, "Roman Greece," pp. 407–8; Heichelheim, *Schwankungen*, pp. 91–97, especially 93, 96; G. Glotz, in JDS, XI (1913), 18.

silver and lead were produced in the mines at Laurium.[126] It was mainly in the instance of bronze that Athens was compelled to import raw materials essential–for industry. This was, of course, a distinct handicap to the bronze-working trade, which, however, had already been in decline at Athens for some years before the beginning of the third century. In the Hellenistic period the new trend was toward making the more expensive vases of metal. Despite the sharp decline in the value of metals these vases were accessible only to the purchasers of luxury articles.[127] The poor had to be content with imitations in clay. In the face of competition and even moderate transportation charges Athens was unable to export with profit the more expensive vases made of bronze, but in the sphere of the cheaper clay vases and of silver vases[128] the city was to hold some share in the market throughout the third and much of the second centuries.

Our knowledge concerning laborers and the conditions of labor at Athens in the third century B.C. is scanty. The lot of the laborer was trying, for, as we observed above, wages had declined and remained low even in the second half of the century when prices were rising. Moreover, with the decline of foreign markets the number of workers required by the city's industries grew smaller. And although a number of Athenians had emigrated to foreign parts, that emigration had not proceeded to the extent that the city suffered from a shortage of labor. On the contrary, Athens, it seems likely, had

[126] The ore mined at Laurium was argentiferous galena, which usually has a lead content of 65 percent. The finding, however, of only a small amount of litharge at Laurium makes it evident that the ancients produced lead there as well as silver. Consequently, despite the fact that lead from Laurium is not attested by our literary authorities—Davies, however, suggests the emendation of Λαυρίων for Τυρίων in Aristotle, *Econ.* 1353a, 15—there is good reason for believing that most of the lead consumed in Greece proper came from the Attic mines. See Davies, *Roman Mines*, pp. 246–47.

[127] H. A. Thompson, in *Hesperia*, III (1934), 312. For the decline in the price of metals induced by the distribution of the Persian treasure, see F. M. Heichelheim, in *Economic History: a Supplement to the Economic Journal*, III (1935), 1–3; *Schwankungen*, pp. 40–41.

[128] There are no extant silver vases of this period which may be assigned to Athens. But we are justified in assuming that some such wares were produced in the most important center of silver mining in the Greek world. Cf. Ardaillon, *Mines du Laurium*, pp. 115–17, who suggests that at least some of the silver phialae that were offered as votives at various sanctuaries must have been made at Athens.

to deal with an unemployment problem. Probably contributory to unemployment—but how greatly we cannot determine—was the situation in the ceramic industry, especially in that branch which produced Megarian bowls, where something akin to modern methods of mass production prevailed.[129] No longer did an individual artisan work on the decoration of each vase; the decorations were now impressed upon the vase through the employment of molds. Thus a smaller number of workmen was required. Possible proof that the unemployment problem was met in part by enrolling poor citizens as members of the frontier garrisons is to be found in the organization of the Athenian armed forces at the end of the third century B.C. Thus, the fact that, in one instance which is known to us, a general made a prepayment [πρόδομα] to the soldiers[130] seems to show that the Athenians in question were of the poorer classes.[131] The number of slaves employed at Athens at this time cannot be estimated. In general in Greece at this time the number of slaves had fallen off, especially in those districts in which industry had declined.[132] However, there is no doubt but that there were still slaves in Attica; they were employed in the mines at Laurium, in the households of the wealthy, and possibly in small numbers in industry and agriculture.[133] To what extent the employment of slaves deprived free laborers of work we are unable to estimate. As for the type of work done by the individual workers at Athens we have little specific information, but it is likely that specialization was in vogue here as elsewhere in the Hellenistic world. One indication of this is to be found in certain families at Athens where the trade of sculptor was hereditary between the third and the first centuries.[134] As for the ingenuity and initiative of

[129] For the methods employed in the production of Megarian bowls, see P. V. C. Baur, in A JA, XLV (1941), 245–48.

[130] IG, II–III², 1304, ll. 34–38.

[131] Griffith, *Mercenaries*, p. 85. In the latter part of the fourth century B.C. the poor welcomed army service as a source of livelihood. See Diodorus, XVIII, x, 1; cf. H. W. Parke, *Greek Mercenary Soldiers from the Earliest Times to the Battle of Ipsus* (Oxford, 1933), p. 204.

[132] Westermann, "Sklaverei," col. 935.   [133] *Ibid.*, cols. 931–32, 934.

[134] Glotz, *Ancient Greece at Work*, p. 321. For the Eubulides-Eucheir family, see C. Robert, in RE, VI, 870–75, Nos. 9–11. For the Dies-Caicosthenes family, see C. Robert, in RE, V, 477, No. 3; Lippold, in RE, X, 1503. For Athenian sculptors of the third and second centuries B.C., see Ferguson, *Athens*, p. 246, note 4.

Attic artists and skilled workers, it has for some time been customary to consider (and wrongly so) that these qualities were lacking
at Athens in the third century. Thus in the instance of the ceramic
industry, although the glaze on the vases was less carefully applied,
the fabric was still better than most local fabrics in the Greek
world, the designs of Megarian bowls were so excellent that they
were imitated by foreign schools of potters,[135] and the molds produced by the Athenians were so highly thought of that there was a
foreign demand for them.[136] As regards Athenian sculptors of the
third century, it seems likely that they were more accomplished
than we have hitherto thought. Some works of merit that were not
altogether subservient to tradition were produced at Athens in the
first part of the century.[137] But many sculptors followed their trade
in other cities. At this time three Athenian sculptors, Telesinus,[138]
Niceratus,[139] and Phyromachus,[140] are known to have worked at
Delos. Of these, Telesinus worked also at Tenos,[141] and Niceratus
and Phyromachus at Pergamum.[142] During the middle years of the
third century, between about 277 B.C. and 239 B.C., the Athenian
sculptor Parthenocles executed commissions at Delos,[143] and at the
end of the third century, after 229 B.C., other Athenian sculptors

[135] H. A. Thompson, in *Hesperia*, III (1934), 458–59.

[136] *Ibid.*, p. 459; cf. note 123, above. However, this point should not be over-
emphasized. Actually only one imported Athenian mold has been reported from
Delos. See Courby, *Vases grecs*, p. 333.

[137] Ashmole, in Beazley and Ashmole, *Greek Sculpture and Painting*, pp. 68–69
(=Ashmole, in CAH, VIII, 669–70).

[138] IG, XI, iv, 514, ll. 2–10, and 1201b; Durrbach, *Choix*, No. 16. Cf. M. Lacroix,
"Les Étrangers a Délos pendant la période de l'indépendance," *Mélanges Gustave
Glotz*, II, 501–25, especially 513.

[139] IG, XI, iv, 1105, l. 7, and 1212; Durrbach, *Choix*, No. 32. Wrongly assigned
to the time of Eumenes II by M. Fraenkel, *Die Inschriften von Pergamon* (1890;
Altertümer von Pergamon, VIII, i), No. 132. See P. Roussel's comments on IG,
XI, iv, 1105.

[140] IG, XI, iv, 1212; Durrbach, *Choix*, No. 32. Wrongly assigned to the time of
Eumenes II by M. Fraenkel, *Die Inschriften von Pergamon*, p. 69. See P. Roussel's
comments in IG, XI, iv, 1212.

[141] See the commentary on IG, XI, iv, 1201, by P. Roussel; Durrbach, *Choix*, No.
16, with commentary, pp. 23–24.

[142] See the commentary on IG, XI, iv, 1212, by P. Roussel; Durrbach, *Choix*,
No. 32, with commentary, pp. 39–40. Cf. M. Fraenkel, *Die Inschriften von Pergamon*, No. 132.

[143] IG, XI, iv, 1098, l. 7.

received contracts outside of Athens.[144] Athenian contractors, also, seem to have been employed in various foreign districts.[145] It seems obvious that there was little for a sculptor to do at Athens in the third century, and that he was forced to find employment elsewhere.[146] This circumstance will explain in part the fact (concerning which Pliny commented),[147] that little art of value was produced in mainland Greece between the beginning of the third and the middle of the second centuries B.C.

As we have seen, Athens lost much of its commerce and trade during the third century—the loss (which became extremely severe between c.260 B.C. and 229 B.C.) being caused in part by the unwillingness of the Athenians and resident foreigners to venture upon substantial business risks in the face of the political uncertainty and disorganization which existed in Attica during the period of Macedonian domination. Contributing to this severe decline were also the loss of foreign markets and the shifting of the important centers of trade and industry to the East. When Athens regained its independence in 229 B.C., and when the uncertainty with regard to the political situation was removed, citizens and resident foreigners took part again in what was left of the transit trade. But Athens was never again to attain the degree of property which it had experienced during the fifth century and at the end of the fourth century under Demetrius of Phalerum. Moreover, the progressive concentration of land in the hands of fewer and fewer individuals and the impoverishment of the laboring class served to draw the

[144] Ferguson, *Athens*, p. 246, note 4, counted the names of fifty-seven Athenian sculptors of the third and second centuries B.C. who worked in cities other than Athens. For the Athenian sculptor Archestratus, who worked at Rhodes, see F. Hiller von Gaertringen, "Rhodos," RE, Supplementband V, 731–840, especially 829. Some Alexandrian tombstones of the period immediately following the foundation of the city were produced either by immigrant Athenian sculptors or were imported from Athens. See E. Pfuhl, "Alexandrinische Grabreliefs," AM, XXVI (1901), 258–304, especially 264; cf. A. W. Lawrence, "Greek Sculpture in Ptolemaic Egypt," *Journal of Egyptian Archaeology*, XI (1925), 179–90, especially 182.

[145] One may be cited at Peparethus, in an inscription (IG, XII, viii, 640) dated shortly after 197 B.C. Similar conditions may be assumed for the closing years of the third century. Cf. Ferguson, *Athens*, p. 246, note 4.

[146] Cf. Ashmole, in Beazley and Ashmole, *Greek Sculpture and Painting*, pp. 68–70 (=Ashmole, in CAH, VIII, 669–72).

[147] NH XXXIV, lii.

political lines ever more tightly between a small class of the very wealthy (always a relative term when applied to Greece) and another group, the very poor, who formed the mass of the population. This situation had existed in Greece long before the third century B.C.,[148] and was destined to become even more aggravated under Roman domination.[149]

In 203 B.C. Antiochus the Great entered into a secret agreement with Philip of Macedon which provided for partition of the realm of Ptolemy V Epiphanes, for a free hand for Philip in the Aegean (limited only by the latter's respect for Syrian interests there), and for mutual assistance in the event of an attack upon either party to the compact. Late in 201 B.C., when the existence of this agreement became known, the Senate decided to intervene to maintain the *status quo* in Greece and in the Aegean, the domination of which by a strong foreign power the Senate considered dangerous to Rome.[150] The Senate was not only fearful of the powerful support which Philip received from Antiochus and from his alliance with Hannibal, but also looked askance at the signs of Philip's naval power, evidenced by his victories at Lade and Chios.[151] Hence, in 200 B.C. Rome entered upon the Second Macedonian War, which was brought to an end, in 197 B.C., by the battle of Cynoscephalae. In the following year, at the Isthmian festival,

[148] H. Francotte, *L'Industrie dans la Grèce ancienne* (Brussels, 1901), II, 312–15.

[149] See A. Passerini, "Studi di storia ellenistico-romana, VI: i moti politico-sociali della Grecia e i Romani," *Athenaeum*, XI (1933), 309–35; Aymard, *Premiers Rapports*, pp. 31 (note 6), 32, 135 (note 6), 158–59; cf. Larsen, "Roman Greece," 421–22.

[150] The best discussion of Rome's intervention in the East at this time is by A. H. McDonald and F. W. Walbank, "The Origins of the Second Macedonian War," JRS, XXVII (1937), 180–207, where full citations of important earlier discussions are given. The relation of Athens to this momentous event is discussed especially on pp. 200–3, where the historical implications of the honorary decree for Cephisodorus, recently found in the Agora at Athens and published by B. D. Meritt, in *Hesperia*, V (1936), 419–28, are treated. The standard discussion of Rome's relations with eastern states in the third century is by M. Holleaux, *Rome, la Grèce et les monarchies hellénistiques au IIIe siècle avant J.-C.* (*273–205*) (1921; Bibliothèque des Écoles françaises d'Athènes et de Rome, CXXIV); cf. CAH, VII, 822–57, and VIII, 116–240.

[151] The Senate's concern over Philip's naval power is pointed out by G. T. Griffith, "An Early Motive of Roman Imperialism," *Cambridge Historical Journal*, V (1935), 1–14.

proclamation was made of the "freedom" of the Greeks.[152] But it was freedom only in name.[153] Henceforth the Greeks—and among them the Athenians—were to be under Roman domination.

[152] Polybius, XVIII, xlvi, 5 and 15; Livy, XXXIII, xxxii, 5, and xxxiii, 7; cf. Larsen, "Roman Greece," p. 274.

[153] J. A. O. Larsen, "Was Greece Free between 196 and 146 B.C.?" *Classical Philology*, XXX (1935), 193–214, especially 209; cf. M. Holleaux, in CAH, VIII, 195.

CHAPTER II

SECOND CENTURY TO THE

ACQUISITION OF DELOS:

200-166 B.C.

AT THE BEGINNING of the second century B.C. the members of the governing class, who were men of considerable wealth, were pro-Roman in sympathy, but the Athenian populace at large, the poor, were anti-Roman.[1] And in this respect the Athenian poor shared the sentiments of the poor in Greece at large, who thought of the Romans as the mainstay and support of their oppressors, the wealthy, and were therefore ready to throw their support to the enemies of Rome, the foremost of these at the moment being Antiochus the Great of Syria.[2] The Romans had tried, by various diplomatic means, to persuade Antiochus to withdraw from Europe, but the Seleucid king's ambitions in Thrace seemed likely at any moment to embroil him in war with the great power of the West.[3] Moreover, it seemed quite likely that Antiochus would come to Greece to attack the Romans and would wish to use the Piraeus as a naval base. At this juncture the demagogue Apollodorus, in an attempt to further the cause of Antiochus, urged the Athenians to overthrow the pro-Roman government and, as was natural in an appeal to the proletariat, made promises of gifts of large sums of money to come from the Seleucid monarch.[4] Apollodorus apparently met with some success, for the situation became so serious that the government made an appeal for aid to the Roman commissioners who had been sent to

[1] Ferguson, *Athens*, pp. 281–83.   [2] M. Holleaux, in CAH, VIII, 196.
[3] *Ibid.*, pp. 199–203.
[4] Livy, XXXV, 1; cf. M. Holleaux, in CAH, VIII, 198.

aid Flamininus in arranging the affairs of Greece. These commissioners arrived soon at Athens—at about the same time that Eumenes II of Pergamum appeared on the scene with a large fleet.[5] The threatened revolt was suppressed, and Apollodorus was sent into exile. But the possibility of another outbreak seemed so imminent that, in the winter of 192/1 B.C., it was considered necessary to place a garrison of 500 Achaeans in the Piraeus to assure the continuance of the government in power.[6] Since the wealthy governing class had espoused the cause of Rome, it was natural that Rome would continue her support of them; and it was with this support that members of those families who were then in office continued in positions of power until well into the latter half of the second century.[7] The members of this ruling class remained constant in their allegiance to Rome, and for this loyalty Athens was to be rewarded in 166 B.C.

The various officials of the government at this time, whether selected by lot or by vote, were usually wealthy men.[8] And although liturgies had been abolished by the reforms of Demetrius of Phalerum, the officeholders were expected to make liberal contributions out of their own means towards the support of various forms of public services, such as festivals and the repair of public buildings.[9] Their concept of the function of the officeholder was, therefore, that which was to obtain under the Roman Empire. There are several external indications of the wealth of these men and of the fact that that wealth was now being expended considerably less sparingly than during the third century. At the end of the fourth century Demetrius of Phalerum had, in promulgating his sumptuary legislation, forbidden extravagant expenditures on family plots in the cemeteries and the erection of elaborate grave monuments: he permitted the use of only a small round pillar, a plain stele, or a vase.[10] But in the first part of the second century the aristocratic

[5] Livy, XXXV, xxxix; Plutarch, *Cato Maior*, 12; Ferguson, *Athens*, pp. 283–84.
[6] Livy, XXXV, l, 3–4.   [7] Ferguson, *Athens*, p. 288.
[8] *Ibid.*, p. 289.   [9] *Ibid.*, p. 289; cf. 55–56.
[10] Cicero, *De leg.* II, 64–66. For the elaborate family plots and a detailed discussion of all matters pertaining to the cemetery outside the Sacred Gate, the most important cemetery at Athens in the classical period, see Brückner, *Der Friedhof am Eridanos;* cf. AM, LI (1926), 130–31; H. Diepolder, *Die attischen Grabreliefs* (Berlin, 1931).

families resumed the practice of erecting costly sculptured tombstones in their family plots in the cemetery.[11] They also had a
penchant for horse racing and must have gone to considerable expense in breeding and training horses for competition in the contests
held at the state festivals.[12] Moreover, in addition to the contributions which they made in their capacity as officeholders, the members of the aristocratic families made contributions toward various
public undertakings which were carried out by means of funds
raised by voluntary (?) subscription.[13] Yet another manifestation
of their wealth is to be found in their creation of endowments—a
practice highly developed in Greece by the second century[14]—
which provided funds for permanent support of various public and
private institutions and services. An instance of such an endowment
at Athens in the second century is the gift of 1,000 drachmas that
was made for the purpose of defraying the cost of the monthly
sacrifices of the *Dionysiastae* in the Piraeus.[15]

The New Style coinage, the issuance of which had been instituted

[11] H. Möbius, *Die Ornamente der griechischen Grabstelen klassischer und nach-
klassischer Zeit* (Berlin-Wilmersdorf, 1929), p. 46. For ornamented (some with
sculpture) sepulchral stelae of the second century which have recently been identified, see J. Kirchner, in AE, 1937, pp. 338–40. Kirchner has also recognized ten
stelae of the third century that are adorned with ornaments or palmettes. All the
latter are monuments of foreigners, and for that reason Kirchner suggests that only
Athenians were specified in Demetrius' sumptuary edict.

[12] For the equestrian contests held during the second century B.C. in conjunction
with the Panathenaea, see IG, II–III², 2313–17; Gardiner, *Greek Sports*, pp. 229,
235–36; Klee, *Agone*, pp. 28–29; A. Martin, *Les Cavaliers athéniens* (1887; Bibliothèque des Écoles françaises d'Athènes et de Rome, XLVII), pp. 226–72; cf.
Ferguson, *Athens*, pp. 291–94; Mommsen, *Feste*, pp. 85–98. For a discussion of the
families represented among the individuals who took part in these contests, see
Martin, *Les Cavaliers athéniens*, pp. 273–81. Other equestrian contests were held in
connection with the Theseia, records of which are extant from the period between
161–130 B.C. IG, II–III², 956–66; Ferguson, *Athens*, pp. 294–95; Klee, *Agone*, p. 40;
Mommsen, *Feste*, pp. 278, 296–98.

[13] E.g. IG, II–III², 2331–32; cf. Kuenzi, p. 31. Rostovtzeff, in his *Social and
Economic History of the Hellenistic World*, maintains that neither the making of
these contributions nor the establishing of endowments was really a voluntary act;
both were exacted in some way or other by the community.

[14] Cf. Larsen, "Roman Greece," pp. 361–68. A complete treatment of the entire
subject is to be found in Laum, *Stiftungen*, Vols. I–II.

[15] IG, II–III², 1325 (a decree of the association voted during the lifetime of the
donor, 185/4 B.C.) and 1326 (a decree of the association voted in 176/5 B.C., after
the death of the donor); cf. Laum, *Stiftungen*, Vol. II, No. 20.

in 229 B.C., soon gained wide currency and asserted its primacy in Greece. And between 229 B.C. and the time of Sulla Athens was surpassed, with respect to volume of coinage, only by Syria and Egypt. The first class, which was issued between 229 B.C. and 196 B.C., found almost immediate acceptance among merchants, and c.200 B.C. imitations of it were made by the Cretan cities of Cnossus, Cydonia, Gortyn, Hierapytna, Polyrrhenium, and Priansus.[16] The volume of all classes of the currency and their wide circulation are conclusively shown by various facts, among which are the existence of numerous hoards—some of them quite large— which have been found in widely separated places. In northern Greece a hoard of silver tetradrachms of the New Style has been found at Anthedon in Boeotia,[17] and a very large hoard, consisting of 969 silver tetradrachms at Halmyros, near Larissa Kremaste in Thessaly.[18] In Macedonia two very large hoards have been found, one near Aecaterini,[19] consisting of 600 silver tetradrachms, the other at Zaroba,[20] consisting of 1,000 silver tetradrachms. Farther north, at Benkovski in Bulgaria,[21] silver tetradrachms of the second period (196–186 B.C.) of the New Style coinage were discovered in 1933. In Euboea two hoards of New Style coinage have been found, one at Carystus,[22] buried at about 88 B.C., consisting of seventy silver coins out of a total of 103 coins of various mints, and one at Haghia Varvara,[23] consisting of 231 bronze coins. Hoards including numerous New Style coins have also been unearthed in Crete,[24] Aegina,[25] Naxos,[26] and Delos.[27] Most of the coins from

[16] Seltman, *Greek Coins*, pp. 260–61; Head, *Hist. Num.*, p. 462; Svoronos, *Les Monnaies d'Athènes*, Pl. CXIII.

[17] Noe, *Bibliography*, No. 53.

[18] M. L. Kambanis, in BCH, LVIII (1934), 101–31; LIX (1935), 101–7, 244; Noe, *Bibliography*, No. 478. The hoard contained 969 silver tetradrachms.

[19] *Ibid.*, No. 18. The hoard contained 600 silver tetradrachms.

[20] *Ibid.*, No. 1184; cf. M. L. Kambanis, in BCH, LVIII (1934), 131–35; LIX (1935), 108–20. The hoard contained 1,000 silver tetradrachms.

[21] Noe, *Bibliography*, No. 145. The hoard contained 270 silver tetradrachms.

[22] *Ibid.*, No. 212. The hoard contained 70 silver tetradrachms.

[23] *Ibid.*, No. 473. The hoard contained 231 bronze coins.

[24] *Ibid.*, Nos. 282, 433 (from Hierapytna). No. 433 contained 50 ± silver tetradrachms.

[25] *Ibid.*, No. 19, where the number of New Style coins is very small.

[26] *Ibid.*, No. 733, which contained 31 silver tetradrachms.

[27] *Ibid.*, Nos. 303 (containing 43 silver tetradrachms), 304 (three separate hoards

Delos, however, belong to the period after 166 B.C., but there are also some dating from the period preceding the Athenian cleruchy.[28] Large hoards of these coins have also come to light in Attica[29] and in Salamis;[30] the number found in the Agora at Athens and identified as of 1935 amounted to 902 coins.[31] The evidence now in our possession suggests that the New Style coins may not have circulated in the Peloponnesus. Two large hoards found there contained no coins of this type,[32] but later evidence may show Athenian coins there just as it has recently shown, contrary to the accepted opinion, that Athenian coins circulated in at least some parts of Asia.[33] A study[34] of twelve hoards found in Asia had disclosed only one Athenian New Style coin, a silver tetradrachm, but recently a hoard buried c.95 B.C. and containing ten New Style silver tetradrachms of the period 229–187 B.C., out of a total of seventy coins, has been found in Syria.[35] And even before the finding of this

---

containing a total of 30 silver tetradrachms), 305 (a very small hoard), 306 (containing 314 silver tetradrachms, 120 silver drachmas, and 23 triobols), 308 (containing 39 silver tetradrachms, drachmas, and hemidrachms), 309 (a very small hoard), 311 (a very small hoard), 312 (a very small hoard), 313 (a very small hoard), 315 (containing 92 silver tetradrachms), 316 (containing 50 ± silver tetradrachms), 318 (containing 250 silver tetradrachms), 319 (containing 18 silver tetradrachms and 2 drachmas). Cf. Roussel, DCA, p. 48, note 4.

[28] Noe, *Bibliography*, Nos. 303–4; Roussel, DCA, p. 48, note 4.

[29] Noe, *Bibliography*, Nos. 102 (containing 40 bronze coins), 105 (containing 244 bronze coins), 106 (containing 45 bronze coins), 818 (containing 13 bronze coins); A. R. Bellinger, *Two Hoards of Attic Bronze Coins* (1930; Numismatic Notes and Monographs, No. 42), treats Noe's Nos. 105 and 106; cf. W. Schwabacher, in *Numismatic Chronicle*, 5th series, XIX (1939), 162–66.

[30] Noe, *Bibliography*, No. 890 (containing 24 silver tetradrachms and 5 silver drachmas).

[31] J. P. Shear, in *Hesperia*, V (1936), 150.

[32] Larsen, "Roman Greece," p. 330. For the huge hoard containing 9,171 silver coins found at Zougra (ancient Pellene), see Noe, *Bibliography*, No. 1186. The hoard found at Caserta, Italy, in 1889–90 was apparently carried there from the Peloponnesus and buried c.146 B.C.; it contained 499 silver coins. A. Löbbecke, in ZFN, XXVI (1908), 275–303; Noe, *Bibliography*, No. 213.

[33] However, other evidence tends to show that the trade relations of the city were predominantly with northern Greece.

[34] K. Regling, "Hellenistischer Münzschatz aus Babylon," ZFN, XXXVIII (1928), 92–131. The hoard (Noe, *Bibliography*, No. 116) analyzed in this article consisted of 100 silver tetradrachms, which were buried c.150 B.C.; among them was only one Athenian New Style coin. Eleven other hoards from Asia, analyzed by Regling, contained no New Style coins.

[35] F. Thureau-Dangin and M. Dunand, *Til Barsib* (Paris, 1936), pp. 81–82.

hoard we possessed evidence which tended to indicate that New Style coins had penetrated as far as southern Arabia, for at the end of the second century B.C. they were being copied by the Himyarites who dwelt in that region.[36] So favored were the New Style coins that—the Peloponnesus probably excepted—the silver tetradrachms were employed as standard currency throughout Greece.[37] Contributory to the high favor in which these coins were held were undoubtedly the scrupulous maintenance of weight, adhering on the average closely to 17 gr.,[38] and the high percentage of tin, which produced a hard alloy and thereby assured exceptionally good preservation of the coins.[39] A striking indication of the repute of this coinage is to be found in the fact that the coinages most frequently singled out for explicit mention in the lists of booty brought to Rome after the campaigns of the end of the third and the beginning of the second centuries were the Athenian tetradrachms and the Philippei.[40] In taking this action the Romans were merely recognizing the fact that the New Style coinage had already attained to wide currency in Greece. More explicit recognition of its primacy was to be made at the end of the second century in the decree of the Delphic Amphictyony, which prescribed the exchange value of the Athenian tetradrachm in all districts of Greece which were represented in the Amphictyony.[41] A further indication of the dominance of this coinage is to be observed in the fact that coins of the same standard, but issued by another authority, were

[36] G. F. Hill, "The Ancient Coinage of Southern Arabia," *Proceedings of the British Academy*, VII (1915), 1–28, especially 7, 8; *British Museum Catalogue of the Greek Coins of Arabia, Mesopotamia and Persia* (London, 1922), pp. liv–lxii; cf. Svoronos, *Les Monnaies d'Athènes*, Pl. CXII.

[37] Larsen, "Roman Greece," p. 330.

[38] *Ibid.*, p. 327, where the calculation is based on the weights given by Svoronos, *Les Monnaies d'Athènes*, Pl. XXXIII–LXXVIII, where the various types of New Style coins are pictured. Segrè, *Metrologia*, p. 228, maintains that the normal weight of the tetradrachm was 17.46 gr. This coin was ordinarily equated with four Roman denarii. *Ibid.*, p. 389. Coins of smaller denomination than the tetradrachm were probably used only for local currency, for their weight varies considerably. Larsen, "Roman Grèece," p. 327.

[39] Caley, *Greek Bronze Coins*, Table IV, p. 26; Table VI, p. 41; cf. J. P. Shear, in *Hesperia*, V (1936), 288.

[40] Larsen, "Roman Greece," p. 331.

[41] FDD, III, ii, 139. For the date, between 124 B.C. and 100 B.C., see Daux, *Delphes*, p. 388.

at times listed as "Athenian tetradrachms."[42] In the list of booty
that adorned the triumphal procession of Flamininus at the end of
the Second Macedonian War we find mention of 84,000 Athenian
tetradrachms, but of no Macedonian silver coins.[43] Likewise, in the
list of the booty carried in the triumphal procession of M. Fulvius
Nobilior at the end of the Aetolian Wars (192–189 B.C.) mention
is made of Athenian tetradrachms and of Philippei, but not of Aetolian coins.[44] In each case it is likely that other coinages were
lumped together with the Athenian coinage under the term "Athenian tetradrachms." At about 196 B.C. Athens began to issue the
second class of this coinage,[45] which was soon to be imitated by
various cities in Asia Minor, of which we may note especially the
Ionian cities of Heraclea, Lebedus, and Priene;[46] and in 186 B.C. it
began to mint the third class.[47] To ensure the maintenance of high
standards of weight and purity a careful system of checks was
worked out.[48] A number of names and devices appeared on each
coin. First of all there were the names of two officials, one an ex-
archon, accompanied by a device selected by the official whose name
stood in the first position.[49] Responsibility for the coinage was
placed upon a committee selected from the Areopagus; the members of this committee, twelve in number, served one each month,
and each month the name of the responsible member—thus a
third name—was placed on each coin.[50] The lunar month in which
the coin was issued was also specified on each coin.[51] Finally, on

[42] Larsen, "Roman Greece," pp. 331–32, who cites the report (Livy, XXXIX,
vii, 1) that Cn. Manlius Vulso brought 127,000 Athenian tetradrachms back from
Asia Minor—but at a time when Athenian coins seem not to have circulated there.

[43] Livy, XXXIV, lii, 4–8.   [44] Livy, XXXIX, v, 14–17.

[45] Head, *Hist. Num.*, pp. 381–82; Seltman, *Greek Coins*, p. 261.

[46] *Ibid.*, p. 261.

[47] Head, *Hist. Num.*, pp. 382–85; Seltman, *Greek Coins*, p. 262.

[48] Head, *Hist. Num.*, pp. 378–80; Seltman, *Greek Coins*, p. 262.

[49] The officials were selected from influential families, pairings of father and son,
or two brothers, often being found on the coins. And at times visiting foreign
potentates were chosen. Head, *Hist. Num.*, p. 379; Sundwall, *Untersuchungen*, II,
16. It is Sundwall's view that these officials were not strictly magistrates, but,
rather, honorary superintendents upon whom the obligation was imposed of meeting, out of their own means, part of the expenses involved in the duties attached
to the office.

[50] *Ibid.*, p. 69; Head, *Hist. Num.*, p. 379.

[51] G. Macdonald, in *Numismatic Chronicle*, 1899, p. 288.

each coin, below the amphora, there was an indication, in the form of letters, of the mine from which the silver employed in minting that particular coin came.[52] As a distinguished numismatist has recently remarked,[53] such a complicated system of accounting is found on no currency before the era of the modern paper note. Moreover, the necessity of changing each month the name of the responsible mint official and of the lunar month shows that the dies were changed each month. This is, of itself, an indication of the exceptionally wide circulation of the coinage.

Although the finances of the state were greatly strengthened by the revenue derived from the activity of the mines at Laurium, the deficiencies of the fiscal system remained to plague the city.[54] It was, accordingly, found necessary to take resort to various measures to meet pressing current expenses. The magistrates were required, we have seen, to contribute toward various public services. Moreover, resort was had to the *epidosis*, a system of contributions called voluntary, but, in actuality, probably compulsory.[55] Thus, in 183/2 B.C. a fund was raised, for what purpose we do not know, by subscriptions collected from both citizens and foreigners.[56] And in 172/1 B.C. another fund was raised, also by popular subscription, this time for the purpose of repairing a tower in the walls which, apparently, formed a part of the fortifications of the Piraeus.[57] The state treasury could not even maintain the defenses of the city! Possibly another method of replenishing the treasury is to be deduced from an inscription of 176/5 B.C. which honors a foreigner for selling grain and oil to the state at a low price:[58] the

[52] Sundwall, *Untersuchungen*, II, 18, note 2; Head, *Hist. Num.*, p. 379; G. F. Hill, *Handbook of Greek and Roman Coins* (London, 1899), p. 130, took these signs to be an indication of the shop in which the individual coins were struck. The silver used by the mint was supplied by thirty to forty mines, but the output of only about one-half of them was needed consistently. Head, *Hist. Num.*, p. 380.

[53] Seltman, *Greek Coins*, p. 262.   [54] Ferguson, *Athens*, p. 369.

[55] For the nature of the ἐπίδοσις, see Kuenzi, pp. 1–6. Cf. note 13, above, and chap. i, note 65.

[56] IG, II–III², 2332. For the date of the archonship of Hermogenes, see Dinsmoor, *Archon List*, pp. 23, 187; Ferguson, *Cycles*, p. 28; Pritchett and Meritt, *Chronology*, p. xxviii.

[57] IG, II–III², 2331. For the date, see Dinsmoor, *Archon List*, pp. 8–9, 23, 189; Ferguson, *Cycles*, p. 29; Pritchett and Meritt, *Chronology*, p. xxviii.

[58] IG, II–III², 903; cf. A. von Premerstein, in AM, XXXVI (1911), 73–86,

state may have made a profit on the transaction by disposing of the commodities at a higher price.

A striking phenomenon of the second century was the holding of a large number of international festivals throughout the Hellenistic world.[59] The festivals held at Athens constituted one of the greatest expenditures undertaken by the state. While some of the old festivals had been abandoned, many of them still flourished and new ones were added to their number.[60] The Athenians now raised the Eleusinia to the rank of an international festival,[61] with the result that four great festivals, the Dionysia,[62] the Ptolemaea,[63] the Panathenaea,[64] and the Eleusinia,[65] were celebrated in the city, two each year. The games connected with the festivals—in particular with the Panathenaea[66]—were attended by visitors and competitors[67] from widely separated foreign districts. Even ruling kings and princes eagerly entered their horses in the races, each with an

---

especially 78–79. For the date, see Dinsmoor, *Archon List*, pp. 9, 23, 188, 189; Ferguson, *Cycles*, p. 29; Pritchett and Meritt, *Chronology*, pp. xxviii, 117, 119–21.

[59] Tarn, *Hellenistic Civilization*, pp. 104–6; cf. P. Boesch, Θεωρός (Berlin, 1908), pp. 14–17. See the interesting inscription, recently found in the Agora at Athens, in honor of the athlete Menodorus of Athens; S. Dow, in *Hesperia*, IV (1935), 81–90. Menodorus won prizes in contests at eighteen different festivals. An almost precisely similar monument was erected to the same athlete at Delos. L. Bizard and P. Roussel, in BCH, XXXI (1907), 432–35. For a list of similar inscriptions of the period ranging between the end of the third and the beginning of the first centuries B.C., see S. Dow, in *Hesperia*, IV (1935), 89.

[60] Ferguson, *Athens*, pp. 290, 295–96.

[61] P. Foucart, "La Fête des Éleusinia," REG, XXXII (1919), 190–207, especially 203–4.

[62] Deubner, *Attische Feste*, pp. 138–42; Mommsen, *Feste*, p. 428. The festival was celebrated annually.

[63] Deubner, *Attische Feste*, pp. 235–36; Dinsmoor, *Archon List*, p. 192; W. S. Ferguson, in *Klio*, VIII (1908), 338–45. The festival was celebrated in the first year of every Olympiad.

[64] Deubner, *Attische Feste*, pp. 22–35. The festival was celebrated in the third year of every Olympiad.

[65] *Ibid.*, pp. 91–92. The festival was celebrated in the second and fourth years of every Olympiad.

[66] See note 12, above.

[67] More than half of the non-Athenian victors at the Panathenaea came from Ionia and Caria. Klee, *Agone*, p. 119. Greek athletes had, by this time, become professionals and attempted to compete in as many festivals as possible. See C. A. Manning, "Professionalism in Greek Athletics," *Classical Weekly*, XI (1917), 74–78; E. N. Gardiner, *Athletics in the Ancient World* (Oxford, 1930), pp. 105–6; *Greek Sports*, pp. 160–61. Cf. note 59, above.

eye to interests, we shall see, not necessarily related to sports. Not long after 191 B.C. Ptolemy Epiphanes entered a horse in the races held in connection with the Panathenaea.[68] Four years later King Eumenes II and his three brothers entered horses and won four prizes.[69] Some years later Mastanabal, son of King Massinissa of Numidia, was listed among the victors at the Panathenaea;[70] and in the same year Ptolemy Philometor I entered a colt which took first prize.[71] To conclude the list, we may take notice of the two victories won by Antiochus V of Syria in 162 B.C.[72] Although the magistrates in charge of the games contributed generously toward the expenses, it was still necessary for the state to meet a substantial part of the costs. Nevertheless, the benefits that accrued to the Athenians were rather great, for opportunities for trade were greatly enhanced at Greek festivals. Moreover, the influx of visitors added greatly to the trade of local merchants, hucksters, innkeepers, and other business men. The Athenians realized, perhaps even better than moderns, the possibilities for profit in the institution of the fair.

During the first half of the second century the most powerful Hellenistic kings attempted in various ways to curry favor with the Athenians. We find them not only bestowing costly gifts upon the city, but also accepting Athenian citizenship and appointment to posts in the official service of the city,[73] as well as taking part in the contests held at the public festivals and attending lectures at the schools of philosophy.[74] The Athenians, of course, accepted the homage of the distinguished foreigners—and turned it to their own advantage. Indeed, Polybius seems to imply that the Athenians unblushingly asked for gifts.[75] It was sufficient for them to show their gratitude with a fulsome honorary decree or a statue.

[68] IG, II–III², 2314, l. 41.

[69] IG, II–III², 2314, ll. 84, 86, 88, 90, and Addenda, 1931. Cf. W. S. Ferguson, in *Klio*, VIII (1908), 351–54.   [70] IG, II–III², 2316, ll. 43, 44.

[71] IG, II–III², 2316, l. 45; cf. W. S. Ferguson, in *Klio*, VIII (1908), 355.

[72] IG, II–III², 2317, ll. 37, 47.

[73] Thus, e.g., Antiochus IV Epiphanes served as first mint magistrate, apparently in 176 B.C. Head, *Hist. Num.*, p. 382. Ariarathes V of Cappadocia and Attalus II both received Athenian citizenship before accession to their respective thrones. SIG, 666; cf. Ferguson, *Athens*, p. 300.

[74] *Ibid.*, pp. 298–307; *Klio*, VIII (1908), 349–55.

[75] Polybius, XXVIII, xix, 4.

The most splendid and, at the same time, the most ostentatious gifts that Athens received from her royal benefactors were those made by the kings of Pergamum.[76] We have already had occasion to observe the gifts of Attalus I. However, his immediate successors surpassed him by far in generosity. Thus, Eumenes II (197–159 B.C.) constructed the large and splendid stoa to the south of the Acropolis which served as an adjunct to the theater of Dionysus,[77] and his brother, Attalus II (159–138 B.C.), erected the imposing stoa which bounded the market square on the east.[78] Another great royal benefactor was Antiochus IV Epiphanes of Syria, a sincere admirer of Athenian culture in all its aspects, who became possessed of the ambition to carry through to completion the great temple of the Olympian Zeus, which had been left unfinished by the Pisistratids at the end of the sixth century.[79] But the project was immense and at his death was still far from final realization. Although no striking gifts of the Ptolemies are attested in our sources,[80] the honors conferred upon them by the Athenians and the celebration of the Ptolemaea at Athens[81] make it quite clear that their gifts were by no means unsubstantial. Gifts were also

[76] The details have already been adequately set forth and discussed by Ferguson, *Athens*, pp. 299–300.

[77] Vitruvius, V, ix, 1; Judeich, *Topographie*, pp. 94, 325–26. It is not known whether the stoa was built before or after 166 B.C. The date of the ex-voto, consisting of four sculptured groups and dedicated on the Acropolis at Athens by one of the Attalids, is still much discussed. B. Schweitzer, *Das Original der sogenannten Pasquino-Gruppe* (Leipzig, 1936; Abhandlungen der sächsischen Akademie der Wissenschaften zu Leipzig, philologisch-historische Klasse, XLIII, No. 4), pp. 96–101, maintained that work on them was begun under Attalus I (241–197 B.C.) and completed under Eumenes II (197–159 B.C.). R. Horn, in RM, LII (1937), 150–62, assigns them to the time of Attalus II (159–138 B.C.) and Attalus III (138–133 B.C.), while A. Schober, in RM, LIV (1939), 82–98, places them in the time of Attalus II. For additional bibliography, see the citations in these articles.

[78] IG, II–III², 3171; cf. Judeich, *Topographie*, pp. 354–56.

[79] *Ibid.*, pp. 382–83. For a complete discussion of Antiochus' relations with Athens, see Ferguson, *Athens*, pp. 302–7.

[80] Polybius, XXVIII, xix, 4, mentions an Athenian embassy sent in 170 B.C. to thank Ptolemy Philometor for a gift whose nature is unspecified. For the date, see Ferguson, *Athens*, p. 298. Recognition of a gift of undisclosed nature from the same ruler was made by an equestrian statue which the Athenians set up on the Acropolis. IG, II–III², 983; cf. W. S. Ferguson, in *Klio*, VIII (1908), 338–39. For the relations of the Ptolemies with Athens during the first half of the second century, see Ferguson, *Athens*, pp. 298–99.

[81] *Ibid.*, p. 299; *Klio*, VIII (1908), 338–45.

received from Ariarathes V of Cappadocia and his queen Nysa, members of a dynasty which had for some time been attracted to Athenian culture.[82] I shall devote more attention to the final dynasty to be considered, not because more splendid gifts were made by it, but because the inscription which attests its benefactions has recently been studied anew by several scholars. In 160/59 B.C. the Athenians honored King Pharnaces and Queen Nysa of the Pontic dynasty with crowns of gold and with bronze statutes which were set up at Delos.[83] And they delegated an embassy to convey to the royal couple the decree that had been passed in their honor by the Demos. There is some dispute concerning the circumstances which occasioned the decree, but the facts seem to be somewhat as follows. Between 183 B.C. and 181 B.C. Pharnaces, the sixth king of the Pontic dynasty and the grandfather of Mithradates VI Eupator, conquered and annexed Sinope, Tius, Paphlagonia, and part of Galatia. In 179 B.C. he was compelled to return to their original owners all the lands he had seized except Sinope and its colonies[84] and to pay an indemnity of nine hundred talents to Morzius and Ariarathes, the kings of Paphlagonia and Cappadocia respectively, as well as three hundred talents to Eumenes II to be applied toward the expenses of the war, along with a like amount to Mithradates, the satrap of Armenia.[85] Before these strenuous reparations had been exacted from him Pharnaces had incurred some sort of financial obligation toward the Athenians, but the exact nature of his commitment is not known. It seems quite certain, however, that repayment of a loan does not enter into the question, for the financial condition of Athens was such as to certainly prevent the city from lending money.[86] It seems more probable that Pharnaces had promised a sum of money to be paid every year for some such purpose as the endowment of a festival or a gymnasium. But the oppressive terms of the treaty of

[82] Ferguson, *Athens*, pp. 300–1. Their gifts were made after 166 B.C.

[83] IG, XI, iv, 1056; OGIS, 771; Durrbach, *Choix*, No. 73, with commentary, pp. 97–105; cf. R. Laqueur, *Epigraphische Untersuchungen zu den griechischen Volksbeschlüssen* (Leipzig, 1927), pp. 55–57; A. Wilhelm, in JOAI, XXIV (1929), 168–74.

[84] Polybius, XXV, ii; cf. XXIV, xiv–xv; Robinson, *Ancient Sinope*, p. 251.

[85] Polybius, XXV, ii.

[86] Durrbach, *Choix*, pp. 101–2; OGIS, 771, note 9.

179 B.C. made it impossible for him to meet his obligations. Consequently, after the lapse of some time, an Athenian embassy took up with Pharnaces the matter of the payments which he had not made. Thereupon the king entered into a new agreement, in pursuance of which he paid the Athenians a certain sum as an installment and treated them as preferred creditors.[87] During the first quarter of the second century, then, Athens had received gifts from Pharnaces, and these gifts were to be continued in the period following 166 B.C.

What were the reasons that underlay this lavish bestowal of gifts upon Athens by the Hellenistic kings? Two explanations have heretofore been offered.[88] Athens had acquired such great prestige through its glorious past that it came to be regarded as the source from which the highest culture of mankind stemmed. When the kings honored Athens, they, at the same time, attracted honor and glory to themselves. Secondly, but of lesser importance, by favoring Athens the kings solidified the support, within their own kingdoms, of the Hellenic element of the population. It is very difficult, however, to believe that the kings were swayed so greatly by mere considerations of sentiment. Consequently, while the two explanations just set forth may be partially valid, a third seems to be even more to the point.[89] If we consider first the Pergamene kings, we shall see that although they were philhellenes and sincere admirers of Greek culture, the policy they followed toward the Greek cities of Asia Minor—not only the subject cities, but also the allied Greek cities—was a calculating policy; their loans and their gifts were made for the purpose of strengthening their own power.[90] Hence it is a point worth considering whether some economic motive may have prompted their gifts to Athens. It is well known that their policy towards Rhodes and Delos was very cordial. Moreover, those two cities were flourishing commercial centers in

[87] Durrbach, *Choix*, pp. 101–3; W. Dittenberger, commentary on OGIS, 771; A. Wilhelm, in JOAI, XXIV (1929), 168–74.

[88] See Ferguson, *Athens*, pp. 307–10.

[89] I am gratified to find that this interpretation, which I had set forth in the first version of my manuscript, has the weighty support of Rostovtzeff in his *Social and Economic History of the Hellenistic World*.

[90] M. Rostovtzeff, in CAH, VIII, 613–18; "Notes on the Economic Policy of the Pergamene Kings," *Anatolian Studies* (Ramsay), pp. 359–90, especially 389–90.

the first half of the second century. And Athens, although it had undoubtedly suffered a great loss in trade since the days of Demetrius of Phalerum, was still one of the leading centers of trade in the Aegean. For further substantiation of the thesis that the gifts of the kings were, in part, prompted by the desire to further the commerce of their own realms we may observe that several times during the second century—in 191/0 B.C., 188/7 B.C., 185/4 B.C., c.181–170 B.C., and c.170 B.C.—men in high favor with the Ptolemies were honored with decrees at Athens for their services in aiding Athenians who had traveled to Alexandria, Cyprus, and Cyrene, all of which were territories controlled by the Ptolemies.[91] It is natural to assume that a goodly number of these travelers were merchants, and the assumption is probably confirmed by the fact that one of the decrees honors a certain Timarchus of Salamis in Cyprus, member of a wealthy family of traders who were active at Delos in the latter half of the second century.[92] Another of the decrees in honor of friends of the Ptolemies is paralleled—even in phraseology—by a recently published inscription from the Agora at Athens which honors a friend of Seleucus IV (187–175 B.C.) of Syria,[93] apparently for his aid to Athenian merchants who traveled in the realm of that king. In the latter half of the century there is evidence of Athenian traders receiving privileges at Pergamum[94] and honors from the ruler of the Pontus.[95] Evidently Athenian traders were of considerable importance. But it was by no means a one-way trade that the city enjoyed, for numerous foreign traders established themselves at Athens to sell their wares there and elsewhere in Greece. Indeed, more of these foreigners resided in the city and at the Piraeus now than at any other time since the be-

[91] IG, II–III², 889 (dated 191/0 B.C.), 891 (dated 188/7 B.C.), 893 (dated 188/7 B.C.), 897 (dated 185/4 B.C.), 908 (dated c.181–170 B.C.), and 909 (dated c.170 B.C.); cf. Ferguson, *Athens*, p. 298.

[92] IG, II–III², 909; cf. Durrbach, *Choix*, Nos. 127–28.

[93] This inscription is published, without comment on the historical implications, by Pritchett and Meritt, *Chronology*, pp. 117–18; cf. IG, II–III², 897.

[94] IG, II, 438b.

[95] An Athenian who was probably a trader, Dionysius, son of Boethus, was given the title of φίλος by Mithradates Euergetes shortly before 120 B.C. Durrbach, *Choix*, No. 100. See further the discussion of the relations of Delos with various parts of the Hellenistic world in chap. iii.

ginning of the third century. This fact appears, among other indications, from a comparison of the number of foreign contributors to the fund raised during the archonship of Diomedon,[96] soon after the middle of the third century, where five foreign names may be observed out of a total of 133 legible entries, with the contributors to the fund raised during the archonship of Hermogenes (183/2 B.C.),[97] where there are twenty-seven names of foreigners out of 358 entries. Other reminders of the presence of numbers of foreigners exist in the numerous foreign cults—the same ones that were there in the third century—in Athens and the Piraeus, and in the foreign names on tombstones found in Attica.

The directions of the city's foreign trade are clearly reflected by the place of origin of the various foreign contributors to the fund raised in 183/2 B.C.,[98] where five were from Rhodes, four from Cyzicus, three from Antioch on the Orontes, two each from Mytilene, the Chersonese, and Tenos, and one each from Acarnania, Adramyttium, Apollonia (in Thrace?), Ephesus, Paphos, Salamis (in Cyprus), Scyrus, Seleucia (in Pieria?), and Tanagra. The same directions of trade are indicated, even more completely and conclusively, by the names of foreigners that appear on Attic sepulchral stelae. On these stones names of individuals from the following districts may be read:

1. Bithynia, Pontus, and the Black Sea region
2. The Hellespont, Bosphorus, and Thrace
3. All districts of northern Greece
4. Southern Greece (mainly from Corinth and Argos)
5. Rhodes, Crete, Cyprus, and the islands of the Aegean
6. Syria (mainly Antioch), Phoenicia, and Palestine
7. Alexandria

[96] IG, II–III². 791. For the date of the archonship of Diomedon, see the citations in chap. i, note 63.

[97] IG, II–III², 2332. However, it must be admitted that the force of this argument is somewhat reduced by the fact that contributors to the fund raised in the archonship of Diomedon subscribed amounts varying between 50 and 200 drachmas, whereas in the archonship of Hermogenes most of the subscriptions were in the amount of 10 drachmas, with only a very few individuals contributing more than that amount. For the date of the archonship of Hermogenes, see note 56, above.

[98] Cf. notes 56 and 97, above.

8. Cities of coastal and inland Asia Minor
9. Italy and Sicily (few in number)[99]

Consequently, it appears that Athens enjoyed trade relations with the important trading cities of the Hellenistic world, as well as with the cities of Greece proper. The city was, apparently, a center of transit trade, and foreign merchants settled there to carry on trade with the cities of mainland Greece, more especially with the cities of northern Greece.[100] As regards the West, Italy and Sicily in particular, although numerous Romans visited Athens in the first part of the second century B.C.,[101] the great movement of Italian *negotiatores* into the East was not to begin until about the middle of the century.[102]

We have specific information concerning the activities of one of these foreign merchants in an inscription of 176/5 B.C. in which the city honored a resident foreigner for selling grain to it at a low price and delivering, at a time of extraordinary scarcity, a cargo of 1,500 metretes of oil which he had collected at Aegean ports for transportation to the Pontus.[103] It is interesting to observe, in passing, the financial outlay undertaken by the trader.[104] The value of the oil, reckoned on the basis of the price of oil at Delos in 179 B.C., which fluctuated between 16 and 18 drachmas per metretes,[105] would amount to 24,000–27,000 drachmas, or between 4 and $4\frac{1}{2}$ talents. But the inscription is more important in that it shows that in ordinary years Athens shipped oil to the Pontus and took grain in return.[106] Athens had for many years depended upon South Russia for its grain supply, but at this time the supply from that region was an uncertain matter, as Polybius informs us.[107] In some

[99] See the analysis of these names in chaps. i and iii.

[100] I shall elaborate upon this point in chap. iii. Note should also be taken of the probability that some of the prosperity of Athens at this time came from participation in the trade of Delos. Roussel, DCA, pp. 11–12.

[101] Ferguson, *Athens*, p. 312.   [102] Hatzfeld, *Trafiquants*, p. 30; cf. pp. 17–20.

[103] IG, II–III², 903; cf. A. von Premerstein, "Athenischer Ehrenbeschluss für einen Grosskaufmann," AM, XXXVI (1911), 73–86; P. Roussel, "Note sur un décret attique," REA, XIV (1912), 39.

[104] Cf. A. von Premerstein, in AM, XXXVI (1911), 83.

[105] IDD, 442A, ll. 182–84, 189–94.   [106] Cf. Polybius, IV, xxxviii, 5.

[107] IV, xxxviii, 5; cf. Minns, *Scythians and Greeks*, p. 443; Rostovtzeff, *Iranians and Greeks*, pp. 70–71, 147.

years the crops were good, whereas in others the incursions of the Sarmatians and intertribal warfare restricted them to such an extent that it was necessary to import grain. Various eastern lands which had relied upon South Russia were now compelled to look elsewhere for their supply. To meet this need grain was shipped to the East from Numidia during the first part of the second century.[108] Additional grain probably came from Pergamum, whose kings are known to have possessed large stores at this time,[109] and from Egypt and Syria. Of course, in many years much grain was still brought from South Russia. Consequently, as Rostovtzeff suggests,[110] it seems probable—although the evidence is not conclusive—that the flattery implicit in the participation of the Ptolemies, the Attalids, the Seleucids, and Mastanabal, son of Massinissa of Numidia, in the contests held at the Athenian games, and the gifts, noted above, that were made by the various rulers had for their purpose the cultivation of an extensive grain trade that was centered at Athens. Athens would, in that event, have recovered a large part of that grain trade in which it had enjoyed such a dominant position in the fourth century. At first blush it might seem very improbable that a city which was beset so often with the problem of meeting a serious deficiency in grain could have been, at the same time, an important distributing center for grain. However, as ironical as such a state of affairs would seem, we must not overlook the fact that in our own times we have faced the anomaly of "starvation in the midst of plenty."[111] In addition to trade in grain and oil, we find that the same products were exported as in the third century, while only a few items in the list of imports—the *lagynos*, a special type of vase which was brought from the Aegean islands or Asia Minor,[112] and

[108] Durrbach, *Choix*, Nos. 68–69, pp. 91–92; F. Heichelheim, "Sitos," RE, Supplementband VI, 819–92, especially 854–55; *Wirtschaftsgeschichte*, I, 463–65.

[109] M. Rostovtzeff, "The Economic Policy of the Pergamene Kings," *Anatolian Studies* (Ramsay), pp. 359–90, especially 389–90; CAH, VIII, 608.

[110] In his *Social and Economic History of the Hellenistic World*.

[111] When Ziebarth, *Beiträge*, p. 71, and F. Heichelheim, in RE, Supplementband VI, 855, hold that the two traders in grain who were honored by Oropus at the end of the third century B.C. (IG, VII, 4262) were established at the Piraeus, they would seem to agree with Rostovtzeff's thesis.

[112] H. A. Thompson, in *Hesperia*, III (1934), 450–51; cf. G. Leroux, *Lagynos: Recherches sur la céramique et l'art ornemental hellénistique* (Paris, 1913), p. 101.

lamps possibly from Rhodes[113]—differ from those of the preceding century.[114]

It remains for us now to consider how the individual Athenian fared during the first decades of the second century. There was now much more work to be done than in the third century. The benefactions of the Hellenistic kings had produced work for stonecutters, contractors, architects, sculptors, and other workers. The renewal of the practice of adorning tombstones with sculptured reliefs provided a new stimulus for the trade of the sculptor.[115] And yet some Athenian sculptors still found it necessary to obtain employment elsewhere.[116] In the field of ceramic wares the Athenian worker was still able to produce Megarian bowls that not only held the home market, but also were so highly regarded that they continued to be exported elsewhere and that the molds from which they were produced were copied in various other places.[117] In the field of metal working, it is likely that silver from the mines at Laurium was employed in manufacturing at least some of the silver vases which were highly favored during the Hellenistic period both as products of art and as dedicatory offerings in sanctuaries. As regards the employment of slaves, it seems probable that two or three slaves were often employed in shops and that a similar number was employed by individual wealthy families in domestic service.[118] Of course, we know definitely that they were employed in the mines at Laurium, for twice during the second half of the century Athens found it necessary to quell their revolts there.[119] Whether the employment of some slaves, together with the displacement of workers occasioned by the employment of molds in the manufacture of Megarian bowls, contributed materially to an unemployment problem cannot be satisfactorily ascertained. However that may

[113] H. A. Thompson, in *Hesperia*, III (1934), 461–62.

[114] See my account in chap. i. Possibly some Parian amphorae were still imported (V. Grace, in *Hesperia*, III [1934], 276), but no Thasian amphorae of a date later than 200 B.C. have been found in the Agora at Athens.

[115] See note 11, above.

[116] See the discussion in chap. i along with the citations in notes 136–44 of that chapter.

[117] H. A. Thompson, in *Hesperia*, III (1934), 459; cf. chap. i, note 123.

[118] Westermann, "Sklaverei," cols. 934–35.

[119] Ferguson, *Athens*, pp. 378–79, 427–28.

be, there seems to be no doubt that numerous workers were unemployed, but in smaller numbers than in the third century B.C. Moreover, there was a substantial body of workers who were dissatisfied because of their declining standard of living. Wages, we remember, declined sharply between 300 B.C. and 250 B.C., and thereafter did not rise.[120] On the other hand, the price of grain, the most important element in the worker's diet, had risen greatly by the first part of the second century.[121] It seems very evident that at Athens, as elsewhere, the laborer received but little benefit from the wealth of the Hellenistic world. When we turn to the farmer, we find that very much the same conditions prevailed as during the third century. Wheat, which had sold for 4 drachmas per medimnus in 250 B.C.,[122] was now priced at 10 drachmas.[123] Barley followed the same trend, being valued at about half the price of wheat.[124] Wine was low in price,[125] and vineyard owners found even their home market invaded by wines from Rhodes and Cnidus.[126] Oil, which had sold for 16–18 drachmas per metretes at the depth of the general decline of prices at about 250 B.C.,[127] reached its lowest price, 11–12 drachmas, in 190–180 B.C.[128] and after that time rose somewhat to 22 drachmas in 169 B.C.;[129] the average price during the first third of the century was approximately 16 drachmas, at which the producer probably enjoyed a small margin of profit. Hence, with exportation of oil not very profitable, the wine market invaded by foreign products, and the price of grain high, only those farmers who produced a respectable proportion of grain in their total crop would prosper.[130] These farmers would be, in the main,

[120] G. Glotz, in JDS, XI (1913), 206–15, 251–60; Heichelheim, *Schwankungen*, pp. 97–98; Larsen, "Roman Greece," pp. 408–12.

[121] Heichelheim, *Schwankungen*, pp. 51–52; Larsen, "Roman Greece," pp. 383–86.

[122] This is a deduction of *ibid.*, p. 386.

[123] Heichelheim, *Schwankungen*, pp. 51–52; Larsen, "Roman Greece," p. 386.

[124] See chap. i, note 42.

[125] Larsen, "Roman Greece," pp. 391–92.

[126] V. Grace, in *Hesperia*, III (1934), 201, 214–75.

[127] IG, XI, ii, 287A, ll. 43, 47, 54, 58, 63, 65, 68, 74, 76, 79, 82.

[128] IDD, 440, ll. 7, 9, 15–16, 18, 22.

[129] *Ibid.*, 461Ab, ll. 6, 12, 18; cf. Larsen, "Roman Greece," p. 390.

[130] Larsen, "Roman Greece," p. 407; *Classical Philology*, XXXVI (1941), 165, note 21.

those individuals who were so fortunate as to own land in one of
the four Attic plains. While during the third century B.C. only the
farmers of the Mesogeia and of the plain of Marathon had been
prosperous, during the first part of the second century B.C. the
farmers of the Thriasian and of the Athenian plain also prospered,
now that their lands were no longer subjected to periodic raids. In
any event, landholders were still among the wealthiest and most
influential citizens of Athens. For it is not without significance that
the city had not yet resumed the dispatch of the Pythais to Delphi,
whereas the wealthy landholders of the Marathonian Tetrapolis
continued to send to Apollo's sanctuary the Pythais which they had
originated in the latter part of the third century.[131] It is also significant that the descendants of the wealthy landholders who gained
control of the government during the third century B.C. in turn
retained the power in their hands until well into the second half of
the second century B.C.[132]

Greece as a whole had not suffered from the wars occasioned by
the intervention of Rome in the East at the end of the third and
the beginning of the second centuries B.C. Only individual districts
had been devastated, and Athens was not one of these.[133] And even
the devastated regions were not affected to such an extent that the
remainder of Greece suffered from the indirect effects of the wars.
The fact that the country was not deprived of most of its capital by
the imposition of indemnities by the Romans and by the carrying
away of booty on the part of their armies is conclusively shown by
the prevailing rates of interest, which indicate an ample supply of
money.[134] In the fourth century B.C. 12 percent was the common
rate of interest in Greece.[135] By the third century B.C. the rate had
fallen to 10 percent,[136] and in the first half of the second century
B.C. lower still, a low rate of $6\frac{2}{3}$ percent being attested at Delphi.[137]
Moreover, the general trend of prices, as we know it from the
Temple accounts at Delos, manifests none of the symptoms of

---

[131] Boethius, *Die Pythaïs*, pp. 38–51; Daux, *Delphes*, pp. 532–40.

[132] Ferguson, *Athens*, p. 288; cf. the citations in chap. i, note 62, above.

[133] Larsen, "Roman Greece," pp. 382–83.   [134] *Ibid.*, pp. 374, 383.

[135] Billeter, *Geschichte des Zinsfusses*, p. 58.   [136] *Ibid.*, p. 58.

[137] This rate of interest was earned by the endowments of the Attalids at Delphi.
The latest edition and discussion of the inscription is that of Daux, *Delphes*, pp.
502–9, 682–98; cf. SIG, 671, 672; Laum, *Stiftungen*, Vol. II, Nos. 28 and 29.

having passed through the violent fluctuations which are brought about by any war that really affects the economy of a country.[138] Indeed, conditions for trade had become more favorable throughout the eastern half of the Mediterranean world soon after the beginning of the second century. In mainland Greece the disastrous wars of the third century had been brought to an end by Rome, peace held sway in Asia Minor, while in the Aegean Rhodes became the leading political and commercial power and with its navy suppressed the piracy which had been a serious deterrent to trade.[139] In the revival of trade that took place at this time Athens played a leading part.

This survey of economic conditions at Athens during the first decades of the second century tends to show that foreign trade revived somewhat, that some few fortunate landholders continued to prosper, and that some few business men fared well; but that, on the other hand, the lot of the worker was extremely poor. However, it seems that no strong movement toward migration developed—at least not to the extent of bringing about a problem of depopulation —for despite the fact that Athenian citizens settled in the new quarter of Antioch which was built by Antiochus IV Epiphanes[140] and that in 166 B.C. the Athenians sent settlers to Haliartus and Delos,[141] we do not find the city suffering from a shortage of labor in the period following 166 B.C. The first decades of the second century were a period of recovery from the depression of the third century, and were to be followed by renewed prosperity in the years following the acquisition of Delos.

[138] Larsen, "Roman Greece," pp. 382–83.
[139] M. Rostovtzeff, in CAH, VIII, 627–30. It should be noted, however, that Rostovtzeff does not subscribe to the description of comparatively favorable economic conditions on the mainland at this time as set forth in the text, above.
[140] Niese, *Geschichte der griechischen und makedonischen Staaten*, III, 95; Ferguson, *Athens*, p. 304.
[141] Polybius, XXX, xxi; cf. Ferguson, *Athens*, pp. 315–20; Roussel, DCA, pp. 7–18.

CHAPTER III

FROM THE ACQUISITION OF DELOS

TO THE SACK OF ATHENS:

166-86 B.C.

URING the first decades of the second century Athens had never departed from a course of the utmost constancy toward Rome, and when the Third Macedonian War broke out in 172 B.C., the Athenians at once sent a few ships and men to take part in the war. But the Roman commanders rudely rejected the offer and demanded instead a contribution of 100,000 modii (c.27,500 bushels) of grain.[1] Similar exactions were made from other Greek cities which were *amici* of Rome.[2] In consequence, Athens and the other cities made complaints to the Senate at Rome, which decreed in 169 B.C. that thereafter requisitions should be legal only in case they were made in accordance with a decree of the Senate.[3] However annoying these requisitions may have been, it is most unlikely that the economy of Greece was seriously upset by them or by the devastation wrought by the war, for the prices in the Temple accounts at Delos at this time experienced no violent fluctuations and interest rates were at such a low point as to suggest a plentiful supply of ready capital.[4] At the end of the war Athens was rewarded for its loyalty. At their own request, as Polybius informs us, the Athenians received in 166 B.C. Delos, Lemnos, and the territory of Haliartus.[5] Either at the same time, or possibly a few years later, the islands of Imbros and Scyrus were also allocated to them.[6] Somewhat of an addition was

[1] Livy, XLIII, vi, 3. [2] Cf. Larsen, "Roman Greece," pp. 290–93.
[3] Livy, XLIII, xvii, 2. [4] Larsen, "Roman Greece," p. 324.
[5] Polybius, XXX, xx; Strabo, IX, 411. [6] Ferguson, *Athens*, pp. 315–22.

made thereby—excluding Delos for the moment—to the population and revenues of the city.[7] And what is more important, a considerable supply of grain from Lemnos, Imbros, and Scyrus became available in addition to the meager supply produced in Attica.[8]

Before 166 B.C., Athens had benefited somewhat from the prosperity of Delos, albeit in a very indirect way, by the participation of some of its citizens in the trade of that island.[9] During the remainder of the second century the city was to enjoy a high degree of prosperity. To what extent did Delos contribute to this state of well-being? The allocation of the island to Athens was not an act of pure altruism on the part of the Senate; rather, it was a premeditated expedient for the destruction of the prosperity of Rhodes, in line with the policy adopted by Rome of preventing the growth of any dominant power in the East.[10] Consequently, the Athenians received the island with the stipulation that it was to be a free port;[11] and so, no revenue came to Athens from port dues at Delos. Furthermore, when the Romans required the native Delians to depart from the island, they allowed them to take away their movable property. But difficulties arose over the interpretation of the property included under the stipulation laid down by the Romans. Meanwhile, upon their withdrawal from the island the dispossessed Delians became citizens of the Achaean League and attempted to secure indemnification for their losses under the terms of a treaty between Athens and the League which provided for arbitration of cases arising between private citizens of the respective states. But the Athenians refused to arbitrate, maintaining that

[7] *Ibid.*, pp. 317–20. Vitruvius, VII, vii, informs us that the Lemnians paid taxes to Athens in accordance with the arrangements specified by the Romans. And from IG, II–III², 1223, we learn that the islanders helped in meeting the expenses incurred in various festivals held at Athens.

[8] M. Cary, in *Mélanges Gustave Glotz*, I, 142, has suggested that the Senate at Rome also showed its favor toward Athens by closing the Macedonian silver mines at about the middle of the second century B.C. He rejects the statement of Livy, XLV, xviii, 3–5, to the effect that the Senate acted in the interest of the Macedonians by keeping the publicans from exacting royalties from the proceeds of the working of the mines.

[9] Roussel, DCA, p. 35.

[10] M. Rostovtzeff, in *American Historical Review*, XLI (1936), 243; CAH, VIII, 631.

[11] Polybius, XXX, xxxi, 10; Strabo, X, 486.

the alleged damages had been incurred before the Delians had become Achaean citizens and that the terms of the treaty were not
retroactive. However, the Achaeans allowed the Delians to seize
property held by the Athenians within the territory under their
jurisdiction, and the Athenians permitted their citizens to secure
recompense by seizing property held in Athens by Achaeans. These
seizures continued until the Athenians and the Achaeans sent embassies to the Senate at Rome, which decided, in 157 B.C., that
whatever decisions the Achaean League made concerning the
Delians in accordance with their own laws were to be binding.[12] It
is this circumstance that led Polybius to state that in acquiring
Delos the Athenians, as the proverb went, "got the wolf by the
ears."[13] In view, therefore, of the losses suffered by the Athenians
during the course of this extended dispute and of the expense involved in the maintenance of a staff of officials on the island along
with, supposedly, the necessity of maintaining harbor equipment
without any recompense in the way of customs, the question has
been raised whether Delos was not a burden, rather than an asset,
to the Athenians at large.[14]

What expenditures were incumbent upon the Athenians in connection with their administration of Delos? Toward the physical
equipment of the town and the port, the Athenians undertook
comparatively slight outlays.[15] Adjoining the Portico of Philip the
Athenians built between 166 B.C. and 150 B.C. a portico which was
designed to serve the needs of commerce in the port, but not in
the agora, of Delos.[16] Thereafter, in 126/5 B.C. the so-called Agora

[12] Polybius, XXXII, vii; cf. Ferguson, *Athens*, pp. 323–24; Niese, *Geschichte der griechischen und makedonischen Staaten*, III, 191.

[13] Polybius, XXX, xx.

[14] Cf. Ferguson, *Athens*, pp. 329–30; M. Rostovtzeff, in CAH, VIII, 643–44.
Rostovtzeff holds, in his *Social and Economic History of the Hellenistic World*, that
the Athenians probably collected harbor dues at Delos, and that additional revenue
may have come to them from petty taxes and from the renting of storehouses and
houses which, he thinks, the Athenian government may have owned.

[15] A detailed consideration of the question may be found in Roussel, DCA, pp.
294–302.

[16] R. Vallois, *Les Portiques au sud du Hiéron, Première Partie, le Portique de
Philippe* (Paris, 1933; Exploration archéologique de Délos, VII), pp. 163–64; cf.
153–54. For the port of Delos, see Lehmann-Hartleben, *Antike Hafenanlagen*,
pp. 154–61.

of Theophrastus was built adjacent to the Sacred Harbor; it was strictly not an agora, but a quay built to improve the facilities of the harbor.[17] This quay, on which no buildings of consequence were constructed, was probably built in large part with funds provided by the Athenian state. Nevertheless, at least part of the funds needed for completion of the work seems to have been contributed by the *epimeletes* Theophrastus out of his own means.[18] Beyond the two building projects just mentioned we have no knowledge of any additional expenditures for physical equipment undertaken at Delos by the Athenians. The newly arrived inhabitants seem rather to have made use of the buildings already on hand and to have erected, at their own expense, new structures as the need for them arose.[19] So much for the physical equipment of the island. But what of the expense involved in the maintenance of officials at Delos to attend to matters of local administration? We are informed by Strabo that the Athenians provided a very adequate administration of the island.[20] However, very little information has come down to us concerning the details of this administration. Executive supervision of the island was placed in the hands of an *epimeletes*.[21] The market was placed under the control of a college of *Epimeletae* of the Emporium, at first composed of three members, but later reduced to one.[22] Also associated with the supervision of the market were the agoranomi, at first three, later two in number.[23] Two *hieropoei* were entrusted with the administration of the Temple property;[24] moreover, in charge of the public bank, which was apparently closely associated with the financial administration of the Temple property, we find a manager, who seems to have been a very important official.[25] At first glance, then, it might seem— especially since our information concerning the administration of the island is admittedly very incomplete—that the maintenance of a rather large and expensive staff of administrators at Delos was

---

[17] IDD, 1645 (=Durrbach, *Choix*, No. 95); cf. Roussel, DCA, pp. 297–300.

[18] *Ibid.*, p. 298.

[19] *Ibid.*, pp. 300–2.   [20] Strabo, X, 486.   [21] Roussel, DCA, pp. 123–25.

[22] *Ibid.*, pp. 179–82, 184–85.   [23] *Ibid.*, pp. 182–85.

[24] *Ibid.*, pp. 126–35. Among the duties of these functionaries were maintenance of the physical properties and supervision of the ceremonies of the cult. *Ibid.*, pp. 134–35; Ferguson, *Athens*, p. 347.

[25] Roussel, DCA, pp. 138–39.

incumbent upon the Athenians. We must, however, bear in mind the important fact that at this time Athenians were very eager to hold appointments at Delos and that, in consequence, the conditions which adhered to the holding of a magistracy at Athens were also effective in the case of appointments at Delos, that is to say, substantial contributions toward public enterprises were expected of officeholders. In the instance of the administrators of the Temple property at Delos we have explicit evidence that the office involved a financial outlay on the part of the incumbent,[26] and, as we have observed in the instance of Theophrastus, the same conditions probably applied to the tenure of the *epimeletes* of the island. It appears, therefore, that neither from the maintenance of administrative officials, nor from the construction and upkeep of physical properties, were the Athenians called upon for considerable expenditures at Delos. However, we must always bear in mind the fact that an expenditure which would seem very moderate in the case of another city would constitute a real burden for Athens, especially since the Athenian budgetary system had for some time been quite inadequate.

Soon after 166 B.C. an Athenian cleruchy was formed at Delos,[27] but the method of its formation is quite uncertain. While in the fifth and fourth centuries B.C. cleruchies were formed by the division of the land into lots for poor citizens, it is not at all certain that the same conditions obtained in the second century. Indeed, a study of the tenant farmers, of the renters of Temple houses, and of borrowers from the Temple and their guarantors, in the years immediately after 166 B.C. has shown that, while the cleruchs were not members of wealthy and prominent Athenian families, they were certainly not altogether poor; rather, that they should probably be classified as *bourgeoisie*.[28] Belief that the cleruchs were of this class is made all the more reasonable by the facts that even before 166 B.C. Athenians of means had been attracted by the commercial possibilities of the island and that possibly a measure of the increased prosperity at Athens in the first decades of the second century is to be accounted for in this way.[29] On the other hand, the assumption has been made that the cleruchs upon their arrival

[26] IDD, 1838.   [27] Roussel, DCA, pp. 33–35.   [28] *Ibid.*, pp. 37–41.
[29] *Ibid.*, p. 35, note 5; cf. pp. 11–12.

were poor, but within ten years were enriched by a rapid rise in real estate values.[30] However, this is a very uncertain matter, for we have no explicit information concerning real estate values at Delos at this time.[31] On the whole the more likely conclusions would seem to be that the original cleruchs were possessed of some means, that there was some appreciation—how much we can not even estimate—in real estate values, especially in the region surrounding the commercial harbor, and that this appreciation redounded in part, as Ferguson suggests,[32] to the benefit of Athenian citizens, inasmuch as Attic law did not permit foreigners to own real estate, and in part to the Temple, seeing not all the property of the dispossessed Delians fell to the cleruchs.

A few additional comments may be made concerning the chief administrative officer of the island, the so-called *epimeletes* or "*epimeletes* of the island." This official, who was designated for a term of one year, had often previously held the office of archon or of general at Athens,[33] but he was not necessarily a member of the Areopagus, as Sundwall has assumed.[34] And especially in view of the facts that Delos was predominantly a center of commerce and that Theophrastus, the *epimeletes* noted above, was responsible for the enlargement of the commercial facilities of the Sacred Harbor,[35] it seems probable that the *epimeletes* devoted much of his attention to matters connected with business.[36] Indeed, it is very likely that the various families whose members held the office of *epimeletes* at Delos were not only interested in commerce, but possibly even founded their family fortunes there.[37] The most prominent in-

[30] Ferguson, *Athens*, pp. 348, 354–55.

[31] Roussel, DCA, p. 41, who maintains that the rise in prices was not as great as Ferguson suggested. Moreover, the fact that there was no considerable rise in rents at Delos after 166 B.C. (Larsen, "Roman Greece," p. 402) militates against Ferguson's thesis.

[32] Ferguson, *Athens*, pp. 348–49.

[33] A careful study of the incumbents of this office has been made by Roussel, DCA, pp. 97–125.

[34] Sundwall, *Untersuchungen*, I, 71.

[35] IDD, 1645 (= Durrbach, *Choix*, No. 95); cf. Roussel, DCA, pp. 297–300.

[36] Cf. Laidlaw, *Delos*, p. 180.

[37] In chaps. iv and v we shall have occasion to observe various members of prosperous families whose wealth is to be traced to commercial activity at Delos in this period. For prominent Athenians engaged in business at Delos, see Roussel, DCA, p. 66; Ferguson, *Athens*, pp. 421–22; *Klio*, IV (1904), 12.

cumbent of the office was that Medeius who was one of the leading members of the oligarchical party at Athens at the end of the second and the beginning of the first centuries B.C.[38]

Careful accounts were published by the Delian administrators of the sacred property during the period of independence (i.e., before 166 B.C.), and a number of valuable studies of wages and prices have been based upon them.[39] But with the coming of the Athenians the accounts were displaced with inventories from which little has been deduced concerning the administration of the Temple, the finances of the city, wages, and prices.[40] Thus it happens, most ironically, that in the most thriving period of the history of Delos we are reduced, in the main, to the most indirect items of evidence concerning the history of the island—evidence such as, for example, ethnics, which indicate merely the directions of trade and the extent and importance of the foreign colonies, and honorary inscriptions and dedications, which provide only indirect information concerning business activities—whereas in the preceding period, when Delos was by no means so prosperous, information on economic matters is relatively abundant.

The yearly income of the Temple was derived principally from the renting of landed properties and houses, and from the interest on sums of money loaned from a special fund that was kept in the Temple. The landed properties, which were located on the islands of Rheneia and Myconos, as well as at Delos, consisted of farms with farm buildings [χωρία and ἐποικίαι] and gardens and orchards [κῆποι].[41] In 179 B.C. the Temple collected 6,980 drachmas 2 obols from the renting of these properties,[42] but for the following period satisfactory evidence concerning the rents is lacking.[43] The following types of buildings were owned by the Temple in 157/6 B.C.

[38] Roussel, DCA, p. 112; PA, No. 10098; NPA, p. 127.

[39] The most important of these studies are: G. Glotz, "Le Prix des denrées à Délos," JDS, XI (1913), 16–29; "Les Salaires à Délos," ibid., pp. 206–15, 251–60; Heichelheim, Schwankungen, especially pp. 48–103. Larsen, "Roman Greece," pp. 334–48, 379–414.

[40] Roussel, DCA, pp. 20–29; Larsen, "Roman Greece," p. 334.

[41] IDD, 1416, 1417; Roussel, DCA, pp. 145–46, 157, and the tabulation on 149–56.

[42] IDD, 442A, ll. 145–52.

[43] Larsen, "Roman Greece," p. 404; cf. Heichelheim, Schwankungen, pp. 82–83; Roussel, DCA, pp. 145–47.

and 156/5 B.C.:⁴⁴ houses [οἰκίαι, οἰκήματα, συνοικία, συνοικίδια],⁴⁵ workshops [ἐργαστήρια]—among these were a surgery [ἰατρεῖον] and shipbuilders' yards [ναυπήγια]—and warehouses [ἐγδοχεῖα]. In 179 B.C. the *hieropoei* collected rent from seventeen houses, which brought in 1,735 drachmas 5⅔ obols,⁴⁶ whereas in 157/6 B.C. and 156/5 B.C. thirty or more buildings brought in a total of somewhat more than 5,000 drachmas.⁴⁷ The evidence concerning the trend of rents in the period following 166 B.C. is almost entirely lacking.⁴⁸ The money that was loaned by the Temple came from the so-called ἱστιατικὸν ἀργύριον, which consisted of funds given to the Temple over a period of years for the support of various sacred rites and ceremonies.⁴⁹ The earliest of these endowments at Delos that is now known to us is the income from a landed parcel worth 10,000 drachmas which was given to the Temple by the Athenian general Nicias in the latter part of the fifth century B.C.⁵⁰ This endowment, we learn from an inscription, was yielding income as late as 161/0 B.C.⁵¹ Some years after Nicias made his gift various kings and individuals otherwise prominent and wealthy presented the Temple with funds designed to support various sacred rites, which have ordinarily been called "vase festivals."⁵² Among the donors of these funds the names of various monarchs of Macedon, Egypt, and

⁴⁴ IDD, 1416–17; Roussel, DCA, p. 157, and the tabulation on pp. 149–56.

⁴⁵ The designations οἰκία and οἴκημα seem to have received rather flexible meanings, so as to refer, in some instances, also to ἐργαστήρια and ἐγδοχεῖα; *ibid.*, p. 157.

⁴⁶ IDD, 442A, ll. 140–45; cf. Heichelheim, *Schwankungen*, p. 115, Table V, and Larsen, "Roman Greece," pp. 400–2, where the authors set forth a condensation of the conclusions reached by S. Molinier, *Les "Maisons sacrées" de Délos au temps de l'indépendance de l'île, 315–116/5 av. J.-C.* (Paris, 1914; Bibliothèque de la Faculté des Lettres de l'Université de Paris, XXXI).

⁴⁷ For the figures, which are incomplete, see IDD, 1416–17; Roussel, DCA, p. 159, and the tabulation on pp. 149–56.

⁴⁸ Larsen, "Roman Greece," p. 402.

⁴⁹ F. Durrbach, in BCH, XXXIV (1910), 160–62; commentary to IDD, 366A, ll. 53–86; Roussel, DCA, pp. 173–76; E. Schulhof, in BCH, XXXII (1908), 101–19; E. Ziebarth, "Delische Stiftungen," *Hermes*, LII (1917), 425–41; cf. Dinsmoor, *Archons*, pp. 496–99.

⁵⁰ Plutarch, *Nic.* 3; cf. Laum, *Stiftungen*, Vol. II, No. 53. L. Kirtland, in *Proceedings of the American Philological Association*, LXIX (1938), xli, maintains that the plot of land in question was probably purchased at about the end of the fourth century B.C., rather than at the time of Nicias.

⁵¹ IDD, 1421Bcd, I.

⁵² Roussel, DCA, pp. 173–76, and the citations in note 49, above.

Pergamum are to be noted, and although the funds were treated as sacred, it seems quite likely that they were diverted to uses other than those for which they were given after the power of the various dynasties had declined. Lesser amounts of money came to the Temple from the coins which pilgrims inserted in the *thesauri*, or collection-boxes, which were placed in the various Delian temples.[53] After the Temple's receipts had balanced expenditures, any surplus that remained was placed in a reserve fund.[54] But apart from these moneys the Temple possessed two additional reserves. The first of these consisted of a sum of money amounting to approximately 100,000 drachmas which was kept in a lettered series of jars.[55] A wide variety of coinages formed the fund. The largest amount came from Histiaea in Euboea, a good amount from Rhodes; and there are several other varieties which have not yet been satisfactorily identified. No Athenian money was kept in the jars, but in the published accounts of the contents the value of the various coinages was stated in terms of Athenian money. The money in the jars was kept in the combined sacred and public "chests" into which receipts had been distributed in the period before 166 B.C. in accordance with the purpose for which they were to be expended. With the advent of Athenian control the two chests seem to have been combined, and the moneys withdrawn from circulation and treated as a sacred fund, which was probably finally dissipated when the island was sacked in 88 B.C. The second reserve comprised various votives in metal which had been presented to the Temple.[56]

The value of the entire Temple property in 279 B.C. has been estimated at 5,500,000 drachmas.[57] By far the greater part of this sum was invested in various sacred buildings and equipment which brought in no income. The total income-yielding capital amounted to about 200,000 drachmas, at the highest, but the liquid assets to be let out on loan probably did not, in general, exceed 50,000 drachmas. The resources of the Temple after 166 B.C. were, of

[53] Roussel, DCA, pp. 166–68; T. Homolle, in BCH, XIV (1890), 456.
[54] Roussel, DCA, p. 176.
[55] IDD, 1429B, II; 1432Bb, I, and Ba, II; 1443B, I; 1449Ba, I; Roussel, DCA. 168–73; Larsen, "Roman Greece," pp. 348–49.
[56] Roussel, DCA, p. 168.
[57] This estimate was made by T. Homolle, in BCH, XV (1891), 164–68.

course, somewhat greater. The Temple's liquid assets formed the reserve of a public bank [δημοσία τράπεζα], which was, at the same time, the agency that handled the rents from the Temple properties.[58] Little is known concerning the services the bank was intended to perform[59] and the manner in which it operated, but it may be assumed that it resembled the various public banks of this period, concerning which we have some information.[60] In any event, the working capital of the bank was so small that it was unable to undertake speculative risks, and it certainly could not have operated on the scale on which the banks established by foreigners carried on their business.[61] It had no share, therefore, in the lucrative business of making loans to traders engaged in commercial ventures.

A short account of the procedure followed in the leasing of Temple property and the granting of loans from Temple funds will be of interest. During the period of Delian independence the failure of debtors to pay had for various reasons been frequent. Consequently, in 157/6 B.C. new regulations were formulated to govern these transactions. The terms of leases were henceforth to be for five years.[62] Rents were to be due every three months. The contract listed in detail the different repairs to be undertaken, and all of them were the responsibility of the lessee. If, upon termination of his tenancy, any trees were shown to have been cut down or otherwise destroyed or removed, the lessee was obligated to pay appropriate damages. The lessee was also subject to fine in case he failed to keep cattle out of the vineyard. Renting of more than one Temple property at a time by the same individual was not permitted. The lessee must maintain residence on the island; other-

[58] Roussel, DCA, pp. 176-77; cf. IDD, 1416B, I, ll. 39-42.

[59] Ferguson, *Athens*, p. 350, suggested that the bank was established with an eye to exchange in a community where a multiplicity of coins issued by various authorities must have circulated, while F. Durrbach, in REG, XXXI (1918), 125, thought it was introduced for the purpose of placing Athenian money in circulation.

[60] E. Ziebarth, "Hellenistische Banken," ZFN, XXXIV (1924), 38-42; cf. Laum, in RE, Supplementband IV, 81. Note also the public bank at Athens at the end of the second century; IG, II-III², 1013, l. 4.

[61] Roussel, DCA, p. 177.

[62] For the leases and their terms, see IDD, 1416B, I, ll. 1-56; cf. Roussel, DCA, pp. 160-64; E. Ziebarth, in *Hermes*, LXI (1926), 105-9; Larsen, "Roman Greece," pp. 402-3.

wise the contract was to be annulled. Finally, the more important clauses of the contract could be changed only with the consent of the government at Athens. As regards loans from the Temple funds,[63] the term was for five years, and the interest amounted to 10 percent paid annually. By way of security for the loan the borrower was required to convey to the Temple administrators a mortgage on a specific piece of property. He was also required to secure a guarantor to endorse the contract. In case of default in payment of interest or installments of principal, all the property of the borrower—and of his guarantor as well—could be attached without court action, under the procedure known, in Greek law, as *syngraphe*.[64] The contract which governed the loan was made in the presence of three witnesses, then turned over to a banker; it was finally deposited in the Metroum at Delos.

The trade of Delos increased greatly after 166 B.C., in large part because the Romans had declared the island a free port. In taking this action the Romans hoped, as we have seen, to strike at the power of Rhodes, the great center of transit trade in the Aegean area, but the amount of trade that was diverted to Delos can not be satisfactorily estimated. In a speech reported by Polybius,[65]

[63] IDD, 1416B, II, ll. 68–118; 1416C; cf. Roussel, DCA, pp. 164–66; Larsen, "Roman Greece," pp. 375–76.

[64] Cf. R. Dareste, "Sur la συγγραφή en droit grec et en droit romain," BCH, VIII (1884), 362–76; F. Durrbach, "La Ἱερὰ Συγγραφή à Délos," REG, XXXII (1919), 167–78; E. Schulhof, in BCH, XXXI (1907), 80–84; E. Ziebarth, "Die ΙΕΡΑ ΣΥΓΓΡΑΦΗ von Delos," Hermes, LXI (1926), 87–109.

[65] Polybius, XXX, xxxi, 10–12. There has been some question concerning the proper reading of this passage. The view set forth in the text follows the reading of W. R. Paton in the Loeb Library edition of Polybius, and the interpretations of Beloch, Griechische Geschichte, IV, i, 291, note 4; M. Rostovtzeff, in CAH, VIII, 631; Ferguson, Athens, p. 333, note 1; P. M. Benecke, in CAH, VIII, 290; Larsen, "Roman Greece," p. 356. On the other hand, Hultsch and Büttner-Wobst, in their editions of Polybius, emend the passage so as to make the reduction in revenues 150,000 dr. rather than 850,000 dr., and they are followed by G. De Sanctis, Storia dei Romani (Turin, 1907–23), IV, 356, note 317; H. van Gelder, Geschichte der alten Rhodier (Hague, 1900), p. 156; Niese, Geschichte der griechischen und makedonischen Staaten, III, 196. Paton's reading seems preferable for the following reasons. A center of transit trade is peculiarly susceptible to any slight dislocation of trade that may occur in any district with which it enjoys relations, and a fluctuation of 15 percent in volume of business from year to year would not be at all exceptional. Cf. Ferguson, loc. cit. Moreover, the ambassadors complained less about the loss of 120 talents (=720,000 dr.) which Rhodes had formerly collected from

ambassadors of the Rhodians are represented as protesting to the
Senate at Rome because their harbor dues, which they had previously been able to farm out at 1,000,000 drachmas, now—because
Delos had been made a free port—brought in only 150,000 drachmas. If it be assumed that the harbor dues were levied at the rate
of 2 percent—a reasonable assumption for a center of transit trade
such as Rhodes—the value of the island's foreign trade would have
fallen from 50,000,000 drachmas to 7,500,000 drachmas per year.[66]
Of course, not all the trade that Rhodes lost came to the Delians,
but a very substantial part of it must have fallen to their lot. The
importance of this new trade receives further emphasis when we
call to mind the far-flung districts for which Rhodes had served as
a clearinghouse, namely, Egypt and the Black Sea, Syria and the
West.[67] The destruction of Corinth in 146 B.C. resulted in the diversion of additional trade to Delos; and to the same island came
most of the Syrian trade with the West after the destruction of
Carthage. And, after the formation of the province of Asia in
133 B.C., Delos attained to its greatest prosperity.[68] By the second
century B.C. the Italian market had become the most lucrative of
all the markets of the Mediterranean, and it was in its capacity
as the chief center of trade with that market that the greatest importance of Delos lay.

There were numerous foreign traders at Delos even before 166
B.C.,[69] but after that date they increased rapidly in numbers.[70]
With the great influx of Italian traders that began after the es-
tablishment of the free port, the Italian colony grew very strong.[71]

Stratonicea and Caunus than about the loss of the harbor dues—a fact which cannot be satisfactorily explained if the decline of the latter amounted to only 150,000
drachmas. Larsen, *loc. cit.*

[66] Larsen, "Roman Greece," p. 356.

[67] M. Rostovtzeff, "Alexandrien und Rhodos," *Klio*, XXXVII (1937), 70–76;
CAH, VIII, 619–32.

[68] M. Rostovtzeff, in CAH, VIII, 644; Roussel, DCA, p. 20.

[69] M. Lacroix, "Les Étrangers à Délos pendant la période de l'indépendance,"
Mélanges Gustave Glotz, II, 501–25; Roussel, DCA, pp. 84–85.

[70] Roussel, DCA, pp. 72–96; Hatzfeld, *Trafiquants*, pp. 31–37.

[71] The earliest study of the Romans at Delos was made by T. Homolle, "Les
Romains à Délos." BCH, VIII (1884), 75–158. The standard work on the subject
is now Hatzfeld, "Les Italiens résidant à Délos mentionés dans les inscriptions de
l'île," BCH, XXXVI (1912), 5–218; cf. the same author's *Tranfiquants*, pp. 31–37.

Near the end of the second century B.C. the members of this colony
built a meeting-hall, the *Italike Pastas*, which served as a center
for their various religious and social activities.[72] But even before
this time the Italians had grouped themselves together in associations of a religious and social character, which possessed, at the
same time, a distinctly nationalistic flavor. The most important
of these associations had for their patron divinity Mercury, Apollo,
or Neptune, and are more commonly known by the Greek form of
their names, as *Hermaistae, Apolloniastae,* and *Poseidoniastae.*[73]
Distinct from these groups was a college known from inscriptions
of the beginning of the first century B.C., the *Competaliastae,*[74] most
of whom were slaves. Then there were guilds of oil sellers[75] and wine
sellers,[76] traders in two of the most important export products of
Italy toward the end of the Republic. But while some Italians are
thus known to have been traders in wine and oil, the occupations
of others are scarcely known at all.[77] It is quite likely, however,
that many of them, like numerous *negotiatores* in other parts of the
Greek East, were bankers.[78] Most prominent among the Italian
bankers of Delos were Maraeus Gerillanus[79] and L. Aufidius.[80] The
Italian bankers undoubtedly occupied a very favorable position at

---

This subject is also treated by H. O. Kompter, *Die Römer auf Delos: ein Beitrag
zur Geschichte des Römertums im hellenistischen Zeitalter* (Münster, 1913); Roussel,
DCA, pp. 73, 75–84, 317.

[72] J. Hatzfeld, in BCH, XXXVI (1912), 109–10; Lapalus, *L'Agora des Italiens,*
pp. 97–98.

[73] Roussel, DCA, pp. 75–81; and the new material by E. Ziebarth in Bursian's
Jahresbericht über die Fortschritte der klassischen Altertumswissenschaft, CXCIII
(1922), 70–75. For dedications of the *Hermaistae,* see IDD, 1731–50; *Apolloniastae,*
see IDD, 1730; *Poseidoniastae,* see IDD, 1751–52; for dedications by the three
groups combined, see IDD, 1753–59.

[74] IDD, 1760–71; cf. Hatzfeld, *Tranfiquants,* p. 342; BCH, XXXVI (1912),
157–58; Roussel, DCA, pp. 81–82.

[75] Durrbach, *Choix,* No. 141 (=CIL, III, 14203, 6); IDD, 1712–14; cf. J. Hatzfeld, in BCH, XXXVI (1912), 143. For the numerous Italian amphorae found at
Delos, see Durrbach, *Choix,* p. 230.

[76] IDD, 1711 (=Durrbach, *Choix,* No. 142); cf. J. Hatzfeld, in BCH, XXXVI
(1912), 144, note 2; Roussel, DCA, pp. 95, note 6, and 274.

[77] J. Hatzfeld, in BCH, XXXVI (1912), 140–46.

[78] Roussel, DCA, p. 82. For *negotiatores* as bankers in the East, see Hatzfeld,
Trafiquants, pp. 193–212.

[79] IDD, 1725–27; cf. J. Hatzfeld, in BCH, XXXVI (1912), 37.

[80] IDD, 1728, 1729; cf. J. Hatzfeld, in BCH, XXXVI (1912), 19.

Delos.[81] Moreover, the fact that the Syrian banker Philostratus of Ascalon became a citizen of Naples suggests the possibility that those bankers who were known as Italians enjoyed a larger volume of business.[82] While we can proceed no further in identifying the occupations of Italians at Delos, we are at least in a position to observe that one fundamental characteristic of Roman trade in general probably obtained also at Delos, for an analysis of the names of 231 "Romans" at Delos which shows that 88 were free, 95 freedmen, and 48 slaves would seem to indicate that trade was left largely in the hands of slaves and freedmen, who acted as agents of their masters, some of whom must have been *equites* at Rome.[83] The Greeks gave these traders—even the Greeks from southern Italy and Sicily—the name 'Ρωμαῖοι; but they were Roman only in allegiance.[84] Whereas the Greeks usually stated, in connection with their names, their place of origin, and thus are known to have come from Magna Graecia, the traders of Italian origin gave no indication of their homeland.[85] However, a comparative study of the names of the latter has shown that most of them came from southern Italy, especially from Campania and Apulia, and that only a very few had been inhabitants of central Italy.[86]

Elements of population at Delos, aside from Italians and Greeks of southern Italy, together with the directions of the trade of Delos with regions other than the West are clearly shown by a wide variety of documentary evidence. First of all, in the Temple accounts of 157/6 B.C. and 156/5 B.C. we find that a very substantial proportion of the tenants of Temple property and the guarantors of Temple loans were "Greeks" other than Athenians and Athenian cleruchs at Delos.[87] The very terms imposed upon the tenants and guarantors of Temple property that we have already observed makes it obvious that the residence of these individuals at Delos

[81] Roussel, DCA, p. 82, held that the majority of the bankers at Delos were Italians, but this cannot have been true until the later years of the Athenian cleruchy. Cf. Larsen, "Roman Greece," p. 359.

[82] *Ibid.*, p. 359. For Philostratus, see IDD, 1717–24; Durrbach, *Choix*, No. 132; J. Hatzfeld, in BCH, XXXVI (1912), 67; XLV (1921), 472.

[83] Hatzfeld, *Trafiquants*, p. 247.

[84] J. Hatzfeld, in BCH, XXXVI (1912), 132.   [85] *Ibid.*, p. 130.

[86] *Ibid.*, p. 131; cf. Hatzfeld, *Tranfiquants*, pp. 238–42.

[87] The tabulation in the text is adapted from Roussel, DCA, p. 85.

must have been more or less permanent. These foreign tenants and guarantors hailed from the following places:

1. Mainland Greece: Corinth
2. Islands of the Aegean and eastern Mediterranean: Naxos, Paros, Tenos, Euboea, Crete, Chios, Cos, and Cyprus
3. Thrace: Aenus
4. Asia Minor: Miletus, Halicarnassus, Stratonicea, Myndus, Soli, and Phaselis
5. Syrian littoral: Sidon
6. Towns with location not definitely determined, but fairly certainly identified: Apollonia (Pontus), Heraclea (Pontus), Antioch (Syria), and Laodicea (Syria)

Second, the ethnics which appear in various dedications, catalogues, and ephebic inscriptions add the names of many more foreign towns whose natives frequented Delos. A list of such names follows:[88]

1. Mainland Greece: Megalopolis and Megara
2. Islands of the Aegean and eastern Mediterranean: Amorgos, Andros, Corcyra, Crete (Cnossus, Hierapytna, Lyttus, and Polyrrhenia), Cyprus (Carpasia and Salamis), Euboea (Chalcis), Melos, Myconos, Samos, Syros, Tenedos, and Thera
3. Thrace: Byzantium
4. Asia Minor (including the Pontus): Alabanda, Amisus, Athymbra (in Caria), Cnidus, Ephesus, Erythrae, Maeonia, Magnesia, Mallus, Mylasa, Nicaea, Nicomedia, Nymphaea (on the Tauric Chersonesus), Patara, Pessinus, Phaselis, Pitane, Sinope, Smyrna, and Teos
5. Syrian littoral: Antioch, Apamea, Aradus, Ascalon, Berytus, Damascus, Hieropolis, Laodicea, Marathus, Sidon, and Tyre
6. Egypt: Alexandria and Pelusium
7. Towns with location not definitely determined: Amphipolis,

---

[88] The tabulation in the text has been compiled from Roussel, DCA, p. 86, and from the list given by L. Pernier, "Delus," De Ruggiero, *Diz. ep.*, II, ii, 1604–22, expecially p. 1615.

Anthedon, Nicopolis, Ptolemais, and Seleucia (in Pieria or on the Tigris)

The towns most frequently encountered in the inscriptions are Tyre, Sidon, Ascalon, Antioch (on the Orontes), Laodicea, Berytus, Hieropolis, and Alexandria.[89] Third, evidence that Delos was used as a trade center by merchants from the Pontus,[90] Bithynia,[91] Syria,[92]

[89] Roussel, DCA, p. 89.

[90] IG, XI, iv, 1056 (= Durrbach, *Choix*, No. 73): a decree of Athens in honor of King Pharnaces and Queen Nysa of the Pontus; IDD, 1558 (= Durrbach, *Choix*, No. 99): a dedication, by the gymnasiarch Seleucus, in honor of Mithradates V Euergetes; IDD, 1559 (= Durrbach, *Choix*, No. 100): a dedication, by an Amisene, of a statue in honor of an Athenian, who was a φίλος of Mithradates V Euergetes; IDD, 1560 (= Durrbach, *Choix*, No. 113): a dedication, by a gymnasiarch, of statues of Mithradates VI Eupator and his brother Chrestus; IDD, 1561 (= Durrbach, *Choix*, No. 114): a dedication to Zeus Ourius in behalf of Mithradates VI Eupator and his brother Chrestus, apparently in recognition of his aid to sailors and traders; IDD, 2039 (= Durrbach, *Choix*, No. 137): a dedication of a shrine to Serapis in behalf of the Athenian people, of the Roman people and of Mithradates VI Eupator; IDD, 1552, 1562, 1563, 1569–74, 1576 (= Durrbach, *Choix*, Nos. 133–36): dedication, made by Helianax, priest of the Cabiri, in behalf of the Athenians and Romans on Delos, of a temple to Mithradates VI Eupator, to whom the title Dionysus was given, along with various shields and medallions in honor of kings who were friendly toward, and allied with Mithradates, and in honor of officers of the court of Mithradates (IDD, 1563 = Durrbach, *Choix*, No. 134 was made in recognition of the benefactions of Mithradates towards the Athenian people). For other Delian inscriptions that honor the kings of the Pontus, see IDD, 1555–57, 1564–68. For the relations of Delos with the Mithradatic dynasty, see Roussel, DCA, pp. 88, 317–23. For the colony of Amisene merchants at Delos, see Durrbach *Choix*, pp. 170–71.

[91] IDD, 1579 (= Durrbach, *Choix*, No. 101): dedication, by the gymnasiarch Dioscourides, in honor of Nicomedes III; IDD, 2038 (= Durrbach, *Choix*, No. 102): dedication, by the priest Sosion of Athens, of a temple and statue of Isis Nemesis, in behalf of the Athenian people and of Nicomedes III; IDD, 1580 (= Durrbach, *Choix*, No. 104): ephebic dedication of statue of Nicomedes, son of Nicomedes III; IDD, 1577 (= Durrbach, *Choix*, No. 93): statue of King Massinissa, of Numidia, dedicated by Nicomedes Epiphanes, son of Prusias, of Bithynia. For the relations of Delos with Bithynia, see Roussel, DCA, pp. 67, 88.

[92] IDD, 1540 (= Durrbach, *Choix*, No. 87): dedication, by Alexander, son of Apollodorus, of a statue of Antiochus IV Epiphanes, in return for the monarch's benevolence towards the Athenian people; IDD, 1541: dedication of a statue of Antiochus IV Epiphanes; IDD, 1543 (= Durrbach, *Choix*, No. 88): dedication by a synod in honor of Menochares, who was a courtier in the service of Demetrius I; IDD, 1544: dedication of a statue of the Athenian Lysias, who was a courtier and officer of Demetrius I or Demetrius II; IDD, 1547, 1548 (= Durrbach, *Choix*, Nos. 109, 110): dedications in honor of Antiochus, who later became Antiochus IX;

and Egypt[93] may be clearly adduced from an imposing list of dedications made at Delos in honor of kings, and high officers of kings, of these regions, apparently in recognition of favors granted to traders, as well as of dedications in honor of individuals of private station. One of these dedications, by which οἱ καταπλέοντες εἰς Βιθυνίαν ἔμποροι καὶ ναύκληροι consecrated a statue of Meleager, son of Zmertomarus of Nicaea, to Apollo, Artemis, and Leto, provides explicit evidence of the trade relations of Delos with Bithynia.[94] Fourth, evidence of the residence of foreigners on the island for the sake of commerce is to be found in the inscriptions relating to various corporations of Oriental merchants, which resemble the Italian associations which we have already observed. The most important associations of easterners at Delos in the period follow-

IDD, 1549 (= Durrbach, *Choix*, No. 120): dedication of statue of Antiochus VIII by his courtier Bithys; IDD, 1550 (= Durrbach, *Choix*, No. 121): dedication, by Antiochus VIII, in honor of Cn. Papirius Carbo, the proconsul; IDD, 1551 (= Durrbach, *Choix*, No. 122): dedication, by the people of Laodicea in Phoenicia, of a statue of Antiochus VIII; IDD, 1552 (= Durrbach, *Choix*, No. 136h): dedication, by the priest Helianax, of a bust of Antiochus VIII in a temple consecrated to Mithradates VI Eupator; IDD, 1553; dedication, by an Athenian, of a statue of Seleucus VI Epiphanes. For other Delian inscriptions involving the Seleucids, see IDD, 1542, 1546. For the relations of Delos with Syria, see Roussel, DCA, pp. 12, note 3, 86, 88, 93–94, 252–53.

[93] IDD, 1525 (= Durrbach, *Choix*, No. 90): dedication, by Areius of Athens, of a statue of Chrysermus of Alexandria, who was a courtier and high official of Ptolemy VI; IDD, 1526 (= Durrbach, *Choix*, No. 105): dedication, by Italian ναύκληροι καὶ ἔμποροι of Alexandria, of a statue of a high courtier of Ptolemy VIII Euergetes II; IDD, 1527 (= Durrbach, *Choix*, No. 106): dedication, by two Romans, of a statue of a courtier of Ptolemy VIII Euergetes II; IDD, 1528 (= Durrbach, *Choix*, No. 108), IDD, 1529: dedication, by a synod of warehousemen in Alexandria, of a statue of Crocus, a high courtier and official of Ptolemy VIII Euergetes II; IDD, 1530: dedication, by Ptolemy VIII Euergetes II, of a statue of his cousin, Queen Cleopatra; IDD, 1531 (= Durrbach, *Choix*, No. 124): dedication, by Ptolemy X Soter II, of a doorway in a gymnasium; IDD, 1532 (= Durrbach, *Choix*, No. 126): dedication, by a citizen of Alexandria, of a statue of Ptolemy X Soter II; IDD, 1533 (= Durrbach, *Choix*, No. 128): dedication, by Stolus of Athens, of a statue of Simalus, his friend and a high courtier of Ptolemy X Soter II; IDD, 1534 (= Durrbach, *Choix*, No. 127): dedication, by Simalus of Salamis in Cyprus, of a statue of his friend, Stolus of Athens, who was a courtier and high official of Ptolemy X Soter II. For other Delian inscriptions involving the Ptolemies, see IDD, 1535–39; Durrbach, *Choix*, No. 125. For the relations of Delos with Egypt, see Roussel, DCA, pp. 5–6, 10, 88; Leider, *Der Handel von Alexandria*, p. 30; M. Rostovtzeff. in *Journal of Economic and Business History*, IV (1932), 751.

[94] IDD, 1705 (= Durrbach, *Choix*, No. 103).

ing 166 B.C. were the Tyrian *Heracleistae*, merchants and shippers,[95] and the *Poseidoniastae* of Berytus, merchants, shippers, and warehousemen.[96] At about 110 B.C. the *Poseidoniastae* built, to the northwest of the Sacred Lake, an elaborate establishment which contained shops or storerooms, a club-house, and various rooms devoted to religious observances.[97] Another association, which was of lesser importance at Delos, was that of the Alexandrian warehousemen.[98] Fifth, the strength of various foreign cults provides an indication of the existence of considerable colonies of foreigners from certain districts. That the number of Egyptians at Delos was quite large is shown, aside from other evidence, by the strength of the Egyptian cults there, particularly the cults of Isis and Serapis, which were highly favored among the Hellenic element in Egypt.[99] Likewise the strength of the Syrian cults attests the prominence of the Syrian community.[100] Finally, the presence of a Jewish colony at Delos is established by various items of literary and archaeo-

---

[95] IDD, 1519 (=Durrbach, *Choix*, No. 85); cf. Roussel, DCA, pp. 89–90; Ziebarth, *Beiträge*, p. 93; C. Picard, in BCH, XLIV (1920), 293–95.

[96] IDD, 1772–96 (1774 =Durrbach, *Choix*, No. 119); cf. Roussel, DCA, pp. 90–92; M. N. Tod, in JHS, LIV (1934), 140–59; Ziebarth, *Beiträge*, pp. 93–95. This association replaced an earlier association (of the early part of the second century B.C.) of shippers of Laodicea (the name, for a time, of Berytus). Cf. Durrbach, *Choix*, No. 72, with commentary.

[97] C. Picard, *L'Établissement des Poseidoniastes de Bérytos* (Paris, 1921; Exploration archéologique de Délos, VI); BCH, XLIV (1920), 263–311.

[98] IDD, 1528 (=Durrbach, *Choix*, No. 108), 1529; cf. Ziebarth, *Beiträge*, pp. 95–96.

[99] P. Roussel, *Les Cultes égyptiennes à Délos* (Paris, 1916); DCA, pp. 249–52.

[100] *Ibid.*, pp. 252–70. The prominence of the Syrian element in the population, known from other evidence to have been great, is confirmed by an inscription of 119/8 B.C. published by P. Roussel, in BCH, LV (1931), 438–49, which records a list of 41 ephebes, 28 παρεύτακτοι, and 22 *hieropoei* of the Apollonia. The Syrian representation appears in the following tabulation:

City	No. of Ephebes	Παρεύτακτοι	Hieropoei
Antioch	7	5	4
Tyre	3	1	2
Aradus	2	1	
Berytus	2	1	
Sidon	2		
Ptolemais	1	2	
Laodicea	1		
Anthedon	1		
Apamea		1	

logical evidence.[101] This colony, which seems to have attained to a relatively important position at Delos only after 88 B.C., when its synagogue was built, was made up of fairly poor tradesmen. We have, therefore, found abundant evidence to show that important groups of traders from the Pontus, Bithynia, Syria, and Egypt utilized Delos as a center for trade with the important Italian market. The traders from the Pontus and Bithynia probably dealt in grain and other products that had for many years bulked large in their trade, as well as in Oriental products brought to their cities over the northern trade routes which led to the East.[102] The traders from Syria came from cities that were located on the important caravan routes which led to the East,[103] while the merchants from Alexandria brought to Delos products that came from the interior of Africa, as well as from India and from other countries of the East by way of the Red Sea.[104] Thus during the latter part of the Hellenistic period the far-flung commerce of the Mediterranean world with regions located at all points of the compass came into the hands of traders who utilized Delos as a clearing-house for commerce with Italy and the West.[105] To Cicero we owe a succinct description of the articles that bulked largest in this trade.[106] He states that *mercatores* brought to Italy purple from Tyre, incense, perfume, Syrian clothing, pearls and precious stones, wines from Greece and slaves from Asia. In some instances Oriental traders brought their products, perfumes, spices, and aromatics, directly to Delos, dispensing with the services of the Greek traders of Syria and Egypt. Thus we find evidence at Delos in the second half of the second century B.C. of the presence of Nabataean, Minaean, and Gerrhaean traders. At this time two Minaean traders from Khidâb (?) dedicated an altar to their national god, Oddus or Oaddus, at Delos;[107] an "Arab," who was, apparently, a

---

[101] Durrbach, *Choix*, pp. 263–65; Roussel, DCA, pp. 94–95, 271–72, 306.

[102] Cf. chap. i, note 114. For the northerly trade routes leading to the East, see Charlesworth, *Trade Routes*, pp. 104–9.

[103] Cf. chap. i, note 103.   [104] Cf. chap. i, note 104.

[105] For Hellenistic commerce and the various regions involved, see Heichelheim, *Wirtschaftsgeschichte*, I, 458–531; II, 1083–87.

[106] Cicero, *In Verr.* II, v, 146.

[107] Durrbach, *Choix*, No. 129. For the Minaeans and their commerce, see Strabo, XVI, 768, 776.

Nabataean, dedicated an offering to Helius;[108] and a certain Temellatus of Gerrhae consecrated two offerings in the Sarapieum along with two others in the Artemisium.[109]

The city of Delos was relatively unimportant, but the harbor teemed with the activities of a multitude of traders. The important business of the island was transit trade, as is well illustrated by the storehouses which abut on the quay in the so-called Merchant Harbor.[110] Facing each warehouse was a court enclosed by walls that extended from the warehouse to the water-line, leaving almost no access to the town. The goods brought into port by cargo ships apparently reached the Delian agora only with infrequency. The two commodities which bulked largest in the trade of Delos were slaves and grain. Strabo, while writing about the scourge of piracy, has the following to say:

The market, which was large and rich in property, was not extremely far away. I mean Delos, which could both admit and send away ten thousand slaves on the same day; whence arose the proverb, "Merchant, sail in, unload your ship, everything has been sold." The cause of this was the fact that the Romans, having become rich after the destruction of Carthage and Corinth, used many slaves; and the pirates, seeing the easy profit therein, bloomed forth in great numbers, themselves not only going in quest of booty but also trafficking in slaves. The kings both of Cyprus and of Egypt cooperated with them in this, being enemies to the Syrians. Neither were the Rhodians friendly to the Syrians, and they therefore afforded them no assistance. And at the same time the pirates, pretending to be slave-dealers, carried on their evil business unchecked.[111]

The frequency of the resort of pirates to Delos, and the prominence of the trade in slaves there, may be accepted as facts; otherwise one must adopt certain reservations in his interpretation of the passage. In the first place, one should be very chary in believing that as many as ten thousand slaves changed hands there in a single day. Actually, there is no need to interpret the passage in

[108] Roussel, DCA, p. 432, No. 62.

[109] IDD, 1442B, ll. 57–58; 1444Aa, ll. 45, 51. For the wealth of the Gerrhaean merchants and the important part they played in the trade of Arabia, see Strabo, XVI, 766, 768.

[110] Roussel, DCA, pp. 300–301; A. Jardé, in BCH, XXIX (1905), 35–36. For the harbor equipment, see also J. Paris, "Contribution à l'étude des ports antiques du monde grec: II. Les Établissements maritimes de Délos," BCH, XL (1916), 5–73.

[111] Strabo, XIV, 668. The translation is that of H. L. Jones in his Loeb Library edition of Strabo.

that fashion, for the word μυριάδας, above translated literally by "ten thousand," is commonly used also to express "a very large number." In any event, so thriving was the trade in slaves at Delos that the island acquired the very unsavory reputation which is reflected in Pausanias' description of it as "the common market of Greece."[112] Secondly, the destruction of Corinth and Carthage should not be taken as the cause of more extensive use of slaves on the part of the Romans.[113] As regards the grain trade, Delos was an important center for such commerce as early as the third century B.C., at which time the Delians were very careful to maintain amicable relations with various cities in the region of the Hellespont, the Bosphorus, and the Black Sea.[114] In the first half of the second century B.C., in addition to the supplies of wheat from the Pontus, which had become intermittent owing to intertribal warfare in those regions and a new invasion of the Sarmatians,[115] grain from Numidia appeared on the market at Delos.[116] In 179 B.C., apparently for the purpose of securing an outlet for his surplus supplies of grain in future years, Massinissa, king of Numidia, made a gift to Delos of a large amount of wheat, which the city sold for 9,919 drachmas $5\frac{3}{12}$ obols.[117] No evidence is at hand for the period following 166 B.C., but we are probably safe in concluding that large amounts of grain were still sold on the Delian market. We do not have explicit evidence concerning other products which were sold there, but as we have seen above the presence of Syrian and Egyptian, Nabataean, Minaean, and Gerrhaean merchants implies that unguents, perfumes, frankincense, gums, spices, and other Oriental products were transshipped at Delos. As regards the products of local industry, our evidence is very meager and difficult of interpretation.[118] Pliny informs[119] us that perfumes were produced there, but one wonders whether these were not of Oriental origin, the

[112] VIII, xxxiii, 2.   [113] Cf. Larsen, "Roman Greece," p. 352.
[114] Durrbach, Choix, Nos. 46–50, with commentaries.
[115] See the citations in chap. ii, note 107.
[116] See the citations in chap. ii, note 108.
[117] IDD, 442A, ll. 100–6; cf. Durrbach, Choix, Nos. 68, 69; Jardé, Céréales, p. 180. The suggestion that Massinissa was attempting to secure a regular market for his grain at Delos was offered by Larsen, "Roman Greece," p. 351.
[118] See the concise survey by Hatzfeld, Trafiquants. pp. 32–33.
[119] Pliny, NH XIII, i, 4.

name Delian being associated with them merely because of their prominence on the Delian market. Another fact which Pliny records, namely that Polyclitus' statue of Jupiter Tonans was made of bronze which came from Delos,[120] would indicate that the bronze industry had enjoyed some prosperity there during the fifth century B.C. In the writings of Cicero we encounter *vasa Deliaca* and *suppellex Deliaca*,[121] but they must have been produced at some place other than Delos,[122] for by his time the island had become a very small and unimportant settlement; they were either collector's pieces of the type that Romans were eagerly buying up in the first century B.C., or, perhaps, articles of bronze produced in one of the leading bronze working centers of the time which carried on the tradition that had obtained at Delos in earlier times.[123] Our literary testimony, therefore, fails to provide any evidence of industrial production on the island during the second and first centuries B.C. Moreover, the assertions have been made that no instance of production on the scale of a factory is attested by archaeological evidence and that the island was almost certainly not an industrial center.[124] It is probably true that manufacturing did not develop there to any extent, but we must remember that at this time few industrial establishments were developed to the extent that they could be compared to a modern factory.[125] However, in recent years investigation has disclosed the existence on the island of a ceramic industry which was well developed by 200 B.C. and, between that date and the time of the sack of the island in 88 B.C., exported considerable amounts of the relief ware that was so highly favored at the time to various islands of the Aegean, Egypt, Asia Minor, South Russia, Italy, and Thrace.[126] Indeed, it has been assumed that Ariston, one of the leading producers of relief ware during the

---

[120] *Ibid.*, XXXIV, ii, 9–10.

[121] Cicero, *In Verr.* II, xxxiv, 83; lxxii, 176; *Pro Rosc. Amer.* 133.

[122] However, F. Oertel, in CAH, X, 403, maintains that bronzes were made at Delos in late Hellenistic and Roman times, while Heichelheim, *Wirtschaftsgeschichte*, I, 484, holds that bronze statues and furniture were brought to Rome from Delos in the second and first centuries B.C. Laidlaw, *Delos*, p. 292, does not make his position clear.

[123] Cf. Hatzfeld, *Trafiquants*, p. 33.   [124] *Ibid.*, p. 33.

[125] Cf. M. Rostovtzeff, in CAH, VIII, 656.

[126] Courby, *Vases grecs*, pp. 392–98.

Hellenistic period, operated a factory at Delos.[127] However, reëxamination of the evidence has shown that, while certainty is not yet attainable, his factory was probably located on the island of Rhodes.[128] But potters' shops were not the only ones to be found at Delos. There was, of course, opportunity for many small artisan shops to produce articles to meet the immediate needs of the community. Moreover, the trade of the sculptor flourished. Many sculptors were attracted to the island in the period following 166 B.C., but no Delian school of art developed.[129] Very few of the works that came from the studios were of at all high merit, but were most often realistic portraits of very commonplace functionaries and business men.[130] We may note in passing that the trade of the sculptor was, as elsewhere in the Hellenistic world, a hereditary craft in certain families which were domiciled on the island.[131] As regards agriculture, one must remember that Delos was a small and comparatively barren island, and that it was always necessary for it to import considerable amounts of food. To be sure, a certain amount of wine and, contrary to the assertion often made, some olive oil were produced on the Temple lands,[132] some of which were located on the neighboring islands of Rheneia and Myconos. But the wine was not highly favored—even at Delos—and foreign wines were imported in large amounts. In the Temple accounts of the third and the first part of the second centuries B.C. we find listed various purchases of Cnidian and Coan wines for use at Delian festivals,[133] and, although the accounts are lacking for the period following 166 B.C., we are justified in concluding that the purchases were not discontinued. Moreover, a large number of Cnidian amphorae have been found on the island.[134] On the other hand, no Coan

[127] *Ibid.*, p. 365; Broneer, *Lamps*, pp. 64–65.

[128] H. A. Thompson, in *Hesperia*, III (1934), 463–64.

[129] Lawrence, *Later Greek Sculpture*, pp. 32–39; F. Mayence and G. Leroux, in BCH, XXXI (1907), 389–419, especially p. 419.

[130] Lawrence, *Later Greek Sculpture*, p. 33.

[131] Roussel, DCA, pp. 287–88.

[132] Durrbach, *Choix*, p. 280, calls attention to the production of oil on a domain of the Temple located on Myconos.

[133] IG, XI, ii, 144A, l. 30; 154A, l. 15; 199A, l. 22; IDD, 406, l. 70; 440A, l. 62; 445, l. 4; 461Bb, l. 51; cf. G. Glotz, in JDS, XI (1913), 20; Larsen, "Roman Greece," pp. 392–94.

[134] Roussel, DCA, p. 29, note 4.

jars have been identified there. However, Coan wine was so cheap that, in all probability, the merchants and producers did not take the pains—or the expense—to label their jars.[135]

There is no available evidence to enable us to estimate the amount of trade carried on at Delos, but it must have been very large. Nevertheless, the prosperity produced thereby seems to have been limited, in the main, to a few very wealthy merchants and bankers.[136] And inasmuch as Delos was one of the most important commercial centers of the Hellenistic period, we are justified in concluding that these wealthy Delians amassed fortunes that equalled those of wealthy business men in other parts of the Hellenistic world.[137] Moreover, there is rather explicit evidence from Delos to bear out this conclusion. When Stolus, the Athenian, dedicated a statue to his friend Simalus, a wealthy business man of Salamis in Cyprus, he had an epigram composed which compared his friend's home in Salamis with the palace of Alcinous.[138] Two branches of the family are known, both of which were very prominent.[139] At c.170 B.C. Simalus' father had been singled out for special honors at Athens because of his services to Athenians who had traveled in Cyprus.[140] Another branch of the family was established at Tarentum.[141] The names of the sons of both the Tarentine and the Cyprian families are listed among the students who were enrolled in the school of Staseas at Delos;[142] and one of the youths was also enrolled in the ephebia at Athens.[143] Further indication of the circles in which Simalus moved is afforded by the fact that both he and his friend Stolus were high officers and courtiers [συγγενεῖς] of Ptolemy X Soter II.[144]

It is very difficult to form a satisfactory estimate of the population of Delos. Beloch estimated it[145] at 50,000, on the basis of a

---

[135] Larsen, "Roman Greece," p. 394.
[136] M. Rostovtzeff, in CAH, VIII, 643–44.
[137] *Ibid.*, pp. 649–50.
[138] IDD, 1533 (= Durrbach, *Choix*, No. 128).
[139] Durrbach, *Choix*, pp. 205–7; Ferguson, *Athens*, p. 408, note 1.
[140] IG, II–III², 909.
[141] Cf. Ferguson, *Athens*, p. 408, note 1.
[142] Durrbach, *Choix*, No. 117.
[143] IG, II–III², 1028, l. 145, where Simalus, son of Simalus, of Tarentum is listed.
[144] IDD, 1533, 1534; Durrbach, *Choix*, Nos. 128, 127, with commentary.
[145] Beloch, *Bevölkerung*, p. 182.

passage in Appian[146] which informs us that 20,000 men were slain by the forces of Mithradates' general Archelaüs at Delos and other places in the Aegean area. However, Beloch failed to take into account the fact that men from places other than Delos were included in the 20,000,[147] with the result that his estimate falls to the ground. The evidence to be derived from the ephebic lists is no more satisfactory, as Roussel has recently concluded after a study of an inscription of 119/8 B.C. which lists the names of forty-one ephebes, among whom six were Athenians.[148] If the proportion of one ephebe to 112 of total population were valid, as Dumont assumed years ago,[149] this inscription would indicate a population of about 5,000 at Delos. However, valid actuarial calculations can not be applied to these lists, for the ephebic training was no longer compulsory, and only sons of wealthy families were enrolled in the corps.[150] Moreover, at least some of the Athenian residents probably sent their sons to be enrolled in the Athenian ephebia.[151] This would seem to be true in the instance of the present inscription, where only 6 out of 41 ephebes were Athenians. And possibly sons of foreign families as well were sent to Athens for this training, for we have evidence, beginning with the very year of this inscription, of the enrollment of foreigners in the Athenian ephebia.[152] In any event, a population of 50,000, as suggested by Beloch, would presuppose a greater density of population than that which one finds in present-day Paris, and for that reason Roussel rightly rejects[153] the figure and suggests a total population of 20,000 to 30,000, which is the most satisfactory estimate that can be reached.

While the members of the Italian community at Delos were inclined to live more to themselves, the Greeks and Orientals seem to have intermingled freely.[154] Athenians participated with frequency in the rites of the Oriental cults,[155] and there were numerous

[146] Appian, *Mithr.* 28.   [147] J. Hatzfeld, in BCH, XXXVI (1912), 119.

[148] P. Roussel, in BCH, LV (1931), 438–49.

[149] A. Dumont, in JDS, 1871, p. 643.

[150] E. Ziebarth, *Aus dem griechischen Schulwesen* (Leipzig and Berlin, 1909), pp. 74–75. See my discussion of this question in the Appendix.

[151] Larsen, "Roman Greece," p. 350.

[152] Reinmuth, *The Foreigners in the Athenian Ephebia*, p. 12.

[153] P. Roussel, in BCH, LV (1931), 442–43.

[154] Roussel, DCA, pp. 69–71.   [155] *Ibid.*, p. 71.

instances of the erection of statues of Athenians by foreigners and
of foreigners by Athenians.[156] Moreover, intermarriage between
Athenians and Orientals occurred with some frequency, and the
children of such unions were not deprived of any of the rights which
a child of Athenian parentage on both sides possessed.[157] Consequently, it is not surprising to learn that there are a number of
instances of acquisition of Athenian citizenship by foreigners.[158]
The extent to which the cosmopolitanism of Delos progressed is indicated by the number of foreign names adopted by Athenians, a
circumstance notable also at Athens at this time.[159] This cosmopolitanism reacted upon the Athenian community in such a manner
as to contribute toward the disappearance of the formal organization of the cleruchy. The latest extant evidence we have of the
functioning of the cleruchy is derived from the year 144/3 B.C.,
while the first inscription to show a wider grouping of inhabitants
belongs to 126/5 B.C.[160] Precisely when the change took place it is
impossible to say. The Athenian families which had held offices at
Delos, or had been tenants or farmers of Temple property, or borrowers, or guarantors of Temple loans in the first decade of the
cleruchy had largely disappeared from Delian records of later years.
Consequently, when Roussel investigated the names of Athenians
in five catalogues of the later period, he found that it was impossible
to differentiate between Athenians who had taken up residence at
Delos and Athenians who continued to reside in their native city.
Moreover, he drew the very plausible conclusion that the Athenian
proportion of the population of Delos consisted largely of officials
and merchants whose term of residence was quite brief, in contrast
with the foreigners, whose abode at Delos was of longer duration.[161]
Among the Athenians who now frequented the island were many
individuals who were prominent in the public life of the mother
city, and who were founding fortunes which were to aid in maintaining their prominence at Athens for some years to come. Noteworthy among the Athenians who appear in Delian documents of

---

[156] *Ibid.*, p. 70, note 8.   [157] *Ibid.*, pp. 70–71; cf. Ferguson, *Athens*, p. 423.
[158] Roussel, DCA, pp. 69–70.
[159] *Ibid.*, p. 70; cf. W. S. Ferguson, in *Klio*, VIII (1908), 354; *Athens*, pp. 423–24.
[160] Roussel, DCA, pp. 50–55, 362; cf. Ferguson, *Cycles*, p. 173.
[161] Roussel, DCA, pp. 64–66.

this date are Medeius, son of Medeius, of the Piraeus,[162] Sarapion, son of Sarapion, of Melite,[163] and Theodotus, son of Diodorus, of Sunium, [164] all of them leaders in the oligarchical movement at Athens. It seems, therefore, that, owing to the great influx of foreigners, the growing cosmopolitanism, and the change in the nature of the residence of Athenians at Delos, the organization of the cleruchy disappeared not long after 140 B.C.[165]

An important consequence of Athenian participation in the life—social as well as commercial—of Delos was the penetration into Athens of the cosmopolitanism which we have observed at work in the island community.[166] Social and religious practices experienced very great changes. Women now received a greater amount of freedom than had ever before fallen to their lot at Athens. Religious associations with both citizen and foreign membership were introduced, and even upper class Athenians, who had formerly been of conservative bent, entered into them. Not only did foreign cults thrive[167]—many of them had been introduced into Athens as early as the fourth century B.C.—but foreign divinities, given Greek names through a kind of syncretism, found worshipers among the various associations.[168] Moreover, the barriers to intermarriage of Athenian men and women with foreigners were now lowered.[169] No longer were foreigners a class apart! Under the circumstances it is not surprising to find changes in Athenian nomenclature, but one would not have anticipated the extent to which these changes were made.[170] In many instances children were given theophoric names[171]

---

[162] *Ibid.*, p. 112; cf. PA, No. 10098.

[163] Roussel, DCA, pp. 110–11; PA, No. 12564.   [164] Roussel, DCA, p. 110.

[165] *Ibid.*, p. 55; Ferguson, *Cycles*, p. 173, commits himself merely to a date between 144/3 B.C. and 130 B.C.

[166] An excellent description of this movement is given by Ferguson, *Athens*, pp. 421–26; cf. U. Kahrstedt, *Staatsgebiet und Staatsangehörige in Athen* (Stuttgart and Berlin, 1934), pp. 286–87.

[167] Although it should be brought up to date, a unified portrayal of foreign cults at Athens between the third and the first centuries B.C. is to be found in Clerc, *Les Métèques athéniens*, pp. 140–46. For modern studies of limited portions of the field see S. Dow, "The Egyptian Cults in Athens," *Harvard Theological Review*, XXX (1937), pp. 183–232; A. Wilhelm, in JOAI, V (1902), 127–39.

[168] Thus the Syrian Atargatis became Aphrodite Hagne. IG, II–III², 1337; cf. Ferguson, *Athens*, p. 423, note 5.

[169] *Ibid.*, p. 423.   [170] *Ibid.*, pp. 423–24; *Klio*, VIII (1908), 354.

[171] For a recent study of these names see S. Dow, in *Harvard Theological Review*, XXX (1937), 216–24.

—the divinity most often being foreign, such as Isis or Serapis—or names of famous foreigners of exalted station. Thus it is that names such as Alexander, Attalus, Ariarathes, Byttacus, Cleopatra, Ptolemy, Pyrrhus, and Seleucus are common at Athens at the end of the second century B.C. Indeed, the prevalence of such names gives the impression, upon superficial inspection, of a population more polyglot than it really was.[172]

In addition to the evidence of a large number of foreigners that is afforded by the cosmopolitan movement and the presence of foreign cults, there are other indications that the number of resident foreigners at Athens at this time was large, although not as large as at the time of Demetrius of Phalerum. In the first place, the presence of a large colony of "Roman" *negotiatores* is well attested, specific reference to it being made in one inscription which is now extant; possibly also in a second. In the first inscription, which is written in Greek, a certain priest is honored for having provided a feast for members of his own tribe and the [κατοικ]οῦντας ʿΡωμαίους.[173] The second inscription, which is written in Latin, records the honors paid the military tribune Cn. Pollienus by the Athenians and the Cives Romani.[174] Moreover, a fairly large number of "Romans" who resided at Athens are known from a series of dedications, tombstones, and other inscriptions.[175] The members of the colony were, in many instances, apparently related to families that resided at Delos, for Hatzfeld found, both at Athens and at Delos, the following *nomina*: Annius, Aufidius, Babullius, Caecilius, Castricius, Crepereius, Granius, Mundicius, Ofellius, Orbius, Paconius, Trebellius, and Valerius.[176] Moreover, Hatzfeld was able to point to some instances where members of the Athenian colony had also been residents of Delos. For example, the two sons of the banker Heracleides of Tarentum, who lived at Delos with his family, also

---

[172] However, granting of citizenship to foreigners had become a very common practice in Greece by the latter part of the second century B.C.; Tarn, *Hellenistic Civilization*, pp. 94–95.

[173] AE, 1883, p. 101, ll. 8–9.

[174] CIL, X, 7350. Although the inscription was found in Sicily, the Corpus editor, T. Mommsen, offers the reasonable deduction that it was carried thence to Athens. The restoration of C R—to be expanded into Cives Romani—is not beyond question.

[175] Hatzfeld, *Trafiquants*, pp. 41–43.   [176] *Ibid.*, p. 42, and notes 1–13.

resided at Athens, where they received awards of proxeny.[177] And
in some instances families that resided at Delos sent their sons to
Athens for ephebic training.[178] These facts make it very evident
that the Italian community at Athens was closely connected with,
and dependent upon, that of Delos.[179] How is this close connection
between the Italian colonies at Delos and at Athens to be explained?
A partial explanation might be that the traders found Athens, with
its great cultural reputation and its metropolitan life, a more
pleasant place to live in. But a more compelling motive in their
choice of the metropolis for their residence is probably to be found
in the trade which they anticipated finding there. It is a noteworthy fact that the prosperous districts of Greece at this time may
be identified by ascertaining the localities where colonies of *negotiatores* had taken up residence—and Athens was no exception to the
rule. But it was not only strictly local Athenian business that attracted the *negotiatores*, for there is reason to believe that Athens was
a strategic center for carrying on trade with other cities of the
Greek mainland. In this connection it cannot be without significance
that, whereas numerous Greeks from cities on the mainland resided
at Athens, apparently for purposes of trade, these individuals are
not known to have frequented Delos, as Roussel has convincingly
shown. From a study of the tenants of Temple property and of the
guarantors of Temple loans in the accounts of 157/6 B.C. and
156/5 B.C., he was able to ascertain that, aside from Athenians, the
inhabitants of only two cities of mainland Greece and Euboea,
namely, Corinth and Histiaea, were settled permanently at Delos.[180]
But, there is no possibility that Corinthian traders were active at
Delos during the latter half of the second century B.C., for Corinth
was destroyed in 146 B.C., and her trade dispersed to other centers.
Next, from an investigation of seven catalogues and ephebic dedications ranging in date between 144/3 B.C. and the end of the second
century B.C., Roussel found that, aside from Athenians, the inhabitants of only two cities of mainland Greece and Euboea,

[177] IG, II–III², 979; cf. Hatzfeld, *Trafiquants*, pp. 42–43.

[178] Thus, Simalus, son of Simalus, of Tarentum, whose family resided at Delos,
was an ephebe on the island in 102/1 B.C., and then enrolled in the Athenian ephebia
in the following year. IG, II–III², 1028, l. 145. Cf. J. Hatzfeld, in BCH, XXXVI
(1912), 78–79.

[179] Cf. Hatzfeld, *Trafiquants*, pp. 43–44.   [180] Roussel, DCA, p. 85.

namely, Megalopolis and Chalcis, took up more or less permanent abodes at Delos.[181] But the conjecture has been made that, inasmuch as the mainland was so near the island, permanent residence was not a prerequisite to trading there; that the Greeks did not like the odor of the slave trade, which was so prominent on the island, and for that reason were content to trade at Delos only at the time of the annual festival.[182] However, the only available evidence that bears on the point does not support this theory. Thus, only one possible votive offering that could have been dedicated at Delos by such a merchant, a votive dedicated by an inhabitant of Larissa, has been found—and this Larissa may not be the Thessalian city of that name![183] Only infrequently, therefore, did traders of mainland Greece other than Athenians and citizens of one or two other places frequent Delos. Instead, these traders purchased, from agents of the Delian merchants, whom they met at Athens, the products which were sold on the Delian market. It is not difficult to ascertain the identity of these agents. Some were, as we have already seen, Italian *negotiatores;* others were Athenians who plied their trades both at Athens and at Delos;[184] others still came from various cities of the East.

But to gain a more adequate idea concerning the merchants who were active at Athens, it will be of aid to consider in detail the composition of the resident foreign colony at Athens. The provenance of the members of this colony may be ascertained from an inspection of a number of sepulchral inscriptions which have been found in Attica.[185] Out of the 775 names to be considered, approximately 90 percent are published in the second volume of *Inscriptiones Graecae*, where most of the sepulchral inscriptions are dated only in a very general way, within the period between 403 B.C. and the time of Augustus, and only a few are assigned to a more

[181] *Ibid.*, p. 86.   [182] By Ferguson, *Athens*, p. 359.
[183] Roussel, DCA, p. 87.   [184] *Ibid.*, p. 67.
[185] The names which are considered in the text appear on stones published in IG, II, Fasc. 3 and 5; also on stones published in substantial number as follows: Brückner, *Der Friedhof am Eridanos*, pp. 47–52; B. D. Meritt, in *Hesperia*, III (1934), 87–96 (these inscriptions are largely undated); D. M. Robinson, in AJP, XXXI (1910), 377–403; SEG, I–III. I have been unable to consult IG, II–III[2], Part III, Fasc. 2 (Berlin, 1940), which is Kirchner's new edition of Attic sepulchral inscriptions.

specific date. Obviously, therefore, much caution must be exercised in drawing conclusions concerning the second and first centuries B.C. from this body of inscriptions. However, the dates of the remaining 10 percent are known to fall within these two centuries; and it is significant that they show the same relative distribution— that is, as to district of provenance—of names as is shown by the 90 percent which are not specifically dated. The figures to be set forth below must, therefore, be considered as indicative of the relative strength, rather than of the absolute numbers, of each of the foreign contingents. But the following facts should be noted before the figures are set down; for it must not be thought that most of these names belong to the fourth century B.C., when the number of foreigners at Athens was very large, rather than to the second and first centuries B.C. First, some cities that were named in these inscriptions—such as, for example, Alexandria, Antioch and Seleucia—were foundations of the Hellenistic kings; others attained to their greatest prosperity only in Hellenistic times. It is extremely unlikely that many men from these cities would have reached Athens by the end of the fourth century; it is likewise improbable that more than a moderate number of them were attracted to the city in the lean third century. Consequently, it is to be concluded that the names from these cities belong, in large part, to the second and first centuries B.C. Second, there is also forthcoming specific evidence from four inscriptions, which are definitely dated within the period between 166 B.C. and 86 B.C., to show that numerous foreigners resided at Athens during the last two centuries before our era. A bilingual inscription, the Semitic portion of which is dated in 97/6 B.C., attests the worship of the god Bel by a club of Sidonians in the Piraeus.[186] In an inscription which lists the names of members of an association of *Sabaziastae* at the Piraeus in 103/2 B.C., the names of seventeen foreigners appear; four of them were slaves whose origin is not stated, while the others were natives of Aegina, Antioch, Apamea, Laodicea, Macedonia, Maronea, and Miletus.[187] An inscription of 113/2 B.C. discloses the presence at

[186] *Corpus inscriptionum Semiticarum ab Academia inscriptionum et litterarum humaniorum conditum atque digestum* (Paris, 1881), I, 118. For the date see E. Renan, in RA, 1888, p. 5. The Greek inscription (IG, II–III², 2946) is dated at the end of the third or the beginning of the second century B.C.

[187] IG, II–III², 1335.

the Piraeus of a guild of foreign merchants who worshipped Zeus Xenius.[188] The fourth inscription, which was engraved c.135 B.C., lists the names of ninety-one members of an *eranos* which was established at Athens.[189] The *archeranistes* of the club was a certain Irenaeus of Antioch, while eighty-five other members, apparently for the most part slaves, were foreigners whose place of origin is not stated. When, at last, we come to the names in the sepulchral inscriptions,[190] we find from Bithynia, the Pontus, and the Propontis 183 names, prominent among which are 96 from Heraclea, 24 from Sinope, 10 from Byzantium, 8 from Cius, and 6 from Cyzicus. Thrace is represented by 20 names. In northern Greece we find the Chalcidice, excluding Olynthus, represented by 34, Thessaly by 16, Aetolia by 4, Epirus by 12, and Boeotia by 61, of which 33 are from Thebes, 6 from Plataea, and 4 each from Thespiae, Orchomenus, and Oropus. The Peloponnesus is less well represented. We find 39 names from the Argolid, of which 18 are from Corinth, 13 from Sicyon, and 5 from Argos. There are 6 or 7 names from Messenia, and 4 from Laconia. A strikingly large percentage of the Aegean islands is represented on these stones, the most prominent being Euboea with 12, of which 6 are from Carystus 5 from Eretria, and 1 from Chalcis; Aegina has 13 names, Samos 6, and Lesbos 5. From Cyprus there are 26 names, from Crete 8, and from Rhodes 4. Asia Minor, aside from Bithynia and the regions of the Pontus and the Propontis, is represented by approximately 125 names, prominent among which are 48 from Miletus, 15 from Ephesus, 8 from Ancyra, and 5 each from Apamea and Halicarnassus. From Syria we have 50 or more names, 39 of them being from Antioch, 2 from Hieropolis, and 4 from Seleucia (in Pieria?). Possibly, however, the names from Seleucia should be attributed to Seleucia on the Tigris, then a very important commercial city. Phoenicia and Palestine are represented by approximately 15 names, of which 11 are from Sidon. Alexandria is represented by 7 names and Naucratis, in the Nile delta, by 4. The names of two Arabs on the tombstones[191] remind us of the Minaeans, Nabataeans, and Gerrhaeans at Delos.

---

[188] *Ibid.*, 1012.   [189] *Ibid.*, 2358.
[190] See the citations in note 185, above.   [191] IG, II, 2827, 2828.

We find, therefore, that the foreign colony at Athens consisted of substantial groups of individuals from the following regions:

1. Southern Italy and Sicily.
2. Bithynia, the Pontus, and the Propontis.
3. Northern Greece.
4. Islands of the Aegean.
5. Asia Minor.
6. Crete, Cyprus, and Rhodes.
7. Syria and Phoenicia.
8. Alexandria.

This distribution of foreigners resembles closely the distribution which we have already noted at Delos. But, with respect to numbers, the foreign contingent is relatively much weaker at Athens than at Delos. However that may be, it is obvious that the directions of trade at Athens were much the same as those of its subject colony. But the deduction should not be drawn from this fact that all the trade of Athens with all regions except the Greek mainland and some of the islands of the Aegean was carried on through Delos. Strabo's statement[192] that Delos was located at a place which was convenient for those who sailed from Italy and from Hellas to Asia now takes on added significance. Athens was no longer located on the main trade route between the East and the West—Delos now enjoyed that good fortune—but it was on a spur, so to speak, which was closely attached to that route. Athens was now a mainland center for the operations of those traders— or their agents, or business associates—who were active on the Delian market; it was there that they met traders from cities of the mainland, especially from northern Greece.

There is additional, and conclusive, evidence of the participation of Athens in the trade of Delos. Not only do we have the explicit statement of Posidonius that a wealthy resident at Athens at the beginning of the first century B.C., Dies (?) by name, made his fortune at Delos,[193] but a wide variety of additional information points towards the same conclusion. Conclusive numismatic evidence is available to us. Numerous "finds" of Athenian New Style

[192] Strabo, X, 486.
[193] Posidonius, in Athenaeus, V, 212d. But the reading of the name in the MSS is uncertain.

silver coins have been made at Delos,[194] as is natural, seeing the silver coinage of the island was provided by the mother city. On the other hand, 118 bronze coins of smaller denomination struck by the cleruchy had been found in the Agora at Athens by 1935.[195] When one considers that only 902 Athenian New Style coins had been found in the Agora by this time,[196] it becomes readily apparent that the intercourse between Athens and Delos must have been very extensive. From epigraphical sources evidence of a different kind is to be drawn. Very specific testimony to the presence of Athenian traders on the island in numbers is to be found in a dedicatory inscription composed, in part, of Athenian ἔμποροι and ναύκληροι.[197] At least some of the regions in which these merchants and shipowners carried on their trade may be deduced from other evidence at our disposal.[198] In an inscription of the latter half of the second century there is recorded the dedication of a statue of a certain citizen of Nicaea by οἱ καταπλέοντες εἰς Βιθυνίαν ἔμποροι καὶ ναύκληροι.[199] While the identity of these individuals is not more precisely indicated, there are indications from other sources that there must have been some Athenians among them. Not long before 120 B.C. a certain Hermogenes of Amisus dedicated at Delos a statue of Dionysius, son of Boethus, of Athens, who had been honored with the title of φίλος by Mithradates V Euergetes, apparently at a time when he was engaged in trade in the regions around the Black Sea.[200] Numerous other dedications made at Delos by Athenians testify to the liberality of Nicomedes III of Bithynia and of his son,[201] and of Mithradates V Euergetes and Mithradates VI Eupator[202] toward the Athenians at Delos, and serve to confirm the impression of close trade relations between the Athenians of Delos and the peoples of Bithynia and the Pontus. Close relationship with the Ptolemies during the latter part of the

[194] See the citations in chap. ii, note 27.
[195] J. P. Shear, in *Hesperia*, V (1936), 150.
[196] *Ibid.*, p. 150.   [197] IDD, 1645.   [198] See Roussel, DCA, pp. 66–68.
[199] IDD, 1705 (= Durrbach, *Choix*, No. 103).
[200] IDD, 1559 (= Durrbach, *Choix*, No. 100).
[201] Cf. note 91, above. Note may be taken of the tombstone of an Athenian, who was probably a merchant, at Cyzicus; it is dated in the second or first century B.C. AM, X (1885), 209; F. W. Hasluck, *Cyzicus* (Cambridge, 1910), p. 280.
[202] Cf. note 90, above.

second and the beginning of the first centuries B.C., and the conduct of trade through Delos, are suggested by the exchange of statutes between Stolus of Athens, a courtier and high military official of Ptolemy X Soter II, and Simalus of Salamis in Cyprus, one of the very wealthy traders who was active on the Delian market.[203] A final proof that the Athenians carried on an extensive trade through Delos is to be found in an instructive list of the *epimeletae* of the *Disoteria* in the Piraeus,[204] where several names may be identified as those of individuals who had interests at Delos as well. Indeed, after c.140 B.C. the Athenians at Delos were, as Roussel has pointed out, largely officials and merchants, and their abode was so transitory that it is often difficult to determine, from epigraphic evidence, whether a specific Athenian resided in Delos or at Athens.[205]

Additional evidence may be cited concerning the directions of Athenian trade—whether through Delos or directly with the regions to be mentioned, it is difficult to determine. The evidence of trade with Egypt is especially clear. Shortly before the middle of the second century B.C. the relations of Athens with the Ptolemies were very close. The Ptolemaea were celebrated with pomp and ceremony,[206] and the cordial relations that existed between Ptolemy VI Philometor and the Athenians are shown by a dedication made at Delos by a certain Areius of Athens in honor of Chrysermus of Alexandria, a courtier of Ptolemy who served as director of the Museum, as supervising officer in charge of the medical corps, and as *exegetes*.[207] But in 146/5 B.C. Ptolemy VIII Euergetes II, upon his succession to the throne in Egypt, had to put down frequent revolts, in the course of which his troops slew large numbers of Greeks, hence an estrangement between Athens and the Ptolemies, signalized by the abandonment of the celebration of the Ptolemaea.[208] However, in 102/1 B.C. a pro-Greek policy was reëstablished by Ptolemy X Soter II, whereupon the anti-Greek movement came to an end, and the Athenian government became recon-

---

[203] IDD, 1533, 1534 (= Durrbach, *Choix*, Nos. 128, 127).
[204] IG, II–III², 1939, 1940; cf. Roussel, DCA, p. 67.   [205] *Ibid.*, p. 64.
[206] W. S. Ferguson, in *Klio*, VIII (1908), 338–41.
[207] IDD, 1525 (= Durrbach, *Choix*, No. 90).
[208] Ferguson, *Athens*, pp. 368–69; *Klio*, VIII (1908), 341–43.

ciled with the Ptolemies.[209] The celebration of the Ptolemaea was resumed at Athens, a number of statues of the Ptolemies were restored at Delos, and new statues, at Athens and at Delos, were dedicated to Soter in return for his benefactions toward the Athenians and Delians.[210] Soter, who had come to the throne in 116 B.C., but had, through a succession of intrigues, been banished for some years (108–88 B.C.) to Cyprus, had already, in 111/0 B.C., shown his good will toward Athens by making a gift of a doorway in a gallery in a gymnasium to the Athenian community at Delos.[211] Consequently, even before 102/1 B.C. Athens enjoyed the favor of the ruler of at least a part, namely Cyprus, of the realm of the Ptolemies. And a most significant indication of the commercial privileges which followed upon these cordial relations is the exchange of statues at Delos between Stolus of Athens and his friend Simalus in Cyprus to which reference has already been made.[212] A further indication of the importance of Athenian trade with the eastern part of the Mediterranean—as well as with the West—has been seen in the report of Diodorus of Halae, who was appointed in the last decade of the second century B.C. to draw up a new system of regulations to govern Athenian weights and measures.[213] The new regulations, it was assumed, "established a simple method of converting the Aeginetan or commercial and the Solonian or mint systems of weights and coinage both into terms of one another and into terms of the Roman and Phoenician systems,"[214] and were

[209] *Ibid.*, pp. 341–45; Ferguson, *Athens*, p. 435.

[210] BCH, XXXIII (1909), 480; VI (1882), 343; A. Plassart, *Les Sanctuaires du mont Cynthe* (Paris, 1928; Exploration archéologique de Délos, XI), pp. 104–5; cf. note 93, above. For the bronze statues of Soter and his sister Berenice in front of the Odeum at Athens, see Pausanias, I, viii, 6; ix, 3; cf. W. S. Ferguson, in *Klio*, VIII (1908), 338–45.

[211] IDD, 1531 (=Durrbach, *Choix*, No. 124); cf. Roussel, DCA, p. 293.

[212] IDD, 1533, 1534 (=Durrbach, *Choix*, Nos. 128, 127).

[213] IG, II–III², 1013; cf. Ferguson, *Athens*, pp. 434–35. But see note 215, below.

[214] Ferguson, *Athens*, pp. 429–30; *Klio*, IV (1904), 8–10, especially p. 8, note 8. The content of the commercial mina (μνᾶ ἐμπορική) was defined as 138 standard drachmas (Στεφανηφόρου δραχμαί), and it was prescribed that when the old standard mina was not definitely specified in a contract, it was to be understood that the commercial mina was meant to apply to the transaction in question. Moreover, it was prescribed that when the commercial mina was used in business transactions, it was to be increased by an addition of twelve standard drachmas. And for ready equation of other parts of the commercial with the old standard

drawn with an eye to international trade at Delos—trade with Syria, Egypt, and other Ptolemaic possessions, and with the lands in the western part of the Mediterranean which employed the Roman standard. However, this interpretation rests upon a reading of Diodorus' report which is highly questionable.[215]

But additional evidence is available to demonstrate Athenian trade with, and through, Syria and Palestine, and extending as far as southern Arabia and the Persian Gulf. In 106/5 B.C. Theodotus of Sunium, a wealthy business man and leader in the oligarchical movement of the last decade of the second century, proposed a decree in honor of Hyrcanus I, high priest of the Jews between about 135 B.C. and 105 B.C.[216] The decree was, apparently, prompted in large part by the business interests of Theodotus and other

---

system it was prescribed that one mina be added to the five-mina weight, and five minas to the commercial talent. However, the new regulations established not only the relation to obtain between the commercial and the old standard systems, but also—although this fact is not mentioned in Diodorus' report—tacitly provided for the ready conversion of Athenian weights and measures into both the Roman and the Phoenician. For the μνᾶ ἐμπορική and the μνᾶ ἀγοραία, see Segrè, *Metrologia*, pp. 128–30; O. Viedebantt, *Forschungen zur Metrologie des Altertums* (Leipzig, 1917; Abhandlungen der königlichen Sächsischen Gesellschaft der Wissenschaften zu Leipzig, philologisch-historische Klasse, XXXIV, No. 3), pp. 35, 40, 57, 112–13. W. Giesecke, *Antikes Geldwesen* (Leipzig, 1938), pp. 7–8.

[215] A large part of the inscription is known only from a transcription made by Fourmont, which is, in many respects, unsatisfactory. Unfortunately, the fragment recently found in the Agora (B. D. Meritt, in *Hesperia*, VII [1938], 127–31) contains only lines 49–62, while the part of the inscription apposite to the point at issue falls within lines 32–41. Ferguson's interpretation (see the preceding note) assumes additions as follows: 12 dr. to the commercial mina, 1 mina to the commercial 5-mina weight, and 5 minas to the commercial talent. Segrè, *Metrologia*, p. 128, note 2, called attention to the disproportionate additions, but failed to offer an explanation. He had, apparently, not seen the article of O. Viedebantt, "Der athenische Volksbeschluss über Mass und Gewicht," *Hermes*, LI (1916), 120–44, who, through an arbitrary restoration of lines 37–38, suggested that *proportionate* additions were provided as follows: 12 dr. to 1 commercial mina; 60 dr. to 5 commercial minas; 1 commercial mina to 12 commercial minas; 5 commercial minas to 1 commercial talent. For the commercial mina, see also the preceding note. It is Viedebantt's conclusion (*ibid.*, pp. 137–38) that the effect of the provisions was to facilitate the conversion of the Attic system of weights and measures into the Roman.

[216] Josephus, *Antiq. Iud.* XIV, viii, 5; cf. A. Wilhelm, in *Philologus*, LX (1901), 487–90. For the date of the decree, and the identification of the priest honored therein as John Hyrcanus I, rather than Hyrcanus II, see Dinsmoor, *Archons*, p. 277.

Athenians in the East; by flattering Hyrcanus they hoped to protect their trade not only with Palestine, but also with Arabia, for trade with the latter region passed through the territory of the Jews.[217] The possibility that Athenians enjoyed trade relations with Arabia is indicated, as shown above, by the presence of the tombstones of two Arabs at Athens.[218] Conclusive confirmation of this possibility is forthcoming from other sources. Merchants from certain districts of Arabia, especially the Sabaeans of southern Arabia and the Gerrhaeans of the western coast of the Persian Gulf, were very prosperous in Hellenistic times. Indeed, we learn from Agatharchides that much of the carrying trade to and from Asia was concentrated in their hands.[219] Much of this trade came under the control of the Nabataeans at Petra.[220] And when, in the latter part of the second century B.C., the power of the Ptolemies and the Seleucids declined and the Nabataeans had, in turn, received a freer hand, they extended their commercial ventures into the Aegean area. We have already observed their presence at Delos.[221] Elsewhere in the Aegean area we find proxeny and a crown granted a Nabataean by the city of Tenos,[222] and a citizen of Priene honored by his native city for his services on an embassy which it had sent to Petra.[223] It should not, therefore, be surprising to find Arabian merchants at Athens. But the evidence is more nearly conclusive still. At about 115 B.C. the Himyarites of southern Arabia began to strike imitations of Athenian New Style coins.[224] Obviously Athenian coins circulated in trade in southern Arabia. Trade with Syria is evidenced by the finding in Syria of a hoard of seventy coins,[225] which was buried c.95 B.C. and included ten New Style silver coins.

[217] T. Reinach, in *Revue des études juives*, XXXIX (1899), 23–25.

[218] IG, II, 2827–28.

[219] Agatharchides, *De Mari Erythraeo*, frg. 102, in C. Müller, *Geographi Graeci minores*, I.

[220] M. Rostovtzeff, in *Journal of Economic and Business History*, IV (1932), 741–47.   [221] See notes 107–9, above.

[222] P. Graindor, in *Musée belge*, XIV (1910), 34, No. 16.

[223] F. Hiller von Gaertringen, *Inschriften von Priene* (Berlin, 1906), No. 108, l. 168.

[224] See the citations in chap. ii, note 36.

[225] See the citations in chap. ii, note 35. However, it may be that Delian trade carried the coins thither. See M. Rostovtzeff, "Some Remarks on the Monetary

The growth of the foreign trade of Athens finds itself reflected in a renaissance of the Piraeus which outstrips by far the revival that the port town had experienced during the first half of the second century B.C. Numerous Athenians who had before that time pursued their businesses elsewhere were now attracted to the port town by the splendid prospects of trade, and numerous foreigners came as well.[226] Moreover, guilds of merchants somewhat like those at Delos were formed there, but of course in much less significant numbers.[227] A guild of foreign merchants and shipowners whose patron divinity was Zeus Xenius so appreciated the favors shown them by their patron, Diodorus of Halae—he was at the same time superintendent of the Piraeus—that, in 112/1 B.C., they sought and obtained leave from the Boule to place a painted portrait of him in his office.[228] Another guild of merchants and shipowners, about whom we have no further information, made a dedication c.97/6 B.C. to Argeius son of Argeius, the general ἐπὶ τὸν Πειραιᾶ.[229] A club of Sidonians who carried on rites at the Piraeus in honor of their native divinity Bel is attested by a Semitic inscription of the beginning of the first century B.C.[230]

There are numerous additional indications that a considerable prosperity was being enjoyed by Athens between 166 B.C. and the end of the century. The repair of public buildings is frequently mentioned in our sources,[231] and various new buildings were erected as well. At some time prior to the decade between 160 B.C. and 150 B.C. the Parthenon was rebuilt—it had been swept by fire in the first half of the century—and in it a new statue of Athena Parthenos was erected c.165–160 B.C.[232] About 150 B.C. the theater

and Commercial Policy of the Seleucids and Attalids," *Anatolian Studies* (Buckler), pp. 277–98, especially p. 298.

[226] See the excellent portrayal of the prosperity of Athens at the end of the second century B.C. given by Ferguson, *Athens*, pp. 374–77. However, his proof of the return of traders to the Piraeus is not to be accepted, for by this time the deme name may not be considered a reliable indicator of one's place of residence. Cf. Gomme, *Population*, p. 40, note 4.

[227] Cf. Ferguson, *Athens*, p. 375.   [228] IG, II–III², 1012.

[229] *Ibid.*, 2952.   [230] See the citations in note 186, above.

[231] Cf. Ferguson, *Athens*, p. 370.

[232] W. B. Dinsmoor, in AJA, XXXVIII (1934), 98–103, 106; XLV (1941), 425–27. In the second of the articles Dinsmoor holds that the statue was the work of Damophon of Messene.

in the Piraeus was repaired,[233] and between 147/6 B.C. and 143/2
B.C. improvements were carried out on the Acropolis, in the Odeum
of Pericles, in the Anacium, and in an unnamed stoa.[234] And in
125/4 B.C. the Dionysiac artists undertook some remodeling in
their temenos.[235] Moreover, a goodly amount of new construction
was undertaken during this period. At about the middle of the
century the Agora square was largely rebuilt,[236] and in it were
erected the Stoa of Attalus II,[237] the so-called South Stoa,[238] and
the Hellenistic Metroum.[239] Somewhat later in the second century
the bema in front of the Stoa of Attalus[240] and the portico of the
second temple of Apollo Patrous were also built in the Agora.[241]
Possibly the great stoa located to the south of the Acropolis and
near the Dionysiac theater[242] was given to Athens by Eumenes II
(197–159 B.C.) after 166 B.C., but of the exact date we cannot be
certain. All these building activities should not be interpreted as
evidence of improved public finances at Athens. On the contrary,
the fiscal system remained as inefficient as it had been in the first
half of the century;[243] now, just as then, the public works program

[233] IG, II–III², 2334. Fiechter, *Dionysos-theater*, p. 78, holds that the parascenia
of the Theater of Dionysus were removed in the second century and a proscenium
added; he makes the suggestion that the cost of the work may have been met by
Eumenes II (197–159 B.C.) or Attalus II (159–138 B.C.) of Pergamum.

[234] *Ibid.*, 968. Of the decrees contained in this inscription, the earliest is dated
by the archonship of Archon, the latest by that of Theaetetus. For the dates of these
archons, as employed in the text, see Dinsmoor, *Archon List*, pp. 176–78; Ferguson,
Cycles, p. 30; cf. *Athens*, p. 370, note 1; Pritchett and Meritt, *Chronology*, pp.
xxx–xxxi.

[235] *Ibid.*, 1332.

[236] H. A. Thompson, in *Hesperia*, VI (1937), 223.

[237] IG, II–III², 3171; cf. Judeich, *Topographie*, pp. 354–56.

[238] T. L. Shear, in *Hesperia*, V (1936), 4–6; VI (1937), 357–58.

[239] H. A. Thompson, in *Hesperia*, VI (1937), 192–95.

[240] T. L. Shear, in *Hesperia*, VII (1938), 324; cf. Athenaeus, V, 212f.

[241] H. A. Thompson, in *Hesperia*, VI (1937), 90. The well house of the Clepsydra
at the northwestern corner of the Acropolis, was reconstructed at some time during the Hellenistic period. T. L. Shear, in *Hesperia*, VIII (1939), 225. In "late
Hellenistic" times a stoa was built along the northern side of the Agora, adjoining
the Stoa of Attalus. *Ibid.*, p. 213. Also in "late Hellenistic" times a stoa was built
in the enclosure of the Asclepieum, to the south of the Acropolis. Judeich, *Topographie*, p. 322.

[242] Judeich, *Topographie*, pp. 325–26.

[243] This situation was characteristic of Greek cities in the Hellenistic period. See
Tarn, *Hellenistic Civilization*, pp. 107–10.

was left largely to private initiative.[244] The Stoa of Attalus—and possibly, I would suggest, also the South Stoa—was constructed with funds donated by the Pergamene kings. And various other gifts were made to Athens by foreign monarchs, but we are unable to associate them with specific buildings in the city.[245] Resort was also had to the *epidosis*. Thus, the expense of repairing the theater in the Piraeus was met with funds raised by popular subscription.[246] Other public needs were cared for with the contributions which were required of the various magistrates.[247]

Another indication of the prosperity of Athens in the period following 166 B.C. is the wide circulation of Classes III and IV (a) of the New Style coinage.[248] A large number of coins was now issued —more especially in the years following 125 B.C.—apparently because of the need of an abundant coinage at Delos.[249] Nevertheless, so scrupulous was the care taken to maintain the purity and honest weight especially of the tetradrachm, that not only was it employed in quantity at Delos, but it also served as standard currency, along with Macedonian issues, throughout most of continental Greece, excepting possibly the Peloponnesus and the islands of the

[244] This practice was common in the Hellenistic world (*ibid.*, pp. 99–100). Greek cities generally found their finances inadequate for undertaking public works. *Ibid.*, pp. 109–10.

[245] Nysa, the queen of Ariarathes V of Cappadocia was honored by the Athenians for some gift or favor she had bestowed upon them. IG, II–III², 1330; cf. L. Robert, in BCH, L (1926), 497–98; Robert, *Études anatoliennes*, p. 449; Robert, *Études épigraphiques et philologiques* (Paris, 1938; Bibliothèque de l'École des Hautes Études, Fasc. 272), pp. 38–45; A. Wilhelm, in JOAI, XXIV (1929), 184–86. The much-wedded Queen Stratonice of Pergamum was honored by the Athenians with a statue at Delos at some time between 138 B.C. and 134 B.C., when she was dowager queen. Apparently she had conferred some gift upon Athens. IDD, 1575; cf. Durrbach, *Choix*, No. 89, with commentary, pp. 149–51. A colossal female statue which has been tentatively identified as one of this queen has recently been found in the Agora at Athens. T. L. Shear, in *Hesperia*, IV (1935), 385–87. Antiochus IV Epiphanes of Syria seems to have been carrying on the work of completing the Olympieum at the time of his death in 164 B.C. Judeich, *Topographie*, pp. 94, 382–83. The Athenians also received in the period following 161/0 B.C. gifts of money, for purposes not as yet identified, from King Pharnaces and Queen Nysa of the Pontus. See chap. ii, notes 88, 91, 92.

[246] IG, II–III², 2334.   [247] Ferguson, *Athens*, pp. 289–90, 370.

[248] Seltman, *Greek Coins*, pp. 260, 262; cf. Head, *Hist. Num.*, pp. 382–86.

[249] The silver from approximately six mines seems to have supplied the ordinary needs of the mint. In periods of extraordinary activity twenty additional mines were utilized. Head, *Hist. Num.*, p. 380.

Aegean.[250] The excellence of the coinage, and the extent to which it was employed in trade, is shown, moreover, by the fact that imitations of it were struck by foreign peoples, as, for example, by the Himyarites of southern Arabia in the period following 115 B.C.[251] Its primacy in Greece was first recognized by the Romans after the Third Macedonian War, as is shown by the fact that, in the official lists of booty taken during that war, the two currencies most frequently referred to were Athenian tetradrachms and Philippei.[252] Moreover, this predominance of the coinage was recognized by the Romans a second time—indirectly, however, through Delphi. In the latter half of the second century B.C. the policy of Delphi was really that of Rome:[253] where Rome bestowed its favor, so also did Delphi. It will, therefore, be of interest to take note of a decree which was passed by the Amphictyonic League at Delphi in the latter part of the century, at some time between 124 B.C. and 100 B.C.[254] It makes the following provisions. The exchange ratio of four silver drachmas for the Attic tetradrachm was made binding upon all Greeks who came under the supervision of the League. Any free person who should not abide by this regulation was to pay a fine of two hundred silver drachmas, and any slave who was guilty of infringement was to be scourged. The magistrates in the various cities and the *agoranomi* were to aid in collecting the fine, half of which was to be turned over to the informer who brought the culprit before the magistrate, the other half to the city. If the magistrates in the various cities, or at the national festivals, should not honestly enforce the provisions of the decree, they were to be tried before the Amphictyons. And if the money-changers [$\tau\rho\alpha\pi\epsilon\zeta\hat{\iota}\tau\alpha\iota$] in the cities, and at the festivals, should not adhere to the provisions of the decree, they were to be brought before the magistrates. If the latter should not do their duty, they were to be tried before the Amphictyons. Copies of the decree were to be sent to all Greek states. One copy was to be inscribed on the

---

[250] See my discussion of this coinage in chap. ii.

[251] See the citations in chap. ii, note 36.

[252] Larsen, "Roman Greece," p. 331.   [253] Daux, *Delphes*, p. 577.

[254] FDD, III, ii, No. 139. An excellent commentary on this inscription is given by T. Reinach, "L'Anarchie monétaire et ses remèdes chez les anciens Grecs," *Mémoires de l'Académie des Inscriptions et Belles-Lettres*, Vol. XXXIII, Part 2 (1911), 350–64; cf. Daux, *Delphes*, pp. 387–91.

Athenian treasury at Delphi, and another was to be set up on the Acropolis at Athens. The practical effects of the decree were the recognition of the Athenian tetradrachm as the standard currency of Greece, prevention of speculation in Athenian money, and the curbing of the money-changers.[255] Final recognition of the excellence of the Athenian tetradrachm came when, between 93 B.C. and 88 B.C., the Roman officials of Macedonia began issuance of their coinage on the same standard.[256] The Delphic decree has sometimes been taken as an endorsement of the revision of the Athenian coinage that was carried out in the last years of the second century B.C. by a special commissioner, Diodorus of Halae, who was appointed to regulate the weights, measures, and coinage of the city.[257] This is, however, not altogether certain, for the relative chronology of the two decrees is not definitely established. As noted above, the Delphic decree can be assigned only to some undetermined date between 124 B.C. and 100 B.C.,[258] while the Athenian decree seems to have been promulgated soon after 106/5 B.C.[259] However that may be, the provisions made in the Athenian decree for the ready equation of Roman and Athenian coinage established even more firmly the predominance of the New Style coinage in commercial transactions throughout Greece.

Another indication of prosperity at Athens at this time is to be found in the increased activity of the Dionysiac artists.[260] Soon after the middle of the second century B.C. the guild voted a decree in honor of Ariarathes V of Cappadocia and his queen Nysa, placed the king's statue in their shrine, and celebrated the birthdays of the royal couple in recognition of the gifts which the artists had received from them.[261] Somewhat later in the century a dispute arose between the Attic and Isthmian guilds of the artists.[262] In the

[255] See the article of T. Reinach cited in the preceding note; cf. Daux, *Delphes*, p. 387; Larsen, "Roman Greece," p. 332.

[256] H. Gaebler, *Die antiken Münzen Nordgriechenlands* (Berlin, 1906, 1935), Band III, Heft i, Nos. 224–25; III, ii, No. 9; cf. J. Friedländer, in ZFN, III (1876), 179–80; Larsen, "Roman Greece," p. 333.

[257] Ferguson, *Athens*, p. 430.   [258] Daux, *Delphes*, p. 388.

[259] W. S. Ferguson, in *Klio*, IV (1904), 8–9.   [260] Ferguson, *Athens*, p. 370.

[261] IG, II–III², 1330. For the most recent discussions of this inscription, see the citations in note 245, above.

[262] G. Colin, in BCH, XXIII (1899), 1–55; FDD, III, ii, No. 70, with com-

spring of 277 B.C. a decree of the Amphictyonic League at Delphi
had pledged the Athenian guild inviolability of person and property
[ἀσυλία and ἀσφάλεια] and exemption from taxes and military service [ἀτέλεια] in perpetuity.[263] By 134 B.C. the Athenian artists
were, apparently, experiencing difficulties in maintaining their
privileges in the districts in which the Isthmian guild was strong.
Consequently, they requested a reaffirmation of the privileges of
ἀσυλία and ἀσφάλεια.[264] The Amphictyons, who were on good
terms with the Isthmian association, answered, not too enthusi-
astically, with a reaffirmation of the privileges requested, but with
the qualification that the bestowal should be conditioned upon its
acceptability to Rome.[265] Meantime, the Athenian association
took a prominent part in the Pythais of 128/7 B.C.[266] Influenced
by this action, Delphi soon experienced a change of heart: at about
125 B.C. the Amphictyons issued a fulsome decree in honor of the
Athenian branch, which they characterized as the first and foremost guild of the Dionysiac artists, and the city of Athens as a
dispenser of culture and morality.[267] The quarrel with the Isthmian
guild continued until, in 118 B.C., the Athenian association made
formal accusations against it before C. Cornelius Sisenna, the
proconsul of Macedonia.[268] He required the Isthmian guild to send
four delegates before him to answer the charges, but it was not
until 112 B.C. that the quarrel was finally settled, when ambassadors
representing both guilds appeared before the Senate at Rome.[269]
Such great importance did the Athenians attach to the welfare of
the Athenian artists that the city placed its entire prestige behind
the guild, sending its own ambassadors to appear before the Senate

---

mentary; G. Klaffenbach, *Symbolae ad historiam collegiorum artificum Bacchiorum*
(Berlin, 1914), pp. 29–46; Daux, *Delphes*, pp. 356–72.

[263] FDD, III, ii, No. 68, lines 67, 70, 72–73, 81 (in this inscription, which is the
copy at Delphi, lines 61–94 set forth the provisions of the decree passed in 277
B.C., lines 1–61 the text of 134 B.C.); IG, II–III², 1132 is the Athenian copy, where
the text of the decree of 277 B.C. is set forth in lines 2–39, the text of 134 B.C. in
lines 52–94. Cf. Daux, *Delphes*, p. 357, notes 1 and 3; A. Wilhelm, in JOAI, XXIV
(1929), 184–85.

[264] FDD, III, ii, No. 68, ll. 36–37.   [265] *Ibid.*, No. 68, ll. 59–61.

[266] FDD, III, ii, No. 47; cf. Boethius, *Die Pythaïs*, pp. 84–85; Daux, *Delphes*,
pp. 722–26.

[267] FDD, III, ii, No. 69.   [268] Daux, *Delphes*, pp. 362–63.

[269] *Ibid.*, pp. 360–61.

in the interest of the artists.[270] The decision of the Senate favored
the Athenian association; it was destined henceforth to be the
dominant guild within the League of the Dionysiac artists. The
action of the Senate was but added confirmation of Roman favor,
which had already been manifested indirectly by the Delphic decree
of c.125 B.C. But the most tangible reflection of the prosperity of
the Athenian artists at this time is to be seen in their participation
in the various Pythaids between 128/7 B.C. and 98/7 B.C.[271] In
128/7 B.C. the guild dispatched a choir of thirty-nine members,
along with flute-players and citharists who were to provide the
accompaniment, to chant the paean in honor of Apollo. Other
artists declaimed epic poetry or engaged in dramatic presentations
on the stage of the theater at Delphi. In all sixty-one members of
the guild participated in this embassy.[272] The guild also sent contingents in the Pythaids of 106/5 B.C. and 97/6 B.C., the number
of participants in the latter year reaching the figure of eighty-eight.[273]

The renewal of the practice of dispatching a Pythais to Delphi
is another indication of the increasing prosperity of Athens at this
time. Before 138/7 B.C. only three Pythaids are attested, all of
them in the fourth century.[274] Between the fourth century and the
latter part of the second century B.C. the interruption of the practice was occasioned by various factors, important among which
were the seizure of Delphi by the Aetolians, the Macedonian
domination at Athens, and the declining prosperity of the Athenians.[275] However, the prosperity of the city made possible the resumption of the practice in 138/7 B.C.[276] Another, and more splendid,
Pythais was dispatched in 128/7 B.C.,[277] after which the practice

[270] *Ibid.*, pp. 368–69.

[271] *Ibid.*, pp. 564–67; Boethius, *Die Pythaïs*, pp. 58–59, 66, 84–87, 110–13, 123–24.

[272] Daux, *Delphes*, p. 564.   [273] *Ibid.*, p. 565.

[274] Boethius, *Die Pythaïs*, pp. 13–33.

[275] Daux, *Delphes*, p. 532. Instead, embassies were sent on occasion by the
Marathonian Tetrapolis. FDD, III, ii, Nos. 18–22; Boethius, *Die Pythaïs*, pp.
38–46; Daux, *Delphes*, pp. 532–40.

[276] FDD, III, ii, Nos. 7, 11, 23, 29 (grouped together in SIG, 696); also a small
fragment, given by Daux, *Delphes*, p. 542; cf. pp. 540–43; Boethius, *Die Pythaïs*,
pp. 53–57, 59–62.

[277] FDD, III, ii, Nos. 3, 8, 12 (and addendum), 24, 27 (and addendum) 33,
34–42, 46, 47, 50, 137, 138 (= SIG, 697–99); cf. Boethius, *Die Pythaïs*, pp. 61–73;
Daux, *Delphes*, pp. 543–45.

was interrupted—we do not know why—until 106/5 B.C. At that time the most splendid embassy of all was sent forth;[278] a total of approximately 400 individuals participated, among them the nine archons of Athens, the hoplite general, various priests, 97 ephebes, 78 knights, along with *theori, pythaistae* (adults), *canephori*, a delegation of Dionysiac artists (including the choir which chanted the paean), a choir of boys [πυθαϊσταὶ παῖδες], and financial officials. Thirty foot-soldiers and nine cavalrymen provided protection for the participants in the embassy. The expense of this huge undertaking—and to it must be added the first fruits [ἀπαρχαί] presented to Apollo—was met by contributions from the magistrates of the city, from the priests, and from other participants. The Dionysiac artists met themselves the expense involved in their participation in the embassy.[279] Then, there are indications that the families of the *canephori*, or maidens who carried the baskets filled with the sacred objects, and of the choir of boys [πυθαϊσταὶ παῖδες] met the expense of their children's participation.[280] And it is interesting to note several pairs of sisters among the *canephori*, along with several pairs of brothers among the πυθαϊσταὶ παῖδες.[281] These boys and girls were children of wealthy families, who could well afford to contribute toward the expense involved in sending the Pythais. Finally, among the *theori* and the *pythaistae* were some individuals who were elected by lot to represent the state, others who represented certain noble families, and still others who represented the Marathonian Tetrapolis.[282] These individuals, too, contributed toward the expenses of the Pythais. The fourth, and final, Pythais sent to Delphi by the Athenians occurred in 98/7 B.C.; it was considerably smaller and less expensive than its predecessors.[283]

[278] FDD, III, ii, Nos. 4 (and addendum), 5, 9, 13, 14 (=IG, II–III², 1941), 15 (and addendum), 25, 28, 30, 43, 44, 49, 51 (all these inscriptions are grouped together in SIG, 711), and IG, II–III², 1136; cf. Boethius, *Die Pythaïs*, pp. 91–110, especially pp. 110 and 139–40; Daux, *Delphes*, pp. 545–46.

[279] Boethius, *Die Pythaïs*, p. 100.

[280] The names of children of wealthy families appear very frequently in the lists of participants in the Pythaids. *Ibid.*, pp. 57–58.

[281] *Ibid.*, p. 57.   [282] *Ibid.*, pp. 117–18; Daux, *Delphes*, pp. 548–54.

[283] FDD, III, ii, Nos. 2, 6, 10, 16, 17, 26, 31, 32, 45, 48, 53, 54; cf. Boethius, *Die Pythaïs*, pp. 91–123, *passim*, especially pp. 117, 122; Daux, *Delphes*, p. 561. Daux points out that the decline of the Pythaïs is to be attributed to the political crises at Athens.

Thus far we have been concerned with the indications of prosperity at Athens and with the directions of Athenian trade. But what were the articles of trade? Our information is rather limited, but what there is of it is fairly definite. From the coastal towns of Asia Minor came a variety of ceramic wares, which included two types of *terra sigillata*,[284] a special type of gray ware,[285] lamps,[286] and, possibly, a special type of vase, the *lagynos*,[287] which was much favored at Athens in the latter half of the second century B.C. That wine from Cnidus gained some favor at Athens is shown by the

[284] It would seem that further studies of this pottery are needed before definitive results can be obtained. For the present, see the studies and classifications of the Agora examples by F. O. Waagé, in *Hesperia*, II (1933), 280–93; J. H. Iliffe, "Sigillata Wares in the Near East," QDAP, VI (1936), 4–53 (this article will, in this note, be referred to as Iliffe—QDAP); cf. Iliffe, "Hellenistic and Sigillata Ware in the Near East," JHS, LVI (1936), 234–35 (to be referred to as Iliffe—JHS). Iliffe contends (Iliffe—JHS, p. 234) that the identification of "Samian" and "Pergamene" wares has not yet been established. However, in Iliffe—QDAP, pp. 10–12, he admits the probability of the manufacture of his "Group i" ware at Samos and assigns it to a date possibly as early as the second century B.C. F. O. Waagé, "Vasa Samia," *Antiquity*, XI (1937), 46–55, defends the identification of Samian ware, and maintains (p. 52) that it was produced rather early in the first century B.C. He discusses "Pergamene" ware in *Antioch-on-the-Orontes* (Princeton, 1934; Publications of the Committee for the Excavation of Antioch and Its Vicinity, I), pp. 68–70, concluding that it was widely exported in the third and second centuries B.C., and that, while its place of origin is still uncertain, it was probably manufactured in Asia Minor. See, also, F. O. Waagé's review of Iliffe—QDAP, in AJA, XLIII (1939), 539–43; H. Comfort, "Terra sigillata," RE, Supplementband VII, 1295–1352, especially 1297–1306. Vessels stamped with the inscriptions ΔΩPON and KAΛΛ seem to have been imported into Athens from Samos in the first and, possibly, the second centuries B.C. (Iliffe—QDAP, pp. 32, 37; F. O. Waagé, in *Hesperia*, II [1933], 291–92; cf. Waagé, in AJA, XLIII [1939], 541, for the stamp KAΛΛ; for ΔΩPON see also H. Comfort, in JAOS, LVIII [1938], 40; H. Comfort, in RE, Supplementband VII, 1303); possibly also those stamped with the name ?IΛTPOΣ (Iliffe—QDAP, p. 36). Other *terra sigillata* wares which were imported from Asia Minor or the East ("Pergamene"?) as early as the second century B.C. were stamped with names as follows: ENϒ . . (Iliffe—QDAP, p. 34); MATPECV (Iliffe—QDAP, p. 39); NEIKOMAXOΣ (Iliffe—QDAP, p. 41); ΩPAIOΣ? (Iliffe—QDAP, p. 53). One shard of imported Pergamene relief ware of c.100 B.C. has also been found in the Agora at Athens. See H. A. Thompson, in *Hesperia*, III (1934), 422–26. Additional examples of sigillate wares from Athens—they are not dated—may be found in Iliffe—QDAP and in H. Comfort, "Supplementary Sigillata Signatures in the Near East," JAOS, LVIII (1938), 30–60.

[285] H. A. Thompson, in *Hesperia*, III (1934), 471.

[286] *Ibid.*, pp. 461–62.   [287] *Ibid.*, pp. 450–51.

numerous Cnidian amphorae that have been found in the Athenian Agora.[288] Again from the Aegean area various plain ware cooking utensils were imported.[289] What the Athenians imported from Rhodes remains uncertain; but it seems likely that some lamps[290] and, possibly, some wine[291] were purchased. Traders from the East who, as noted above, appeared in numbers at Athens, probably sold to the Athenians those articles which bulked largest in the trade of their native lands, such products as unguents, spices, and incense. Tangible evidence of the importation of unguents is to be seen in the Syrian fusiform unguentaria which have been found at Athens.[292] Trade relations with Egypt were, as noted above, close, and, although little direct and specific evidence is at hand for this period, we are justified in assuming that the Athenians imported those articles which are known to have played a large part in the trade of Alexandria, specifically, grain, linen, papyrus, faience, glass, and various Oriental products which were transshipped there.[293] Trade relations with the regions of the Propontis and Pontus remained close, but again we have no direct and specific evidence of the commodities imported during the period with which we are now concerned. It is very probable, however, that grain and other commodities in which that region had specialized for many years were imported.[294] From the West *negotiatores* began to import Italian wine at the beginning of the first century B.C.[295]

[288] V. Grace, in *Hesperia*, III (1934), 241. The number of Cnidian amphorae of the late second or first century B.C. found in the Agora is much smaller than that of earlier dates. This is probably to be explained by the decline of Greek vintages and the importation of Italian wines. See note 295, below. Note, however, the recent discovery, in the Agora at Athens, of additional stamped Cnidian amphora handles—this time of the first quarter of the first century B.C. T. L. Shear, in *Hesperia*, VIII (1939), 225.

[289] H. A. Thompson, in *Hesperia*, III (1934), 464–68.   [290] *Ibid.*, pp. 463–64.

[291] V. Grace, in *Hesperia*, III (1934), 201, 220. It is, however, not certain that any of the Rhodian amphorae found in the Agora are to be assigned to a date later than 166 B.C.   [292] H. A. Thompson, in *Hesperia*, III (1934), 472–74.

[293] See the citations in chap. i, note 104; also Leider, *Der Handel von Alexandria*, p. 23; Lewis, *Industrie du papyrus*, pp. 82–85; M. Rostovtzeff, in *Journal of Economic and Business History*, IV (1932), 748. For glass vases imported from Egypt, see Kisa, *Das Glas im Altertum*, I, 164.

[294] See the citations in chap. i, note 114.

[295] There may be some doubt concerning the date. The following inscriptions on Italian amphora handles found at Athens may be noted: CIL, III, Supplement I,

Other commodities that must have been imported were copper, probably largely from Cyprus, and tin, both of which were essential to the production of the bronze alloy that was employed in the smaller denominations of the New Style coinage, and in the production of the bronze furniture and statuary to which reference is made in the following paragraph.

It is because of a marine disaster that we know of various commodities which played an important part in the export trade of Athens at this time. At the beginning of the first century B.C. a ship bearing a cargo of various manufactured products set sail from Athens for Italy, but foundered off the coast of Tunisia, near Mahdia, before reaching its destination.[296] Included in the cargo were statues, statuettes, and reliefs, some of marble, others of bronze,[297] various articles of furniture made of bronze, such as beds, candelabra,[298] and small statuettes designed as ornaments for furniture, dressed and decorated blocks of marble, columns, column bases and capitals, huge marble craters, and vases and candelabra made of marble. The bas-reliefs, candelabra, and craters decorated with sculptured reliefs are typical of the work done by the Neo-

---

6545, 1–25, 7309, 1–26. *Ibid.*, 7309, 27–28 come from Laurium. These amphorae are usually assigned to the same period as those found at Brundisium, namely, the end of the Republic, CIL, IX, p. 613; cf. O. Bohn, in *Germania, Korrespondenzblatt der römisch-germanischen Kommission*, VII (1923), 14–16. However, amphora handles of approximately the same date as those at Brundisium and at Athens have been found at Delos (Hatzfeld, *Trafiquants*, p. 214, note 4), and some of them must be assigned to the end of the second and the beginning of the first centuries B.C. when an association of Italian wine-sellers is known from epigraphical evidence to have been active on the island. IDD, 1711 (= Durrbach, *Choix*, No. 142; cf. the commentary, pp. 230–31); cf. IDD, 1713, 1714. It would seem, therefore, that at least some of the Italian amphorae at Athens should be assigned to such a date. Note may be taken of the epitaph of an Athenian, who was probably a merchant, at Puteoli; it is dated in the second century. IG, XIV, 842.

[296] A. Merlin, in CRAI, 1908, pp. 245, 522; 1909, pp. 650–71; 1910, pp. 585–89; 1911, pp. 556–65; 1913, pp. 469–81; *Antiquity*, 1930, pp. 408–11; A. Merlin and L. Poinssot, in CRAI, 1909, p. 386; cf. Lippold, *Kopien*, pp. 71–73.

[297] For the bronzes of the Mahdia cargo, see A. Merlin and L. Poinssot, in *Monuments Piot*, XVII (1909), 29–57; A. Merlin, *ibid.*, XVIII (1910), 5–17; A. Merlin and L. Poinssot, *Cratères et candélabres de marbre trouvés en mer près de Mahdia* (Paris, 1930), pp. 3–11; Lamb, *Greek and Roman Bronzes*, pp. 206–8. For various objects of marble in the cargo, see the work of Merlin and Poinssot.

[298] For the marble candelabra found at Mahdia, see A. Merlin and L. Poinssot, in RA, XIV (1921), 1–12; and their work mentioned in the preceding note.

Attic sculptors who were active at Athens at this time. The marble statues were produced for the foreign market, we may be sure, since they were made of several pieces that were to be put together at a later time. Also produced for the export market were sculptured heads destined to be attached to statues of more than life size. The presence in the cargo of a bronze statuette of an Eros which reflects Lysippean influence is significant in that it illustrates a trend that was to grow in importance in the first century B.C. and later. So popular were Greek works of art becoming in Rome that Athenians found a ready market for works of art of an earlier age, and when the supply of originals approached exhaustion, the demand arose for copies no matter how eclectic their style. Thus it was that Neo-Attic sculptors flourished at Athens and became active even in Italy.[299] Another item in the cargo which illustrates the Roman craving for things Greek is a collection, taken from a building probably located in the Piraeus, of Greek inscriptions that was destined for the cabinet of a Roman scholar. While the inscribed ingots of lead that were found in the Mahdia cargo may not be Attic in origin, the probability exists that some lead from Laurium was exported, inasmuch as the mines there seem to have been the main source of lead in the Greek world.[300] It is, moreover, not unlikely that at least some of the vases and other objects of silver

[299] The fundamental work on Neo-Attic sculpture is F. Hauser, *Die neu-attischen Reliefs* (Stuttgart, 1889). In this work Hauser asserted that the center of Neo-Attic work was located at Rome, but later (JOAI, XVI [1913], 53–54) he recognized that most of the Neo-Attic sculptures were produced at Athens. Only some of the more recent discussions of the Neo-Attic school will be cited here. E. Loewy, *Neuattische Kunst* (Leipzig, 1922); Lippold, *Kopien*, pp. 55–70; Picard, *Sculpture antique*, pp. 218, 222–28. The beginnings of the Neo-Attic school are placed a little before the end of the second century B.C. by Lawrence, *Later Greek Sculpture*, pp. 49, 128. Neo-Attic works were exported not only to Italy (cf. W. Deonna, in Daremberg-Saglio, IV, 1501), but also to Africa, where they have been found at Thuburbo Maius (L. Poinssot, in *Bulletin archéologique du Comité des Travaux historiques et scientifiques*, 1922, pp. 67–71) and between Tripolis and Leptis, in Tripolis (S. Reinach, *Monuments nouveaux de l'art antique*, II [Paris, 1925], 89–90). For the shipment of Greek art to Italy between 200 B.C. and the time of Augustus, see Fuhrmann, *Philoxenos von Eretria*, pp. 216–21. The fact that a statue made by Boethus of Chalcedon was included in the cargo leads Rostovtzeff to suggest, in his *Social and Economic History of the Hellenistic World*, that works of art from other Greek communities were assembled at Athens for shipment to Italy.

[300] Davies, *Roman Mines*, pp. 246–47.

that were so popular in Hellenistic times were produced at Athens from the output of the mines at Laurium.

In spite of the declining quality of its wares, the Athenian ceramic industry still enjoyed an export market. Megarian bowls were exported to South Russia, and possibly to Asia Minor,[301] as well as to various other districts which can not be identified at present. Athenian agricultural products were still being exported, but we do not know to what districts—aside from Delos, and even there the market for Attic oil and other farm products could not have been large. While it is true that Delos was a comparatively barren island, and that it was far from able to feed its resident population, it is also true that, in addition to the wine, oil,[302] and figs produced on Temple lands, much Italian oil and wine, and large amounts of Coan and Cnidian wine found their way onto the Delian market.[303] The natural presumption would, therefore, be that the Italians, who formed the preponderant element of the population soon after 140 B.C., would prefer the products of their native land, and that, accordingly, the demand for Athenian agricultural products would have been limited in the main to the members of the Athenian colony. However that may be, Athenian oil maintained an extensive foreign market in the face of competition, and was still being exported in quantity at least as late as the time of the Emperor Hadrian.[304] Likewise, honey from Hymettus retained its foreign market well into the period of the empire.[305]

We have observed manifold evidences of prosperity at Athens in the period following the acquisition of Delos. It remains for us now to determine, in so far as it may be possible, the distribution, among the various economic groups which constituted the population of Attica, of the wealth upon which this prosperity was based. Since the middle of the third century B.C. the members of certain wealthy landholding families had held the chief offices of state.[306] In the last years of the second century B.C. these individuals were displaced by men whose interests lay in the sphere of commerce.[307]

[301] H. A. Thompson, in *Hesperia*, III (1934), 459.   [302] See note 132, above.
[303] See notes 133–35, above.
[304] See my discussion of Hadrian's oil law in chap. v.
[305] See chap. vii.   [306] Ferguson, *Cycles*, pp. 93–94; *Athens*, pp. 231–32.
[307] Ferguson, *Athens*, p. 426, calls attention to the facts that the father of Theodotus of Sunium had belonged to an association composed mainly of Easterners

Upon first consideration one might be tempted to conclude that this change should be attributed to a decline in agricultural well-being; and the appearance of Italian oil and wine on the Delian market, and probably at Athens as well, would seem to support this conclusion, especially since oil had for long been the chief export crop of the Athenian farmer. More careful consideration, however, tends to show that such a conclusion is not warranted. Athenian oil, as noted above, continued to hold its foreign market in the face of competition at least down to the time of Hadrian. And, although we have no information concerning the price of farm products at this time, the likelihood exists that farm prices had been carried upward by the prosperity the city was enjoying. In all probability, the producers of oil now secured more than the meager margin of profit that had fallen to their lot in the century preceding 166 B.C. At any rate, just as in the third century B.C., those farmers who could market a reasonably large proportion of grain continued to prosper. Indeed, the dispatch of a Pythais to Delphi by the Marathonian Tetrapolis[308]—on two separate occasions at about the middle of the second century B.C.—indicates that landholders continued to prosper for some years after 166 B.C.; and their participation in the Athenian Pythais as late as 106/5 B.C.[309] shows that not even by that time had their prosperity declined to any appreciable extent. The explanation of the loss of office on the part of the landholders is probably twofold. First, the revival of commerce had been so brisk that the prosperity of the traders now outstripped that of the farmers. Second, the formation of the new government was encouraged by the Romans, who favored oligarchical governments in

------

(IG, II–III², 2358, l. 22), that he had been priest of Aphrodite Hagne at Delos (BCH, XXXII [1908], 430, No. 42), and that he had proposed the Athenian decree in honor of John Hyrcanus (see notes 216, 217, above); that Diodorus of Halae had been patron of a guild of foreign merchants at the Piraeus during his tenure of the office of superintendent in the port town (IG, II–III², 1012); also that the leaders of the oligarchical movement are known to have been active at Delos. Roussel, DCA, p. 66, note 4, points out that the names of Theodotus and Diodorus are often Jewish, and suggests that they were possibly of Jewish descent, with a consequent interest in trade.

[308] FDD, III, ii, Nos. 21, 22; cf.Daux, *Delphes*, pp. 535–36; Boethius, *Die Pythaïs*, pp. 43–45. For the lot of the farmer in the first third of the century, see my discussion in chap. ii, including notes 122–30.

[309] *Ibid.*, pp. 139–40; Daux, *Delphes*, pp. 549–51.

their subject communities[310] and consequently supported the business men against the landholders, who adhered to democratic
principles. Athenian industry enjoyed its share of the current prosperity throughout the period following the acquisition of Delos. In
the ceramic trade the makers of Megarian bowls were able to hold
the home market, and to export some of their products, until about
100 B.C., by which time the Athenian ware had been so cheapened
that foreign products gained a foothold on the local market.[311] The
lessees of mines at Laurium experienced a high degree of prosperity.
Not only were large amounts of silver required for the New Style
coinage, but some of the metal was probably also employed for
making silver vases, inlays, and feet for couches. It is probable,
also, that a goodly amount of lead was produced in the mines at
this time. Certainly the ore from which the silver was extracted at
Laurium contained a large amount of lead, and shortly before the
time of Augustus the old slag heaps were being worked over to
secure the lead that remained in them.[312] Moreover, included in the
cargo of the ship which foundered off the coast of Tunisia were five
ingots of lead,[313] which were, presumably, mined at Laurium; but
the possibility of a Spanish origin has been raised.[314] However, the
probability that the ingots were mined in Spain, carried to Greece,
and reloaded with a cargo of art products destined for Italy seems
not very great. In any event, whether they originated in Laurium
or not, we have already seen that for many years before the second
century B.C. the greater part of the lead used in the Greek world
came from Laurium.[315] But some of these ingots are also interesting
because they are inscribed with the names of two brothers—M ET
L PLANI L F RVSSINI. The name of the latter appears also on
ingots of lead which have been found in Sicily and in Picenum.[316]
It has, therefore, been suggested that the mines at Laurium had
been farmed out to a company of Romans in the second century

[310] Pausanias, VII, xvi, 9.
[311] H. A. Thompson, in *Hesperia*, III (1934), 459. It should be observed that
little is as yet known of Athenian ceramic ware in the first century B.C.
[312] Strabo, IX, 399. See my account in chap. iv.
[313] A. Merlin, in CRAI, 1909, p. 664; in *Mélanges Cagnat*, pp. 383–91.
[314] M. Besnier, in RA, XIV (1921), 100–7; JDS, 1920, p. 268, note 1.
[315] Davies, *Roman Mines*, pp. 246–47.
[316] CIL, IX, 6091; X, 8073, 3.

B.C.;[317] but the evidence at our command is not sufficient to support this conclusion. Actually, Rome seems not to have turned over any of the territory of Athens to publicans.[318] The presence of Planius' name on the ingots from Laurium—if they really are from Laurium —is to be explained on the ground that he was one of the few *negotiatores* who were so fortunate as to secure a lease of a mine at Laurium,[319] or that he was a Roman trader who imported lead from Laurium into Italy. Athenian stone-cutters did not lack employment in the latter half of the second century B.C. Marble from Hymettus and Pentelicus was worked into columns, capitals, and bases, and then shipped to Rome for use in public buildings and private mansions.[320] Additional supplies of marble were absorbed in public building activities at Athens, and in the trade of the Neo-Attic sculptors. After giving the date of the pupils of Lysippus in 296 B.C., Pliny wrote concerning art on the mainland of Greece: *cessavit deinde ars, ac rursus Olympiade CLVI revixit.*[321] That a period of stagnation ensued is a fairly apt statement in the instance of Athens. Throughout the third and the first half of the second centuries B.C. Athenian sculptors devoted themselves, in the main, to the production of portrait statues and of other works of decorative character in the restrained classical style of the fourth century B.C.[322] But popular taste favored not at all the old classical style, looking instead toward the newer and more sensational works of art, such as those that were produced at Pergamum and other leading schools in the East. However, by 156/5 B.C. a reversion of taste had taken place, and, in the meantime, Athens had regained a large

[317] Davies, *Roman Mines*, p. 250; A. Merlin, in *Mélanges Cagnat*, pp. 383–91.

[318] Hatzfeld, *Trafiquants*, p. 224.

[319] Foreigners are known to have received concessions at Laurium. Ardaillon, *Mines du Laurium*, p. 183.

[320] The orator Licinius Crassus had columns of Hymettus marble placed in his house at Rome in 95 B.C., but Pliny's account (NH XVII, i, 6; cf. XXXVI, iii, 7; xv, 114) of Crassus' quarrel with Cn. Domitius Ahenobarbus makes it clear that imported marbles were employed only in small amounts. Cf. Larsen, "Roman Greece," p. 462, note 30. That Attic marble was actually imported into Rome in the first century B.C. is shown by the finding of finished marble columns, capitals, and bases in the Mahdia cargo. Cf. A. Merlin, in CRAI, 1909, pp. 651–54.

[321] Pliny, NH XXXIV, viii, 52.

[322] Ashmole, in Beazley and Ashmole, *Greek Sculpture and Painting*, pp. 68–70; cf. 84–85 (=CAH, VIII, 669–71; cf. p. 684); Dickins, *Hellenistic Sculpture*, pp. 54, 58–59.

amount of its former prosperity, with the result that Athenian sculptors began again to experience a quickening demand for the products of their studios. Works of art were produced not only for the local market, but were also in great demand in Italy.[323] So great was the Italian demand that mass production methods were employed to supply the market—statues were made in pieces, to be assembled at a later time.[324] Under the stimulus of the greatly increased demand for classical works of art, there came into being the so-called school of Neo-Atticists, who specialized in the production of works of eclectic style based on the famous works of the classical periods. Many of these sculptors were active at Athens; some migrated to Italy, a trend which had begun even before the inception of the Neo-Attic school when, in 156/5 B.C., Timarchus of Thoricus and his two sons, Polycles and Dionysius, went to Rome to execute commissions for Metellus Macedonicus.[325] Moreover, the Neo-Atticists were engaged not only in the production of statues and of reliefs, but also of various articles of furniture, such as candelabra and ornaments to be attached to couches and various other items.[326]

Obviously there was much work for Athenian workmen to perform at Athens in the latter half of the second century B.C. But it is by no means certain that the laborer participated to any appreciable extent in the prosperity enjoyed by his employers. Nor is it at all certain that he was always employed. The utilization of methods of mass production, as, for example, in the making of Megarian bowls and of statues for export, must have exercised a depressing influence, the extent of which, however, we are unable to determine,

[323] Ashmole, in Beazley and Ashmole, *Greek Sculpture and Painting*, pp. 93–95 (=CAH, VIII, 692–93); Dickins, *Hellenistic Sculpture*, pp. 68–69. Many Athenian sculptors were also occupied with the execution of statues at Delos. Ferguson. *Athens*, pp. 409, 410, and note 1. The conclusion should, however, not be drawn that Athenian sculptors enjoyed anything like a monopoly of the sculptors' commissions on the island. Roussel, DCA, pp. 288–89.

[324] A. Merlin, in *Antiquity*, 1930, p. 410. The pieces were made with such great haste that little care was taken to see that they fitted together properly.

[325] For Timarchus and his sons, see Pliny, NH XXXVI, v, 35; G. Lippold, in RE, Zweite Reihe, VI, 1238–39, No. 12. For the migration of Athenian sculptors to Rome, see Collignon, *Sculpture grecque*, II, 613; Lawrence, *Later Greek Sculpture*, pp. 63–65.

[326] Note the various objects found in the Mahdia cargo. See notes 296–98, above. Attic safes (ἀσφαλῶνες) containing myrrh—the latter not Attic—are mentioned in an Egyptian papyrus of 150–139 B.C. from the Thebaid. P. Grenf. I, xiv, 8–9.

upon the market for labor. While it is true that we have no direct information concerning the level of either wages or prices after the middle of the second century B.C., we do have good reasons for assuming that the worker fared no better than in the first half of the century. Certainly the revolution which led to the dictatorship of Athenion and the alignment of Athens on the side of Mithradates presupposes widespread social unrest due to maldistribution of wealth. Moreover, if the Athenian worker was not exploited by the employing class at this time, he certainly enjoyed a more favorable position by far than any of his fellow laborers in the Hellenistic world—and that we cannot believe! Whether the lot of the free worker was made appreciably poorer by the competition of slave labor, we cannot assert with assurance of certainty. The number of slaves at Athens at this time cannot be estimated, but that there were many of them is quite certain, for twice during the latter third of the second century, in 130 B.C. and 103 B.C., the Athenians were put to the trouble of suppressing revolts of the slaves, somewhat more than one thousand in number, who worked in the mines at Laurium.[327] Only at Laurium were large gangs of slaves employed by the Athenians. Elsewhere, we may suppose, possibly two or three slaves were employed by owners of small shops or at domestic tasks in the service of a well-to-do family.[328] Beyond this we are unable to deduce the nature and the extent of their employment. It seems to emerge, therefore, from our survey of the available evidence, that there were two main groups of Athenians, the very poor, constituting by far the bulk of the population, and the very rich, who represented only a very small percentage. However, despite the hardships which oppressed the poor, no considerable exodus of population seems to have taken place at this time. This is strikingly illustrated in Egypt, where, in the period preceding 150 B.C., a moderate proportion of Athenian names appears in Egyptian documents which relate to the Greek inhabitants of the country, while, after that date, Athenian names have practically disappeared.[329]

[327] The first revolt is attested by Orosius, V, ix, the second by Posidonius in Athenaeus, VI, 272e-f; cf. Ferguson, *Athens*, pp. 379, 427–28; H. Last, in CAH, IX, 11–16, 153. Only a few slaves may be recognized with certainty in the inscriptions of the period.   [328] Westermann, "Sklaverei," cols. 934–35.

[329] The names of thirty-seven Athenians appear in early Ptolemaic documents,

Two further questions prompt themselves. Is the presence of numerous foreign traders who dealt in luxury products from the Orient to be explained entirely by the existence of a small local demand on the part of a few well-to-do Athenians, and by the convenience of Athens as a center from which to carry on trade with other cities of the mainland of Greece? The answer is negative. Brilliant festivals continued to attract numerous visitors to the city as in the years preceding the acquisition of Delos.[330] Numerous students were attracted by the famous schools of philosophy that were located in the city,[331] and visitors came in number, lured by the great reputation of the city as the cultural capital of the world. Moreover, in 119/8 B.C., there began a trend which was to grow in importance, the resort of foreigners to the Athenian ephebia.[332] The floating population represented by all these individuals naturally provided an excellent market for products from the Orient, as well as for the local products of Athenian industry. The second question relates to the size of Athenian families. A frequently quoted passage from the writings of Polybius sets forth the complaint that in the historian's time Greece was suffering from a severe decline in population, owing to the preference of men for the pleasures of an idle life, and to their desire to enjoy luxuries, even if it should be necessary to curb the size of their families to secure that end.[333] There is, however, no need for us to undertake a detailed consideration of this passage, for whatever the situation may have been elsewhere in Greece, the evidence is fairly conclusive that there was no dearth of children at Athens during the latter half of the second century B.C. Ferguson was able to conclude from a study of Athenian families listed in the Prosopographia that wealthy families were rearing

but after 150 B.C. there are only two. See Heichelheim, *Auswärtige Bevölkerung*, pp. 84–85.

[330] See chap. ii, notes 12, 60–72. The Ptolemaea were omitted between 146/5 B.C. and 102/1 B.C. See the citations in notes 208–9, above. The records of the Panathenaea in 166/5 B.C. and c.160 B.C. (IG, II–III², 2316, 2317) are extant, but after the latter date do not survive. The records of the Theseia are extant between 161 B.C. and c.130 B.C., but foreigners do not often appear in them; the names of only four non-Athenian prize winners are recorded in them. IG, II–III², 956–65; cf. H. Pope, *Non-Athenians in Attic Inscriptions* (New York, 1935; dissertation), p. 34.

[331] Cf. Ferguson, *Athens*, p. 326; Walden, *Universities*, pp. 51–52.

[332] Reinmuth, *The Foreigners in the Athenian Ephebia*, pp. 12–13.

[333] Polybius, XXXVI, xvii, 1–11.

"three or four sons and the usual complement of daughters."[334]
Moreover, it is especially interesting to note the number of sisters
among the *canephori*, and the number of brothers among the
πυθαϊσταὶ παῖδες—as well as the number of *canephori* and πυθαϊσταὶ
παῖδες who were brothers and sisters—who appear in the lists of
participants in the various Pythaids dispatched to Delphi by the
Athenians.[335] If, then, one takes into account the fact that the
poorer classes are hardly ever found with fewer children than their
wealthy compatriots, it becomes evident that the revived Athenian
prosperity of the latter half of the second century was accompanied
by the practice of rearing respectably large families.[336]

We are now in a position to answer the question posed at the
beginning of this chapter: To what extent did Athens benefit from
the acquisition of Delos? We have seen that the Demos did not find
it necessary to undertake much in the way of expense toward the
equipment of the port and the town of Delos. We have also seen
that Athenians were eager to hold public office at Delos, and that
contributions were expected of the incumbents of those offices. It is,
therefore, likely that the state was involved in very little expense
through the acquisition of the island. Of course, even a respectably
small expenditure would have been relatively large for the Athenian
state, in view of its chronic inefficiency in matters of taxation and
administration of public finance. So much for the state. Did the
Athenian populace at large derive any benefits from Delos? It has
been suggested that the creation of the free port at Delos worked
as much to the disadvantage of the Piraeus as of Rhodes,[337] but
that is difficult to believe. In the last analysis the damage done the
trade of the Piraeus was occasioned by a number of factors, most
important of which was the shifting of trade routes and centers of
trade—and this trend had begun long ago, at the beginning of the
Hellenistic period, when Rhodes supplanted the port town of
Athens as the leading commercial center of the eastern Mediter-

---

[334] Ferguson, *Athens*, p. 374. J. Sundwall collected (cf. NPA, p. 1) materials for
an article on the number and naming of children, and on the age of marriage, at
Athens, but it has, to my knowledge, never been published; the materials are, however, set forth in his NPA.
[335] Boethius, *Die Pythaïs*, p. 57.   [336] Cf. Ferguson, *Athens*, p. 374.
[337] M. Rostovtzeff, in CAH, VIII, 643–44.

ranean. Moreover, the disturbed political conditions incidental to the domination of the Macedonians at Athens had also contributed to the decline of trade. When this situation was remedied in 229 B.C., the Piraeus was able to reassert its activity in commerce to the extent that its position on the trade routes permitted, and from that date until 166 B.C. a distinct revival took place. However, inasmuch as the commercial activity in the Piraeus became much greater in the period following 166 B.C., we are bound to conclude that the creation of the free port at Delos did not have a deleterious effect upon Athenian commerce. The reason why Rhodes fared differently was that the hostility of Rome towards the islanders was well known, whereas, on the other hand, Athens basked in the favor of the dominant power in the Mediterranean world. Indeed, if Delos had remained independent, it is very probable that Athenian traders would not have enjoyed the ready association with foreign traders which was vouchsafed to them under the arrangements that came into effect in 166 B.C. It is true, of course, that the number of Athenians to profit directly from trade at Delos was small when compared with the entire population of the city, and that these individuals were, in the main, bankers and traders of the type that benefited mostly from speculation on the international market.[338] But an increase in the prosperity of even a small number of individuals tends to reflect itself in the temporary well-being of a much wider group. In a city such as Athens, where the wealthy were elected to the chief offices of state and were expected to contribute to various public causes, it would follow that the newly acquired wealth of the leading citizens would in part be placed in circulation in the construction of public buildings, in the maintenance of shrines and gymnasia, in the conduct of festivals, and for other public purposes. Correspondingly, elsewhere in the Hellenistic world the lion's share of profits fell to a very restricted group of individuals, and yet that world may by no means be considered devoid of prosperity. The various indications of prosperity at Athens set forth above cannot be accounted for merely by forces at work within Attica.

The destruction of Corinth in 146 B.C. was undoubtedly responsible for the diversion to Athens of some of the trade which the city

[338] *Ibid.*, pp. 643-44.

on the isthmus had formerly enjoyed. Moreover, the favor of Rome, which had been abundantly manifested not only by the gift of Delos in 166 B.C. but also by the various acts of deference toward the Athenians on the part of Delphi,[339] contributed largely to a feeling of confidence which could only attract foreign trade to the Piraeus.[340] The harbor of Athens was a convenient stopping place, especially for vessels which were transported across the Isthmus of Corinth by means of the Diolcus.[341] Thus, in 102 B.C. Marcus Antonius had his fleet hauled across the Isthmus and then proceeded to the Piraeus, where he halted for some time, and then sailed on to the East to attempt to curb the activities of the Cilician pirates.[342] But by no means all the trade which Corinth had enjoyed found its way to Athens—in fact only a comparatively small part of it did. A large part of the traffic by way of Corinth, especially that between Asia Minor and Syria, on the one hand, and the West, on the other, was diverted to Delos. Cargoes of ships which sailed up the Gulf of Corinth were unloaded and hauled over still other routes, which led to northern Greece, avoiding Athens. One of these routes was by way of an important commercial road which ran from Creusa, the port of Thespiae, to the Euripus, a journey of one day, and thence to various cities of Euboea and of northern Greece.[343] Another route which accommodated part of this trade was that which ran from Pagae to Megara and from there to Thebes.[344] The importance of the terminal points of these routes is shown by the establishment of important colonies of *negotiatores* at Pagae and Thespiae in the first century B.C.[345]

In the last years of the second century B.C. a significant change in the government of Athens took place.[346] This change was brought

---

[339] Daux, *Delphes*, pp. 370–71; "Athènes et Delphes,"in *Athenian Studies*, pp. 37–69.

[340] Cf. Ferguson, *Athens*, p. 375.

[341] For the Diolcus, see Strabo, VIII, 335, and the citations in the following note.

[342] Cicero, *De orat.* I, 82; A. B. West, *Latin Inscriptions 1896–1926* (Cambridge, Mass., 1931; Corinth: Results of Excavations Conducted by the American School of Classical Studies at Athens, VIII, Part 2), No. 1.

[343] Ephorus in Strabo, IX, 400; cf. Ps.-Scymnus in Müller, *Geographi Graeci minores*, I, 216, ll. 490–95. Livy, XLIV, i, 4, states the length of the journey; cf. Hatzfeld, *Trafiquants*, p. 70.

[344] Strabo, VIII, 334; Plutarch, *Quaest. nat.* 59.

[345] Hatzfeld, *Trafiquants*, pp. 68–70 (Thespiae), 73–74 (Pagae).

[346] Ferguson originally ("The Oligarchical Revolution at Athens of the Year

about ultimately as a result of the cosmopolitan movement which swept over Athens and of the commercial prosperity which came with participation in the international trade of Delos, both of which led to the growth of a party of business men with new political ideas who succeeded in overthrowing the democratic government then in power—what Ferguson calls the "tory democracy"—and establishing an oligarchical regime. And in their endeavors these men had the support of Rome, which preferred timocratic governments in those subject communities to which it had left a modicum of freedom in matters of local administration.[347] The advent to power of this new group fanned into hostility the hatred for Rome which had long been rampant among the masses at Athens, who felt that the Romans were the abettors of the wealthy exploiters of the poor.[348] In face of the threat from the masses a succession of changes in the constitution was forced through between 106/5 B.C. and 101/0 B.C. Election by lot was abolished. The prohibitions against the holding of a magistracy more than once and of a senatorship more than twice were abandoned. Magistrates were no longer to be required to submit to an accounting before the courts, and for this ordeal an accounting before the Boule was substituted. The practical effect of the change last mentioned was, of course, to put an end to the most vital check that the democracy possessed on the influential officers of state.

103/2 B.C.," *Klio*, IV [1904], 1–17; *Athens*, pp. 418–29) maintained that an oligarchical revolution took place at Athens in 103/2 B.C. His argument was based, in part, on the dating of the archon-group Theocles-Heraclitus (IG, II–III², 2336) in 102/1–95/4 B.C. In the meantime it has been shown (Dinsmoor, *Archons*, pp. 240–46; *Archon List*, p. 203; Pritchett and Meritt, *Chronology*, p. xxxv) that this group is to be dated instead in 103/2–96/5 B.C., and Dinsmoor has contended that, therefore, no revolution or revolutionary change of government took place at Athens in 103/2 B.C. (*Archons*, p. 246). Ferguson now (*Cycles*, pp. 147–54) accepts the altered dating of this archon-group, and modifies his account of the changes in government at Athens at the end of the second and the beginning of the first centuries B.C. to the extent that he insists that a succession of crises—not just one c.103 B.C. —took place in the period preceding 89/8 B.C. *Ibid.*, p. 154, note 1.

[347] Pausanias, VII, xvi, 9. For the intervention of the Romans, see Appian, *Mithr.* 39; Ferguson, *Cycles*, p. 153.

[348] See my account at the beginning of chap. ii. The democrats may also have begun at this time to toy with the idea of attaching themselves to the cause of Mithradates. Ferguson, *Athens*, pp. 427, 438, note 2; Durrbach, *Choix*, No. 114, with commentary.

The fact that the new oligarchical government was much interested in trade and commerce is shown by the revision of the system of coinage, weights, and measures carried out under the supervision of a commissioner chosen from among their own number, Diodorus, son of Theophilus, of Halae, in the last years of the century.[349] The provisions of the decree which embodied Diodorus' recommendations are as follows. Any person who employed counterfeited measures was to be liable to arrest, and if he should be a free man, his property was to be sold at auction; if a slave, he was to receive fifty strokes of the lash. The counterfeited measures in question were to be destroyed by the magistrates, and if the magistrates should not bring the culprit to justice, the Council was to act. Specific provision was made that all who sold in the Agora, whether in workshops [ἐργαστήρια], wine shops or wine-cellars [οἰνῶνες], taverns or petty shops [καπηλεῖαι], or storehouses [?οἰκήματα] were to employ standard wet and dry measures, and that, if the magistrates failed in their duty of enforcing the employment of these measures, they were to be liable to pay 1,000 drachmas to Demeter and Cora. The magistrate's declaration of his holdings [ἀπογραφή] was to be accessible to all Athenians to facilitate their coöperation in enforcing the fine. In order that there might be continued supervision toward the end of preventing the use of illegal measures, the Council was delegated to conduct a survey each year during the first month of the Attic year. Detailed provisions were made concerning the type of measure to be used by dealers in various products. A grain measure containing one and one-half choinices (approximately two and one-quarter pints), with a depth of five dactyls ($3\frac{1}{2}$ inches), and a brim one dactyl ($\frac{7}{10}$ inch) in width, the measure to be filled not level, but heaping full, was to be employed by dealers in the

[349] IG, II–III², 1013; cf. Ferguson, *Athens*, pp. 429–30. A few minor corrections in the reading of this decree have been made on the basis of a fragmentary copy of lines 49–62 recently found in the Agora at Athens. B. D. Meritt, in *Hesperia*, VII (1938), 127–31. For the interpretation of those sections of the decree which are discussed in this portion of the text, see A. Boeckh, *Die Staatshaushaltung der Athener*, II (3d ed., by M. Fränkel, Berlin, 1886), 318–32; Roberts and Gardner, *Greek Epigraphy*, Part II, No. 64, pp. 170–76; O. Viedebantt, "Der athenische Volksbeschluss über Mass und Gewicht," *Hermes*, LI (1916), 120–44; Segrè, *Metrologia*, pp. 130–31. Metrological problems are discussed in the two treatments last cited; cf. O. Viedebantt, "Die athenischen Hohlmasse," *Festschrift für August Oxé* (Darmstadt, 1938), pp. 135–46.

following products: walnuts [Περσικαὶ ξηραί], dried almonds [ἀμύγδαλαι (ξηραί)], hazelnuts ['Ηρακλεωτικὰ κάρυα], the edible seed of the type of pine called πίτυς [κῶνοι], chestnuts [καστάναια], Egyptian beans [κύαμοι Αἰγύπτου], dates [φοινικοβάλανοι] and like products, lupines [θέρμοι], olives, and edible pine nuts [πυρῆνες]. A wooden measure twice the size of that just described, and with a rim one and one-half dactyls ($\frac{3}{4}\frac{1}{6}$ inch) in width, the measure to be filled not level, but heaping full, was prescribed for dealers in fresh almonds [ἀμύγδαλαι αἱ χλωραί], newly harvested olives, and dried figs. If another type of measure should be employed in selling these products, it might not be smaller than a medimnus grain measure (c.12 gallons). If a smaller measure should be employed, the magistrates were enjoined to seize it, together with its contents, destroy it, and turn the corresponding value over to the state bank. The section of the decree which provided means for the ready conversion of the commercial, old standard, and Roman systems of weights and measures and coinages one into the other has been described above. Safe preservation of the standard measures was assured by the provision that they be kept in the Tholus and at Eleusis. The public slaves were to be appropriately punished in case they did not carefully guard the measures. At the termination of the tenure of the officials in charge of the supervision of the standard measures, the magistrates were obligated to render a written account of their stewardship and file it in the Metroum; and any official found guilty of misconduct would not henceforth be allowed to receive compensation for public service. The obvious intent of the new regulations was to assure full weight and full measure to purchasers, and to prevent any sharp dealing as far as the value of coinage was concerned. The new regulations were made necessary, at least in part, by the presence at Athens of numbers of foreign traders who were accustomed to other standards of weight, measure, and coinage. Although it is not specified that the measures were to be made available at Delos, there can be no doubt that they were intended to govern commercial transactions there,[350] for the provisions relating to the ready conversion of the

---

[350] The dedication of a number of *secomata* at Delos c.100 B.C., the date of the Athenian inscription, would seem to be not without significance. For these *secomata*, see IDD, 1820 (= Durrbach, *Choix*, No. 143), IDD, 1827–29; cf. Durrbach, *Choix*, p. 229.

Roman and Athenian standards, as noted above, would be most advantageous in an international trading community such as that on the island.[351]

The succession of constitutional changes which began in 106/5 B.C. continued down to the siege of Athens by Sulla.[352] As the discontent of the masses grew, the authority in the government became restricted to progressively fewer men until a "dictatorship" was established in 91/0 B.C., when Medeius became archon and held office for three successive years without interruption.[353] Already, at some time between 106/5 B.C. and 101/0 B.C., as we have seen, the courts had been deprived of the power of calling the magistrates to account, but now civil liberties were restricted even further in order to strengthen the hand of the oligarchs, apparently with the connivance of Rome. When Medeius became archon, the Assembly was dissolved, shrines were closed, ceremonies of cult were halted, and restrictions were placed upon the philosophical schools and, apparently, upon rights of public assembly.[354] Thereupon, the popular party sent an unofficial ambassador, in the person of a Peripatetic philosopher named Athenion, to the court of Mithradates VI Eupator.[355] Beginning at this juncture the story may best be told through a few excerpts from the account of Posidonius, as quoted by Athenaeus.[356] It will be readily apparent that Athenion appealed, after the fashion of the true demagogue, to the discontent of the masses that had its roots in the maldistribution of wealth which had, in all probability, become even more pronounced than in previous times.

He [i.e. Athenion] was then elected an ambassador by the Athenians at the time when their interests were inclining to the side of Mithradates, and insinuating himself in the king's good graces he became one of his intimates, receiving the highest promotion. Wherefore he began through letters to unsettle the Athenians with false hopes, as though he possessed the greatest influence with the Cappadocian monarch—an influence which would enable them not only to live in peace and concord, freed from the fines in which they were mulcted, but even to recover their democratic constitution and receive large doles individually and as a community.

---

[351] Cf. Ferguson, *Athens*, p. 430.
[352] Ferguson, *Cycles*, pp. 149–54; cf. *Athens*, pp. 440–47.
[353] Dinsmoor, *Archons*, p. 281; Ferguson, *Cycles*, p. 151.
[354] Posidonius in Athenaeus, V, 213d.
[355] *Ibid.*, V, 212a.
[356] Posidonius is our sole ancient authority for these events.

All this the Athenians were loudly boasting, convinced that the Roman rule had been completely overthrown.[357]

The latter part of 89/8 B.C. witnessed the dramatic return of Athenion. His speech to the multitude follows:

"Men of Athens, the situation of affairs and the interest of my native land compel me to report the facts which I know; and yet the enormous importance of what is to be said, on account of the unexpected turn of circumstances, embarrasses me." When the crowds standing around shouted to him to have no fear, but to speak out, he said: "Very well, then; I speak of things never hoped for or even conceived of in a dream. King Mithradates is master of Bithynia and Upper Cappadocia; he is master of the whole continent of Asia as far as Pamphylia and Cilicia. And kings form his bodyguard, Armenian and Persian, and princes ruling over the tribes who dwell round the Maeotis and the whole of Pontus, making a circuit of three thousand six hundred miles. The Roman commander in Pamphylia, Quintus Oppius, has been delivered up and now follows in his train as a captive; Manius Aquilius, the ex-consul, who celebrated a triumph after his Sicilian campaign, bound hand and foot by a long chain to a Bastarnian seven and a half feet tall, is dragged along on foot by a man on horseback. Of all the other Roman citizens, some are prostrated before the images of the gods, while the rest have changed their dress to square cloaks and once more call themselves by the countries to which they originally belonged. And every community, greeting him with more than human honours, invokes the god-king; oracles from all quarters predict his supremacy over the civilized world. Wherefore he is dispatching great armies even to Thrace and Macedonia, and all parts of Europe have gone over to his side in a body. Yes, ambassadors have come to him not only from Italic tribes, but even from the Carthaginians, demanding that they be allies to accomplish the destruction of Rome."[358]

Continuing:

"What, now, am I to advise you? Tolerate no more the anarchical state of things which the Roman Senate has caused to be extended until such time as it shall decide what form of government we are to have. And let us not permit our holy

[357] *Ibid.*, V, 212a-b. The translation is that of C. B. Gulick, in the Loeb Classical Library. That Mithradates actually sent subsidies to Athens is shown by the series of gold coins stamped with the names of the king and of Aristion as monetary magistrates; they are dated in 87/6 B.C. Head, *Hist. Num.*, p. 385. Ferguson, *Athens*, pp. 427, 437–40, stresses the close relationship that had existed between the Pontus and Athens for several centuries as a factor that encouraged the Athenians to attach themselves to the cause of Mithradates. (For the gifts received by Athens from King Pharnaces of the Pontus, see chap. ii, note 83). But it seems more likely to have been a *mariage de convenance*: the power of Mithradates seemed to the Athenians to be the most likely means of destroying the power of Rome and rectifying the distressing economic conditions which oppressed the city.

[358] Posidonius in Athenaeus, V, 212f–213c. The translation is that of C. B. Gulick, in the Loeb Classical Library. The implication in "square cloaks," as Gulick points out, is that of "turncoat." That is, they had given up the toga for Greek dress.

places to be kept locked against us, our gymnasia in squalid decay, our theatre deserted by the Assembly, our courts voiceless, and the Pnyx, once consecrated to sacred uses by divine oracles, taken away from the people. Nor let us, men of Athens, permit the sacred voice of Iacchus to remain sealed in silence, the august temple of the Two Divinities to remain closed, and the schools of the philosophers to stand voiceless."[359]

Thereupon, the multitude selected Athenion as hoplite general. Posidonius' account continues:

And this Peripatetic, coming forward in the theatre "with a stride like that of Pythocles," thanked the Athenians and said: "To-day you are your own commanders, although I am at your head. And if you will lend your assistance, I shall have the combined strength of all of you." With these words, he appointed the other officers in his own interest, proposing by name those whom he desired. Not many days after, he made himself dictator . . .[360]

Upon the establishment of this dictatorship, which made a pretence of employing democratic forms, a reign of terror was instituted.[361] Sympathizers with the oligarchical government—almost all the wealthy inhabitants of the city—attempted to escape, but Athenion set a guard over the walls to prevent their departure and attempted to round up those who had already made their way out of the city. A number of wealthy suspects were executed, and others were thrown into prison. To these terroristic actions there was added a widespread confiscation of property, with the result, as we are informed by Posidonius, that Athenion "gathered together money in such amounts as to fill several wells."[362] Moreover, Athenion's greed led him on to send the philosopher Apellicon to Delos with an armed force to seize the treasures on the island. But so great was the inefficiency of Apellicon that a defending force under the leadership of a certain Orobius was able easily to overcome the assault of the expeditionary force from Athens.[363] However, where

[359] *Ibid.*, V, 213c-d. The translation is that of the Loeb Classical Library.

[360] *Ibid.*, V, 213e-f. The translation is that of the Loeb Classical Library.

[361] *Ibid.*, V, 213f–214d.

[362] *Ibid.*, V, 214b. Hyperbole is, of course, to be expected here. See note 386, below.

[363] *Ibid.*, V, 214d–215b. The leader of the Delian forces is given the name Orobius in this passage. T. Mommsen, in his commentary on CIL, III, Supplement, 7225 and 7234, identified him with Lucius Orbius, the well-known merchant who resided at Delos. For the various dedications at Delos made by Orbius, or in his honor, see Durrbach, *Choix*, pp. 235–36. The members of the family of the Orbii at Delos were engaged in the selling of wine or the making of amphorae. J. Hatzfeld, in BCH, XXXVI (1912), 61, note 2. Mommsen's identification of Orobius with

the Athenian expedition failed, Mithradates' fleet succeeded. The Temple treasures were seized and sent to Athens, the island was thoroughly plundered, and a large number of the resident Italians were slain.[364] But before this great disaster the island had regained its independence from Athens.[365] Possibly—for we can not be certain of it—the business interests of the members of the Athenian colony and the residence there of a dominant colony of Italians led to the island's adherence to the cause of Rome rather than to that of the democrats at Athens.[366] Following, and perhaps as a result of, the defeat of Apellicon, Athenion was succeeded in the dictatorship at Athens by the philosopher Aristion, a partisan of Mithrades who arrived on the scene with the treasures of Delos.[367]

There is some reason to believe that the political disturbances of the first decade of the first century B.C. were accompanied by a decline in the prosperity of the city. It was not a rapid decline, nor can we be certain of the extent of it. Indeed, it has been assumed that, to the contrary, the period between 103 B.C. and 90 B.C. was one of "commercial expansion."[368] In support of this contention we are reminded of the holding of the ceremony of the weaving of the *peplos* for Athena in 103/2 B.C. and, supposedly, in 94/3 B.C.[369]—

Orbius has been accepted by Roussel, DCA, p. 324; Ferguson, *Athens*, pp. 445–46; J. Hatzfeld, in BCH, XXXVI (1912), 123. However, Durrbach, *Choix*, pp. 235–36, contends that the leader of the defending force was not a resident of Delos, but the commander of a Roman fleet then patrolling the Aegean. The title στρατηγὸς 'Ρωμαίων given Orobius by Posidonius supports Durrbach's view.

[364] Appian, *Mithr.* 28; Pausanias, III, xxiii, 2; Plutarch, *Sulla*, 11; cf. Roussel, DCA, pp. 324–27; Laidlaw, *Delos*, pp. 262–63.

[365] Roussel, DCA, pp. 320–23.

[366] Ferguson, *Athens*, pp. 426–27, suggests the economic motive. Roussel, DCA, pp. 317–23, maintains that we can not be certain as to the factors which motivated the action of the Athenian colony on the island. However, Dies (?), who made his fortune at Delos, was anti-Roman, for Aristion was entertained in his house upon his return from the Pontus; Posidonius in Athenaeus, V, 212d.

[367] Appian, *Mithr.* 28; cf. Ferguson, *Athens*, pp. 446–47. It is not relevant to the purposes of the present discussion to inquire whether Athenion and Aristion were one and the same, or different individuals. For this question, see *ibid.*, p. 447, note 1; U. von Wilamowitz-Moellendorff, "Athenion und Aristion," *Sitzungsberichte der preussischen Akademie der Wissenschaften, philosophisch-historische Klasse*, 1923, pp. 39–50.

[368] Ferguson, *Athens*, pp. 435–36.

[369] The ceremonies were held during the archonships of Theocles (IG, II–III², 1034) and of Demochares (*ibid.*, 1036). The name of the archon Procles is conjec-

the ceremony is now known not to have been held at the latter date—
of the restoration of the Ptolemaea in 102/1 B.C.,[370] the dispatch
of the Pythais to Delphi in 98/7 B.C.,[371] the activity of an organized
group of Sidonians, obviously merchants, in the Piraeus in 97/6
B.C.,[372] and the reconstruction of the Agora of the Italians at Delos
c.100 B.C.[373] To these considerations may be added the dispatch
of a new Pythais, this time to Delos, in 103/2 B.C.[374] On the other
hand, various factors seem to indicate the *beginning* of a decline in
prosperity soon after 100 B.C. In the first place, the disturbed
political conditions then obtaining at Athens were not conducive
to trade. Secondly, attention may be called to the fact that the
Pythais of 98/7 B.C. was considerably less expensive than its predecessors.[375] Finally, and most important of all, the prosperity of
Athens was adversely affected by the decline of Delos, which, there
are some grounds for believing, set in soon after 100 B.C.[376] The
cause of this decline is to be found in the island's loss of the slave
trade, which came about as a result of the curbing of the pirates,
who were the principal dealers in slaves. The first evidence we have
of stern measures against the pirates on the part of the Romans is
dated in 102 B.C., when Marcus Antonius was dispatched at the
head of an expedition which had for its purpose the curbing of the
activity of the Cilician pirates.[377] While we are not explicitly in-

---

turally restored in *ibid.*, 1034, but for the correct restoration of the name of Theocles,
see Dinsmoor, *Archon List*, p. 181. For the dating of the archonship of Theocles in
103/2 B.C., see note 346, above. Ferguson, *Athens*, p. 436, note 2, maintains 94/3
B.C. as the date of the archonship of Demochares, but the correct date is now seen
to be 108/7 B.C. Cf. Dinsmoor, *Archons*, p. 243; *Archon List*, p. 200; Ferguson,
Cycles, p. 32; Pritchett and Meritt, *Chronology*, pp. xxxiv, 131.

[370] See the citations in note 209, above.

[371] See the citations in note 283, above.

[372] See the citations in note 186, above.

[373] Lapalus, *L'Agora des Italiens*, pp. 97–98; J. Hatzfeld, in BCH, XXXVI
(1912), 109–20.

[374] IG, II–III², 2336, with commentary by J. Kirchner; cf. Daux, *Delphes*, pp.
580–81; Ferguson, *Cycles*, p. 147, note 1; S. Dow, "The First Enneeteric Delian
Pythais, IG, II² 2336," *Harvard Studies in Classical Philology*, LI (1940), 111–24.

[375] See the citations in note 283, above.

[376] Cf. M. Rostovtzeff, in CAH, VIII, 647; *Journal of Economic and Business
History*, IV (1932), 751–52.

[377] Livy, *Epit.* lxviii; Obsequens, 104; Trogus, *Prol.* 39; cf. Ormerod, *Piracy in
the Ancient World*, pp. 208–9; Ziebarth, *Beiträge*, p. 33.

formed concerning the precise results of this expedition, we do know that a patrol was maintained henceforth off Cilicia, as a result of which Delos was lost to the pirates as a market for slaves. Very soon thereafter, c.100 B.C., the Romans took further action, whereby the kings in Cyprus, Alexandria and Egypt, Cyrene, and Syria were required to close their ports against the pirates.[378] While these measures by no means succeeded at this time in curbing the activity of the pirates, the important point, as far as Delos and Athens are concerned, is that the island was deprived of one of its most lucrative sources of trade. From that time onward the foreign traders began to leave the island, for they came gradually[379] to realize that Puteoli, which had begun to develop as an important port by the beginning of the second century B.C.,[380] was a much more convenient center for carrying on trade between, on the one hand, Syria and Egypt, and, on the other, the Italian market, which had become the most promising field for commercial development in the Mediterranean area.

In the summer of 87 B.C. Sulla arrived in Attica with an army of 30,000 men and laid siege to Athens and the Piraeus.[381] In the following spring both the city and its port town fell before his assaults. His army forced its way into the city on the calends of March, and a ruthless slaughter of the inhabitants—irrespective of age and sex—followed. When the soldiers entered the city, Aristion and a few of his followers took refuge in the Acropolis, after setting fire to the Odeum of Pericles to keep Sulla from utilizing its timbers in his assault on the citadel.[382] The city was thoroughly pillaged, but the amount of destruction wrought by the soldiers in other respects can not be ascertained. In any event, we are informed that

[378] SEG, III, 378; cf. Ormerod, *Piracy in the Ancient World*, pp. 242–47; Ziebarth, *Beiträge*, pp. 33–34.

[379] That members of the Italian colony and other foreigners returned to Delos after the sack of the island in 88 B.C. is clearly shown by an inscription which records the subscribers, including, among others, Italians, Greeks, Sidonians, and Tyrians, to the reconstruction of the Agora of the Italians (IDD, 2612), and by a number of other inscriptions which prove the continued existence there of Italian associations (Roussel, DCA, pp. 329–35; Laidlaw, *Delos*, pp. 265–66) and of a Jewish colony (Durrbach, *Choix*, pp. 263–65).

[380] C. Dubois, *Pouzzoles antique* (Paris, 1907), pp. 65–74.

[381] Plutarch, *Sulla*, xii; Appian, *Mithr.* 30–39; cf. Ferguson, *Athens*, pp. 447–52.

[382] Appian, *Mithr.* 38.

Sulla gave instructions that the houses were not to be fired.[383] The Piraeus fared much differently when it was finally seized.[384] Lest the harbor be utilized by the fleet of Mithradates, the docks, ship-sheds, arsenal—in fact almost the entire city—were destroyed; only the temple of Aphrodite Pandemus and the Disoterium remained. After his successful siege of the city Sulla found his supply of money sadly depleted. To replenish his coffers he confiscated the slaves in the city[385] and removed forty pounds of gold and six hundred pounds of silver from the Acropolis.[386] With the terrible calamity of 86 B.C. we arrive at a major turning point in the history of Athens.

[383] *Ibid.*, 38.

[384] Appian, *Mithr.* 41; Plutarch, *Sulla*, xiv, 7; cf. Strabo, IX, 395–96.

[385] Appian, *Mithr.* 38.

[386] *Ibid.*, 39. Rostovtzeff argues, in his *Social and Economic History of the Hellenistic World*, that the fact that even after the confiscations during the reign of terror only this amount of money could be placed in the Acropolis vividly demonstrates the limited resources even of the wealthy citizens.

CHAPTER IV

FROM SULLA TO THE DEATH

OF AUGUSTUS:

86 B.C.-14 A.D.

A T THE END of his account of the devastation of Athens by Sulla's army Pausanias wrote as follows: "In such wise was Athens sorely afflicted by the war with Rome, but she flourished again when Hadrian was emperor."[1] This passage, taken in conjunction with various others, the most representative of which may be quoted here, has formed the basis for the opinion widely held that Athens was an exceedingly poor and wretched city in the period that elapsed between the sack of the city in 86 B.C. and the accession of Hadrian to the throne at Rome. In 45 B.C. Servius Sulpicius wrote to Cicero as follows:

While on my way back from Asia I was sailing from Aegina towards Megara, I began to view the surrounding districts. Behind me was Aegina, in front of me Megara, on the right the Piraeus, on the left Corinth, cities which had formerly been most prosperous, but now lay before my sight prostrate and thoroughly destroyed.[2]

Some years later, at the time of Augustus, Horace wrote incidentally concerning Athens:

A man of ability who has chosen peaceful Athens for his abode and devoted seven years to study and has grown old amidst books and the serious study of philosophy generally turns out more taciturn than a statue and makes the people's sides shake with laughter; here [in Rome] in the midst of the seething waves and turbulent storms of the city may I consider myself fit to weave together words of such a sort as to wake the tones of the lyre?[3]

---

[1] I, xx, 7. The translation is from the Loeb Library edition.
[2] Cicero, *Ad fam.* IV, v, 4. The translation is my own.
[3] *Epist.* II, ii, 81–86:

        Ingenium, sibi quod vacuas desumpsit Athenas
        et studiis annos septem dedit insenuitque

Also during the reign of Augustus the poet Ovid asked, in a passage which laments the sad state in his own time of Greek cities that had enjoyed great renown in former ages:

What remains of Pandionia, unless it be the name [of] Athens?[4]

Again from the time of Augustus we have statements in the work of the geographer Strabo concerning the desolation of the Piraeus. In one passage he writes:

But the numerous wars caused the ruin of the wall and of the fortress of Munychia, and reduced the Peiraeus to a small settlement, round the harbours and the temple of Zeus Soter. The small roofed colonnades of the temple have admirable paintings, the works of famous artists; and its open court has statues.[5]

Again he writes:

But the Peiraeus no longer endures, since it was badly damaged, first by the Lacedaemonians, who tore down the two walls, and later by Sulla, the Roman commander.[6]

Finally, there may be quoted a general statement that is typical of the rhetorical exaggeration of Roman and late Greek writers as regards the condition of Greece as a whole. In the middle of the first century A.D. Seneca had the following to say:

Do you not see how, in Achaia, the foundations of the most famous cities have already crumbled to nothing, so that no trace is left to show that they ever even existed?[7]

Of such a nature are our literary sources for the history of Athens after the time of Sulla. It will be of value, however, to consider the passages quoted above rather closely. Servius Sulpicius wrote his letter to Cicero at about the middle of March, 45 B.C. In it he attempted to console Cicero for the death of Tullia. The general purport of the letter is as follows: "During the course of recent events we have all suffered degradation—especially because our

---

> libris et curis, statua taciturnius exit
> plerumque et risu populum quatit; hic ego rerum
> fluctibus in mediis et tempestatibus urbis
> verba lyrae motura sonum conectere digner?

The translation in the text is my own. In the past certain scholars have interpreted the *vacuas* with extreme literalness—but wrongly, as Wachsmuth, *Die Stadt Athen*, I, 665, note 4, and Graindor, *Auguste*, p. 98, have observed.

[4] *Metam.* XV, 430. The translation is my own.

[5] IX, 395–96. The translation is from the Loeb Library edition.

[6] XIV, 654. The translation is from the Loeb Library edition.

[7] *Epist.* XIV, iii (xci), 10. The translation is from the Loeb Library edition.

country and our honor have been taken away from us. Your grief
for these losses should be so great that this more personal loss of
yours will not add to your sorrow. Besides, I often think of the
comment you used to make, that a painless death would not be an
unwelcome exchange for the sort of life we are now compelled to
live. And why could Tullia have wished a longer life? Anything
that she might have hoped for was already lost to her. However, I
have found some consolation—which I hope you may share—in
observations which I made recently in the course of my travels."
At this point in the letter came the passage quoted above, in which
Sulpicius refers to Aegina, Megara, the Piraeus, and Corinth as
prostrata et diruta. To resume: "When such famous towns have
perished from the earth, why should it ever occur to us that we
are not mortal beings? Other men—famous men—have died. And
Tullia would have died not long hence—for she too was mortal.
You can at least remember that she had the satisfaction of happy
married life with young men of noble station and of seeing her
father regaled with the highest honors in the state. Moreover, she
was fortunate in dying at a time when all that she had treasured
in life had vanished—when the Republic fell. But as you have
helped others in the past with your advice, so now console your-
self with your own wisdom. Time, it is true, moderates all sorrows,
but it is not fitting that a man of your intellectual stature refrain
from employing his wisdom to attain to the same end. Furthermore,
if the dead are really conscious, Tullia will not wish you to grieve
for her. One final point—do not let the idea get abroad that perhaps
you are grieving not so much for Tullia as for the fall of the Republic. It is fitting for a great man to endure sorrow and good fortune with the same dignity." Thus, while Sulpicius urges Cicero to
console himself with philosophy, he paints the world in colors
none too bright, after the fashion of a sympathetic friend who says
—and can, under such circumstances, say no more—that life is,
after all, but a poor and fleeting thing. It would, therefore, seem
quite obvious that there must be a certain amount of exaggeration
in Sulpicius' letter concerning the condition of the cities in question.
But how great was this exaggeration? A brief consideration of the
history of these cities will throw some light on this point. Aegina
had been seized by the Roman admiral P. Sulpicius in 210 B.C.,

during the First Macedonian War; its inhabitants were sold into slavery by the admiral, while the island itself was sold to the Attalids by the Aetolians and the Athenians.[8] At a considerably later date, probably 69 B.C., the island was harassed by the pirates.[9] However, by the time of Augustus it had regained sufficient importance to be granted autonomy by the emperor.[10] In the time of the Severi Aegina issued its own coinage.[11] Although Megara no longer enjoyed the repute and prosperity that it had before the Peloponnesian War, it remained a city of not inconsiderable importance for some two and three quarters centuries following the death of Alexander.[12] But in 48 B.C., after the battle of Pharsalus, the city was sacked by Q. Fufius Calenus, the legate of Caesar, its population severely decimated by the ensuing slaughter, and the survivors sold into slavery.[13] Servius Sulpicius, writing three years later, portrays the condition of the city that resulted from this severe treatment. However, the city was restored before long and regained sufficient importance, during at least part of the empire, to issue its own coinage.[14] Corinth had been ruthlessly sacked by Mummius in 146 B.C.,[15] and no fault may be found with Sulpicius' description of the site, which was still deserted in 45 B.C. But the year following the writing of his letter was marked by the refounding of Corinth by Caesar.[16] As regards the Piraeus, it has been generally maintained that that town was so utterly devastated by Sulla that it did not regain until the reign of Hadrian even a moderate degree of well-being. This is a very complicated question and, for the moment, must be passed over with the comment that there is very good reason to believe that the Athenian port town was being reconstructed as early as c.60 B.C. and that the extent of its recovery was quite considerable by the time of Augustus. Two

---

[8] Polybius, XI, v and xxiii, 8.

[9] IG, IV, 2, with commentary by M. Fraenkel, who argues for the date of 69 B.C.

[10] Dio Cassius, LIV, vii, 2; cf. Graindor, *Auguste*, p. 5.

[11] Head, *Hist. Num.*, p. 398.

[12] E. L. Highbarger, *The History and Civilization of Ancient Megara* (Baltimore, 1928), pp. 201–15.

[13] Dio Cassius, XLII, xiv; cf. Plutarch, *Brut.* viii.

[14] Head, *Hist. Num.*, p. 394; *British Museum Catalogue: Coins of Attica* (London, 1888), pp. 122–24.

[15] Livy, *Epit.* LII; Velleius, I, 13.

[16] Cf. T. Lenschau, in RE, Supplementband IV, 1033–34.

facts emerge very clearly from our attempt to evaluate the statement quoted from Sulpicius' letter. First, a certain amount of
rhetorical exaggeration is manifestly present: Aegina was not to be
described as *prostrata et diruta*; and the same situation probably
existed in the case of the Piraeus. Second, Sulpicius' description is
partially true for his own time but is not valid for any succeeding
time.

Of a somewhat different nature is the evidence concerning Athens
that may be derived from the *Geography* of Strabo, a native of
Amasia in the Pontus, who composed his work near the end of the
reign of Augustus. He traveled very little—this is especially true
for Greece, where he seems to have visited only Corinth—and in
consequence derived most of his information from written and oral
sources.[17] That Strabo had no firsthand knowledge concerning
Attica is clearly shown by his confused description of many of the
coastal districts of that territory,[18] and especially by his statement
that the promontory of Sunium extended nearly as far south as
that of Malea.[19] Furthermore, as we shall have occasion later to
observe, various items of archaeological and epigraphical evidence
make it clear that the Piraeus had recovered to a far greater extent
by the time of Augustus than the account of Strabo would lead one
to believe. We must conclude that, in so far at least as Attica is
concerned, Strabo utilized sources of information that stemmed
from the most depressed period of the civil wars.

Again the passages quoted from Horace, Ovid, and Seneca are
of a different nature. When Ovid states that only the name of
Athens remains, and when Seneca asserts that "the foundations of
the most famous cities have already crumbled to nothing," we must
conclude that they are following the current mode, wherein the
decline of Greece had become a stock in trade of rhetorical decla-

---

[17] J. G. C. Anderson, "Some Questions Bearing on the Date and Place of Composition of Strabo's Geography," *Anatolian Studies* (Ramsay), pp. 1–13; E. Honigmann, "Strabo," RE, Zweite Reihe, IV, 76–151, especially pp. 147–51. See also
H. F. Tozer, *A History of Ancient Geography* (2d ed., edited by M. Cary; Cambridge, 1935), pp. 238–60, especially pp. 238–46; and the citations in the following
note.

[18] C. H. Weller, "The Extent of Strabo's Travel in Greece," *Classical Philology*,
I (1916), 339–56; in AJA, VII (1903), 286; *Athens and its Monuments* (New York,
1913), p. 399.   [19] II, 92.

mations. Under the influence of such exaggerations Horace's *vacuas Athenas* has been unnecessarily misinterpreted. Quite obviously he was not saying that Athens was devoid of population or of buildings. Rather, he was contrasting the relatively peaceful atmosphere of a university city that was devoted to learning—and not necessarily altogether bereft of prosperity—with the hustle and bustle of the capital city of the empire, which teemed with the political, economic, and social endeavors of a multitude of all sorts of men.

By way of summary, therefore, we may observe that the following types of literary evidence are at hand for the economic history of Athens in the period following the destruction of the city by Sulla. First, there are reports, such as those of Servius Sulpicius and Strabo, which describe with some accuracy the condition of Attica at the time of the greatest stress during and immediately following the civil wars. These accounts must not be applied by construction to any later years. Second, there are obvious rhetorical exaggerations, such as those we have observed in the passages quoted from Ovid and Seneca. Third, some passages, such as the one quoted from Horace, have been taken out of context and unnecessarily misinterpreted. Fourth, there are general statements, again obviously exaggerated, that proclaim the decline of all Greece; such is the passage quoted from Seneca. The following procedures must be followed in dealing with such forms of evidence. First, all literary sources must be rigorously examined in the light of archaeological and epigraphical evidence. Second, all contradictions must be ferreted out. Third, care must be taken not to be influenced by comparisons with the great past of Athens, nor with other and more prosperous parts of the empire. Fourth, general statements concerning economic conditions in Greece as a whole must be subjected to close scrutiny before being applied to Athens. While due allowance is, of course, to be made for a limited amount of economic interdependence between various parts of the province of Achaea, the fact of wide variation in resources and in economic activity between different sections of the country must be recognized. Any treatment of the economic history of Greece during the empire must, of necessity, be regional in nature. Fifth, allowance must be made for the propensity of ancient writers to perpetuate pessimistic statements made by their predecessors, even after conditions had improved.[20]

After Athens had fallen before the army of Sulla numerous Athenians were slain by the Roman soldiers, while still others committed suicide.[21] Even before the siege had begun, a number of citizens were slain by Athenion;[22] others took refuge with relatives and friends outside of Athens.[23] The net decline of the city's population was not great, however, for many individuals probably returned soon after peaceful conditions were restored. The Piraeus was unmercifully razed,[24] but the public buildings of the city suffered relatively little damage. Substantially the same constitution was restored to the Athenians as that which had existed before the dictatorships of the first decade of the century.[25] However, in conformity with Roman policy in their dependencies, the government was made distinctly aristocratic. The changes in the constitution were apparently carried through upon the return of Sulla to Athens in 84 B.C., and at this time, as well as at the time of the sack of the city, many objects of art were carried away by the Romans. From the unfinished Olympieum Sulla removed a number of columns to Rome.[26] To adorn his triumph, he removed from the Stoa of Zeus Eleutherius the shields of Athenian patriots that were dedicated there, and carried away paintings and statues from other buildings.[27]

After the departure of Sulla the city was by no means without woes. For some years it suffered from maltreatment at the hands of various Roman officials, first of all at the hands of the notorious Verres, who removed a large sum of gold from the Parthenon;[28] later the city was victimized by L. Calpurnius Piso, proconsul of Achaea in 59–57 B.C.[29] That this form of maltreatment persisted

[20] Compare the excellent statement of Larsen, "Roman Greece," pp. 465–67, concerning the nature of our literary sources for the economic history of Greece during this period.

[21] Plutarch, *Sulla*, xiv.   [22] Athenaeus, V, 214.

[23] Plutarch, *Luc.* xix, tells us that some betook themselves to the Pontus.

[24] Appian, *Mithr.* 41; Plutarch, *Sulla*, xiv, 7; cf. Strabo, IX, 396.

[25] Appian, *Mithr.* 39; cf. Strabo, IX, 398; Ferguson, *Athens*, pp. 455–56; *Cycles*, p. 150.

[26] Pliny, NH XXXVI, vi, 45.   [27] Pausanias, X, xxi, 6.

[28] Cicero, *In Verr.* I, xvii, 45; cf. V, lxxii, 184.

[29] Cicero, *In L. Pis.* xl, 96.

at least until the middle of the century is made evident by two
letters written by Cicero, one in 51 B.C.,[30] in which he takes satisfaction from the fact that he and his staff had not, like other tran-
sient Roman officials, been a burden to the Greeks; the other,[31]
written in 49 B.C., expresses the fear that no place in Greece would
be left unplundered. Moreover, Greece suffered from the disruption
of commerce by the pirates and from the exactions of Roman
generals during the course of the campaigns to clear the seas of the
marauders. As Appian[32] specifically informs us, even cities that
were independent and exempt from tribute were called upon to pay
contributions during the Mithradatic and pirate wars. While we
have no direct testimony to the effect that contributions were
exacted from Athens, the likelihood exists that some were collected. Indeed, several additional items of evidence show that the
Athenians fared very badly at this time. Soon after the sack of the
city in 86 B.C. the Athenians found it necessary to sell the island
of Salamis.[33] And the city even resorted to the selling of its citizenship.[34] Both of these acts do not necessarily mean that the Athenians were poor, but rather that the state was poor[35]—which was not
at all a unique situation at Athens. That the state was poor is
indicated, also, by the fact that the city found it necessary to bor-
row through an intermediary whose credit was good, T. Pomponius
Atticus, in order to secure loans at a reasonably low rate of interest.[36]
That Atticus also distributed grain to the citizens of Athens[37] re-
veals that the city was in dire straits and that a severe depression
was wreaking havoc upon its citizens. But this argument is by no
means weighty, for Athens for centuries past had experienced much
difficulty with its grain supply and found it necessary frequently to
carry out the distribution of free grain to its citizens. There is no
reason, however, to doubt that the revenues of the city had declined severely. One fact alone would be sufficient to prove this:
the loss of revenue occasioned by the exhaustion of the mines at
Laurium. The supply of silver seems to have approached exhaus-

---

[30] *Ad Att.* V, x, 2; cf. V, xi, 5.   [31] *Ad Att.* IX, ix, 2.   [32] *Bell. civ.* I, i, 2.
[33] Strabo, IX, 394; cf. Graindor, *Auguste*, pp. 8–9.
[34] Dio Cassius, LIV, vii, 2.
[35] Cf. Graindor, *Auguste*, p. 161.   [36] Cornelius Nepos, XXV, ii, 4.
[37] Cornelius Nepos, XXV, ii, 4.

tion there c.86 B.C.[38] In conclusion it may be readily admitted that the normal economic life of Athens had been greatly disrupted by the decline of Delos, by the sack of the city by Sulla, by the exactions of various Roman officials, and by the infestation of the seas by the pirates. But care must be taken to avoid exaggeration of the difficulties that beset the city, for even during these distressing times certain alleviating factors may be observed. In 84 B.C., upon his return from Asia, Sulla restored to Athens the islands of Imbros, Lemnos, Scyrus, and Delos.[39] Apparently in return for this beneficence the Athenians celebrated a new festival, the Sylleia, in Sulla's honor.[40] In the same year the Roman general was initiated into the Eleusinian Mysteries.[41] Henceforth the Mysteries became increasingly important, with consequent benefit to Athens through the large number of visitors attracted thither at the time of the celebration of the rites of the Greater and the Lesser Mysteries. A long series of influential Romans now came to be initiated into the Mysteries. Among the prominent individuals, aside from Sulla, to appear for this purpose during the first part of the first century B.C. were Cicero, T. Pomponius Atticus, and Antony.[42] By 82/1 B.C. the Athenians had recovered so far from the events of 87/6 B.C. as to be able to restore various sacrifices.[43] More important still were the numerous students who were attracted to Athens by the renown of its teachers, for from them Athens was henceforth to derive a goodly amount of its prosperity. During the period with which we are now concerned Cicero could refer to Athens as the *domicilium studiorum*;[44] and many other passages might be cited to show the importance of Athens as a university town during these troubled times.

In 67 B.C. the pirates were finally cleared from the seas. Following this date the evidences of recovery at Athens are considerably more imposing. In 62 B.C. Pompey presented the city with fifty talents with which to restore its monuments,[45] and, significant as

---

[38] See my discussion below, including chap. iv, notes 105, 222.

[39] Ferguson, *Athens*, p. 454.   [40] IG, II–III², 1039, l. 57.

[41] Plutarch, *Sulla*, xxvi; cf. G. Giannelli, in *Atti della reale Accademia delle Scienze di Torino*, 1914–15, pp. 321-22; Graindor, *Chronologie*, p. 42, note 1.

[42] G. Giannelli, in *Atti della reale Accademia delle Scienze di Torino*, 1914–15, pp. 320–25.   [43] Cf. IG, II–III², 3489.

[44] *De orat.* III, xi, 43.   [45] Plutarch, *Pomp.* xlii, 5–6.

an indication of at least a partial revival of commerce after the subjection of the pirates, part of this sum was employed in rebuilding the Deigma in the Piraeus. Between this date and the beginning of the civil wars a number of new buildings were erected and various projects of restoration were carried out, in part through private initiative, as in the second century B.C. In 52/1 B.C. a shrine of Asclepius was restored.[46] In the following year Appius Claudius Pulcher built a propylaeum at Eleusis.[47] Also at about the middle of the century the Odeum of Pericles, which had been destroyed by Sulla's soldiers in 86 B.C., was restored by C. and M. Stallius and Melanippus at the expense of Ariobarzanes II Philopator (63/2–52/1 B.C.) of Cappadocia.[48] And at some time between 86 B.C. and 48 B.C. the section of the city wall between the Piraic Gate and the Sacred Gate, through which a breach had been made by Sulla's soldiers in 86 B.C., was repaired.[49] So promising had the trade in objects of art become by this time that foreigners established factories there to take part in the trade. One of these factories is mentioned in 50 B.C. by Cicero, who wrote to C. Memmius with the request that C. Avianius Evander be allowed to continue to occupy his property at Athens in order that he might fill many orders for his numerous customers.[50]

The respite which Athens enjoyed beginning with the conclusion of the pirate wars in 67 B.C. was all too brief. In 49 B.C. the civil war between Pompey and Caesar broke upon the scene, and again

[46] IG, II–III², 1046.

[47] CIL, I, 775, III, 547; ILS, 4041; G. Libertini, in *Annuario della reale Scuola italiana archeologica di Atene*, II (1916), 201–17.

[48] IG, II–III², 3426. Various alterations were made in the Theater of Dionysus in the middle of the first century B.C. See Bieber, *History of the Greek and Roman Theater*, p. 240; Bulle, *Untersuchungen*, p. 80; Fiechter, *Dionysos-theater*, I, 62–63; III, 77–78. M. Thompson, in *Hesperia*, X (1941), 223, suggests that this work also may have been paid for by Ariobarzanes, who was honored with an inscription in the Theater (IG, II–III², 3427); or, possibly, that it was paid for by Antony. Note may also be taken here of the reconstruction of the kitchen in the Tholos at some time during the first century B.C. See Thompson, *The Tholos of Athens and its Predecessors*, p. 136.

[49] This is shown by the statement of Dio Cassius, XLII, xiv, 1, to the effect that Caesar's legate Calenus was able in 48 B.C. to seize the Piraeus because it was without walls, but he could not take the city.

[50] *Ad fam.* XIII, ii; cf. xxi; xxvii, 2. Evander, a freedman of M. Aemilius Avianius, was the director of and chief sculptor in his patron's factory at Athens.

the Greeks were harassed by forced levies and contributions. On March 17th of that year Cicero gave voice to the apprehension lest no place in Greece be left unplundered.[51] The Athenians took the side of Pompey, contributing three ships to his fleet.[52] It remains uncertain whether they contributed soldiers to his army,[53] or whether money was requisitioned from them. We have only the information vouched for by Caesar,[54] that Pompey exacted money from the free cities of Achaea.[55] During the course of the war Attica was invaded and devastated by Caesar's legate Q. Fufius Calenus; the Piraeus was seized, but the city held out until after the defeat of Pompey at Pharsalus in 48 B.C.[56] It was at this time that Megara was thoroughly devastated and that the other important ports on the Saronic Gulf (Aegina, the Piraeus, and Corinth) were reduced to the low estate described by Servius Sulpicius in the letter of condolence to Cicero. In spite of their opposition to him, Caesar readily granted pardon to the Athenians[57] and took great interest in the affairs of the city. In 48 B.C. he undertook the restoration of the city's democratic constitution.[58] Later he presented the city with funds for the construction of the so-called Roman Market to the north of the Acropolis.[59] Work on the structure seems to have been started before, or soon after, the assassination of the dictator,[60] but it was not completed until some years after the acces-

---

[51] *Ad Att.* IX, ix, 2.　　　[52] Lucan, III, 181–83; Caesar, *Bell. civ.* III, iii, 1.

[53] Appian, *Bell. civ.* II, 70 and 75, lists Athenians among Pompey's auxiliaries, but they are not mentioned in this connection by Caesar, *Bell. civ.* III, iv.

[54] *Bell. civ.* III, iii, 2.

[55] "Achaea" here means Greece. Cf. Larsen, "Roman Greece," p. 431, note 18.

[56] Dio Cassius, XLII, xiv.　　　[57] Appian, *Bell. civ.* II, 88.

[58] W. S. Ferguson, in *Klio*, IX (1909), 340; Kolbe, *Die attischen Archonten*, p. 149; J. Kirchner, commentary to IG, II–III², 1043.

[59] Graindor, *Hérode*, pp. 6–7, suggests that Caesar gave the money to the Athenians when he visited Athens in 47 B.C., after his expedition against Pharnaces (Dio Cassius, XLII, xiv). Graindor also suggests (p. 7) that Caesar's purpose in making the gift was to outdo Pompey, who had given the city fifty talents for the restoration of its monuments (Plutarch, *Pomp.* xlii, 5, 6).

[60] The dedicatory inscription on the gateway of the Market (IG, II–III², 3175) states that the Market was built with funds given by Caesar and Augustus, and that it was dedicated during the archonship of Nicias son of Sarapion, of Athmonon, when Eucles of Marathon was hoplite general. Eucles had succeeded his father, Herodes, in charge of the work and had fulfilled the function of ambassador. Consequently, in accordance with this interpretation of the inscription, work on the Market began under Herodes, who had been *archon eponymus* in 60/59 B.C. (Dins-

sion of Augustus to sole power. It is quite impossible to believe that
the Market was built merely for the purpose of adorning the city.[61]
Rather, it is most likely that the funds were donated by Caesar,
first because of a desire to help the Athenians, and second in order
to carry out a single project in his larger scheme of furthering the
commerce of the empire with the aid of the state.[62] The prospects
for trade at Athens had brightened considerably after the conclusion of the pirate wars, and Caesar's gift seems almost certainly to
have been intended to meet the new demands.[63] With the renewal
of the civil wars, however, commerce was again stifled, funds ran
out, and completion of the Market, no longer required by immediate needs or prospects of trade, was deferred. The projected
Market was probably but a part of a larger scheme for the development of the Athenian market place,[64] for at about the same time one
other building was built in this general region, the so-called Tower
of the Winds, located immediately to the east of the new market

moor, *Archons*, pp. 280–82) and was well along in years at the time of Caesar. The
work was suspended when the funds given by Caesar ran out. Later, during the
archonship of Nicias, Herodes' son Eucles, in the capacity of an ambassador,
secured from Augustus the funds for the completion of the Market. This is the very
satisfactory interpretation of Graindor, *Hérode*, pp. 5–8, and *Auguste*, pp. 31–32.
Graindor, *Chronologie*, pp. 48–49, assigned the archonship of Nicias to a date between 10 B.C. and 2 A.D., but Dinsmoor, in *Hesperia*, IX (1940), 50, note 114,
places it in 11/10 B.C. or 10/9 B.C. That work on the Market was begun in the time
of Caesar is confirmed by technical similarities between the architecture of the
Market and that of the Tower of the Winds, which could not, since it is mentioned
by Varro, *De re rustica*, III, v, 17, have been built after 37 B.C. Cf. Graindor, in
Musée belge, XXVIII (1924), 115; *Auguste*, p. 197. The attempt by Bagnani, as reported by A. della Seta, in *Bolletino d'arte*, ser. 2, Vol. I (1922), pp. 531–33, to prove
that only the gateway was built in the time of Augustus and that the remainder of
the structure was a gymnasium of Hadrianic date has been confuted by Graindor,
in *Musée belge*, XXVIII (1924), 109–21, and *Auguste*, pp. 191–98.

[61] As Wachsmuth, *Die Stadt Athen*, I, 670, assumed; cf. Graindor, *Auguste*, pp.
164–65.

[62] For Caesar's economic policy, see Frank, *Economic History of Rome*, pp. 348–
50, and "Rome and Italy of the Republic," pp. 311–12. See also Heichelheim,
Wirtschaftsgeschichte, I, 677–79.

[63] An excellent description of the Market is given by Graindor, *Auguste*, pp. 184–
98, and in *Musée belge*, XXVIII (1924), 109–21. Cf. Judeich, *Topographie*, pp.
371–74.

[64] Cf. W. B. Dinsmoor, in *Hesperia*, IX (1940), 51, who suggests, on slightly
different grounds, that the plans for the Agora had their beginnings in the time of
Caesar.

building.[65] The Tower of the Winds was designed—actually it was a horologium—to serve as a convenience to individuals who frequented the market place.[66] On the outside of the building, on each of its eight sides, there were the markings of a sundial along with the gnomon of that device, while in the interior of the building there was a clepsydra, or water clock. It was, therefore, possible to ascertain the time of day both in clear and in cloudy weather. The structure was erected by Andronicus of Cyrrhus in Macedonia at the expense of the people of Athens.[67] In view of the facts that the horologium was built near, and at the same time with, the market building and that Caesar is known to have been greatly interested in astronomical matters,[68] it is quite possible to attribute the erection of the horologium to the Roman dictator.[69]

But Athens was destined to enjoy only a few years of peace and undisturbed economic activity. After the assassination of Caesar in 44 B.C. the wars broke out anew. Despite the benefactions of Caesar the Athenians were able to hail his death with elation. In the market place, alongside the statues of the Tyrannicides, they erected bronze statues of Brutus and Cassius,[70] thus expressing a blatant partisanship in the impending struggle, a partisanship which under ordinary circumstances might have turned out disastrously. Nevertheless, the Athenians were able to range themselves on the

[65] For the date of the erection of the building, see Graindor, in *Musée belge*, XXVIII (1924), 109–21; *Auguste*, p. 197. Judeich, *Topographie*, pp. 97, 375, favors a dating of this building not long after 86 B.C. The attempt of F. Wirth, in AM, LVI (1931), 47–49, to assign the building to the early years of the century, before 80 B.C., on the ground that paintings of the so-called First Style were employed in it is to be rejected. Cf. J. Day, in *Classical Weekly*, XXVI (1933), 139, note 31.

[66] For a description of the building, see Judeich, *Topographie*, pp. 374–75. Graindor's suggestion (*Auguste*, p. 198) that the weather vane surmounting the building was erected especially for the purpose of keeping the merchant shippers who traded in oil informed of the winds and of the prospects for good sailing weather seems rather fanciful.

[67] IG, II–III², 1035, l.54: οἰκίαν τὴν λεγομένην Κυρρηστοῦ ἦν ὁ δῆμος προσκατασκε[ύασε].

[68] For Caesar's interest in astronomy and his written works dealing with that subject, see Pliny, NH XVIII, xxv, 211; xxvi, 234, 237; Macrobius, *Sat.* I, xvi, 29, 39.

[69] This is the suggestion of Graindor, *Auguste*, p. 197.

[70] Dio Cassius, XLVII, xx, 4; cf. Plutarch, *Brut.* xxiv, 1.

side of Antony after the battle at Philippi[71] and were so fortunate as to persuade him to add the islands of Aegina, Ceos, Icus, Peparethus, and Sciathus to their domain.[72] It may be noted in passing that in 38 B.C. Antony restored the aristocratic constitution at Athens.[73] The story that Antony, when he was likened by the Athenians to Dionysus and was joined in symbolical marriage to Athena, exacted from the city a large sum of money, variously stated to be a thousand talents or a million drachmas, is best explained, following Larsen, as propaganda spread by Antony's enemies.[74]

Soon the Actium campaign, which inflicted upon Greece the greatest hardships of all the wars of the first century,[75] again threw the country into turmoil. To what extent Athens was affected is uncertain.[76] But the fact that Octavian, after his victory, sailed to Athens to distribute what was left of the grain (which had been requisitioned during the war) to the Greek cities that had been despoiled by Anthony seems to indicate that Athens, along with the remainder of Greece, had suffered severely.[77] That grain was distributed in the city at this time is also made evident by the existence of a number of tesserae which were struck for the purpose.[78]

[71] There is no direct or certain evidence that the Athenians suffered from exactions during the Philippi campaign. For the exactions from Greece at large at this time, see Larsen, "Roman Greece," pp. 432–34.

[72] Appian, *Bell civ.* V, 7: 'Αθηναίοις δ' ἐς αὐτὸν ἐλθοῦσι μετὰ Τῆνον Αἴγιναν ἔδωκε καὶ Ἴκον καὶ Κέω καὶ Σκίαθον καὶ Πεπάρηθον. Cf. Graindor, *Auguste*, p. 5. The conclusion should not be drawn from Dio Cassius, LIV, vii, 2, that Eretria belonged to Athens in the first century B.C. and was separated from the city by Augustus.

[73] Dio Cassius, XXXVIII, xxxix, 2; Graindor, *Auguste*, p. 95; Kolbe, *Die attischen Archonten*, p. 142; J. Kirchner, commentary to IG, II–III², 1043.

[74] Seneca, *Suasor.* I, 6; Dio Cassius, XLVIII, xxxix, 2; Zonaras, X, 23; cf. Larsen, "Roman Greece," p. 434. Dio and Zonaras give the amount as a million drachmas, Seneca as a thousand talents, amounts which, in either case, it would have been far beyond the ability of Athens to pay. W. W. Tarn, in CAH, X, 53, who doubts the reliability of the story, aptly reminds us that the tale appears in a *suasoria*.   [75] Larsen, "Roman Greece," p. 434.

[76] Of course, many Greeks served in Antony's army. Cf. Larsen, "Roman Greece," p. 435.

[77] Plutarch, *Ant.* lxviii; cf. Larsen, "Roman Greece," p. 434, note 24.

[78] For these tesserae, see M. Rostovtzeff, "Augustus und Athen," *Festschrift zu O. Hirschfeld* (*Klio*, Band III [1903]), pp. 303–11. Some of them were struck in 31 B.C., after the battle of Actium, others in 19 B.C. Graindor, *Auguste*, p. 37, note 2, and p. 118.

There is some confusion in our sources concerning Augustus' treatment of Athens after the battle of Actium. In one passage[79] Dio Cassius informs us that, after that battle, Augustus punished or rewarded the Greek cities depending, in general, upon the part they had taken in the war; but when he goes on to say that the emperor exacted money from them and took away the powers of the popular assemblies, his statements seem to be far removed from fact, at least as far as Athens is concerned. In the first place, the story of a forced levy upon the city does not agree with the known fact that Augustus distributed grain there at that time.[80] In the second place, contrary to the statement of Dio, the Assembly still played an important part in the Athenian government at the beginning of the Empire.[81] In another passage,[82] where he recounts the activities of Augustus in the year 21 B.C., Dio states that the emperor forbade the Athenians to sell their citizenship and deprived them of sovereignty over Aegina and Eretria. That sale of their citizenship was forbidden seems to be beyond doubt, but the statement with regard to Aegina and Eretria is at best only partly true. Aegina seems to have been a free city during the early empire but nevertheless to have been attached in some way to Athens.[83] On the other hand, there are reasons for doubting that Eretria ever belonged to the domain of Athens.[84] In the early part of the first century B.C. the city was not an Athenian possession, as is shown by the fact that an Eretrian is listed among the foreign ephebes in an inscription which is dated between 83 B.C. and 78 B.C.[85] Shortly after the middle of the century, in 42/1 B.C., a number of foreign communities were placed under Athenian control, but the name of Eretria does not appear in the list which is given us by Appian.[86] Nevertheless, in order to explain Dio's statement that Augustus removed Eretria from Athenian control, it has been assumed, unjustifiably I believe, that Appian omitted the name of Eretria

---

[79] LI, ii, 1.   [80] Plutarch, *Ant.* lxviii, confirmed by the tesserae (see note 78).
[81] Hermann and Thumser, *Lehrbuch*, pp. 788–89; cf. Graindor, *Auguste*, pp. 102–4.
[82] LIV, vii.   [83] Pliny, NH IV, xii, 57; Graindor, *Auguste*, p. 6.
[84] Graindor, *Auguste*, p. 5; cf. Philippson, in RE, VI, 423–25; E. Ziebarth, in IG, XII, ix, pp. 162–65.
[85] IG, II–III², 1039, a¹, 4; cf. Graindor, *Auguste*, p. 5, note 7.
[86] *Bell. civ.* V, 7.

through inadvertence.[87] But it is to be observed that Dio himself implies, through the insertion of a qualifying ὥς τινές φασιν, that he does not place too great reliance upon his sources.

To support the view that Augustus, because of the resentment he felt against them, treated the Athenians very harshly, an undated passage in Plutarch's writings has been cited; in it Augustus is represented as having written to the Athenians that he had spent the winter at Aegina because he was offended with them.[88] If this incident is assigned to 31 B.C., it will be necessary to find some way to reconcile Plutarch's statement with Dio's assertion[89] that Augustus spent the winter of that year in Samos. This difficulty might, of course, be readily resolved by assuming that part of the winter was spent in Aegina and the remainder in Samos.[90] But how are we to account for Plutarch's specific statement that Augustus neither did nor said anything to the Athenians other than to inform them that he felt resentment toward them?[91] Apparently Augustus' resentment was little more than pique. Our examination of Dio's testimony has revealed that the only measure certainly taken against the Athenians was one to forbid them to sell their citizenship—and this need not be taken as evidence of severe hostility on his part. Moreover, when Plutarch informs us that Augustus distributed grain to the Greek cities after the battle of Actium, he specifically states that the Roman leader had become reconciled with them.[92] One additional fact should be noted in connection with Dio's testimony. The passage in which he states that Augustus forbade the Athenians to sell their citizenship and deprived them of their sovereignty over Aegina and Eretria recounts the events of the winter of 21 B.C., when Augustus was sojourning in Samos a second time.[93] If Augustus' acts are to be taken as indicating severe resentment toward the Athenians, how are we to explain the fact

---

[87] Cf. Hertzberg, *Geschichte Griechenlands*, I, 471, 501; Wachsmuth, *Die Stadt Athen*, I, 664, note 1.

[88] Plutarch, *Reg. et imp. apophth.* 207f.

[89] LI, iv, 1.   [90] Cf. Graindor, *Auguste*, p. 17.

[91] *Reg. et imp. apophth.* 207f: τοῦ δὲ Ἀθηναίων δήμου ἐξαμαρτηκέναι τι δόξαντος, ἔγραψεν ἀπ' Αἰγίνης οἴεσθαι μὴ λανθάνειν αὐτοὺς ὀργιζόμενος· οὐ γὰρ ἂν ἐν Αἰγίνῃ διαχειμάσειεν. Ἄλλο δὲ οὐδὲν οὔτε εἶπεν αὐτοὺς οὔτε ἐποίησε.

[92] *Ant.* lxviii: . . . καὶ διαλλαγεὶς τοῖς Ἕλλησι τὸν περιόντα σῖτον ἐκ τοῦ πολέμου διένειμε ταῖς πόλεσι . . .   [93] Dio Cassius, LIV, vii.

that this resentment was manifested not in 31 B.C., but in 21 B.C., long after the participation of the Athenians on the side of Antony and after Augustus had already gone to Athens in 31 B.C. to be initiated into the Eleusinian Mysteries? As early as 30 B.C. Augustus had become reconciled with the Alexandrians—and they had been considerably more guilty than the Athenians![94] Possibly the difficulty is not as great as it seems to be. Dio may have transferred his account of Augustus' actions against the Athenians from the passage where he recounts the events of 31 B.C.[95] to the later passage, where he recounts the events of 21 B.C.,[96] for dramatic reasons —that is, to contrast Augustus' harsh treatment of the Athenians with his kindly treatment of the Spartans, who had supported Augustus in the Actium campaign.[97] We may, therefore, reconstitute the sequence of events in 31 B.C. as follows: After the battle of Actium Augustus sailed to Athens, and, when he had become reconciled to the Greeks, distributed grain to the indigent population of Athens and other Greek cities. While in Athens he was initiated into the Mysteries, but, even after his severe resentment had been appeased, a remaining element of pique led him to withdraw for the duration of the winter to Aegina and later to Samos. Perhaps during this winter he forbade the Athenians to pursue the practice of selling their citizenship. That Augustus' pique persisted for long is very unlikely. In 27/6 B.C., or soon thereafter, the Athenians passed a decree which provided for the celebration of the Emperor's birthday, the twelfth of Boedromion,[98] the day on which the Athenians annually celebrated the anniversary of the return to the city of that Thrasybulus who had restored freedom to the Athenians.[99] Since this very obvious association of the two anniversaries could not have been overlooked by the Athenians, one may conclude that by the year 27/6 B.C., or soon thereafter, the Emperor's pique had subsided. The frequent assimilation of Augustus to Zeus or Apollo Eleutherius—titles which the Greeks would hardly have bestowed upon the Emperor had he not granted

---

[94] Dio Cassius, LI, xvi, 3–4; Plutarch, *Ant.* lxxx; Plutarch, *Apophth. Aug.* 3.
[95] LI, ii–iv.   [96] LIV, vii.
[97] This is the suggestion of Graindor, *Auguste*, p. 18.
[98] IG, II–III², 1071; cf. Graindor, *Auguste*, pp. 25–28.
[99] Plutarch, *De glor. Athen.* 7; cf. Mommsen, *Feste*, p. 178, note 2.

freedom to the Greeks in general and to Athens in particular—
also indicates that, in any event, a complete reconciliation had
taken place early in the reign of Augustus.[100] Moreover, at least
two acts on the part of the Emperor during the twenties of the first
century B.C. show clearly that his attitude toward the Athenians
was distinctly friendly. First, some time between 31 B.C. and 20
B.C., but nearer 31 B.C., Augustus, upon the urging of the ambassador Eucles, granted the Athenians the funds that were required for the completion of the Market that had been begun with
funds given by Julius Caesar.[101] Second, an act of the Emperor
that is more significant still may be cited. When Augustus undertook to organize the imperial mint system, he allowed various
municipalities to strike bronze coinage to serve as local currency,
with the stipulation that each coin bear on its obverse the image
of the emperor.[102] On the other hand, a number of cities—not so
limited as heretofore thought[103]—were granted the privilege of
issuing an autonomous coinage on which the portrait of the emperor was not required.[104] The fact that Athens was one of the
cities of the latter group seems now to be assured, for it is established that the first issues of the Athenian autonomous coins
appeared in 27/6 B.C., or soon thereafter.[105] Had the Athenians

[100] OGIS, 457; cf. P. Riewald, *De imperatorum Romanorum cum certis dis et
comparatione et aequatione* (Halle a. d. S., 1912; Dissertationes philologicae Halenses,
XX, No. 3), pp. 287–94.

[101] Graindor, *Auguste*, p. 32.

[102] H. Mattingly, *British Museum Catalogue: Coins of the Roman Empire* (London, 1923), I, xxvii.

[103] Mattingly, *Roman Coins*, pp. 183, 196–99; cf. Larsen, "Roman Greece," p.
441 and note 10.

[104] Head, *Hist. Num.*, p. 389; cf. Svoronos, *Les Monnaies d'Athènes*, Pls.
LXXXII–XCIX; J. P. Shear, in *Hesperia*, V (1936), Pls. II–VIII, and Figs. 1–2,
8–22, 24–31.

[105] J. P. Shear, in *Hesperia*, V (1936), 285–93. Mrs. Shear demonstrates conclusively the falsity of the view, heretofore dominant, that Athens was without a
local coinage between the time of Augustus and that of Hadrian. Indeed, there is
now no justification for assuming that Augustus ever deprived the Athenians of
the privilege of minting, notwithstanding Graindor, *Auguste*, p. 38; Sundwall,
Untersuchungen, II, 23; J. P. Shear, in *Hesperia*, II (1933), 270. Sundwall, in ZFN,
XXVI (1908), 274, dates the latest series of Athenian silver coins in the early years
of the reign of Augustus, and calls attention to the fact that it consists entirely of
drachmas; he contends that the striking of larger silver coins must have come to
an end by that time. Until recent years the latest New Style coins have been dated

been in disfavor with the Emperor, they would not have been granted this privilege.

After the battle of Actium the Athenians, along with the rest of the Greeks, were able to recuperate from the exhaustion induced by the long-drawn-out wars.[106] No changes were made in the political administration of the country as a whole,[107] and Athens continued to enjoy the status of a "free and allied city,"[108] the most advantageous arrangement a subject city could hope for.

---

as follows. The Architimus-Pammenes series of New Style silver coins has been assigned to c.30 B.C. by Head, *Hist. Num.*, p. 386; Sundwall, in ZFN, XXVI (1908), 274; Sundwall, *Untersuchungen*, II, 23, 45. On the other hand, for similar bronze coins A. R. Bellinger, in *Numismatic Notes and Monographs*, No. 42 (1930), 7–8, suggests a date before 87 B.C., while J. P. Shear, in *Hesperia*, II (1933), Pl. VII, Class II λ, favors a date of c.88 B.C., but with reservations. (The bronze coins are dated by comparison with the silver issues.) The Demochares-Pammenes series has been assigned to a date after 30 B.C. and during the reign of Augustus by Head, *Hist. Num.*, p. 386; J. Sundwall, in ZFN, XXVI (1908), 274; Sundwall, *Untersuchungen*, II, 23; cf. 61. J. P. Shear, in *Hesperia*, II (1933), Pl. VII, Class III, assigns the similar bronze coins to the same date. The Dionysius-Demostratus series (only drachmas of this series are extant) is assigned to the time of Augustus by Head, *Hist. Num.*, p. 386; Sundwall, in ZFN, XXVI (1908), 274; cf. Sundwall, *Untersuchungen*, II, 65. J. P. Shear, in *Hesperia*, II (1933), Pl. VII, Class III o, assigns the similar bronze coins to the same date. On the basis of these dates the issuance of New Style silver and bronze coins would be shown to have been continued into the first years of Augustus' reign. Consequently, Graindor, *Auguste*, p. 38, maintains that the emperor may have restricted the coinage rights of the Athenians late in his reign, at the time of a serious revolt at Athens. However, there is no evidence whatsoever to justify the assumption that the issuance of imperial bronze issues, which first appeared in 27/6 B.C. or soon thereafter, was ever interrupted. However, note should be taken of the fact that M. L. Kambanis, in BCH, LXII (1938), 60–84, has assigned the latest New Style silver coins (the Dionysius-Demostratus series) to about the middle of the first century B.C. and contended (p. 84) that New Style coinage was not struck after that time. But M. Thompson, "Some Athenian 'Cleruchy' Money," *Hesperia*, X (1941), 199–236, especially 224–28, has shown that various bronze coins which Svoronos, *Les Monnaies d'Athènes*, Pl. XXV, attributed to various Athenian cleruchies were really struck by the mint at Athens and especially that certain fractional bronze coins attributed to Peparethus are to be dated c.40 B.C. Miss Thompson expresses the opinion (p. 230, note 96) that the imperial bronze coinage followed the New Style with no intervening period of inactivity at the mint.

[106] For the exhaustion induced by the Actium campaign, see Larsen, "Roman Greece," pp. 434–35.

[107] Larsen, "Roman Greece," p. 437.

[108] Pliny, NH IV, vii, 24; Tacitus, *Ann.* II, liii; Strabo, IX, 398; cf. Graindor, *Auguste*, pp. 130–32.

The bestowal of this "freedom"—which consisted of a generous autonomy in administering the. internal affairs of the city—was made through a treaty and, theoretically, could not be withdrawn.[109] In practice, however, the privileges granted by treaty were often recalled or modified, but only in case Rome should feel displeasure with the city and seek a pretext for rescinding the previous action. While, as stated above, administration of internal affairs was left, by and large, to the individual "free" cities, the Romans, nevertheless, never hesitated to intervene to maintain law and order, giving their support to the wealthier element of the population, which, as in the past, maintained steadfast loyalty toward Rome.[110] Consequently, social and political revolutions, which were so characteristic of earlier periods of Greek history, were no longer to play a part in the history of Athens. For that reason we shall henceforth seldom find it necessary to consider political movements in their relation to economic factors. A final point should be noted in connection with the status of the "free" city, namely, the extent to which it was subject to taxation at the hands of Rome. Our information concerning this matter is not at all satisfactory, and only the following summary statement may be made. While it seems that "free" cities were, in the main, not liable to taxation,[111] there were innumerable occasions on which contributions of various kinds were exacted from them. But it may be that Athens and a few other favored cities received especial consideration, whereby they were, on the whole, relieved of this burden.[112]

The return of peaceful conditions under Augustus was accompanied by a revival of building activity. First to be mentioned is the only monument of any importance—and that not an expensive one—erected by the Athenians in the time of Augustus, the small round temple of Roma and Augustus which was built on the Acrop-

[109] For the rights of these cities, see Abbott and Johnson, *Municipal Administration*, pp. 39–46; H. Last, in CAH, XI, 450–56; A. H. M. Jones, "Civitates Liberae et Immunes in the East," *Anatolian Studies* (Buckler), pp. 103–17, especially p. 109; A. N. Sherwin-White, *The Roman Citizenship* (Oxford, 1939), pp. 149–63; H. Horn, *Foederati* (Frankfurt am Main, 1930), pp. 47–51, 65–70; Larsen, "Roman Greece," pp. 445–49.

[110] Rostovtzeff, *Roman Empire*, p. 54.

[111] Abbott and Johnson, *Municipal Administration*, p. 40; Larsen, "Roman Greece," p. 457.   [112] *Ibid.*, p. 459.

olis some time between 27/6 B.C. and 18/7 B.C.[113] A monumental group of a quadriga surmounted by a statue of M. Vipsanius Agrippa, the friend and close adviser of Augustus, was also erected by the Athenians at about the same time.[114] The group, which occupied a prominent position on a high pedestal placed immediately to the west of the Pinacotheca, at the entrance to the Acropolis, occasioned the Athenians no great expense, for the pedestal was re-used, having been erected originally in the early part of the second century B.C., probably to bear statues of Eumenes II of Pergamum and his brother, later Attalus II.[115] The Athenians dedicated the group to Agrippa in return for his benefactions to the city,[116] but precisely what these benefactions were we cannot be sure. However, a clue is to be found in the works of a writer of the second century A.D., who refers to a building in the Ceramicus called the Agrippeum, in which the sophists were wont to deliver lectures and recitations.[117] The building was, apparently, a covered theater of standard Roman type, in which declamations and recitations of unpublished books were delivered, after the fashion at Rome in the time of Augustus.[118] The Agrippeum has, at times, been associated with the so-called Odeum in the Ceramicus,[119] but objections have been raised to the identification.[120] However, the Odeum has now been brought to light, and although the excavators at first assigned the structure to c.50 B.C.,[121] drawing their deductions from technical architectural similarities between certain features of the Odeum and the neighboring Tower of the

[113] IG, II–III², 3173; Graindor, *Auguste*, pp. 180–84; Judeich, *Topographie*, pp. 256–57; G. A. S. Snijder, in *Mededeelingen van het Nederlandsch Instituut te Rome*, III (1923), 73–112 (résumé in RA, XIX [1924], 223–26). For the date, see Graindor, *Auguste*, pp. 30–31; Graindor, *Chronologie*, p. 34.

[114] IG, II–III², 4122; Graindor, *Auguste*, pp. 48–49; Judeich, *Topographie*, pp. 216–17. For the date, between 23 B.C. and 13 B.C., see Graindor, *Auguste*, p. 49.

[115] W. B. Dinsmoor, in AJA, XXIV (1920), 83.

[116] IG, II–III², 4122.

[117] Philostratus, *Vit. soph.* 571, 579.

[118] Dessau, *Geschichte der römischen Kaiserzeit*, I, 561–74; V. Gardthausen, *Augustus und seine Zeit* (Leipzig, 1891–1904), I, 1244; II, 841, note 22.

[119] W. Dörpfeld, in AM, XVII (1892), 258–59; Judeich, *Topographie*, pp. 98, 350. The Odeum is mentioned by Pausanias, I, viii, 6, the Agrippeum by Philostratus, *Vit. soph.* 571, 579.

[120] C. Wachsmuth, "Agrippeion," RE, I, 898; Graindor, *Auguste*, p. 180.

[121] T. L. Shear, in *Hesperia*, V (1936), 6–14, especially 10; cf. IX (1940), 304–5.

Winds, the technical data do not at all preclude a date, for the Odeum, as late as the time of Agrippa. Indeed, it seems preferable to adhere to the view recently set forth by Professor W. B. Dinsmoor,[122] that the Odeum is to be identified with the Agrippeum and that it was probably dedicated during the period of Agrippa's regency in the East,[123] more precisely in 16 B.C., at the time of his visit to Athens.[124] The suggestion may, therefore, be ventured that the Agrippa monument in front of the Propylaea was set up to express the gratitude of the Athenians for Agrippa's erection of the Odeum. The Odeum probably formed part of a larger plan for the development of the Athenian market place, representing a resumption and further elaboration of plans which may have been originated by Julius Caesar.[125] As we have already observed, the Market of Caesar and Augustus was begun before March 15, 44 B.C. under the superintendence of Herodes of Marathon, but, apparently because of insufficient funds, the work was suspended soon thereafter, to be resumed at a later date under the supervision of Herodes' son Eucles, who, at some time before 20 B.C., secured from Augustus the funds required for the completion of the structure. The Market was finally completed and dedicated during the archonship of Nicias son of Sarapion, of Athmonon, in 11/10 B.C. or 10/9 B.C.[126] Also to be associated with this larger plan for the development of the market place is the removal, in the time of Augustus, of the Temple of Ares from its original location to a new site to the south of the Altar of the Twelve Gods.[127] Other building activity to be

[122] In *Hesperia*, IX (1940), 51. Renewed study of the excavations has brought confirmation of this date. T. L. Shear, in *Hesperia*, IX (1940), 304–5.

[123] Between 17/6 B.C. and 13 B.C. Agrippa held the *maius imperium* in the East. See M. Reinhold, *Marcus Agrippa* (Geneva, N. Y., 1933), pp. 106, 170.

[124] For the date of this visit, see *ibid.*, pp. 106–10.

[125] W. B. Dinsmoor, in *Hesperia*, IX (1940), 51; cf. note 64, above.

[126] IG, II–III², 3175. For the date of the archonship of Nicias, see W. B. Dinsmoor, in *Hesperia*, IX (1940), 50, note 114. Graindor (*Auguste*, p. 32, and note 3; *Chronologie*, pp. 48–49) placed the archonship of Nicias between 10/9 B.C. and 2 A.D., but favored a date of c.10 B.C. Judeich, *Topographie*, p. 371, assigns the dedication of the Market to some time between 12 B.C. and 2 A.D., the dates respectively of the adoption by Augustus and the death of L. Caesar, whose statue surmounts the gateway to the Market. Cf. IG, II–III², 3251. For a description of the Market, see Graindor, *Auguste*, pp. 184–98; Judeich, *Topographie*, pp. 371–74.

[127] W. B. Dinsmoor, "The Temple of Ares at Athens," *Hesperia*, IX (1940), 1–52. The temple was originally constructed in the age of Pericles. Each stone was

noted in the time of Augustus is the erection of an annex to the Stoa of Zeus Eleutherius.[128] And the thorough renovation of the temple garden of the Temple of Hephaestus should not be overlooked.[129]

The lot of the Piraeus, the port town of Athens, between 86 B.C. and the end of the reign of Augustus must be considered apart from the destiny of Athens. So completely has the idea of the thorough and lasting devastation of the town at the hands of Sulla gained footing that any testimony which indicates even moderate prosperity in the harbor town is often considered as applicable only at some time prior to 86 B.C.[130] or at a much later date, in the time of Hadrian, when the harbor town is definitely known to have been prosperous.[131] We are, however, struck at once with various facts which are not consonant with this view. In 41 A.D., we learn from an inscription, a certain Diocles, during the second year of his incumbency as *epimeletes* of the Piraeus, dedicated a statue to the Emperor Claudius.[132] Is this fact to be taken as indicating that the Piraeus was at that time an important settlement, or that the office of *epimeletes* of the port town was, like that of the *epimeletes* of Delos under the empire,[133] merely an honorary post in a community largely devoid of importance except from a historical or sentimental point of view? Perhaps judgment concerning this point should, for the moment, be suspended. Next, attention may be called to the fact that statues of Augustus and Claudius have

---

carefully lettered and numbered to facilitate its ready reconstruction in its new location.

[128] H. A. Thompson, in *Hesperia*, VI (1937), 64.

[129] D. B. Thompson, in *Hesperia*, VI (1937), 409–11. Excavations have revealed a second period of construction of the well house of the Clepsydra, on the northwestern slope of the Acropolis, in "the early Roman period" (T. L. Shear, in *Hesperia*, VII [1938], 335) and a tunnel belonging to the water system of "the early Roman period" (T. L. Shear, in *Hesperia*, VIII [1939], 218; IX [1940], 295–96). A very fragmentary imperial epistle of the early years of the empire (IG, II–III², 1097) may possibly mention the gift of a building by the emperor. But none of these projects may be definitely assigned to the time of Augustus.

[130] As, for example, by J. Kirchner, in IG, II–III², 1035, cf. II–III², Fasc. IV, p. 22.

[131] For the Piraeus in the second century A.D., see Gurlitt, *Über Pausanias*, pp. 198–248; Wachsmuth, *Die Stadt Athen*, II, 10–12; Frazer, *Pausanias*, II, 14–15; also my account in chap. v, including notes 226–29.

[132] IG, II–III², 3268; cf. Graindor, *Tibère*, p. 82; *Chronologie*, pp. 76–77.

[133] Roussel, DCA, p. 118.

been found in the Piraeus.[134] But the revival of the Piraeus will be seen to be much more conclusive when we observe that water channels belonging to baths of the time of Augustus have been found there,[135] and that baths which may be of the same date have been found near the harbor of Zea.[136] Definitely dated epigraphical and archaeological sources, therefore, attest to a settlement of some importance at the Piraeus in the time of Augustus and of Claudius but do not provide any information concerning the degree of recovery of the harbor town. However, certain isolated statements in the writings of ancient authors and information to be derived from an inscription which, as we shall see, belongs to the time of Augustus make it considerably clearer to us what the condition of the Piraeus was during the period with which we are now concerned. We have already observed that the statement of Servius Sulpicius to the effect that the Piraeus and other ports on the Saronic Gulf were in a state of absolute decay in 45 B.C. is to be taken, not at its face value, but rather to indicate merely that, as a result of the war between Caesar and Pompey, the Piraeus had suffered greatly.[137] We should also observe, in passing, that a passage in another letter written to Cicero by Servius Sulpicius[138] has been unnecessarily misinterpreted. In this letter, written May 31, 45 B.C., Sulpicius states that he went to the Piraeus to take doctors to his friend M. Marcellus, who had been injured in a brawl, and that upon his arrival there he found Marcellus dead and his body stretched out on a bier in the tent in which he had been living. It has been suggested[139] that this passage indicates the Piraeus in such a decayed state that Marcellus was compelled to live in a tent if he wished to stay there. This interpretation is entirely unnecessary. The Piraeus was at no time noted for anything like elegant accommodations in its inns, and it is most probable that in these less glorious days of the port town a traveler of high

[134] Curtius and Kaupert, *Karten von Attika*, "Erläutender Text," I, 33, 50–51; C. Curtius, in *Philologus*, XXIX (1870), 696–97.

[135] Πρακτικά, 1911, pp. 244–46.

[136] *Ibid.*, 1892, pp. 17–29. These both belong, in any event, to a date later than 86 B.C., for they were built over the ruins of the ship sheds destroyed by Sulla.

[137] Cicero, *Ad fam.* IV, v, 4.   [138] *Ibid.* IV, xii, 3.

[139] W. W. How, *Cicero, Select Letters* (Oxford, 1926), II, 435, states that the Piraeus lay in ruins.

station, such as Marcellus, would have lived in a tent out of mere preference—or discretion.[140]

In any event, however we interpret the statement of Sulpicius, we may observe that there is evidence that during the civil war of Caesar and Pompey, only a short time before Sulpicius was writing to Cicero, the Piraeus was more than a town lying in ruins. From Lucan's *Pharsalia*[141] we learn that the Athenians sent their entire navy to join the forces of Pompey, but that the navy was very small, only three vessels being kept in the *Phoebea navalia*. Before drawing deductions from this statement we must take notice of the question of Lucan's reliability in historical matters. There seems now to be good reason to believe that Lucan's chief source— perhaps his only one—was a lost *Civil War* written by Livy;[142] and that his statements on historical matters require the support of independent testimony.[143] Partial substantiation of Lucan's statement may be found in the writings of two ancient authors—Julius Caesar and Plutarch. Caesar informs us that the Athenians contributed ships to Pompey's forces, but he does not state how many.[144] The question then arises whether Lucan exaggerates or underestimates the number of Athenian ships. It would certainly be rash to assume that the Athenian navy consisted of more ships at the middle of the first century B.C. than in the middle of the preceding century, which was a much more prosperous period for Athens; during the earlier century there were only three ships in the Athenian navy.[145] At the same time, seeing that the Athenians

[140] See the commentary of R. Y. Tyrrel and L. Purser, *The Correspondence of M. Tullius Cicero* (London, 1897) on Cicero, *Ad fam.* IV, xii, 3.

[141] III, 181–83.

[142] R. Pichon, *Les Sources de Lucan* (Paris, 1912); J. P. Postgate, *M. Annaei Lucani De bello civili liber VIII* (Cambridge, 1917), pp. xi–xii; cf. G. M. Hirst, in *The Classical Weekly*, XIII (1919), 69.

[143] J. P. Postgate, *M. Annaei Lucani De bello civili liber VII* (Cambridge, 1913), p. ix; cf. W. E. Heitland's introduction to C. E. Haskin, *M. Annaei Lucani Pharsalia* (London, 1887), p. 34; J. W. Duff, *A Literary History of Rome in the Silver Age* (London, 1927), pp. 319–21; M. Hadas, *Sextus Pompey* (New York, 1930), p. 23.

[144] *Bell. civ.* III, iii, 1.

[145] At the beginning of the century Athens had three undecked warships (Livy, XXXI, xxii, 8). At the end of the century it had, apparently, three undecked ships and possibly as many sacred ships. See W. S. Ferguson, in *Klio*, IX (1909), 315–16; Ferguson, *Athens*, p. 377.

actually contributed some warships to Pompey's forces, the poet could hardly have overstated the number of them when he placed it at three. But what of the *navalia*? The exact significance of the word is not certain; like the Greek νεώρια it may describe either wharves or ship sheds or, in a general way, the equipment of a harbor.[146] There were ship sheds in the harbor town in the second century A.D.,[147] but whether any had been rebuilt as early as the middle of the first century B.C. we cannot be certain. In any event, there must have been wharves for docking warships at that time. And we shall see that there were νεώρια (*navalia*) there at about the turn of the era.

When did the Piraeus begin to recover from its devastation at the hands of Sulla? That rebuilding there began in the late sixties of the first century B.C. emerges from a consideration (in conjunction with a line of a very important inscription which remains yet to be discussed) of a passage in Plutarch's life of Pompey. Upon his return from Asia in 62 B.C. Pompey, Plutarch informs us,[148] gave the Athenians fifty talents for the restoration of the city's monuments. That part of this sum was utilized in the rebuilding of the Piraeus is shown by a reference in the above-mentioned inscription to the "Deigma erected by Magnus."[149] It is true that the identification of this Magnus has given rise to some discussion. The name Magnus appears in Athenian inscriptions of both the second century B.C. and the second century A.D., and, accordingly, advocates of a dating of the inscription in either of these centuries have contended that the name was not that of Pompey, but, instead, of an Athenian who, though enjoying a measure of prominence in Attica in his own time, remains obscure to us.[150] On the other hand, the employment of a single name in the inscription

---

[146] Lehmann-Hartleben, *Antike Hafenanlagen*, p. 183, note 4; cf. 105–21; Judeich, *Topographie*, p. 449, note 4. J. Carcopino, in *Mélanges d'archéologie et d'histoire de l'École française de Rome*, 1911, p. 216, argues, on the basis of Servius, *Ad Aen.* XI, 326, that *navale* never means wharf, but always ship shed.

[147] Pausanias, I, i, 2.   [148] *Pomp.* xlii, 5–6.

[149] IG, II–III², 1035, 1. 47; Magnus was, of course, Pompey's third name after 81 B.C.

[150] Gurlitt, *Über Pausanias*, p. 239. For the name of Magnus in the second century B.C., see IG, II–III², 3780. For the name at Athens during the empire, see the indices to IG, III.

indicates that the individual designated was exceptionally - well
known to all Athenians, and, inasmuch as none of the Magni who
are mentioned in Athenian inscriptions was, to our knowledge, exceptionally well known, we must conclude that the Magnus of the
inscription was probably a Roman cognomen, almost certainly
that of Cn. Pompeius Magnus,[151] provided, of course, that the date
of the inscription under discussion permits of that identification.

The date of the inscription in which the name of Magnus is mentioned[152] must be closely considered. The inscription contains parts
of two decrees of the Demos, but, since only a very small part of
the first decree has been preserved, our attention may be limited to
the second decree, which exists in such a fragmentary state that
only the general nature of its contents may be ascertained. In this
decree (lines 3–29) alienation of public lands and of lands belonging to the shrines of gods and of heroes was forbidden, and penalties
for the contravention of the terms of the decree were provided.
Moreover, provision was made that these lands be restored to the
state and to the appropriate shrines, and that any sacred lands
which had been polluted by profane use be appropriately purified.
The carrying out of these provisions was enjoined upon the hoplite
general, Metrodorus son of Xenon, of Phyle, along with the *archon
basileus* and an *exegetes*, who was an interpreter of sacred rites.
The part of the inscription following the decree (lines 30–59) contains Metrodorus' report concerning the lands recovered in pursuance of the directions set forth in the decree. These lands were
located, for the most part, in the Piraeus and in Salamis. The report
was issued during the archonship of a certain --komedes, whose
year has not yet been satisfactorily ascertained. If the archon's
name is to be restored as Λυ]κομήδης, then the report must have
been made somewhere between the years 139/40 A.D. and 170/1
A.D.[153] But this restoration is by no means certain; the name may

---

[151] This view is held by Graindor, *Chronologie*, p. 143; Judeich, *Topographie*, pp.
97, 448; Frazer, *Pausanias*, II, 15; W. Drumann and P. Groebe, *Geschichte Roms in
seinem Übergange von der republikanischen zur monarchischen Verfassung* (2d ed ;
Leipzig, 1899–1929), IV, 487; Wachsmuth, *Die Stadt Athen*, II, 109, thought that
the Deigma survived the catastrophe of 86 B.C. but was repaired through the
munificence of Pompey.

[152] IG, II–III², 1035.

[153] Lycomedes was archon at some time during the incumbency of a certain

as well be Νι]κομήδης. We are thus deprived of the aid of the archon's name in determining the date of the inscription. When we turn in another direction, we observe in the inscription a reference to the "so-called house of Cyrrhestes" (line 54: οἰκίαν τὴν λεγομένην Κυρρηστοῦ), which is the well-known horologium of Andronicus Cyrrhestes, or, to give it its more popular name, the Tower of the Winds. This structure was, as we have seen, built soon after the middle of the first century B.C.[154] From this reference, therefore, we derive the *terminus ante quem* for the inscription. Another possible indication of date has been seen in the employment in the inscription of the "old" style of numerical notation in listing the ayes and nays during the voting on the decree (line 3: μὴ τετρυπημέναι ᵛᵛᵛΧΧΧΗΗΗΗℙΔΙᵛ αἱ δὲ τετρυπημέναι, αἷς οὐκ ἐδόκειᵛᵛᵛΗℙΓᵛᵛ. The latest employment yet observed of this system of notation has been found in an inscription of 38/9 A.D. or a little later.[155] However, this point should not be pressed too closely, for in later times, particularly in the second century A.D., when archaizing was common—even in inscriptions—one might reasonably expect to find the "old" system used occasionally.[156] As regards the orthography of the inscription, there are no significant characteristics which permit of reasonably exact dating.[157] Our last resort must be to the style of lettering employed in the inscription, but this matter too

---

Abascantus as *paidotribes* for life (IG, II–III², 3737). Abascantus' tenure of this office fell between 139/40 A.D. and 172/3 A.D. (Graindor, *Chronologie*, pp. 145–46). But, inasmuch as the archons of 171/2 A.D. and 172/3 A.D. are definitely known, the year of Lycomedes must lie between 139/40 A.D. and 170/1 A.D. (*ibid.*, p. 142).

[154] See note 65, above.

[155] IG, II–III², 2292, frag. f, 52. Kirchner would date the inscription after 45/6 A.D. The date of 38/9 A.D. is maintained by Graindor, *Chronologie*, p. 143. B. Keil, in *Hermes*, XXV (1890), 319, and in *Berliner philologische Wochenschrift*, X (1890), 1258, contended that the latest known employment of the "old" system of numerical notation occurred in 95/4 B.C.

[156] Graindor, *Chronologie*, p. 143. A list of archaizing inscriptions is given by Wilhelm, *Beiträge*, p. 23.

[157] Observe the employment of ι in place of ει in the following instances: κιμ[ένοις] (line 10); Πιραιεῖ (line 15); δίγματος (line 47)); τίχη (line 48). This practice came into vogue c.100 B.C. and continued throughout the empire. L. Meisterhans, *Grammatik der attischen Inschriften* (3d ed., E. Schwyzer; Berlin, 1900), p. 48; cf. W. Gurlitt, in *Berliner philologische Wochenschrift*, X (1890), 843. For the use of iota adscript, see Graindor, *Chronologie*, p. 144, note 2.

has been the subject of much disagreement.[158] Recently Graindor assigned it "possibly" to the period of Claudius,[159] but later changed his mind and assigned it to the second century A.D.[160] On the other hand, Kirchner can assign the lettering to a date between 105/4 B.C. and 103/2 B.C.[161] But this date is, as we have seen, impossible.[162] However, a recent very careful inspection of the inscription at Athens has revealed that the lettering is probably to be assigned to about the period of Augustus.[163] The dating of the inscription at the time of Augustus is also favored by various historical considerations. Disturbed conditions had been prevalent in Attica since before 86 B.C., and as late as 48 B.C. the Piraeus had been occupied by the Roman army under the command of Q. Fufius Calenus, Caesar's legate.[164] It was not until the time of Augustus that stable conditions were finally restored. At that time one might reasonably

[158] Under the influence of Graindor's confident statement that the lettering is undoubtedly that of the second century A.D. (*Auguste*, p. 198, note 1; cf. *Chronologie*, p. 144) I have heretofore maintained that the inscription should be dated between 128/9 A.D. and 137/8 A.D. Cf. *The Classical Weekly*, XXVI (1933), 138–40. Other dates assigned to the inscription are as follows. C. Tsountas, in AE, 1884, p. 168: between 62 B.C. and 117 A.D.; Gurlitt, *Über Pausanias*, pp. 209, 238–39: between 138/9 A.D. and 170/1 A.D.; J. Toepffer, *Quaestiones Pisistrateae* (Dorpat. 1886), p. 21, note 2: after 31 B.C.; H. G. Lolling, "Topographie von Athen," in Iwan von Müller, *Handbuch der klassischen Altertums-Wissenschaft*, III (Nördlingen, 1889), 321, note 4: after 14/5 A.D.; C. Wachsmuth, in *Berichte über die Verhandlungen der königlichen sächsischen Gesellschaft der Wissenschaften zu Leipzig*, philologisch-historische Classe, XXXIX (1887), 374, and Wachsmuth, *Die Stadt Athen*, II, 12, note 1, 58, note 4: about the middle of the first century A.D.; B. Keil, in *Hermes*, XXV (1890), 319, and in *Berliner philologische Wochenschrift*, X (1890), 1258: before 95 B.C.

[159] In BCH, XXXVIII (1914), 280, note 1.

[160] *Auguste*, p. 198, note 1; cf. *Chronologie*, p. 144.

[161] J. Kirchner, commentary on IG, II–III², 1035, and Fasc. IV, p. 22.

[162] Dinsmoor, *Archons*, p. 294, rejects a date before the accession of Augustus for the archonship of [- -]komedes.

[163] My colleague at Barnard College, Professor James H. Oliver, very kindly examined the stone in Athens in the summer of 1938 and communicated his expert opinion to me in a letter from which I quote the following sentences: "When I saw the letters, my immediate reaction was that it could not be Hadrianic. Since then I have compared the lettering with other inscriptions. I would not absolutely eliminate the *bare* possibility that it belonged in the first quarter of the second century after Christ, just as I would be willing to consider arguments for a date in the last quarter of the second century B.C., *but it looks to me just about Augustan*." [Italics are mine.]

[164] Dio Cassius, XLII, xiv, 1.

expect the extensive restoration of shrines and public lands on the scale indicated by Metrodorus' report. Moreover, it was not until the time of Augustus that Salamis, which had apparently been sold by the Athenians soon after 86 B.C.,[165] was restored to the control of Athens through the munificence of Julius Nicanor.[166] What could be more reasonable than to suppose that many lands on Salamis had been alienated from public or from sacred control during the period when Salamis was not under the jurisdiction of Athens, and that upon regaining the island the Athenians found it necessary to rectify conditions there?

With the added confirmation of the dating of the inscription at which we have now arrived, we may safely conclude that the Deigma in the Piraeus was either restored or built anew with the aid of funds given to Athens by Pompey in 62 B.C. Consequently, at least by that time, if not before, the rebuilding of the port town was begun. The settlement continued to grow in importance until, in the time of Augustus, the baths to which reference has already been made[167] were erected there. But a better conception of the Piraeus at this time is provided by the inscription which we have just considered. The harbor equipment was now adequate for the maintenance and repair of ships. Both in the harbor of Zea and in the large harbor there were $\psi \hat{v} \kappa \tau \rho \alpha \iota$, which were apparently contrivances like dry docks, used for the cleaning and calking of ships.[168] In Zea and in the large harbor were $\nu \epsilon \acute{\omega} \rho \iota \alpha$, which are to be construed as various types of marine equipment, including ship sheds, wharves, and workshops.[169] Aside from harbor equipment, attention was given in other ways to the needs of commerce. In this category may be cited the Deigma erected by Pompey.[170] This

[165] See Strabo, IX, 394; cf. Graindor, *Auguste*, pp. 8–9.

[166] Dio Chrysotomus, XXXI, 116; cf. Strabo, IX, 394; Graindor, *Auguste*, pp. 8–10.

[167] See notes 135 and 136, above.

[168] IG, II–III², 1035, ll. 43–45. For the meaning of $\psi \hat{v} \kappa \tau \rho \alpha \iota$, see Lehmann-Hartleben, *Antike Hafenanlagen*, p. 119, note 5. Some see in the word merely the sense of $\psi \upsilon \kappa \tau \acute{\eta} \rho \iota o \nu$. Cf. Liddell and Scott, *Greek-English Lexicon* (ed. H. S. Jones; Oxford, 1925–40).

[169] IG, II–III², 1035, ll. 43, 46. For the meaning of $\nu \epsilon \acute{\omega} \rho \iota \alpha$, see Judeich, *Topographie*, p. 449; cf. Lehmann-Hartleben, *Antike Hafenanlagen*, pp. 105–21.

[170] IG, II–III², 1035, l. 47.

building was employed for the display and exchange of wares which were brought to the Emporium.[171] Indeed, the equipment of the port seems to have been much the same as in former times, for the inscription describes the large harbor as surrounded by *neoria*, the Aphrodisium, and stoae, a description which parallels almost exactly that given by the topographer Menecles (or Callicrates) in the second century B.C.[172] Other buildings in the Piraeus mentioned by the inscription are τὸ ἀρχαῖον βουλευτήριον, σ]τρατήγιον τὸ ἀρχαῖον, and τὸ ἀρχαῖον θέατρον.[173] Not only does the word ἀρχαῖον in τὸ ἀρχαῖον θέατρον imply the existence of a newer theater, but actually a new theater, distinct from the old theater on the western slope of Munychia,[174] had been built near the harbor of Zea at about the middle of the second century B.C.[175] Whether the word ἀρχαῖον used in connection with βουλευτήριον and στρατήγιον may also be construed as indicating that a new Bouleuterion and a new Strategion had been erected is at best very questionable. Also mentioned in the inscription is τὸ προσὸν ὕπαιθρον, ὅπου τύποι καὶ - - -.[176] There is, as yet, no agreement concerning the nature of the τύποι mentioned here, nor concerning the word or words to be restored after καί.[177] In 1890 Gurlitt proposed the restoration of σηκώματα or σύμβολα, thereby seeing in the passage a reference to weights and measures kept in the hypaethron.[178] In support of this interpretation he cited the provision, in the inscription of the end of the second century B.C. which records the readjustment of the system of weights and measures employed at Athens, that copies of the standard weights and measures be kept, among other places, in the Piraeus.[179] Gurlitt also suggested an alternate restoration of γράφαι, the acceptance of which would entail a hypaethron in which statuary and paintings were on dis-

---

[171] Judeich, *Topographie*, p. 448.

[172] IG, II–III², 1035, ll. 45–46; Schol. to Aristophanes, *Pax*, 145; cf. C. Wachsmuth, in *Berichte über die Verhandlungen der königlichen sächsischen Gesellschaft der Wissenschaften zu Leipzig*, philologisch-historische Classe, XXXIX (1887), 373–74; Judeich, *Topographie*, p. 446.

[173] IG, II–III², 1035, ll. 43–44.   [174] Judeich, *Topographie*, p. 451.

[175] Dörpfeld and Reisch, *Das griechische Theater*, pp. 97–100; Bulle, *Untersuchungen*, pp. 203–4; Bieber, *History of the Greek and Roman Theater*, p. 232.

[176] IG, II–III², 1035, l. 47.

[177] No restoration is attempted by Kirchner in IG, II–III², 1035.

[178] Gurlitt, *Über Pausanias*, p. 242, note 17.   [179] IG, II–III², 1013, l. 40.

play.[180] Although the restoration of γράφαι is not to be insisted upon, there is good reason to believe that Gurlitt's second interpretation is substantially correct, for Strabo, in his passing reference to the precinct of Zeus Soter in the Piraeus, writes τοῦ δὲ ἱεροῦ τὰ μὲν στοίδια ἔχει πίνακας θαυμαστούς, ἔργα τῶν ἐπιφανῶν τεχνιτῶν, τὸ δ' ὕπαιθρον ἀνδριάντας.[181] The hypaethron mentioned in the inscription is, therefore, to be associated with the sanctuary of Zeus Soter, which, according to the testimony of Pausanias[182] as well as of Strabo, possessed statuary and paintings of some note. Finally, a number of sanctuaries are mentioned as existing in the Piraeus: the Asclepieum,[183] the Dionysium,[184] a shrine (?) established by Themistocles before the battle of Salamis,[185] and a temenos of Agathe Tyche.[186] But the sanctuary of Zeus Soter—or, rather, the Disoterium, for Zeus was associated here with Athena Soteira —took first place among the cults of the Piraeus and was appropriately located in the very center of the hectic commercial section of the port town.[187]

That the Piraeus should have been largely rebuilt by the time of Augustus should occasion no surprise. With its excellent land-locked harbors, it provided an admirable naval base for the Romans, just as it formerly had for the Athenians. The finding, both in the Piraeus and at Athens, of a number of tombstones of Roman soldiers, sailors, and veterans makes it probable that the Romans actually utilized the harbors as a naval station.[188] But the most important reason for the reëquipment of the harbor and the rebuilding of the town was the necessity of making adequate provision for the reviving commerce of Athens.

[180] Gurlitt, *Über Pausanias*, p. 242, note 17.   [181] IX, 396.   [182] I, i, 3.
[183] IG, II–III², 1035, l. 40; cf. Judeich, *Topographie*, p. 441.
[184] IG, II–III², 1035, l. 42; cf. Judeich, *Topographie*, p. 453.
[185] IG, II–III², 1035, l. 45.
[186] *Ibid.*, 1035, l. 44; cf. Judeich, *Topographie*, p. 435.
[187] I shall discuss in another place the location of the Disoterium and the various topographical implications of the inscription analyzed in the text.
[188] CIL, III, 556a–57; 558 (= 7291); 6108–10; 7288–91; 14203, 18; J. H. Oliver, in *Hesperia*, X (1941), 244–49, Nos. 44–48; Conze, *Die attischen Grabreliefs*, IV, Nos. 2124–31; cf. Mühsam, *Die attischen Grabreliefs*, pp. 55–56. The inscriptions (excepting CIL, III, 6108) belong between 113 A.D. and 120 A.D., and it is probable that the soldiers and sailors named in them halted at Athens and the Piraeus at the time of the Parthian War (114–18 A.D.). See Oliver, *loc. cit.*

In general, the names of the donors of most of the structures which we have noted above have not been preserved, but that the donors were, in large part, wealthy foreigners seems to be indicated by the large number of dedications to such individuals at this period that have been found at Athens.[189] First of all, there are the numerous statues and decrees dedicated to Augustus and various members of the imperial entourage.[190] Of course, many of these dedications are to be construed as attempts to curry favor with the emperor.[191] Second, there are numerous statues and dedications in honor of other Romans.[192] In fact, there are preserved to us from the time of Augustus more Athenian decrees in honor of Romans than from any other period.[193] Third, various foreigners who were not Romans, both rulers and individuals of private station, were honored by the Athenians.[194] One of these individuals, Herod the Great, of Judaea, may be singled out for special notice.[195] From the writings of Josephus[196] we learn that Herod bestowed numerous gifts upon Athens and other Greek cities, but concerning the nature of these gifts we are not explicitly informed. However, inasmuch as this ruler is known to have endowed gymnasiarchies in numerous Greek cities, among them Cos,[197] it seems likely that his gifts to Athens were of the same character.[198]

[189] We have already observed that the only monuments known to have been erected by the Athenians are the horologium of Andronicus Cyrrhestes, the Temple of Roma and Augustus, and the relatively inexpensive monument of Agrippa.

[190] See the complete collection of such dedications given by Graindor, *Auguste*, pp. 45–54; cf. Judeich, *Topographie*, p. 99.

[191] Cf. Graindor, *Auguste*, p. 45.

[192] See the complete collection of such dedications at the time of Augustus given by Graindor, *Auguste*, pp. 55–80. For dedications of the years prior to the time of Augustus, see Judeich, *Topographie*, p. 98. Note, however, that the Jewish high priest John Hyrcanus, who was honored with a decree (Josephus, *Ant. Jud.* XIV, 153), lived during the second century B.C. See chap. iii, including note 216.

[193] W. Dittenberger, commentary on IG, III, 589; cf. Graindor, *Auguste*, p. 55.

[194] See the list and discussion given by Graindor, *Auguste*, pp. 81–93. For the years prior to the accession of Augustus, see Judeich, *Topographie*, pp. 96–97.

[195] For the dedicatory inscription of the statue in which Herodes is called a bene-factor of the city, see IG, II–III², 3440; cf. Graindor, *Auguste*, pp. 82–84; W. Otto, in RE, Supplementband II, 74.

[196] *Bell. Iud.* I, 425.   [197] *Ibid.*, I, 423.

[198] H. Willrich, *Das Haus des Herodes* (Heidelberg, 1929), p. 92. Graindor, *Auguste*, p. 82, suggests that the presence of the statue of King Juba of Mauretania in the Ptolemaeum (Pausanias, I, xvii, 2) should be taken as an indication that that ruler had bestowed some gift upon the gymnasium.

The fact that by far the larger part of the building activity which we have observed at Athens between 86 B.C. and the time of Augustus was made possible by the gifts of wealthy foreigners indicates that there were fewer Athenians able to contribute toward such projects than in former periods; but one must not go so far as to assume that no inferences concerning the internal economy of the city may be made from the fact of these building operations. The expenditure of large sums of money within Attica, from whatever source they were derived, undoubtedly exercised a stimulating effect upon all forms of business activity, just as in the second century B.C., when various Hellenistic kings vied with each other in bestowing gifts upon the Athenians. Moreover, some of the buildings, such as the harbor equipment at the Piraeus and the Market of Caesar and Augustus, were not intended to serve as mere ornaments for a decadent and lifeless city; they were erected to meet the very definite needs of commerce and trade at Athens.

We come now to a consideration of the products of local industry at Athens. The once dominant ceramic industry had, as we have already observed, begun to decline in the fourth century B.C. and continued to deteriorate early in Hellenistic times. The tendency toward progressively more careless execution of the wares of the potter continued unabated until, in the first century A.D., not only were foreign markets lost, but even the home market was flooded with Italian wares and with wares from various districts in the eastern part of the Mediterranean world.[199] A noteworthy exception to the general trend may be observed in the instance of the trade of the lamp maker. This artisan was producing in large quantities at the time of Augustus a cheap lamp which is now referred to as Type XX.[200] A few specimens of this type of lamp have been found at Corinth, but there they were unable to meet the competition of Italian lamps which were being imported in large numbers.[201] On the other hand, the Type XX lamp was able to hold the Athenian market, for none of the Italian lamps of the time of Augustus has been found at Athens.[202] Otherwise, the

[199] H. A. Thompson, in *Hesperia*, III (1934), 434.

[200] For the Athenian examples, see H. A. Thompson, in *Hesperia*, II (1933), 203–4. The classification is that of Broneer, *Lamps*, pp. 70–73.

[201] Broneer, *Lamps*, pp. 70–73.

[202] H. A. Thompson, in *Hesperia*, II (1933), 204.

Athenian potter seems to have contented himself with producing cheaper wares for local consumption, in some instances making cheaper copies of the more expensive imported wares.[203]

In the sphere of sculpture Athenians were very active between 86 B.C. and the time of Augustus. While some sculptors probably migrated to Rome,[204] the majority of the Athenian artists seem to have remained at home, where they were kept busy, as is shown by the numerous dedications, with a multitude of official and private commissions. The Neo-Attic school, which was, as we have seen,[205] active at Athens, continued to execute large orders of statuary and of furniture, such as candelabra, marble vases, beds, and tables for shipment especially to Italy.[206] Wealthy Romans filled their houses with the products of the workshops of these sculptors. Thus, Cicero bought through various agents statues of Bacchantes, a statue of Ares, a Hermeracles (a double bust of Hermes and Heracles), medallions, engraved stone curbs, and a $\tau\rho\alpha\pi\epsilon\zeta\delta\varphi\rho\rho\sigma$ (i.e., a table-stand or sideboard).[207] So great was the demand of the Italian market that entire shiploads were embarked at Athens, just as at the beginning of the first century B.C., when the vessel which later foundered off Mahdia set sail from Athens bearing a cargo of such objects. Indeed, despite the fact that it is no longer thought that the ship which foundered off Anticythera (Cerigotto)[208] in the time of Augustus necessarily sailed from Athens— instead, from some port in the Aegean[209]—the cargo of the ship

---

[203] See, for example, the locally made imitations of genuine Arretine ware recently found on the slope of the Theseum hill; T. L. Shear, in *Hesperia*, IV (1935), 368.

[204] Lawrence, *Later Greek Sculpture*, pp. 63–65.   [205] See chap. iii.

[206] An excellent summary of our knowledge concerning the Neo-Attic sculptors at Athens during the period of Augustus is given by Graindor, *Auguste*, pp. 207–45, who gives a complete list of the sculptors and the places where their works have been found.

[207] Cicero, *Ad Att.* I, iii, 2, X, iii; *Ad Fam.* VII, xxiii.

[208] J. Svoronos, "Die Funde von Antikythera," *Das athener Nationalmuseum* (Athens, 1908), I, 1–85; K. Stais, Τὰ ἐξ Ἀντικυθήρων εὑρήματα (Athens, 1905); Lippold, *Kopien*, pp. 71–73; A. Merlin, "Submarine Discoveries in the Mediterranean," *Antiquity* (1930), 405–15, especially pp. 406–8; C. Picard, *Sculpture antique*, p. 218.

[209] Lippold, *Kopien*, p. 83; O. Rubensohn, "Parische Künstler," JDAI, L (1935), 49–69, especially 60–61. I owe the latter reference to Rostovtzeff's *Social and Economic History of the Hellenistic World*.

affords evidence to show that Athens was the main center of the art trade in the Aegean area, for the statuary which the ship carried was made at Paros after casts of famous works of former days which were probably shipped there from Athens.[210] In other instances it is quite likely that statues produced elsewhere were assembled at Athens preparatory to shipment to Italy.[211] When an Athenian artist made a statue for the foreign market, he took care to engrave his name, not on the base, but on the statue itself.[212] Moreover, he signed works for export with the ethnic Ἀθηναῖος, not with the demotic. The reason that underlay this practice seems to have been that such an indication of a statue genuinely produced by an Athenian sculptor added considerably to the price the statue could command on the Roman market.[213] Many commissions came to the Neo-Atticists from foreigners who visited Athens. Thus, King Juba of Mauretania bought from Athenian artists a number of statues which he employed in the adornment of Caesarea (Cherchel), the capital city of his realm.[214] Indeed, so thriving was the trade in objects of art that foreigners found it profitable to establish art factories in the city at the time of Cicero, who mentions, in one of his letters,[215] the establishment owned by M. Aemilius Avianius and directed by his freedman, C. Avianius Evander.

The marble quarries on Pentelicon and Hymettus were actively worked during the first century B.C. and the time of Augustus; and since they were probably not a part of the imperial patrimony, the profits derived from them came into the purses of Athenians. Pentelic marble, while found only in small amounts at Rome,[216] was widely employed at Athens and throughout Greece during the

---

[210] O. Rubensohn, in JDAI, L (1935), 61–62.

[211] I owe this suggestion to Rostovtzeff's *Social and Economic History of the Hellenistic World*.

[212] Loewy, *Inschriften*, p. 238; P. Hartwig, in RM, XVI (1901), 368; Wilhelm, *Beiträge*, p. 91.

[213] Graindor, *Auguste*, p. 210.

[214] Lippold, *Kopien*, pp. 73–77.   [215] *Ad fam.* XIII, ii.

[216] Dubois, *Étude*, p. 99. Plutarch, *Pupl.* xv, tells of seeing at Athens columns of Pentelic marble that were dressed preparatory to shipment to Rome, where they were to be employed in the reconstruction of the Temple of Jupiter Capitolinus at the time of Domitian. For the very slight evidence of ownership of the Attic quarries by the emperors, see chap. v, including notes 166–67.

Roman period, both for statues[217] and in the construction of buildings.[218] Marble from Hymettus was still being employed at Athens in the time of Augustus. Moreover, it had been introduced into Rome at the beginning of the first century B.C.[219] and was highly prized there at the time of Horace, who describes a very wealthy house as one in which beams of marble from Hymettus rest upon columns of Numidian marble.[220]

One would expect that one of the leading university towns in the world would also be an important center of the book-publisher's trade, and there is actually some evidence, although it is not altogether conclusive, to this effect. In 60 B.C., in a letter which he wrote to his friend Atticus, who was then somewhere in Greece, Cicero mentions the fact that some time before he had sent to Atticus a copy of a book which he had written in Greek concerning his own consulship, and suggests that Atticus, in case the book should appeal to him, see that copies be made available at Athens and other Greek towns.[221] If this passage be taken as satisfactory proof of the existence of the publisher's trade at Athens in the time of Cicero, there is certainly no valid reason for contending that that trade ceased to exist there in the time of Augustus.

The mining of silver at Laurium, a source of revenue which had for many years been one of the mainstays of Athenian prosperity, began to fall off soon after 86 B.C. The Athenian mint seems to have struck coins, in restricted quantities, in most years between 86 B.C. and the time of Augustus,[222] but the last issue of New Style

[217] Cf. Cicero, *Ad Att.* I, viii, where mention of such statues is made. The extant statues made of that marble are far too numerous to mention.

[218] Pentelic marble was employed in the construction of the Temple of Roma and Augustus at Athens (Graindor, *Auguste*, p. 181), in Herodes Atticus' reconstruction of the Panathenaic Stadium at Athens (Pausanias, I, xix, 6; Philostratus, *Vit. soph.* 550) and of the stadium at Delphi (Pausanias, X, xxxii, 1), and in the statues of Demeter and Cora dedicated by the same individual in the Temple of Demeter at Olympia (Pausanias, VI, xxi, 2).

[219] Pliny, NH XVII, vi, XXXVI, vii; Valerius Maximus, IX, i, 4.

[220] *Carm.* II, xviii, 3–5.

[221] *Ad Att.* II, i, 2; cf. Dziatzko, "Buchhandel," RE, III, 981, 983; Graindor, *Auguste*, p. 163.

[222] Sundwall, *Untersuchungen*, I, 106; Head, *Hist. Num.*, pp. 386–87; Seltman, *Greek Coins*, p. 264; M. Thompson, in *Hesperia*, X (1941), 224–28, 230, note 96; cf. note 105, above.

silver coins seems to have been struck c.50 B.C.[223] By that time the
veins of silver at Laurium had been completely exhausted. Strabo,
writing at the time of Augustus, stated that the mines had failed,
and that those who worked them were able, by treating the old
slag by more skillful methods, to extract pure silver from it:
τὰ δ’ ἀργυρεῖα τὰ ἐν τῇ ’Αττικῇ κατ’ ἀρχὰς μὲν ἦν ἀξιόλογα, νυνὶ δ’
ἐκλείπει· καὶ δὴ καὶ οἱ ἐργαζόμενοι, τῆς μεταλλείας ἀσθενῶς ὑπα-
κούσης, τὴν παλαιὰν ἐκβολάδα καὶ σκωρίαν ἀναχωνεύοντες εὕρισκον
ἔτι ἐξ αὐτῆς ἀποκαθαιρόμενον ἀργύριον, τῶν ἀρχαίων ἀπείρως
καμινευόντων.[224] It has been the fashion to interpret this statement
as applying to the time of Augustus.[225] However, we have already
observed that Strabo depended, in his account of Attica, upon
sources which date from the period preceding his own.[226] Moreover,
it is to be noted that he employs the imperfect εὕρισκον, which
would indicate that he was definitely assigning the practice of re-
handling the scoriae to a period prior to the writing of his account.[227] The statement of Plutarch, who wrote almost a century
after the time of Strabo, that "recently" the Attic silver mines
had been exhausted,[228] is not to be taken literally, but rather to
indicate merely that he had himself observed that silver was no
longer produced at Laurium.[229] It may be reasonably concluded
that the silver veins at Laurium had been exhausted by the middle
of the first century B.C. and that by the time of Augustus it was no
longer possible to extract the metal from the old scoriae. It is,
perhaps, erroneous to go so far as to assert that Laurium was entirely deserted. In view of the facts that Laurium was once the
main source of lead in the Aegean area[230] and that the imperial

[223] M. L. Kambanis, in BCH, LXII (1938), 60–84.

[224] "The silver mines in Attica were originally valuable, but now they have
failed. Moreover, those who worked them, when the mining yielded only meager
returns, melted again the old refuse, or dross, and were still able to extract from it
pure silver, since the workmen of earlier times had been unskillful in heating the
ore in furnaces." Strabo, IX, 399, as translated by H. L. Jones in the Loeb Library edition.

[225] See, for example, Davies, Roman Mines, p. 251; Seltman, Greek Coins, p.
264; Ardaillon, Mines du Laurium, pp. 163–64.

[226] See note 17, above, and the beginning of this chapter.

[227] This is the observation of Graindor, Auguste, p. 164, and note 3.

[228] Mor. 434a.   [229] Cf. Larsen, "Roman Greece," p. 487.

[230] Davies, Roman Mines, pp. 246–47.

bronze coinage of Athens contains a much higher lead content than the New Style coinage contains,[231] it is tempting to assume that Laurium was still exploited for lead in early Roman times. But no certainty is attainable in this matter. In any event, the state lost large amounts of revenue which had formerly accrued to it from leasing the mines, and individual contractors lost a fruitful source of profit in working them.

The scanty information that we possess concerning the country population of Attica between 86 B.C. and the time of Augustus suggests that the lot of the farmer remained approximately the same as during the second century B.C. Like all other forms of economic endeavor, agriculture was affected adversely by the wars of the first century B.C. But with the accession of Augustus normalcy returned. Attic honey enjoyed a very high reputation in ancient times,[232] and from the frequency with which it is mentioned by Roman writers we are justified in concluding that it was imported into Italy in no small amounts.[233] However, Pliny's statement that an attempt was made to cultivate thyme from Hymettus in Italy because the fine quality of Attic honey was attributed to the variety of the herb that grew there[234] would seem to show either that the supply of genuine Attic honey was limited, or that the honey commanded a very high price on the market, with the result in either case that resort was taken to substitutes. On the other hand, Petronius' statement[235] that Trimalchio had bees brought to his estate from Attica is not to be taken as an indication that wealthy Italians followed this practice at all widely. Attic oil was still exported in large amounts.[236] Attic wine was never highly favored and, during the first century B.C., just as in the preceding century, was compelled to meet competition from imported wines. Rhodian wine was not imported after the second century B.C.,[237] and Cnidian

[231] J. P. Shear, in *Hesperia*, V (1936), 288.

[232] Dioscorides, II, 82; cf. Pliny, NH XI, xiii, 32; Scribonius Largus, 16; Strabo, IX, 399–400. Strabo makes the assertion that the honey from the district of the silver mines was by far the best of all Attic honey.

[233] Cf. M. Schuster, "Mel," RE, XV, 364–84, especially 378.

[234] NH XXI, x, 57.   [235] *Sat.* 38.

[236] There is definite evidence to show that it was still being exported in the third century A.D. See chap. vi.

[237] Rhodian amphora stamps of a date later than 100 B.C. have not been found in the Agora excavations. See V. Grace, in *Hesperia*, III (1934), 200.

wine was offered on the Athenian market during the first century
B.C. and the early Roman period in smaller quantity than before;[238]
on the contrary, considerable amounts of Roman wine were sold.[239]
The grain supply was, as ever, insufficient to feed the resident population. Grain was, therefore, imported. But it is probably true that, just
as in the second century B.C., the more prosperous farmer was the
one who was so fortunate as to raise a higher proportion of grain.

Concerning the laborer and his condition we have little information. There was probably some unemployment among workers in
the city. In the making of lamps and of imitation Arretine ware
something akin to modern methods of mass production obtained,
with a resultant displacement of workers.[240] Additional free workmen were displaced by slaves, who were most often employed in
those industries in which mass-production methods were utilized.
But the number of slaves employed in industrial, as well as in
domestic, pursuits was comparatively small, as is indicated by the
extreme infrequency with which their names are encountered in
inscriptions.[241] Concerning agricultural laborers we have no information. The laborer who fared best at Athens was the artisan
engaged in the thriving business of producing objects of art for the
foreign market. We may conclude that, in general, the condition
of the laborer was very poor.

Some attention must be paid to the economic benefits which
Athens derived from its dependencies.[242] While we have no direct
information concerning the revenues derived from these possessions, the evidence at our disposal is sufficient to show that Imbros,
Lemnos, Scyrus, Icus, Peparethus, Sciathus, and Ceos contributed
a considerable amount to the welfare of the mother city, Delos
only a little.

The heyday of Delos was, of course, past, but the island was far
from being the deserted place portrayed by Strabo.[243] The Delians

[238] *Ibid.*, pp. 200, 241–42.

[239] See the inscriptions on Roman amphorae in CIL, III, 6545, 1–25; 7309, 1–28
(27 and 28 are from Laurium, the others from Athens).

[240] For the methods of production generally employed in these two industries,
see Frank, *Economic History of Rome*, pp. 220–25.

[241] Westermann, "Sklaverei," cols. 1024–25.

[242] For the domain of Athens during the empire, see Graindor, *Auguste*, pp. 1–11.

[243] X, 486.

had severed their connections with Athens before the sack of the island in 86 B.C., but the metropolis resumed control after the lapse of a comparatively few months.[244] The festivals were reinitiated,[245] and life on the island resumed its normal tenor. Members of the Italian families that had formerly sojourned at Delos, and even some families not hitherto represented in the Roman community, took up their residence there.[246] The Italians began at once to renew their community life. They restored the meeting place of their community, the so-called Agora of the Italians; and part of the expense involved in the undertaking was defrayed with contributions made by Sidonians and Tyrians who still maintained their residence on the island.[247] The continued existence of the associations is attested by an inscription engraved between 84 B.C. and 78 B.C., in which honors were voted to the proquaestor M' Aemilius Lepidus by the Athenians, the Greeks and Romans, and the resident merchants and shippers.[248] Moreover, the Italian colleges survived the catastrophe of 86 B.C., for in 74 B.C. the *Hermaistae*, *Apolloniastae*, and *Poseidoniastae* associated themselves in a combined dedication in honor of Apollo and the Italians;[249] and in 57/6 B.C. the *Hermaistae* dedicated a chapel to their patron divinity.[250] In 74 B.C. the Second Mithradatic War broke out. Mithradates was joined by the pirates, and in 69 B.C. Delos was sacked unmercifully and its inhabitants sold into slavery. A short time later Lucullus' legate Triarius undertook a partial restoration of the town and built a wall around it.[251] But the position of the inhabitants became secure only after Pompey's conquest of the pirates, in gratitude for which the residents formed an association of *Pompeiastae*

[244] Ferguson, *Athens*, p. 452, maintains that Athenian jurisdiction was restored within eighteen months. Roussel, DCA, p. 328, points out that control had certainly been reëstablished by 80 B.C. For the history of Delos following 88 B.C., see Roussel, DCA, pp. 328–40; Laidlaw, *Delos*, pp. 258–74.

[245] Roussel, DCA, p. 329.

[246] J. Hatzfeld, in BCH, XXXVI (1912), 115; cf. Roussel, DCA, p. 329.

[247] IDD, 2612; cf. Roussel, DCA, pp. 322, 329; Lapalus, *L'Agora des Italiens*, p. 100.

[248] IDD, 1659.   [249] IDD, 1758.

[250] IDD, 1737; cf. Roussel, DCA, p. 335.

[251] Phlegon of Tralles, xii, 13, in Jacoby, *Fragmente*, II, 1164. The town surrounded by the wall was much smaller than the settlement that had been destroyed. See Roussel, DCA, pp. 331–32; Laidlaw, *Delos*, p. 273, note 10.

in his honor.[252] By this time many Asiatics, as well as Romans, had left the island.[253] In 58 B.C. the Romans made a final attempt to restore the prosperity of Delos. In that year a decree of the Senate provided for the restoration of temples and shrines on the island and bestowed upon the Delians a grant of *libertas* and of immunity from taxation—*libertas* in a very restricted sense, however, for the island was to be under the control of the Athenians.[254] But the attempt of the Romans was to no avail; the circumstances that had given rise to the artificial prosperity of Delos had now disappeared. By about the middle of the first century B.C. the last of the *negotiatores* had left the island.[255] A small colony of Jews is still attested for the middle of the first century A.D., but they were apparently content to live on incomes that were not attractive to the members of the corporations that had been so prominent at Delos.[256] If Delos contributed anything at all to the prosperity of Athens at this time, it must have been very little,[257] for the island possessed no natural resources and shared no longer in foreign trade.

Scyrus, on the other hand, must have been the source of a very consequential revenue for the Athenians. Although they were not highly favored in Greece, monolithic columns and large slabs of the variegated marble that was quarried on the island were shipped to Rome for use in both public and private buildings.[258] The wine of the island, which was considered efficacious in the treatment of fevers,[259] was also exported to Italy in large amounts, as is interestingly shown by the fact that the cupola of the Baptistery at Ravenna was built with inscribed amphorae that had once held wine from Scyrus.[260] Of the various brands of yellow ocher, which was utilized by painters in producing various shades, that of

---

[252] Durrbach, *Choix*, No. 162.   [253] Laidlaw, *Delos*, p. 268.

[254] SEG, I, 335; E. Cuq, in BCH, XLVI (1922), 198–215; Laidlaw, *Delos*, p. 273.

[255] J. Hatzfeld in BCH, XXXVI (1912), 50.

[256] Josephus, *Ant. Iud.* XIV, 231–32; cf. Durrbach, *Choix*, pp. 263–65.

[257] It should be noted that Graindor, *Auguste*, p. 166, believes otherwise.

[258] Strabo, IX, 437; Eustathius, *Ad Dionys. perieg.* 521; Pliny, NH XXXI, ii, 29, XXXVI, xvi, 130, II, ciii, 233; Dubois, *Étude*, pp. 129–30; Graindor, *Skyros*, p. 16.

[259] K. G. Kühn, *Medicorum Graecorum opera quae exstant* (Leipzig, 1821–33), XV, 648; cf. Graindor, *Skyros*, p. 14.

[260] Graindor, *Auguste*, pp. 165–66; Graindor, in *Byzantion*, III (1926), 251–52.

Scyrus was still highly favored in the time of Pliny.[261] The island also produced considerable amounts of wheat and barley. It was because of their production of these grains that Lemnos,[262] Imbros,[263] Peparethus,[264] and Sciathus[265] were also important parts of the domain of Athens. While no statistics are available for Peparethus and Sciathus, the approximate amount of grain ordinarily produced in Lemnos, Imbros, Scyrus, and Attica may be calculated from an inscription of 329/8 B.C. which lists the first fruits presented to the Eleusinian goddesses in the course of that year.[266] The production was as follows:[267]

Community			Barley (in medimni)	Wheat (in medimni)
Imbros			26,000	44,200
Lemnos[a]	{	Myrina	97,200	28,100
	{	Hephaestia	151,325	28,650
Scyrus			28,800	9,600
		Total	303,325	110,550
Attica[b]			363,400	39,112.5

[a]Myrina and Hephaestia were the two chief settlements on Lemnos.
[b]Including the domain of Amphiaraus.

It will be observed at once that the total production of barley and of wheat in Lemnos, Imbros, and Scyrus was approximately equal to that in Attica. If, then, allowance be made for the grain raised on Peparethus and Sciathus, it becomes apparent that more grain was produced in the foreign dependencies of Athens than in Attica itself. Most of the grain raised on the islands was required for the sustenance of the local populations, but doubtless considerable

[261] Pliny, NH XXXIII, lvi, 159.

[262] The plains of Lemnos were comparatively extensive and fertile, the return of grain per acre being four times that enjoyed by the Attic farmer; see H. F. Tozer, *The Islands of the Aegean* (Oxford, 1890), p. 253; Jardé, *Céréales*, p. 53. The grain was of good quality; see Theophrastus, CP IV, ix, 6.

[263] Approximately one eighth of the surface of Imbros is suitable for cultivation, but the return of crops seems to have been exceptionally high per acre; see E. Oberhummer, "Imbros," *Festschrift für H. Kiepert* (Berlin, 1898), pp. 275–304, especially p. 291; Jardé, *Céréales*, p. 54.

[264] FHG, II, p. 217.

[265] Demosthenes, *Phil.* 49; Livy, XXXI, xlv.

[266] IG, II–III², 1672.

[267] See Jardé, *Céréales*, pp. 36–60; the tabulation is compiled from the table in Jardé, p. 41.

amounts of it were shipped to Athens, where it served to make up for the perennial deficiency in the supply of cereals.

The island of Ceos remains for consideration. Varro informs us[268] that fine garments were made on this island, but it is quite possible, as Larsen suggests, that he is confusing Ceos with Cos, which was considerably more famous for such products.[269] There is no evidence to indicate that the island still produced the vermilion of which the Athenians had, centuries before, held a monopoly.[270]

Athens, therefore, exported objects of art and oil in considerable amounts, marble and honey in smaller amounts, and a few lamps. Its dependency, Scyrus, exported marble and wine, and some yellow ocher. But so great were the imports into the city that the balance of trade was undoubtedly unfavorable. Indeed, its situation in this respect was much more unsatisfactory than in preceding centuries. With the exhaustion of the silver mines at Laurium, Athens had lost a very important source of wealth. The city had, therefore, less with which to pay for its imports. Moreover, it was even more dependent than formerly upon foreign sources of supply, since it was now necessary to import copper for coinage. This accounted, at least in part, for the higher proportion of lead, a metal considerably cheaper than copper, which was employed in the Athenian coins of imperial date.[271] The commodity imported in largest amount was, as usual, grain. At some time during the reign of Augustus, possibly immediately after the battle of Actium, when an acute shortage of grain was experienced,[272] but at least by the last decade of the century a special treasury for the purchase of grain ($\sigma\iota\tau\omega\nu\iota\kappa\grave{o}\nu$ $\tau\alpha\mu\iota\epsilon\hat{i}o\nu$) was created. This is shown by several facts. First, Xenocles son of Theopompus, of Rhamnus, who had been hoplite general four times, is honored by an Athenian decree of the Augustan period for introducing a measure to create this treasury, and for twice purchasing grain for the state.[273] Second, although the precise date of this inscription is not known, we learn from another inscription that the treasury for the purchase of grain was operative

---

[268] As quoted by Pliny, NH IV, xii, 62.

[269] Cf. Larsen, "Roman Greece," p. 486.   [270] IG, II–III², 1128.

[271] Caley, *Greek Bronze Coins*, pp. 144, 190–91. See Tables VI–VIII in Caley. Cf. *Hesperia*, V (1936), 288, note 2.

[272] Plutarch, *Ant.* lxviii.   [273] IG, II–III², 3504.

at some time between 8/7 B.C. and 1 B.C.[274] The funds in this treasury were administered by ταμίαι τῶν σιτωνικῶν,[275] while the various purchases of grain were made by *sitonae*.[276] These officials were, in turn, placed under the supervision of the hoplite general, who, by the time of the empire, had lost his military functions, and whose specific responsibility it now was to see to it that the city's grain supply was adequate.[277] It seems most likely, then, that it was during the reign of Augustus that the hoplite general lost his military duties and took over his new responsibilities. And it was, apparently, in his capacity as general in charge of the grain supply that Xenocles introduced the measure, to which reference is made above, for the creation of the special treasury for the purchase of grain.[278] South Russia remained, as during preceding centuries, one of Athens' most important sources of grain.[279] Another agricultural product that was imported, as we have already observed, was wine from Cnidus and from Italy.[280] Some of the wine from the West was shipped to Athens by merchants whose trade extended over widely separated districts, as is shown by an amphora bearing the initials "T. H. B.,"[281] which appear also on jars found at Carthage,[282] Mainz,[283] and Rome.[284] From Egypt papyrus was imported for use in the production of books. In the

[274] *Ibid.*, 3505, where two ταμίαι τῶν σιτωνικῶν are mentioned. For the date of the inscription, see Graindor, *Chronologie*, p. 51.

[275] IG, II–III², 3505.

[276] *Ibid.*, 3504, ll. 5–6; cf. Graindor, *Auguste*, p. 118, note 5.

[277] Specific literary testimony exists to the effect that in the time of Hadrian it was the function of the general to supervise the grain supply; Philostratus, *Vit. soph.* 526.

[278] IG, II–III², 3504; cf. Graindor, *Auguste*, pp. 117–19.

[279] Rostovtzeff, *Iranians and Greeks*, pp. 153–54. It seems likely, as noted above, that a moderate amount of grain came to Athens from the city's dependencies. The suggestion made by T. Mommsen, *Provinces*, I, 279, that the revolt which occasioned the intervention of Rome at Athens in 13 A.D. was of the nature of riots —in part because of the price of bread—is not susceptible of proof. For this revolt, see St. Jerome's revision of Eusebius' *Chronicon*, Year of Abraham 2028 (Olymp. 197, ed. Helm, p. 170); George Syncellus, *Chron.* 318 C; Orosius, VI, xxii, 2; Paulus Diaconus, *Misc. hist.* VII, 25; Graindor, *Auguste*, pp. 41–45.

[280] See notes 238 and 239.

[281] CIL, III, 7309, 9; cf. O. Bohn, in *Germania: Korrespondenzblatt der römisch-germanischen Komission*, VII (1923), 16.

[282] CIL, VIII, 22637, 47.   [283] *Westdeutsche Korrespondenzblatt*, 1901, p.69.

[284] CIL, XV, 2905; cf. 4657g, 4659.

realm of industrial products, local craftsmen continued to produce the more ordinary articles that were in use, but the finer wares came from Italy, whose manufactured products appeared on Greek markets in large quantities in the time of Augustus,[285] and from various eastern centers. The pottery most in vogue at this time was Arretine ware, named after the city in Italy where the largest amounts of it were first made. Large amounts of this ware were imported and have recently been found in the Agora and in the Ceramicus at Athens.[286] Other industrial products imported from Italy and the West will probably be ascertained among the various articles found in excavations at Athens, but further study is re-

[285] Rostovtzeff, *Roman Empire*, pp. 68–69, 493, note 18; cf. pp. 58–59, 502–3, note 16.

[286] The following dated wares, with name of potter, provenance, and date, have been found at Athens (unless otherwise noted, the page references within parentheses are to J. H. Iliffe, "Sigillata Wares in the Near East," QDAP, VI [1936], 4–53):

Arretine ware. Cn. Ateius, Arretine and Gaulish, Augustan (p. 28); P. Claudius, Arretine (?), first century A.D. (p. 30); Euhodus (at one time a slave of Ateius), Augustan (p. 34); Herophilus, first century B.C. (p. 36); Cn. A. M. (Mahes, slave of Cn. Ateius), Augustan (p. 39); MAMMO[-US], early and pre-Augustan (p. 39); Murtilus, early Augustan (p. 41); Neroth, Augustan (p. 41); ΟΝΗΣΙΜΟΣ (or Onesimus), slave of C. Annius, Augustan (p. 42); M. Perennius, Augustan (pp. 42–43); Rasinius, Augustan (p. 44; cf. CIL, III, 6546, 8; H. Comfort, in JAOS, LVIII [1938], 55); Salvus, Augustan (p. 45; cf. AM, LII [1927], 220–21, Abb. 3, No. 3: with Sextus Annius); Sextus Annius, Augustan (p. 47; cf. CIL, III, 6546, 2; H. Comfort, in JAOS, LVIII [1938], 47; AM, LII [1927], 220–21, Abb. 3, No. 3: with Salvus); Suavis, early Augustan (p. 47); Thyrsus, Augustan (p. 48; AM, LII [1927], 221; with Titius); L. Titius (Tittius), early Augustan, with Hilarus, Suavis, and Thyrsus (pp. 48–49; AM, LII [1927], 221); C. Vibius, early and pre-Augustan (p. 49); L. Vibius, early and pre-Augustan (pp. 49–50); Zoilus, Augusto-Tiberian (p. 53).

Arretine or Puteolian ware. P. Attius, Augustan (p. 29); Hilarus, first century B.C. (p. 36).

Puteolian ware. Epigonus [ΕΠΙΓΟΝΟΣ], first century B.C. (p. 33); Malius, with Sextus, c.50–20 B.C. (p. 39); Sextus, with Malius, first century B.C. (p. 47).

Gaulish ware (?). Avitus, first century A.D. (p. 29). Additional, but undated, examples of sigillate wares from Athens are given by Iliffe (pp. 4–53) and by H. Comfort, "Supplementary Sigillata Signatures in the Near East," JAOS, LVIII (1938), 30–60. For other publications of Arretine ware at Athens, see CIL, III, 6546, 1–18; A. Oxé, "Terra Sigillata aus dem Kerameikos," AM, LII (1927), 213–24, especially 219–22; F. O. Waagé, in *Hesperia*, II (1933), 288; cf. J. H. Iliffe, "Hellenistic and Sigillata Ware in the Near East," JHS, LVI (1936), 234–35. For *terra sigillata* wares in general, see H. Comfort in Frank, "Rome and Italy of the Empire," pp. 188–94; H. Comfort, in RE, Supplementband VII, 1295–1352.

quired definitely to identify them.[287] Various brands of *terra sigillata* which resemble Arretine ware were imported from districts in the eastern part of the Mediterranean.[288] Other manufactured products, such as, for example, terra-cotta figurines, were imported from Asia Minor.[289] Fusiform unguentaria bearing perfumes were still imported from Syria in the first century B.C.[290] That other products were brought from the Orient over the caravan routes of the East is indicated by the fact that a number of individuals hailing from towns in Syria and Palestine took up residence at Athens.[291]

[287] Observe the early Roman terra-cotta figurine recently found in the Agora; it is of a style similar to that of figurines found at Pompeii. See D. B. Thompson, in *Hesperia*, II (1933), 190. Other early Roman figurines have been found in the Agora, but it is not certain whence they were imported (*ibid.*, 190–91).

[288] Inasmuch as the provenance of these fabrics has not, in general, been absolutely determined, it seems best, for present purposes, to designate them, with the exception of a few which are probably from Samos, merely as "Eastern." The two main eastern fabrics of sigillate wares are generally referred to as "Samian" and "Pergamene"; "Tschandarli" ware is a variety of the latter. A number of different types are usually listed under the terms "Pergamene" and "Samian." See J. H. Iliffe, in JHS, LVI (1936), 234. For "Samian" ware, see J. H. Iliffe, in QDAP, VI (1936), 7–9; F. O. Waagé, "Vasa Samia," *Antiquity*, 1937, pp. 46–55; H. Comfort, in RE, Supplementband VII, 1302–4. Some wares now classified as "Pergamene" may have been made at Samos; see J. H. Iliffe, in QDAP, VI (1936), 10–12. "Tschandarli" ware has been satisfactorily identified (*ibid.*, pp. 7–9; H. Comfort, in RE, Supplementband VII, 1301–2). The vases of this type from the Agora at Athens date in the main from the first century A.D.; see F. O. Waagé, in *Hesperia*, II (1933), 290. Signed eastern sigillate vases found at Athens, with provenance, stamp, and date, are as follows (the references within parentheses are, unless otherwise indicated, to J. H. Iliffe, in QDAP, VI [1936]): ΕΡΜΗΣ, Samos (?), Augustan (p. 34); ΚΑΛΑ, Samos (?), first century B.C. (p. 37; *Hesperia*, II [1933], 292); ΠΟΣΙΔΟΝΙΟΣ (Posidonius), Samos (?), Augustan (p. 43); ΧΑΡΙΣ, eastern *or* Samos, Augustan (pp. 50–53). It is to be noted that ΚΑΛΑ and ΧΑΡΙΣ are not names of potters, as Iliffe surmised. See F. O. Waagé's review of QDAP, VI (1936), 4–53, in AJA, XLIII (1939), 539–43, especially p. 541; H. Comfort, in RE, Supplementband VII, 1303. For other publications of eastern sigillate wares which have been found at Athens, see F. O. Waagé, in *Hesperia*, II (1933), 285–87 ("Pergamene"), 291–93 ("Samian"); J. H. Iliffe, in JHS, LVI (1936), 234–35; A. Oxé, in AM, LII (1927), 216–18, 222–23. Occasional undated eastern sigillate wares at Athens are listed by H. Comfort, in JAOS, LVIII (1938), 30–60.

[289] For the present, see the terra-cotta figurine of workmanship characteristic of Smyrna recently found in the Agora at Athens (D. Burr. in *Hesperia*, II [1933], 190). Further study of archaeological finds will probably disclose more evidence to the same effect.   [290] H. A. Thompson, in *Hesperia*, III (1934), 473.

[291] The fact of the residence of these foreigners at Athens is shown by the finding

That business was relatively prosperous at Athens in the first century B.C. and in the time of Augustus is also made evident by the fact of the residence there of a sizable colony of Roman *negotiatores*.[292] These traders never lingered in a community where opportunities for profitable intercourse were absent. The family names of some of these traders who resided at Athens are found among the names of residents of Delos a little before the middle of the first century B.C.,[293] which is a phenomenon that had been considerably more striking in the years preceding 86 B.C., when proportionately large numbers of Italian traders at Athens were related to businessmen at Delos. The decline in such instances of relationship should occasion no surprise, for the island was too poor to attract, or keep, *negotiatores* after the middle of the first century B.C.[294] Of resident Romans whose names are known to us from literary and inscriptional sources some were undoubtedly students, but, on the other hand, some are shown by specific evidence to have been businessmen. It may be of interest to pay passing attention to some few of the latter. It is uncertain whether the brothers Stallius, C. and M., to whom Ariobarzanes of Cappadocia entrusted the reconstruction of the Odeum of Pericles,[295] were architects, contractors, or bankers; at least they were business men.[296] The Matrinius who made a dedication to the Tarsian Apollo[297] apparently hailed from Cilicia, where the cult of Apollo throve[298] and where Roman *negotiatores* are known to have been established in the first century A.D.[299] However, not only are individual business men with interests localized at Athens encountered in our sources, but, so good were the prospects, that men

---

of their inscribed tombstones there. The inscriptions antedating the empire have been discussed in chap. iii; those of the period of the empire will be discussed in chap. v.

[292] Hatzfeld, *Trafiquants*, pp. 74–76.

[293] The Cornelii, Flaminii, Granii, Licinii, Popillii, and Saufeii may be cited. Cf. Hatzfeld, *Trafiquants*, pp. 74–75.

[294] *Ibid.*, p. 75. The following families who now resided at Athens were not represented at Delos: the Braccii, Caesellii, Epidii, Seppii, Terentii, and Turranii.

[295] IG, II–III², 3426.

[296] Hatzfeld, *Trafiquants*, p. 76, and note 3.   [297] IG, II–III², 3003.

[298] O. Gruppe, *Griechische Mythologie und Religionsgeschichte* (Munich, 1906), II, 1258, note 3.

[299] Hatzfeld, *Trafiquants*, p. 76.

with interests in various parts of the world plied their businesses at Athens. Thus, the Titus Pinarius who was voted an honorary decree by the Demos[300] seems to have been the agent of the banker Attius Dionysius,[301] who had business interests also in Africa,[302] Galatia,[303] and Gaul.[304] Mention should also be made of M. Aemilius Avianius, who owned an art factory at Athens managed by his freedman C. Avianius Evander[305] as well as branch factories at Sicyon and at Cibyra. The branch located at Sicyon, which was under the direction of another of his freedmen, C. Avianius Hammonius,[306] probably specialized in work in bronze, while the branch at Cibyra, where Aemilius himself spent four years, may have produced embossed ironware, for which that city was noted.[307] We have already seen that a number of eastern businessmen also resided at Athens at this time. But wherein lay the attraction for businessmen? Our survey of economic activities in the city has shown that Athens had become relatively prosperous by the time of Augustus, but it remains to point out additional factors which underlay that prosperity. Perhaps most important is the fact that Athens was a famous university center. Just as the city had been, as we have seen, a place for the frequent and long-continued sojourning of students in the time of Cicero, so in the time of Augustus numbers of students flocked there, in spite of the fact that other important centers had developed at Antioch, Rome, and Marseilles.[308] Numerous foreigners, too, were attracted by the Athenian ephebia.[309] It is

---

[300] IG, II–III², 4108.　　　[301] Cicero, *Ad fam.* XII, xxiv, 3.

[302] *Ibid.*, XII, xxiv, 3.　　　[303] Cicero, *Ad. Att.* VI, i, 23.

[304] Cicero, *Ad Q. fratr.* III, i, 22. Hatzfeld, *Trafiquants*, p. 76, maintains that Cicero, *Ad Att.* VIII, xv, 1, attests to Pinarius' business interests in Greece. The passage in question seems not, however, to permit of this interpretation.

[305] Cicero, *Ad fam.* XIII, ii.　　　[306] *Ibid.*, XIII, xxi.

[307] *Ibid.*, XIII, xxi, 1; cf. Broughton, "Roman Asia Minor," p. 550.

[308] For the importance of advanced studies at Antioch, Rome, and Marseilles at this time, see Strabo, IV, 181; L. Grasberger, *Erziehung und Unterricht* (Würzburg, 1881), III, 452–53, 498. Philostratus, *Vit. Apoll.* VIII, 15, speaks of students from the whole world coming to Athens, and there would seem to be good reason to assume that as many were present there slightly earlier, at the time of Augustus. Cf. Graindor, *Auguste*, pp. 161–62.

[309] At some year between 90 B.C. and 80 B.C. there were more than 14 foreign ephebes (IG, II–III², 1031); at some year between 83 B.C. and 78 B.C. there were more than 5 foreign ephebes (IG, II–III², 1039); and in 39/8 B.C. foreign ephebes numbered 66 (IG, II–III², 1043). Cf. Reinmuth, *Foreigners in the Athenian Ephebia*, p. 18.

also worthy of note that the city was a very attractive resort for tourists, who were drawn thither by its past glories, by its art and festivals. The Mysteries were a special source of interest to foreigners, as we know from Philostratus,[310] who informs us that, at a slightly later period than that of Augustus, Athens was the most populous city in the world whenever the ceremonies at Eleusis were held. Perhaps no single fact indicates more vividly the renown of the city and of the Mysteries than the story of Zarmarus (or Zarmarochegas) of Bargoza (or Barygoza), who was sent by Pandion (or Porus) as an ambassador to Augustus when the emperor was sojourning at Samos.[311] Zarmarus insisted upon being initiated into the Mysteries, and then committed suicide on a funeral pyre at Athens. The choice of Athens as a setting for this dramatic act demonstrates the renown of the city—a renown that extended as far as India.[312] These tourists, then, drawn from far and wide, provided an inexhaustible source of profit for business men of all kinds, especially for traders in luxury articles from the East.

Many indications, therefore, point to a striking revival of prosperity at Athens by the time of Augustus. The state was poor—in spite of low expenses. No longer was it necessary to maintain an army and navy. The magistracies were honorary and were a financial burden to the incumbent rather than to the state.[313] The chief expenses to be met by the treasury—and they were not inconsiderable—were the maintenance of cults and monuments.[314] While there is no evidence in our sources to indicate that the state experienced extreme financial embarrassment before the second century A.D., at which time the Athenians contemplated selling Delos,[315] it is beyond doubt that the Athenians were so improvident that the Demos was continually pressed with financial difficulties. In the years immediately following the sack of the city by Sulla these difficulties were very trying. Cicero's friend Atticus found it

---

[310] *Vit. Apoll.* IV, 17.

[311] Dio Cassius, LIV, ix, 8–10; Strabo, XV, 719–20 (quoting Nicolaus Damascenus); Plutarch, *Alex.* lxix.

[312] Cf. Graindor, *Auguste*, p. 93.

[313] Graindor, *Chronologie*, pp. 11–12; Keil, *Areopag*, pp. 86–90.

[314] Cf. Graindor, *Auguste*, p. 166.

[315] Philostratus, *Vit. soph.* 527; cf. Graindor, *Auguste*, pp. 166–67; and *Tibère*, p. 131.

necessary to intervene at that time to help straighten out the finances.[316] The role of Atticus was that of an intermediary who was able to secure better rates of interest on loans than the treasury could itself have obtained.[317] A further instance, perhaps, is to be cited to show that the finances of the city were poorly administered. During the reign of Augustus Cn. Pullius Pollion was sent to Athens in the capacity of an imperial legate.[318] It has been reasonably suggested that he was not merely an ambassador sent to a free city,[319] but rather an official with the function of a *corrector*[320] sent to reform the administration of Athenian finances.[321] In addition to its revenues from taxation, port dues, and the like, concerning all of which we have no information, the city derived considerable amounts of money from the sale of its citizenship and from gifts made by wealthy citizens and visiting foreigners. The monetary value placed upon their citizenship by the Athenians is not known. However, Thasus sold its citizenship for one hundred staters, an amount which has been equated with two thousand drachmas.[322] But it seems most likely that this amount should be equated rather with two hundred drachmas,[323] since a much more important city, Ephesus, sold its citizenship in 286 B.C. for only six hundred drachmas.[324] With its great prestige, it seems certain, Athens would not have demanded a smaller amount.[325] When Augustus forbade the Athenians to sell their citizenship,[326] they easily circumvented the prohibition; they accepted gifts from wealthy foreigners, and, in return, bestowed the same honors upon them

---

[316] Cornelius Nepos, XXV, ii, 4.

[317] Holtzmann, in Zimmermann's *Zeitschrift für Altertumswissenschaft*, 1836, pp. 867–71, as cited by W. Drumann and P. Groebe, *Geschichte Roms* (2d ed.; Leipzig, 1899–1929), V, 17, note 4; Hatzfeld, *Trafiquants*, p. 204.

[318] ILS, 916; cf. PIR, III, p. 109, No. 802; Graindor, *Auguste*, pp. 39–41. I have been unable to consult E. Groag, *Die römischen Reichsbeamten von Achaia bis auf Diokletian* (Vienna, 1939; Akademie der Wissenschaften in Wien, Schriften der Balkankommission, antiquarische Abteilung, IX).

[319] T. Mommsen, in *Ephemeris epigraphica*, VII, 447.

[320] This office was, of course, instituted much later by Trajan. Cf. A. von Premerstein, in RE, IV, 1646.

[321] Graindor, *Auguste*, p. 41.   [322] BCH, XLV (1921), 153, No. 6.

[323] Graindor, *Auguste*, p. 104, note 1.

[324] Cf. P. Roussel, in *Revue de philologie*, XXXVII (1913), 332–34; M. Holleaux in REG, XXIX (1916), 29–45.

[325] Cf. Graindor, *Auguste*, p. 104, note 1.   [326] Dio Cassius, LIV, vii.

that they were wont to confer upon wealthy benefactors among the citizen population. In almost servile fashion the state recognized these gifts—they usually took the form of distributions of money or of grain, or even of the erection of a public building—by the dedication of a statue of the donor or by a fulsome honorary decree.[327] In either event the recognition involved no considerable outlay. An honorary decree involved only the expense of carving a stone stele, while the provision of a statue was little more expensive, for the practice now became current of rededicating statues by merely altering the dedicatory inscription and substituting a new head.[328]

Along with the upswing of prosperity that set in at Athens during the time of Augustus came an increase in population.[329] And among the prominent families of the period were many who had been wealthy and prominent in the years preceding 86 B.C. This should occasion no surprise, for the sack of the city by Sulla had by no means destroyed the economy that had prevailed there before that time. It may be of interest to trace the destiny of a few of these

[327] Graindor, *Auguste*, pp. 57 and 160. For example, the epic poet Julius Nicanor, who was a native of Hierapolis but later became a citizen of Athens, purchased the island of Salamis and returned it to the Athenians, for which benefaction the Athenians honored him with the titles of "New Themistocles" and "New Homer." See Dio Chrysostomus, XXXI, 116; IG, II–III², 1069; Graindor, *Auguste*, p. 8, and note 7.

[328] Statues of Eumenes and Attalus of Pergamum were reinscribed with the name of Antony (Plutarch, *Ant.* lx). A statue of Alcibiades was rededicated to Ahenobarbus; see Dio-Chrysostomus, XXXVII, 40; IG, II–III², 4144; G. Hirschfeld, *Tituli statuariorum* (Berlin, 1871), p. 47; Loewy, *Inschriften*, p. 317. Such rededications were being made some years before the founding of the empire (Curtius, *Stadtgeschichte*, p. 260; Wachsmuth, *Die Stadt Athen*, I, 679, note 1; E. Hula, in JOAI, I [1898], 27–30), and during the empire even statues of the emperors were rededicated to other individuals (Graindor, *Auguste*, pp. 45–46, 56–57). Cicero, *Ad Att.* VI, i, 26, expressed his distaste for the practice. The reëmployment of statue bases has been interpreted as an indication of the poverty of the Athenian treasury (E. Hula, in JOAI, I [1898], 30). However, in a place filled with statues to the extent that Athens was, economy of space may have been the decisive factor, as Graindor, *Auguste*, p. 161, suggests.

[329] Graindor (*Auguste*, pp. 97–98), maintaining that there were at least six thousand propertied heads of families at Athens in the time of Augustus, attempts, from this figure, to arrive at an estimate of the population of the city. Although it is impossible to reach any valid approximation, the evidence now available is sufficient to justify the assertion that the population of the city increased during the Augustan period. See Appendix.

families. Diotimus son of Diodorus, of Halae, was archon at Athens in 26/5 B.C.[330] He also took a prominent part in the five Dodecades which were dispatched to Delphi during the reign of Augustus.[331] His brother Theophilus held the archonship in 12/1 B.C.[332] These men were great-grandsons of the Diodorus son of Theophilus, of Halae, who was superintendent of the harbor at the Piraeus in 112/1 B.C.,[333] commissioner in charge of the reform of weights and measures,[334] and one of the leaders of the oligarchy at Athens at the end of the second century B.C.[335] Of all the families to be mentioned the most important is that of the millionaire sophist Herodes Atticus, who lived during the second century A.D. Herodes (II), six generations removed from Herodes Atticus by direct descent,[336] held the archonship in 60/59 B.C.[337] and was superintendent in charge of the building of the Market of Caesar and Augustus at the beginning of work on that structure.[338] He was succeeded in that post by his son Eucles (V),[339] who was archon in 46/5 B.C.[340] This Eucles was one of the most prominent men of his time at Athens.[341] It is also possible that Eucles had a son, Polycharmus by name, who held the archonship at some time near 22/3 A.D.[342] Members of this family had already attained to prominence in the second century B.C.[343] Mention should also be made of the family of Epicrates son of Callimachus, of Leuconoe, who held the archonship at the end of the republic or the beginning of the

---

[330] Dinsmoor, *Archons*, p. 287. Graindor, *Chronologie*, pp. 30–34, had dated his archonship between 26/5 B.C. and 17/6 B.C.

[331] Graindor, *Auguste*, p. 143.

[332] Dinsmoor, *Archons*, pp. 282, 284, 293. Graindor, *Chronologie*, p. 48, dates his archonship in 11/10 B.C.

[333] IG, II–III², 1012. [334] *Ibid.*, 1013.

[335] Ferguson, *Athens*, pp. 421, 425. For the stemma of the family, see NPA, p. 56.

[336] For the stemma of the family, see Graindor, *Hérode*, pp. 4, 8.

[337] Dinsmoor, *Archons*, pp. 280–82.

[338] IG, II–III², 3175; cf. Graindor, *Auguste*, p. 31; and *Hérode*, pp. 5–6.

[339] See the citations in the preceding nôte.

[340] The year is not altogether certain; see Dinsmoor, *Archons*, pp. 280, 281, 284, 285.

[341] Graindor, *Auguste*, pp. 142–43.

[342] Although the tenure of the archonship by Polycharmus is attested only by an inscription in which his name has been restored, Graindor, *Chronologie*, pp. 64–65, maintained that there were various facts at our disposal to show that this restoration was reasonable.

[343] For Eucles (II), Eucles (III), and Eucles (IV), see NPA, p. 78.

empire,[344] and who was twice herald of the Areopagus.[345] An additional indication of his position at Athens is to be found in Cicero's reference to him as *princeps Atheniensium* and as one of the *homines docti*.[346] His grandfather, Epicrates (III), was monetary magistrate soon after 86 B.C.,[347] while his great-grandfather, Callimachus (II), was monetary magistrate c.120 B.C.[348] The family was prominent as early as the beginning of the second century B.C.[349] The remaining individuals to be mentioned are interesting because of the fact that their ancestry may be traced back to men who apparently founded or enlarged their fortunes in business at Delos. Two brothers, Epigenes and Xenon, who were monetary magistrates shortly before 50 B.C.,[350] a fact which indicates their membership in a prominent family, were grandsons of Epigenes son of Dius, of Melite, who had been *epimeletes* of Delos in some year preceding 126/5 B.C.[351] Agathostratus son of Dionysius, of Pallene, *epimeletes* of Delos in 48 B.C.,[352] was a descendant—his exact relationship being unknown—of Dionysius son of Nicon, of Pallene, who had held the same office in 110/9 B.C.[353] Dionysius' son, who had been adopted by his uncle Hermaphilus and had taken the name of Hermaphilus son of Hermaphilus, of Pallene,[354] was *epimeletes* of Delos c.80 B.C.[355] A very important family at Athens during the empire—four members held the archonship—[356] was that of Leonides son of Leonides, of Melite, archon in the year 13/2 B.C.[357] His ancestry may be traced to Athenagoras of Melite, who

[344] Graindor, *Chronologie*, pp. 27–28.

[345] Graindor, *Auguste*, p. 169; Graindor, *Chronologie*, pp. 27–28.

[346] Cicero, *Ad fam.* XVI, xxi, 5; cf. Graindor, *Auguste*, p. 169.

[347] Sundwall, *Untersuchungen*, I, 56–57; II, 21; Head, *Hist. Num.*, p. 386: Callimachus-Epicrates series. The two magistrates may have been cousins. For the stemma of the family, see NPA, p. 105.

[348] Sundwall, *Untersuchungen*, I, 57; Head, *Hist. Num.*, p. 385: Nicogenes-Callimachus series.   [349] PA, No. 8018.

[350] Sundwall, *Untersuchungen*, II, 22; J. Kirchner, in ZFN, XXI (1898), 100; Head, *Hist. Num.*, p. 386: Epigenes-Xenon series.

[351] Roussel, DCA, p. 105, where the stemma of the family is given.

[352] *Ibid.*, p. 116.   [353] *Ibid.*, p. 109.

[354] NPA, pp. 72–73, and 61, where the stemma of the family is given.

[355] Roussel, DCA, p. 115.

[356] See the stemma of the family for the time of Augustus and later, as given by P. Graindor, in BCH, XXXVIII (1914), 429.

[357] Dinsmoor, *Archons*, pp. 282–84, 287. Graindor, *Chronologie*, pp. 39–45, 47, would assign the archonship of Leonides to the year 12/11 B.C.

lived at the beginning of the second century B.C.[358] During the second century B.C. and the first part of the first century B.C. twelve members of this family were mentioned in Delian inscriptions.[359] One inscription informs us that the wife of Athenagoras (III) was honored with a statue at Delos by her two sons and her daughter.[360] Another important family was that of Pammenes son of Zenon, of Marathon, who is mentioned with great frequency in inscriptions of the time of Augustus.[361] This individual served the state in the following capacities: archon at some time between 35 B.C. and 10 B.C.,[362] monetary magistrate at some time after 30 B.C.,[363] agoranomus, hoplite general, priest of Apollo for life, and priest of Augustus and Roma.[364] The Zenon son of Zenon, of Marathon, who was archon in 14/3 B.C., was possibly a member of the same family.[365] Four members of this family were active at Delos during the last quarter of the second century B.C.[366]

We have already had occasion to observe that the dispatch of the sacred embassy called the Pythais to Delphi in the second century B.C. is to be taken as an indication of the prosperity of the city at that time. After the sending of the last great Pythais, in

---

[358] NPA, stemma facing p. 5.

[359] P. Roussel, in BCH, XXXII (1908), Nos. 11, 13, 217, 277–79, 366, 403, 437, 503, 543, 544.

[360] *Ibid.*, Nos. 279, 503, 544.

[361] See the texts and bibliography assembled by P. Graindor, in *Musée belge*, 1923, p. 295, No. 401. For the stemma of the family, see NPA, p. 85.

[362] Dinsmoor, *Archons*, p. 294.

[363] Sundwall, *Untersuchungen*, II, 23; Head, *Hist. Num.*, p. 386: Architimus-Pammenes series.

[364] Graindor, *Auguste*, p. 169; Graindor, *Chronologie*, p. 35.

[365] Graindor, *Auguste*, pp. 46–47.

[366] P. Roussel, in BCH, XXXII (1908), Nos. 93, 185, 273, 274. While no pretense of completeness is made in the treatment of these families, two additional instances may be cited. Polyclitus son of Alexander, of Phlya, was *epimeletes* of Delos in 99/8 B.C. (Roussel, DCA, p. 111). The date is determined by the archon Procles, for whom see Dinsmoor, *Archons*, pp. 280–81; Ferguson, *Cycles*, p. 32. Polyclitus' son Alexander held the same post in 54/3 B.C. (Roussel, DCA, p. 115). Possibly a son of the latter, Polyclitus son of Alexander, of Phlya, was archon at some time during the reign of Augustus, but this is uncertain (Graindor, *Chronologie*, pp. 38–39). For the stemma of the family, see Roussel, DCA, p. 111; NPA, p. 10. Aropus son of Leon, of Azenia, was *epimeletes* of Delos in 96/5 B.C. (?) (Roussel, DCA, p. 112). Members of the family were still prominent in the imperial period. Cf. PA, Nos. 2246, 2247.

97/6 B.C., the Athenians decided to send offerings annually in the future; and this practice was continued up to 88–86 B.C.[367] But after 97/6 B.C. the Pythais lost its splendor—no longer did the wealthy Athenian families who had provided the funds for the embassy spend lavish amounts upon it, and the number of participants grew smaller.[368] The last Pythais, which was a very modest one, was dispatched in 58/7 B.C.,[369] and with that embassy the Pythais was finally abandoned, to be replaced under the empire by the Dodecas.[370] The new embassy was dispatched to Delphi five times during the reign of Augustus,[371] the expense being met by the wealthiest members.[372] But it was considerably smaller and less costly than the Pythais of the period before 97/6 B.C.[373] Hence the Dodecas can by no means be interpreted as an indication of prosperity at Athens during the period of Augustus.

Especially from the time of Augustus onward Athens tended to live more and more upon its past. It was the cultural capital of Hellenism—and, consequently, of the world[374]—and upon this depended in large part whatever measure of well-being it possessed.

[367] Boethius, *Die Pythaïs*, pp. 97, 124–25, 141.   [368] *Ibid.*, p. 141.

[369] FDD, III, ii, No. 56; cf. Boethius, *Die Pythaïs*, p. 125.

[370] For the Dodecas, see Boethius, *Die Pythaïs*, pp. 20–21, 103–4, 125-26; Colin, *Le Culte d'Apollon pythien à Athènes*, pp. 146–47; Graindor, *Auguste*, pp. 139–47.

[371] First Dodecas: FDD, III, ii, Nos. 59 and 60; Graindor, *Auguste*, p. 140. It is dated by the archonship of Architimus at Athens and was, therefore, probably dispatched in 30/29 B.C. (cf. Dinsmoor, *Archons*, p, 293), rather than in 26/5 B.C. or 22/1 B.C., as maintained by Graindor (*Chronologie*, pp. 35–37; *Auguste*, p. 140). Second Dodecas: FDD, III, ii, No. 61; cf. Graindor, *Auguste*, p. 140. It is dated by the archonship of Apolexis at Athens and was, therefore, probably dispatched in 20/19 B.C. (cf. Dinsmoor, *Archons*, p. 293). Graindor (*Chronologie*, pp. 37–38; *Auguste*, p. 140) assigns the archonship of Apolexis to some year between 25/4 B.C. and 18/7 B.C., preferably nearer the latter date. Third Dodecas: FDD, III, ii, No. 62. It is dated by the archonship of Theophilus at Athens and was, therefore, dispatched in 12/1 B.C. (cf. Dinsmoor, *Archons*, p. 293). Graindor (*Chronologie*, pp. 29–45, 48; *Auguste*, p. 140) assigns the archonship of Theophilus to 11/10 B.C. Fourth Dodecas: FDD, III, ii, No. 63. It is dated by the archonship of Apolexis, son of Philocrates, whose year fell between 8/7 B.C. and 1 B.C, (Graindor, *Chronologie*, p. 51; Graindor, *Auguste*, p. 140). Fifth Dodecas: FDD, III, ii, No. 64. It is dated by the archonship of Nicostratus, whose year falls at about the beginning of our era (Graindor, *Chronologie*, p. 52; Graindor, *Auguste*, p. 140).

[372] Graindor, *Auguste*, p. 145.

[373] Boethius, *Die Pythaïs*, pp. 20, 103, 125–26; Graindor, *Auguste*, pp. 142–45.

[374] Cf. Graindor, *Auguste*, p. v.

It was this reputation[375] that attracted to its doors the numerous students, tourists, and wealthy patrons upon whose expenditures the economic life of Athens was so largely based. The city's coinage commemorated its famous festivals and works of art, its religious and artistic glories, its monuments, its past history and legends.[376] And the conscious archaism in its art and architecture[377]—even in its inscriptions[378]—allowed neither the Athenians themselves nor foreign visitors to lose sight of the cultural heritage of the city.

[375] Cf. Cicero, *De fin.* V, i, 1.

[376] J. P. Shear, in *Hesperia*, V (1936), 295–96,

[377] For the archaism to be observed in the Temple of Roma and Augustus, and in the Market of Caesar and Augustus, see Graindor, *Auguste*, pp. 183–84.

[378] Archaizing inscriptions seem to have come into fashion at the time of Augustus; Graindor, *Album*, p. 14, No. 7; Graindor, *Hérode*, p. 95, note 5.

CHAPTER V

ATHENS UNDER THE EMPERORS:

14-200 A.D.

IN THE time of Augustus Greece experienced a remarkable recovery from the exactions and the devastation occasioned by the civil wars of the first century B.C. But our sources for the succeeding years, between Tiberius and Trajan, indicate the prevalence of poverty throughout the country.[1] The emperor Nero stated at Corinth, upon the occasion of his bestowal of "freedom" upon the Greeks, that he regretted that he could not have bestowed this boon upon them at a more prosperous period of their history.[2] Plutarch was more specific when he wrote[3] that in his time the whole of Greece could hardly put in the field as many as three thousand men, which had been the number sent to Plataea by the Megarians to aid in the repulse of the Persians. Seneca went still further when he implied, through a rhetorical question, that the most famous cities of Greece had fallen into utter decay by his time.[4] While some allowance must be made for rhetorical exaggeration in these statements,[5] the fact remains that Greece was far from prosperous in the years between the reign of Augustus and that of Hadrian. Special factors peculiar to Greece were responsible in large part for the economic plight of the country, but they were undoubtedly supplemented by unfavorable factors in the economic condition of the empire at large. The maintenance of the security of the empire from outside attack had been a problem even at the time of Augustus. Wars were undertaken in various quarters to subdue the threats of menacing enemies. Toward the end of the first century

---

[1] Rostovtzeff, *Roman Empire*, pp. 234–35, 561–62, note 96.
[2] ILS, 8794.   [3] *De defectu orac.* 8.   [4] *Epist.* XIV, iii (xci), 10.
[5] Compare the beginning of chap. iv.

A.D., under Domitian, energetic campaigns were again undertaken, but with little success, the chief result being the depletion of the state treasury. Trajan's campaigns were, however, more fortunate. The Dacians were subdued in the course of two wars, and later campaigns brought security to the southern and southeastern frontiers. But the huge outlay involved in the prosecution of these wars was so great as to undermine the financial structure of the empire; and the economic life of the provinces fell to a low ebb in spite of Trajan's attempts to ameliorate the situation.[6]

Concerning the economic situation at Athens during the years between the death of Augustus and the accession of Hadrian there is little direct literary testimony available to us. A single passage, of somewhat uncertain import, may be cited. In an oration written at some time between 79 A.D. and 82 A.D. Dio Chrysostomus states that Athens was at the end of its resources.[7] But in interpreting this passage we must make due allowance for the fact that in this oration, the famous Ῥοδιακός, Dio is belittling Athens to make Rhodes more glorious.[8] However, if the phrase in question was meant to imply that the state treasury was involved in financial difficulties, Dio probably spoke the truth,[9] for in the time of T. Pomponius Atticus, in the first century B.C., the Athenians had been unusually improvident in matters of finance[10] and had found it necessary to sell the island of Salamis;[11] and in the second century

[6] Rostovtzeff, *Roman Empire*, pp. 307–9.

[7] XXXI, 123. Von Arnim, *Dio von Prusa*, p. 218, suggests the date set forth in the text. L. Lemarchand, *Dion de Prusa: les oeuvres d'avant l'exil* (Paris, 1926), p. 84, argues that the oration was originally composed in 70–71 A.D., but that Dio wrote a revised version of it eight to ten years later, toward the end of the reign of Vespasian.

[8] Although the reason for Dio's hostility toward Athens is not definitely known, Graindor, *Tibère*, pp. 55–56, suggests the following plausible explanation. On the occasion of a visit to Athens, the sophist had not been lionized as he thought he deserved. He was especially incensed with the Athenians and reproached them, because, while they did not erect a statue in his honor, they had bestowed the title of "Olympian" upon an unknown Phoenician (see Dio Chrysostomus, XXXI, 116). However, by the time of a later visit c.100 A.D., when he delivered the oration entitled Ἐν Ἀθήναις περὶ φυγῆς (XIII), the sophist had become reconciled to Athens. For the date, see Von Arnim, *Dio von Prusa*, pp. 222, 332, 334.

[9] This position is maintained by Graindor, *Tibère*, pp. 131–33, and is to be preferred to that of Wachsmuth, *Die Stadt Athen*, I, 676, who contends that Dio is guilty of gross exaggeration.

[10] Cornelius Nepos, XXV, ii, 4.　　　[11] See chap. iv, note 33.

A.D., apparently under similar circumstances, they considered selling various other islands then under their control.[12] However this lone item of direct testimony is to be interpreted, the bulk of the literary and archaeological information at our disposal indicates that Athens shared in the vicissitudes of the remainder of Greece between the reigns of Tiberius and Trajan, and—to put it briefly— was largely a university city and a center where artists were active in the production of works that harked back to the greater days of the past. But let us now look at this evidence more closely.

The depletion of Athens' stock of works of art began in the first part of the first century B.C.—if not before—when the Athenians, attracted by the prospect of lucrative profits, began to sell numerous statues that had been produced in earlier times.[13] The process of depletion was soon accelerated by the series of plunderings which began with Sulla. Moreover, in the first century A.D. Caligula, probably, and Nero, certainly, did not spare the city. From Dio Cassius[14] and from Pausanias[15] we learn that Caligula removed works of art from various Greek cities. Neither writer specifically mentions Athens as having suffered in this respect, but, inasmuch as Dio informs us that Claudius returned the statues which Caligula had stolen from the Greeks, and since a number of statues are known from dedicatory inscriptions to have been restored to Athens by Claudius,[16] it is reasonable to assume that works of art were stolen from Athens by Caligula.[17] Tacitus tells us that later in the century, in 64 A.D., Secundus Carrinas and Nero's freedman Acratus, acting under Nero's orders, carried off not only the offerings in the temples of Achaea and Asia but even the images of the gods themselves. Since he says also that Pergamum resisted Acratus' thievery, it would seem likely that Carrinas was sent to Greece.[18] This probability seems to be confirmed by the finding, at Athens, of a dedicatory inscription in honor of the *archon eponymus* C. Carrinas, son of Gaius, in whom Lolling, the first editor of the inscription, would see Nero's envoy.[19] Lolling's suggestion that the

---

[12] Philostratus, *Vit. soph.* 527.   [13] See chap. iii, including note 299.   [14] LX, vi, 8.
[15] IX, xxvii, 3. Pausanias mentions specifically the famous Eros of Praxiteles.
[16] IG, II–III², 5173–79.   [17] Thus Graindor, *Tibère*, pp. 9–10.
[18] Tacitus, *Ann.* XV, xlv; XVI, xxiii, 1.
[19] IG, II–III², 4188; H. G. Lolling, in AΔ, 1891, p. 62; cf. Graindor, *Chronologie*, pp. 91–92.

Athenians made Carrinas archon because he spared the city's works of art is, however, not to be accepted, for Dio Chrysostomus informs us[20] that Nero had most of the statues on the Acropolis carried away. Dio's statement undoubtedly exaggerates the amount of plundering that was done, but the fact remains that some statues were carried away. It would have been too dangerous for Carrinas to disobey the emperor. It is, therefore, most likely that the Athenians made Carrinas archon in the hope that the flattery implicit in the act might make him disposed to carry away fewer works of art than he might otherwise have done.[21] Possibly among the works of art removed to Rome at this time was Myron's famous cow, which was one of the famous masterpieces displayed on the Acropolis.[22] The statue was still in Athens at the time of Cicero,[23] but it is not mentioned by Pausanias in his account of the Acropolis. That it was actually removed to Rome we learn from a later writer, Procopius.[24] In any event, it seems quite definite that the statue was carried away at some date between the time of Cicero and that of Pausanias. In spite, however, of the plundering of works of art which had continued for more than a century and a half, Pliny can report that the proconsul Mucianus related that, even in his time, there were three thousand statues at Rhodes; Pliny then goes on to cite the current belief that there were still no fewer statues at Athens, Olympia, and Delphi.[25]

After the death of Augustus little of importance in the way of building activity was carried on at Athens until the time of Hadrian. Moreover, in those instances where information is available to us it was the Roman emperor, or, at times, some individual without official capacity, who bore the expense of erecting new buildings or of carrying out projects of reconstruction. It is, therefore, reasonable to conclude that, as in the two preceding centuries, building activity was left almost entirely to private initiative. During the reign of Claudius, and possibly at the expense of the emperor, the flight of steps ascending to the Propylaea was erected.[26] Apparently

[20] XXXI, 148.   [21] Cf. Graindor, *Tibère*, p. 15.
[22] Tzetzes, *Chil.* VIII, 371–75; cf. Wachsmuth, *Die Stadt Athen*, I, 681, note 2.
[23] Cicero, *In Verr.* IV, lx, 135.   [24] *Bell. Goth.* VIII, xxi, 14.
[25] Pliny, NH XXXIV, vii, 36.
[26] Graindor, in BCH, XXXVIII (1914), 272–81; Graindor, *Tibère*, 1 p. 160–63; W. B. Dinsmoor, in AJA, XXXIII (1929), 101–2.

in conjunction with this project a monumental stairway was built on the northern slope of the Acropolis and extended by a ramp, from a point near the Clepsydra, to the west, where it joined the steps at the entrance to the Acropolis.[27] Also during the first half of the century a flight of steps was built from the market to the top of Theseum hill.[28] Later in the century the skene of the Theater of Dionysus was rebuilt at the expense of an Athenian who was, at the moment, hoplite general for the seventh time—his name is, unfortunately, not preserved. The skene was dedicated to Dionysus Eleutherius and to Nero.[29] Also during the second half of the century a screen wall was built in the square located to the south of the Bouleuterion,[30] and a small circular temple was built in the part of the Agora to which the American excavators have assigned the label of Section I I.[31] And at an undetermined date within the first century the Clepsydra was thoroughly remodeled.[32] Between 100 A.D. and 102 A.D. T. Flavius Pantaenus, "the priest of the wise Muses," later archon at Athens,[33] dedicated to Athena Polias and to Trajan a library with books, decorations, peristyle, and outer stoae, all given at his own expense.[34] At some time near the beginning of the second century A.D. Demetrius son of Antiochus, of Sphettus, paved, at his own expense, the propylaeum of the Temple

[27] T. L. Shear, in *Hesperia*, VII (1938), 333–34.

[28] H. A. Thompson, in *Hesperia*, VI (1937), 221–22. In "early Roman times" a great amount of reconstruction was undertaken in the section of the city immediately to the north of the Acropolis, which has been designated Section Eta Eta by the American excavators of the Agora (T. L. Shear, in *Hesperia*, VI [1937], 359).

[29] IG, II–III², 3182; Dörpfeld and Reisch, *Das griechische Theater*, pp. 82–92; Bieber, *Denkmäler*, p. 18; Bieber, *History of the Greek and Roman Theater*, pp. 385–87; F. Versakis, in JDAI, XXIV (1909), 194–99; Bulle, *Untersuchungen*, pp. 17–20. For the date (not before 66 A.D.), see Graindor, *Tibère*, p. 164.

[30] H. A. Thompson, in *Hesperia*, VI (1937), 168–69.

[31] T. L. Shear, in *Hesperia*, VIII (1939), 220; VII (1938), 329.

[32] T. L. Shear, in *Hesperia*, VIII (1939), 225.

[33] IG, II–III², 2017; cf. Graindor, *Chronologie*, p. 109. His archonship is to be dated soon after 102 A.D.

[34] For the dedicatory inscription of the library, see T. L. Shear, in *Hesperia*, IV (1935), 330–32. The library, which has now been found immediately south of the Stoa of Attalus (*ibid.*, IX [1940], 294–95), was dedicated also in the name of Pantaenus' children, Flavius Menandrus and Flavia Secundilla. For the inscription which contains the library regulations, see *ibid.*, V (1936), 42.

of Asclepius.[35] Finally, during the reign of Trajan, at some time between 114 A.D. and 116 A.D., the elaborate funereal monument of C. Julius Antiochus Philopappus, son of Epiphanes, the deposed ruler of Commagene, was erected on the summit of the Hill of the Muses.[36]

One of the most important factors in Athenian life during the first century A.D. was the city's schools. In a passage in his life of Apollonius of Tyana[37] which applies to the period of Domitian, Philostratus tells us that youths came from all the world to pursue their studies at Athens. Ample confirmation of this statement is forthcoming from the ephebic lists, if, of course, due allowance is made for the hyperbole. The number of foreigners registered in the ephebia during the latter part of the first and the first part of the second centuries A.D. was as follows (for the sake of comparison, the number of Athenians registered in the various years is added):[38]

Date (A.D.)	Foreigners	Athenians	Source (in IG, II–III²)
84/5–92/3	151 (Milesians)[a]	80	1996
97/8–110/1	12 +	60	2017
96–117	47 (incomplete)	52	2018
111/2	79 (Milesians)	21	2024
115/6	48 (Milesians)	4	2026

[a] For the significance of the term "Milesian," see below in this chapter, including notes 224–27.

Without the expenditures of these students the lot of Athenian businessmen and innkeepers would have been considerably poorer. Athenians also derived a certain amount of revenue from the expenditures of visitors who were attracted by the city's glorious past. Although the number of Roman visitors between the time of Tiberius and that of Trajan was much smaller than in the time of Augustus—the attested numbers being respectively thirty-six and

[35] IG, II–III², 3187. For the date, see Graindor, Tibère, p. 164.

[36] IG, II–III², 3451; CIL, III, 552; Judeich, Topographie, pp. 388–89; Graindor, Tibère, pp. 166–69. For the identity and career of Philopappus, see the stemma given by Honigmann, in RE, Supplementband IV, 986; cf. Graindor, Tibère, pp. 51–52; Graindor, Chronologie, pp. 95–100.

[37] VIII, 15; cf. Juvenal, Sat. XV, 110.

[38] Graindor (in BCH, LI [1927], 306, No. 77; cf. Tibère, pp. 87–88) calls attention to the striking fact that in one ephebic inscription all the foreigners who were registered had received Athenian citizenship during the period of their membership, and suggests that they paid for the honor.

twenty-five[39]—those Romans who did come were very important individuals. After a prosopographical study of them, Graindor noted the following general types: provincial governors, sons of governors or of consuls, an individual destined to become a consul, and a praetor-designate. Also to be noted among the renowned visitors to the city are various well-known Greeks and numerous individuals of royal status. Many of these individuals undoubtedly lavished gifts of various kinds upon the city, in return, of course, for some honor bestowed upon them by the Athenians. The Mysteries at Eleusis also continued to attract many visitors. As Philostratus informs us,[40] when the Mysteries were held, Athens was the most populous city in Greece. The prestige of the Mysteries during the first century A.D. is aptly shown by the fact that the emperor Claudius attempted to transfer the ceremonies from Attica to Rome.[41]

Some note should be taken of the dispatch of the Dodecas to Delphi in the first century A.D. The embassy seems to have been omitted altogether between the time of Tiberius and that of Titus. Then, during the reign of Domitian, the last two Dodecades were sent forth,[42] one at some time between 84/5 A.D. and 92/3 A.D., the other at some time between 86/7 A.D. and 95/6 A.D. But these Dodecades are not at all to be compared with the brilliant Pythaids of the second century B.C.;[43] both the number of participants and the financial outlay involved were considerably smaller—a forceful indication of the striking decline of the prosperity of the city.

The measures undertaken by Trajan to remedy the distressing economic conditions in the provinces were, we have already seen, not at all effective. And it was for the purpose of rectifying this situation that Hadrian, when he came to the throne, lightened the tax burden of the provinces, bestowed generous gifts upon pro-

[39] The chance discovery of inscriptions is probably responsible for these proportions. Graindor, *Tibère*, p. 29; on pp. 30–45, 47–58, he gives lists of individual visitors, with citations.

[40] *Vit. Apoll.* IV, 17.

[41] Suetonius, *Claud.* 25. For the Mysteries between the time of Tiberius and that of Trajan, see Graindor, *Tibère*, pp. 101–5.

[42] FDD, III, ii, Nos. 65, 66; cf. the corrections by Graindor, in RA, VI (1917), 18. For the dates, see Graindor, *Chronologie*, pp. 93–95, 101–2.

[43] For the Dodecas in the first century A. D., see Boethius, *Die Pythaïs*, p. 126.

vincial cities, and attempted in various ways to improve the condition of the poor.[44] The measures undertaken by Hadrian in Greece exercised such widespread and beneficial effects that the Greeks issued a series of bronze coins on which the title of *Restitutor Achaiae* was given to the emperor.[45] Pausanias goes so far as to state[46] that the Megarians were the only people in Greece whom not even Hadrian could make prosperous. Moreover, as his biographer informs us,[47] the emperor was so imbued with Greek culture as to be given the surname *Graeculus*. Not only did he master Attic speech, but he also studied carefully the methods and accomplishments of the Athenians in music and singing, and in medicine, geometry, painting, and sculpture.[48] Even before he became emperor, Hadrian had visited Athens and had been made *archon eponymus*.[49] After he had ascended the throne, he visited the city three times, in 124/5 A.D., 128/9 A.D., and 131/2 A.D., each visit being the occasion for bestowing large and elaborate gifts of various sorts upon the Athenians.[50] Pausanias writes[51] very aptly that Athens, which had been sorely treated by Sulla, flourished [ἤνθησαν] again when Hadrian was emperor. The enormous building program which the emperor carried out in the city provided employment for artists, architects, stonecutters, and laborers of all sorts and set in action economic forces which redounded to the benefit of a large part of the population. Even foreign trade received a stimulus as a result of the emperor's efforts. To cite a few instances, marble, from Phrygia and from Carystus in Euboea, and alabaster were imported for use in the Library of Hadrian,[52] and

[44] For the economic policy of Hadrian, see Rostovtzeff, *Roman Empire*, pp. 315–25; Frank, "Rome and Italy of the Empire," pp. 63–64, 70–74.

[45] Mattingly and Sydenham, *Roman Imperial Coinage*, II, 377, No. 321; 463, Nos. 938–39.   [46] I, xxxvi, 3.   [47] Spartianus, *Vit. Hadr.* i, 5.

[48] *Epit. de Caes.* (Aurelius Victor [?]; ed. Pichlmayr, Teubner, 1911) xiv, 2.

[49] Graindor, *Chronologie*, pp. 116–22. The date of his archonship was 111/2 A.D.

[50] For a thorough discussion, with full bibliography, of the dates and events connected with these visits, see Graindor, *Hadrien*, pp. 1–58.   [51] I, xx, 7.

[52] For the alabaster and the Phrygian marble, see Pausanias, I, xviii, 9 (ed. Hitzig and Bluemner). G. Nikolaidis, in AE, 1888, pp. 60, 62, asserts that some of these materials have been found in the course of excavation of the library. Graindor, *Hadrien*, p. 231, note 3, and p. 233, contends that no fragments of Phrygian marble that were certainly used in the columns have been found. For the marble from Carystus which was employed in some of the columns in the library, see *ibid.*, pp. 214, 232.

marble was brought from Libya to construct the hundred columns
that adorned the gymnasium built by the emperor.[53] The prosperity
of Athens at this time has been compared with that at the time of
Pericles[54]—but not too aptly, for many of the benefactions of
Hadrian evidence in themselves the fundamentally insecure foundations of the city's life.

It was in line with his general policy of public works that Hadrian
expended large sums of money upon the buildings of Athens. From
Pausanias[55] we learn that the emperor built and presented to the
Athenians a temple of Hera, a temple of Panhellenian Zeus, a
library, a gymnasium, and a pantheon. Of these structures only the
library has survived to the present day.[56] His most important undertaking in the way of buildings was the completion of the great
temple of the Olympian Zeus, work on which had been begun by
the Pisistratids in the latter part of the sixth century B.C. and had
been continued in the second century B.C. by Antiochus IV Epiphanes (176–165 B.C.), who died before the work could be finished.[57]
Buildings that had fallen into disrepair, or that had been destroyed
and not reconstructed, also received the emperor's attention. Thus,
he rebuilt the Pompeum, which had been destroyed by Sulla in
86 B.C.;[58] and he may also have undertaken the reconstruction of

[53] Fausanias, I, xviii, 9.   [54] By Gurlitt, *Über Pausanias*, p. 207.

[55] I, xviii, 9: κατασκευάσατο μὲν καὶ ἄλλα 'Αθηναίοις, ναὸν ''Ηρας καὶ Διὸς
Πανελληνίου καὶ θεοῖς τοῖς πᾶσιν ἱερὸν κοινόν, τὰ δὲ ἐπιφανέστατα ἑκατόν εἰσι
κίονες Φρυγίου λίθου . . . . . καὶ γυμνάσιόν ἐστιν ἐπώνυμον 'Αδριανοῦ. Wachsmuth, *Die Stadt Athen*, I, 690, note 1, interprets the passage as meaning that the
emperor had built a common temple of Hera and Zeus Panhellenius; see also W. H.
S. Jones in the Loeb Library edition. Frazer, *Pausanias*, translates the apposite
passage as follows: "a temple of Hera and [another] of Panhellenian Zeus." Frazer's
interpretation is followed by Graindor, *Hadrien*, p. 45, note 1. For the library, see
also Aristeides, XIII (ed. Dindorf, I, 306); St. Jerome's revision of Eusebius'
Chronicon, Year of Abraham 2148 (=132 A.D.; Olymp. 227, ed. Helm, p. 200);
George Syncellus, 349D.

[56] M. Sisson, "The Stoa of Hadrian at Athens," *Papers of the British School at
Rome*, XI (1929), 50–72; Graindor, *Hadrien*, pp. 230–45; Judeich, *Topographie*,
pp. 375–78, where Sisson's article is not cited.

[57] Pausanias, I, xviii, 6; Dio Cassius, LXIX, xvi, 1; Spartianus, *Vit. Hadr.*
xiii, 6; Phlegon of Tralles, Book XV, frag. 19 (in Jacoby, *Fragmente*, II, 166, No.
19); Stephanus Byzantius, *s.v.* 'Ολυμπιεῖον; Judeich, *Topographie*, pp. 101, 382–
84; Graindor, *Hadrien*, pp. 40, 218–25.

[58] K. Kübler, in AM, LIII (1928), 169, 179; Judeich, *Topographie*, pp. 100, 361;
Graindor, *Hadrien*, pp. 45, 248–50. There is no certainty that Hadrian restored

the Diogeneum.[59] Not content with erecting new buildings and restoring old ones, Hadrian laid out a new quarter of the city—variously called Hadrianopolis or New Athens.[60] This quarter,[61] which had, apparently, been enclosed within the walls of the city since the time of Themistocles,[62] thereupon developed rapidly into an attractive residential district with ornate villas and elaborate bathing establishments. Turning his attention to another quarter of the city, the emperor enlarged and remodeled the Pnyx, and the Assembly resumed its former practice of meeting there.[63] Because of his interest in the Eleusinian Mysteries, he built a bridge over the Cephisus,[64] as well as stone dikes to hold back the flood waters of the river,[65] in order that access to Eleusis at the time of the festivals would be assured. Finally, near the end of his reign, he began to build an aqueduct which was to carry water to the city from the southern slope of Pentelicon, but the project was not completed until the time of Antoninus Pius.[66]

the Temple of the Charites. The possibility is based entirely upon the questionable restoration of ἀ[έτωμα] in IG, II–III², 4475. Cf. Graindor, *Hadrien*, p. 144, note 2, and p. 225.

[59] This is problematical, depending upon the restoration of IG, II–III², 1102, by Graindor, in BCH, XXXVIII (1914), 392–96; cf. Graindor, in *Musée belge*, XXVI (1922), 180, note 6; Graindor, *Hadrien*, p. 44, note 4.

[60] Hadrianopolis: Spartianus, *Vit. Hadr.* xx, 4; New Athens: CIL, III, 549; cf. Stephanus Byzantius, *s.v.* Ὀλυμπιεῖον; Schol. Aristeides, I (ed. Dindorf, III, 201); IG, II–III², 5185.

[61] Graindor, *Hadrien*, pp. 33–35, 226–28; Judeich, *Topographie*, 101, 163–64, 177, 381. Cf. note 60, above.

[62] The generally accepted assumption (cf. Judeich, *Topographie*, pp. 163–64) that Hadrian built the wall which enclosed this part of the city is to be rejected. Hadrian seems not to have been responsible for building any part of the walls of Athens; see R. L. Scranton, in AJA, XLII (1938), 536; H. A. Thompson, in *Hesperia*, V (1936), 198.

[63] K. Kourouniotes and H. A. Thompson, in *Hesperia*, I (1932), 139–92, 217; cf. Lucian, *Jup. trag.* 11.

[64] St. Jerome's revision of Eusebius' *Chronicon*, Year of Abraham 2139 (= 123 A.D.; ed. Helm, p. 198); Armenian version of Eusebius' *Chronicon*, Fifth Year of Hadrian (translated by J. Karst, Leipzig, 1911); Dionysius Telmaharensis, 63; George Syncellus, 349A; cf. Graindor, *Hadrien*, pp. 35–36.

[65] D. Philios, in AE, 1892, p. 106; A. Milchhoefer, *Karten von Attika*, Erläutender Text (Berlin, 1881–1900), VII–VIII, 24; Curtius and Kaupert, *Karten von Attika*, Bl. XXVI; Frazer, *Pausanias*, II, 502; Graindor, *Hadrien*, pp. 250–51. The bridge over the Cephisus as it exists today seems not to date from the period of Hadrian; so Kourouniotes, the director of the excavations at Eleusis, informed Graindor.

[66] CIL, III, 549 (= ILS, 337); cf. Judeich, *Topographie*, pp. 203–4.

Aside from the benefactions of the emperor, few structures seem to have been erected or restored at Athens during the reign of Hadrian.[67] Minor changes were made in the Theater of Dionysus at Athens.[68] One private benefactor is attested, Aemilius Atticus of Melite. This Athenian citizen erected the columns, façade, and latticed gates of a temple, apparently of Isis, and a statue of Aphrodite in the temple.[69] The city itself, in continuance of the trend which had begun in Hellenistic times, left the erection of new buildings and monuments and the restoration of old ones to the initiative of the emperor, of foreigners, and of private citizens. To this rule a single possible exception may be noted. The so-called Arch of Hadrian bears on its western face the inscription: "This is the Athens of Theseus, the former city"; on its east face: "This is the city of Hadrian, and not of Theseus."[70] Inasmuch as Hadrian's name never appeared on monuments which he had himself erected,[71] it is reasonable to suppose that the Athenians themselves erected the arch.[72]

Hadrian's gifts to the Athenians did not end with the benefactions which we have already observed. There is evidence to show that the emperor created two endowments which were intended to maintain certain important public functions in years when no wealthy citizens were available to support them. One of these foundations had for its purpose the maintenance of the gymnasiarchy;[73] the other was to support the *agonothesia* of the Panathe-

---

[67] For the buildings of Athens in the time of Hadrian, see the detailed account of Graindor, *Hadrien*, pp. 214–52.

[68] Judeich, *Topographie*, p. 313; Graindor, *Hadrien*, pp. 245–46; Fiechter, *Dionysos-theater*, pp. III, 81–82.

[69] IG, II–III², 4771; cf. Graindor, *Hadrien*, pp. 160–62. Two additional buildings erected in the second century A.D., but not to be certainly attributed to the period of Hadrian, may be mentioned. "Early in the century" a large private house, which was probably intended for the use of the priest of Hephaestus, was erected west of the precinct of the god (D. B. Thompson, in *Hesperia*, VI [1937], 400). At an undetermined time during the second century a small circular building was erected —we do not know its purpose—west of the north end of the Stoa of Attalus (T. L. Shear, in *Hesperia*, VI [1937], 354–56).

[70] IG, II–III², 5185. For the arch, see Judeich, *Topographie*, pp. 381–82.

[71] Spartianus, *Vit. Hadr.* xx, 4.

[72] This is the suggestion of Graindor, *Hadrien*, p. 229.

[73] This is the deduction drawn by Graindor (in BCH, XXXVIII [1914], 396–98; also, *Hadrien*, pp. 45–47) from the following facts. In a dedication at Eleusis L.

naea.[74] Moreover, we learn from Dio Cassius[75] that during his third visit to the city the emperor gave the Athenians large sums of money, yearly distributions of grain, and the entire island of Cephallenia. Although Dio does not specifically state the purpose for which the money was given, it has been suggested that he was referring to the large sum which the emperor may have given to the ephebes of the Diogeneum.[76] As regards the gift of Cephallenia, the historian's statement is to be accepted only with some reserve. Certainly Pale in Cephallenia was not included in the gift, for in an inscription which seems to have been engraved in 131/2 A.D. there is recorded a dedication to Hadrian in the Olympieum by Pale, which characterizes itself as a "free and autonomous city."[77] The most likely conclusion seems, therefore, to be, not that the island was deprived of its independence, but merely that certain revenues from the island were handed over to Athens by the emperor.[78] The gifts of 131/2 A.D. are, of themselves, forceful indications of the limited distribution of wealth at Athens and of the unsound condition of the city's finances. Indeed, the city treasury was so poor that the emperor was compelled to take measures for its rehabilitation by sending P. Pactumius Clemens to Athens in

Memmius is given the title ἐπιμελητὴς γυμνασιαρχίας θεοῦ Ἁδριανοῦ (IG, II–III², 3620). The same title is probably to be restored in two additional inscriptions, one of 209 A.D. (IG, II–III², 1077), the other of the middle of the second century A.D. (IG, II–III², 2888). On the other hand, during the reign of Hadrian and the latter part of the second century A.D. a number of Athenians assumed the title γυμνασιαρχήσας ἐκ τῶν ἰδίων (or οἴκοθεν), which would indicate that they assumed themselves the expense of the liturgy in question. For the sense of οἴκοθεν = ἐκ τῶν ἰδίων, see Wilhelm, Beiträge, pp. 101–2. The contrast between these titles that is implicit in the title of epimeletes would seem to indicate that the gymnasiarchy had been endowed by Hadrian.

[74] This conclusion is to be drawn from an inscription which records the fact that T. Flavius Leosthenes served as agonothetes of the Panathenaea, ἀποδειχ[θέν]τος ὑπὸ θεοῦ Ἁδριανοῦ, while his son fulfilled the same liturgy at his own expense; see IG, II–III², 869; cf. Graindor, in BCH, XXXVIII (1914), 398-401; Graindor, Hadrien, pp. 47–49.   [75] LXIX, xvi, 2.

[76] IG, II–III², 1102; cf. Graindor, Hadrien, p. 44, note 4, and p. 54, whose interpration is highly problematical.   [77] IG, II–III², 3301.

[78] Cf. Larsen, "Roman Greece," p. 475, where the conclusion set forth in the text is described as "probable." Graindor (Hadrien, p. 55; cf. Auguste, p. 10) takes the position that the island was given to Athens outright, with the exception of Pale. But on another page (Hadrien, p. 201) he seems to maintain that merely the revenues from the island were included in the gift.

the capacity of *corrector*.[79] Moreover, the fact that there was a large urban proletariat at Athens would seem to be reflected by Hadrian's action in exhibiting a *venatio* of one thousand beats in the Panathenaic Stadium.[80]

In consonance with his general social policy of improving the condition of the poor,[81] Hadrian undertook to promulgate at Athens various laws which are very significant in connection with the economic and social life of the community. Of these the most important is the famous law which provides for the sale to the state of a specified proportion of the yearly yield of olive oil. An inscription which is now extant[82] sets forth the provisions of this law, which is, apparently, an extract from the constitution Hadrian gave to Athens at the time of his first visit as emperor, in 124/5 A.D.[83] The provisions of the law are as follows. Cultivators of oil must deliver one third of their crop to the state, unless they are owners of portions of the lands of Hipparchus which were confiscated by the Fiscus, in which event they are required to deliver only one eighth (ll. 2–6). The deliveries, which are to be made in partial payments, at the beginning of the harvest, in proportion to the amount of the entire harvest, must be turned over to the special state officials [ἐλεῶναι] who are charged with the purchase of the oil (ll. 6–11).[84] Cultivators are to make a declaration of the

---

[79] CIL, VIII, 7059 (=ILS, 1067); PIR, III, p. 5, No. 25; cf. A. von Premerstein, in RE, IV, 1646; Graindor, *Hadrien*, pp. 112–13. I have been unable to consult the work of Groag cited in chap. iv, note 318, above.

[80] Spartianus, *Vit. Hadr.* xix, 2–4.   [81] Rostovtzeff, *Roman Empire*, p. 323.

[82] IG, II–III², 1100, edited by J. Kirchner; IG, III, 38, edited by W. Dittenberger; CIG, 355, edited by A. Boeckh. Cf. the commentary by Roberts and Gardner, *Greek Epigraphy*, Part II, 245–48, No. 93; the discussions by Graindor, *Hadrien*, pp. 74–79; and Abbott and Johnson, *Municipal Administration*, pp. 411–13, No. 90.

[83] Graindor, *Hadrien*, p. 78, plausibly suggests that the heading of the inscription should be expanded as follows: κε(φάλαιον) νό(μων) θε(ιοτάτου) 'Αδριανοῦ. Thus, the oil law is a law extracted from Hadrian's constitution and is, therefore, to be dated in 124/5 A.D. (*ibid.*, pp. 78–79). A. Wilhelm, in JOAI, II (1899), 275, calls attention to the fact that the letter-forms are similar to those employed in the letter of Plotina, which is dated 121 A.D.

[84] The passage, as restored by Boeckh and Kirchner, reads as follows:

6   καταφε-
ρέτωσαν δὲ ἅμα τῷ ἄρξασθαι συνκο-
[μιδῆς κ]ατὰ μέρος, πρὸς λόγον το[ῦ]
[συγκομιζ]ομένου, τοῖς ἐλεώναι[s]

amount of their crop, possibly—a lacuna in the inscription at this point makes absolute certainty impossible—to the Boule and the herald of the Boule and the Demos (ll. 11–15).[85] The declaration, which is to be signed and made under oath, must also make known the name of the slave or freedman who produced the oil (ll. 15–18), and must state whether it is the owner of the land, or the cultivator, or the purchaser who is selling the oil to the state (ll. 18–20). The man who sells oil on the export market must declare the

---

10 [οἵτινες ἀεὶ] προνοοῦσιν τῆ[ς]
    [δημοσίας χρεία]ς

The lacuna in l. 8 is indicated in IG, III, 38, as being of the same length as that in l. 9. Consequently, Boeckh's restoration of [συγκομιζ]ομένου in l. 9 is too long for the space it occupies. Graindor, *Hadrien*, p. 76, restores instead [ὀφειλ]ομένου, and interprets the passage as meaning that at the beginning of the harvest a beginning of deliveries to the oil buyers was to be made, in proportion to the needs of the state. Actually, later in the text, in ll. 59–67, provision is made that cultivators may keep all or part of their crop in case the harvest is so abundant as to supply readily the needs of the state. In a review of Graindor's *Hadrien* C. B. Welles (in AJA, XXXIX [1935], 423–25, especially p. 425) has pointed out that the restoration of [ὀφειλ]ομένου is one letter too short for the space available and that, since the question of excess production is taken up at the end of the inscription, it was probably not considered at the beginning. His interpretation seems very reasonable, and has been adopted in the text above. The sense is that if the first pressing should, for example, yield one fifth of the estimated total harvest, the farmer should pay to the state what would amount to one fifth of his total obligation; and this was to be done before the entire harvest had been collected.

    [85] This passage was restored by Dittenberger as follows:

11   ἀπογραφέσθω[σαν δὲ]
. .[v.8] . τῆς] συνκομιδῆς πρὸ-
[ς τοὺς ταμίας κα]ὶ τὸν κήρυκα δύο
. . . . .[v.12]. . . . . . ἰδόντες ὑπογρα-
15 φέν.

Kirchner reads ὑπογραφήν in ll. 14–15. Boeckh restored in ll. 12–13: πρὸ[ς τοὺς ἀργυροταμίας κα]ὶ τὸν κήρυκα. But this reconstruction is too long for the space available. Graindor, *Hadrien*, p. 76, note 1, objects to the restorations of Boeckh and Dittenberger both. The latter's restoration does not specify the treasurers, nor does it take into account the fact that they would not have a κῆρυξ. At the period of this inscription only three κήρυκες are attested—that of the Areopagus, that of the Boule and the Demos, and that of the Archon. The κῆρυξ of the Areopagus is not here meant, for sufficient space for such a restoration is not available. Graindor prefers the restoration πρὸς τὴν βουλὴν καὶ τὸν κήρυκα (adopted in the text above) because the Boule is twice specified in the inscription as the authority competent to deal with matters connected with the exportation of oil, and because the herald of the Boule and the Demos was an important official, whereas the herald of the Archon was only a minor functionary.

quantity sold, the name of the purchaser, and the place where the
boat which is to carry the oil is anchored (ll. 20–23). In default of
such a declaration the oil is to be confiscated, even if the state
has already received the quota which it reserves for itself (ll. 23–
26). In the event that the declaration is false, the oil is to be
confiscated and the informer is to receive half of the amount involved. Three types of false declaration are specified: (1) a false
statement of the amount of the crop, (2) a false statement concerning the amount exported, and (3) a false statement to the effect
that the property in question was formerly a part of the lands of
Hipparchus which were confiscated by the Fiscus, made for the
purpose of paying one eighth instead of one third of the entire
harvest (ll. 27–32). Lines 33–36 are fragmentary, but the entire
passage (ll. 33–40) seems to treat of the disposition of undeclared
oil which has been purchased for the export market: if the seller
confesses and if the oil has not yet been turned over to the purchaser, the seller is to be allowed to retain one half of the oil; if
the oil has already been turned over to the purchaser, one half the
purchase price is to be retained by the seller; in either event one
half the value is to go to the state. Furthermore, it is provided that
exporters of oil must declare the amount they are exporting and
the name of the person from whom the oil was purchased; otherwise the oil is subject to confiscation. If the exporter is informed
against after he has left the port, then the Ecclesia is to bring the
matter to the attention of the exporter's native city and of the
emperor (ll. 41–46). If a case involving less than fifty amphorae is
brought to trial, the Boule is to sit in judgment, but if a larger
amount is involved, the case is to go before the Ecclesia (ll. 46–49).
If a member of the crew of a boat should be the informer, the general
is to summon the Boule for the following day, unless the amount
involved is more than fifty amphorae, in which event the Ecclesia
is to be summoned. The informer is to receive half of the oil that
may be confiscated (ll. 49–54). If an appeal is carried to the emperor
or to the proconsul, the Ecclesia is to choose syndics to represent
the state. Finally, the producers of oil shall receive for their product
the market price that is current in Attica (ll. 56–59), and in the
event that the year's crop is so abundant that the specified quota
of one third exceeds the needs of the state, the producer may keep

all of the oil, or at least the part which the ἐλεῶναι or the ἀργυροταμίαι are unwilling to accept (ll. 59–68). The ἀργυροταμίαι
seem to have been the Greek equivalents of the *curatores kalendarii*,
whose function it was to loan state funds to private individuals.[86]
Hence it has been suggested that producers of oil were able to bor-
row state funds, mortgaging all or part of their crop to the ἀργυροταμίαι, with the latter exercising their own discretion as to the
amount of oil to be accepted.[87] The law obviously had two ends in
view. First, it was the intent to assure to the state an adequate
supply, at a reasonable price, of the oil required for various public
services.[88] Second, it was the intent to limit the profits of middlemen, as is shown by the following considerations. Obviously the
current market price to be paid for the oil (ll. 58–59) must have
been fixed at a level lower than that which obtained on the foreign
market; otherwise there would have been no temptation for producers and merchants to circumvent the law by exporting the oil
surreptitiously. Moreover, inasmuch as it appears that the middlemen were not to be paid a higher price than the producer (ll. 18–
20), the producer would have been unwilling to sell his product to
the state through the middlemen in case the latter offered a price
appreciably lower than that which might be obtained by selling
directly to the state. It follows, therefore, that the effect of the
law was to restrain the middlemen from profiting unduly from deal-
ings in an essential commodity.

Another attempt on the part of the emperor to curb the middle-
man is to be seen in the imperial rescript which is concerned with
the regulation of the sale of fish[89] or possibly—the fragmentary
condition of the opening lines makes it difficult to arrive at an ab-

[86] J. Oehler, in RE, II, 802; X, 1567.

[87] Graindor, *Hadrien*, p. 97. Cf. Dio Cassius, LII, xxviii, 3–4, where a speaker
advocates the creation of a state bank which would loan money at a reasonable
rate of interest, especially to landowners.

[88] Graindor, *Hadrien*, p. 75, thinks that some oil may have been used for street
lighting at Athens. Streets are known to have been lighted at Pompeii and in important eastern cities. See Rostovtzeff, *Roman Empire*, p. 527, note 6; H. Lamer,
"Strassenbeleuchtung im späteren Altertume," *Berliner philologische Wochenschrift*, 1927, p. 1472.

[89] IG, II–III², 1103; A. Wilhelm, in JOAI, XII (1909), 146–48; Abbott and
Johnson, *Municipal Administration*, pp. 413–14, No. 91; Graindor, *Hadrien*, pp.
127–29, where a few new restorations are suggested.

solutely certain conclusion—of commodities in general.[90] In lines
1-4 provision is made for freeing fishermen, when they sold their
stocks at Eleusis, from what seems to have been a normal tax of
two obols.[91] Inasmuch as the effect of this provision was to divert
the sale of fish from the Piraeus to Eleusis at times when the demand in Eleusis might be sufficiently large to justify a change in
the place of sale, it seems probable that it was the emperor's intent
to assure an adequate supply of food at Eleusis at the time of the
Mysteries when, because of the great influx of visitors, the food
problem was extraordinarily acute.[92] In the remainder of the
letter provision is made that the retailer must be either the im-
porter or the first purchaser—thereby preventing any rise in price
that might have been occasioned by multiple handling of commodities—and any infringement of the regulations set forth was to
be brought before the Areopagus; finally, the order was explicitly
given that the letter be engraved on a stele and set up in front of
the Deigma at the Piraeus.

Dio Cassius refers especially to one of Hadrian's laws which
forbade any councillor to undertake the farming of taxes, whether
in his own person or through an intermediary.[93] Although Dio
does not specifically state it, it is possible that he had Athens in
mind,[94] for what seems to be an imperial edict of the period of
Hadrian, which has been found there, contains the following regulations which were to govern the activities of tax collectors.[95] If
the farmers of the tax fail to make the payments they have con-
tracted for, they are to be fined. If they refuse to pay this fine,
they are to be assessed at a rate of 12 percent on their defaulted
obligations until a period of three months has elapsed, whereupon
the appropriate magistrates are instructed to sell the securities
that have been deposited, with both the defaulter and the surety

[90] Abbott and Johnson, *Municipal Administration*, pp. 413–14, are inclined toward this view.

[91] Freedom from taxation at Eleusis implies a tax at the Piraeus, where the
letter was displayed in front of the Deigma. Cf. W. Liebenam, *Städteverwaltung im
römischen Kaiserreiche* (Leipzig, 1900), p. 24. This is one of the very few items
of information that we have concerning governmental revenues at Athens during
the imperial period.

[92] Graindor, *Hadrien*, pp. 128–29; Graindor, *Album*, p. 79.   [93] LXIX, xvi, 2.

[94] Cf. Graindor, *Hadrien*, p. 79.   [95] IG, II–III², 1104.

retaining the right to redeem their deposits within a further period of sixty days. If Dio's statement is actually to be associated with this edict, it would seem that members of the Boule who were farming taxes had taken advantage of their official position to pursue the sharp practices so often associated with the tax farmer, or even to defraud the state.

The prosperity of Athens was also enhanced by the great renaissance of the city's religious rites during the period of Hadrian.[96] The visitors who thronged the festivals, coming often from great distances, brought, as ever, opportunities for profits to all sorts of businessmen. The emperor's interest in the city's festivals is partly shown by his establishment, already observed, of endowments in support of the *agonothesia* of the Panathenaea and of the gymnasiarchy. Moreover, it was at his instigation that the Panhellenium was established, whereby Athens became the cultural capital of the Greek world.[97] Also, his interest in the Mysteries at Eleusis was especially keen. Not only did he build a bridge and dikes to insure access to Eleusis even when the Cephisus was at flood stage and undertake to assure an adequate supply of food at the time of the Mysteries, as we have already observed, but he may also have brought about, through the Panhellenes, the restoration of the former practice of contributing tithes to the Eleusinian divinities.[98] Hadrian was, furthermore, the first emperor after Augustus to be initiated into the Mysteries; his initiation took place at the time of his first visit to Athens, in 124/5 A.D.; again, in 128/9 A.D., he attended the rites in the capacity of an *epoptes*.[99] A further indication of the importance that he attached to these rites is to be seen in the fact that he had them transferred to Rome.[100] Finally, although the embassies were not large or costly or very significant as regards the economic life of Athens, mention should also be made of the fact

[96] For the cults of Athens at the time of Hadrian, and their rites, see Graindor, *Hadrien*, pp. 115–73.

[97] For discussion of the Panhellenium, and bibliography, see M. N. Tod, in JHS, XLII (1922), 167–80; Graindor, *Hadrien*, pp. 52–53, 102–11.

[98] Cf. Graindor, *Hadrien*, pp. 125–27.

[99] Graindor, *Hadrien*, pp. 38, 55, 118–19; and for the Mysteries at the time of Hadrian, see pp. 118–35.

[100] Aurelius Victor, *De Caes.* xiv, 4; cf. *Epit. de Caes.* (Aurelius Victor [?]; ed. Pichlmayr, Teubner, 1911) xiv, 2.

that the dispatch of the Dodecas to Delos, which was abandoned (or at least sent only with extreme infrequence) after 88 B.C.,[101] was resumed during the later years of Trajan's reign. Thereafter individual embassies were sent yearly between 113/4 and 125/6 A.D.,[102] again c.140 A.D., and yearly between 152/3 and 155/6 A.D.[103]

Inasmuch as Athens was by and large a university town, it is of importance to observe that Hadrian's interest was also directed toward its teachers and its schools.[104] It is known that he mastered the Attic tongue and became intensely interested, and proficient, in the branches of learning that were pursued at Athens, entering, at the same time, into intimate association with various men of learning.[105] Moreover, his biographer informs us that the emperor bestowed honors upon professors and enriched them with gifts.[106] From the Digest we learn that he reaffirmed the immunity granted professors by his predecessors and granted them additional privileges on his own initiative.[107] But our most tangible evidence of the interest of the emperor and of his mother, Plotina, in the philosophical schools at Athens is to be found in the famous series of letters, in which, at the intercession of Plotina, the emperor granted the Epicurean school the right to choose its director from noncitizens as well as citizens and, in addition, permitted Popillius Theotimus, then head of the Epicurean school, to write in Greek that part of his will in which he designated his successor.[108]

The beneficial effects of Hadrian's great building program throughout the provinces—but especially in the cities—were off-

---

[101] Roussel, DCA, pp. 338–39.

[102] Durrbach, *Choix*, pp. 268–69. For the dates, see Graindor, *Hadrien*, pp. 26–29.

[103] Durrbach, *Choix*, p. 269; Graindor, *Chronologie*, p. 156.

[104] Walden, *Universities*, pp. 83–85.

[105] *Epit. de Caes.* (Aurelius Victor [?]; ed. Pichlmayr, Teubner, 1911) xiv; Spartianus, *Vit. Hadr.* xvi, 10; cf. Aurelius Victor, *De Caes.* xiv, 4.

[106] Spartianus, *Vit. Hadr.* xvi, 8.   [107] L, 4, 18, 30.

[108] IG, II–III², 1099 (the date is 121 A.D.); cf. Graindor, *Hadrien*, pp. 203–7; R. Herzog, "Urkunden zur Hochschulpolitik der römischen Kaiser," *Sitzungsberichte der preussischen Akademie der Wissenschaften*, philosophisch-historische Klasse, 1935, pp. 967–1019. A similar set of documents which has to do with the same general subject has now been identified by J. H. Oliver, "An Inscription Concerning the Epicurean School at Athens," *Transactions of the American Philological Association*, LXIX (1938), 494–99. Oliver ascertained that two texts heretofore published as separate inscriptions (SEG, III, 226, and IG, II–III², 1097) are in reality parts of one inscription.

set by the expense involved in the greatly increased civil service and in the maintenance of security along the eastern frontiers—with the result that no sound basis for prosperity was laid.[109] But money was put in circulation, and for the time being a specious brand of prosperity was created. It was this type of prosperity that the Athenians experienced during the reign of Hadrian; it improved the lot of a few, while cloaking very poorly the poverty of large sections of the population. Indeed, several of the emperor's gifts, as, for example, the endowment of the gymnasiarchy and of the *agonothesia* of the Panathenaea, show the fundamentally unsound economic condition of the city. Upon his accession to the throne, Antoninus Pius, while retaining the elaborate bureaucracy built up by Hadrian, began a policy of retrenchment, especially as regards public building projects.[110] The reign of Antoninus' successor, Marcus Aurelius (161–180 A.D.), was fraught with external danger and internal exhaustion. While the Romans were involved in war with the Parthians tribes of Germans and Sarmatians penetrated into the Danubian provinces, and to meet these formidable threats such large expenditures were undertaken that the state treasury was drained and heavy exactions were levied upon cities throughout the empire.[111] But it was from the plague brought back by soldiers who had taken part in the Parthian war that Athens seems to have suffered most.[112] However, the extent of its ravages at Athens can not be determined, for our only extant literary authority merely states that the Athenians said to Marcus Aurelius at Sirmium: "Blessed are they who died in the plague!"[113]

In line with his policy of retrenchment, Antoninus Pius restricted his building activities at Athens to the completion of the aqueduct which had been begun by Hadrian.[114] Heretofore it has been assumed that work on the large Propylaea at Eleusis was begun under

---

[109] Rostovtzeff, *Roman Empire*, p. 325; Frank, "Rome and Italy of the Empire," pp. 70–74.

[110] Rostovtzeff, *Roman Empire*, p. 325; Frank, "Rome and Italy of the Empire," pp. 75–76.

[111] Rostovtzeff, *Roman Empire*, pp. 325–27; Frank, "Rome and Italy of the Empire," pp. 75–76.

[112] Cf. Wachsmuth, *Die Stadt Athen*, I, 702.

[113] Philostratus, *Vit. soph.* 561.

[114] CIL, III, 549 (= ILS, 337); cf. Judeich, *Topographie*, pp. 203–4.

Antoninus and completed under Marcus Aurelius, but it has recently been shown that the project was carried out in its entirety in the time of Marcus Aurelius.[115] However, owing to the benefactions of the millionaire sophist Herodes Atticus, who lived at the time of Hadrian, Antoninus, and Marcus Aurelius, Athens was beautified by the last splendid buildings that were to be erected during Roman times. In July, 139 A.D., when he received a crown at the great Panathenaea, Herodes promised to rebuild the Panathenaic Stadium in white marble before the next festival,[116] four years later. In carrying out the work, if we may believe Pausanias,[117] the greater part of the quarries on Pentelicus was exhausted. The bridge that carried the road across the Ilissus to the Stadium was built at the time of Herodes,[118] but it is not certain that he was responsible for it. Likewise, the Temple of Tyche, which was built on the heights of Ardettus, to the west of the Stadium,[119] has been attributed to Herodes,[120] but concerning this there is no certainty.[121] However, the sophist was certainly the donor of one of the most splendid buildings in Roman Athens, the Odeum, which was erected at the southwestern foot of the Acropolis in memory of his wife, Regilla, who died c.160 A.D.[122] It was substantially the city that had

[115] O. Deubner, "Zu den grossen Propyläen von Eleusis," AM, LXII (1937), 73–81. For earlier discussions, see Hörmann, *Die inneren Propylaeen von Eleusis*, pp. 115, 118; W. B. Dinsmoor, in AJA, XIV (1910), 155, note 1; F. Noack, *Eleusis*, I (Berlin and Leipzig, 1927), 222; K. Kourouniotis, 'Οδηγὸς τοῦ 'Ελεύσινος (Athens, 1934), pp. 24, 31.

[116] Philostratus, *Vit. soph.* 549–50. For the date, see Graindor, *Hérode*, p. 65, note 2, and p. 67.

[117] I, xix, 6. For the stadium, see also Suidas, *s.v.* 'Ηρώδης; Judeich, *Topographie*, pp. 417–19; Graindor, *Hérode*, pp. 182–83; A. Köster, *Das Stadion von Athen* (Berlin, 1906).

[118] E. Ziller, in Erbkam's *Zeitschrift für Bauwesen*, XX (1870), 492; Judeich, *Topographie*, p. 418.

[119] Philostratus, *Vit. soph.* 550; Judeich, *Topographie*, p. 419; E. Ziller, p. 492 (see the preceding note).

[120] Graindor, *Hérode*, pp. 84, 184.

[121] Philostratus, *Vit. soph.* 550, merely refers to the existence of the temple and its statue without stating by whom it was built.

[122] Philostratus, *Vit. soph.* 551; Pausanias, VII, xx, 6; Suidas, *s.v.* 'Ηρώδης; cf. Judeich, *Topographie*, pp. 326–28; Graindor, *Hérode*, pp. 218–25. Herodes also undertook minor projects in Attica outside of Athens. An undated dedicatory inscription (IG, II–III², 3191) from Merenda, the site of the deme of Myrrhinous, states that Herodes restored a temple of Athena and dedicated a statue to the god-

been embellished by Hadrian and by Herodes that was described by Pausanias, who wrote at about the middle of the second century A.D. And it was to this city that Lucian referred when he wrote of Athens as large and prosperous.[123] Aelius Aristeides, in his Panathenaic oration,[124] which was written during the period of the Antonines, says that at that time Athens approached the glory of the greatest days of its past; he is thinking, however, not of the prosperity of the city, or of its external aspect, but rather of its great fame—and even in that connection he is manifestly guilty of exaggeration. After the time of Herodes we hear only of repairs of the city's buildings and of minor building activity. Thus, at some time before the end of the second century a well house was built for the Clepsydra, along with a stairway leading from it to the Acropolis.[125]

If Antoninus was sparing in his expenditure on public works and on the maintenance of imperial bureaus, the same may not be said of his record in connection with higher education, for he created chairs for rhetoricians and philosophers in various cities, and engaged himself to pay the salaries from the Fiscus in case the cities were unable to meet the expense.[126] Moreover, he made the lot of these scholars more attractive by freeing them from the payment of taxes and from the performance of various public services. As a part of this larger program Antoninus established a chair of rhetoric at Athens, the first incumbent of which was Lollianus of Ephesus,[127] and undertook to pay stipends to philosophers.[128] It is uncertain whether he also established a chair of "grammar"; this action may have been taken, instead, by Marcus Aurelius.[129] At any rate, the

dess. Also, c.150 A.D., the sophist built an aqueduct near Marathon to conduct water to an ornamental springhouse. Cf. E. P. Blegen, in AJA, XL (1936), 263–64. Owing to the incorrect interpretation of an inscription, it has been maintained that Herodes built, or restored, an *agoranomium* in the Agora at Athens (H. G. Lolling, in ΑΔ, 1888, pp. 188–89). For the correct reading, see Graindor, in *Revue belge de philologie*, VI (1927), 754–55. The building was actually erected by the Boule.

[123] Lucian, *Scyth.* 9.   [124] Page 298, ed. Dindorf.

[125] T. L. Shear, in *Hesperia*, VIII (1939), 225.

[126] Julius Capitolinus, *Anton. Pius*, xi, 3. Cf. Walden, *Universities*, pp. 86–89; W. Hüttl, *Antoninus Pius*, I (Prague, Vol. I, 1936; Vol. II, 1933), 331.

[127] Philostratus, *Vit. soph.* 526; cf. O. Schissel, in RE, XIII, 1373–75, and in *Philologus*, LXXXII (1926–27), 181.

[128] Walden, *Universities*, pp. 88–89.   [129] *Ibid.*, pp. 87–88.

latter created another chair of rhetoric and one or more chairs of philosophy in each of the four schools.[130] Thus, the university at Athens was fully developed by the time of Marcus Aurelius.[131] After the reign of this emperor, the university at Athens continued to exist in a flourishing condition during the remainder of the second century A.D. It is, however, difficult to determine the relative extent to which Athens attracted teachers and students as compared with other parts of the Greek world. It has been suggested that philosophers were unwilling to establish themselves in such a poverty-stricken city as Athens.[132] However, we find in Philostratus' *Lives of the Sophists* a long and distinguished list of the teachers who were attracted to the city. Moreover, Philostratus[133] puts words into the mouth of a speaker to the effect that one who was interested in learning the pure Attic speech would have to go to the interior of Attica because the city was filled with youths from Thrace and the Pontus, whereas, on the other hand, the inland was not tainted with the speech of barbarians. That Philostratus was not overstating the number of foreign students is shown clearly by the fact that large numbers of foreigners were registered in the ephebia during this period. A list of the numbers of these foreigners in various years, with the number of citizen ephebes indicated for the sake of comparison, follows:

Date (A.D.) According to Graindor[a]	According to Kirchner[b]	Foreigners	Athenians	Source (In IG, II–III²)
148/9	145/6	4 [?] (Incomplete)	c.106	2052, 2055
150/1		7+	70	2065
155/6	143/4 or 144/5	29+	79+	2050
158/9		109+	106+	2068
164/5	161/2	19+	143 [?]	2085
166/7	163/4	41	95	2086
167/8	c.166/7	60	27	2094
172/3	169/70	154	80	2097
175/6–177/8	172/3 or a little later	109	106	2103
181/2–191/2	180/1–191/2	37	60–65 [?]	2119
186/7–191/2	183/4–191/2	76+	76+	2113
192/3		39	85	2130
c.190–200		104	94	2128

a In *Chronologie.*   b In IG, II-III².

[130] *Ibid.*, pp. 91–92.   [131] *Ibid.*, pp. 93–94.

[132] *Ibid.*, p. 100, note 2.   [133] *Vit. soph.* 553.

During the imperial period the gymnastic aspect of the ephebic system received progressively greater emphasis,[134] but the ephebes continued to attend the lectures of the philosophers. Between 124/5 A.D. and 266/7 A.D. a number of new festivals were introduced,[135] and, although some of the older ones were displaced, the evidence indicates quite clearly that the ephebia was very active and prosperous.[136] The exact intervals at which the ephebic festivals were celebrated are not known; they may have been held annually, but the deciding factor was probably financial.[137] The expense involved in the games was probably rather great and seems to have been met either by one or more of the ephebes of the year in which the festival was held, or by foundations known as σεβαστοφορικά.[138] One and the same ephebe is known to have acted as *agonothetes* of as many as five different festivals,[139] and on one occasion the emperor Commodus served in that capacity.[140]

Before he had ascended the throne, as we are informed by his biographer,[141] the emperor Septimius Severus had studied at Athens, had seen the city's famous antiquities, and had been initiated into the Mysteries; and while there he had been offended by the Athenians, with the result that, upon his accession as emperor in 193 A.D., he deprived the Athenians of some of their privileges. On the basis of this passage from the biography of the emperor, supplemented by a slight amount of additional evidence, it has been assumed that the emperor curtailed the territory of Athens by granting independence to Icus, Peparethus, and Sciathus.[142] Actually, Peparethus

---

[134] Graindor, "Études sur l'éphébie attique sous l'empire," *Musée belge*, XXVI (1922), 165–228, especially p. 168.

[135] *Ibid.*, pp. 173–74.   [136] *Ibid.*, p. 175.

[137] *Ibid.*, p. 174, following R. Neubauer, *Commentationes epigraphicae* (Berlin, 1869), p. 69.

[138] Graindor, in *Musée belge*, XXVI (1922), 170–71.

[139] *Ibid.*, p. 171.   [140] IG, II–III², 2660, l. 18.

[141] Spartianus, *Vit. Sev.* iii, 7. For his initiation into the Mysteries, see P. Foucart, "Les Empereurs romains initiés aux mystères d'Eleusis," *Revue de philologie*, XVII (1893), 207. G. Giannelli, in *Atti della reale Accademia delle Scienze di Torino*, 1914–15, p. 382, note 4, wrongly maintains that proof of the initiation of Septimius into the Mysteries is lacking.

[142] Hermann, *Lehrbuch*, p. 786, note 6. A. von Domaszewski, in *Archiv für Religionswissenschaft*, XI (1908), 239, suggests that Septimius took from Athens its rights and privileges as a *civitas foederata*. An opposing view is held by A. von Premerstein, in JOAI, XVI (1913), 268–69; Graindor, *Marbres*, p. 61.

had received its independence by the time of Commodus, when it resumed the issuance of coinage;[143] there is no evidence to show whether it was made autonomous before that time.[144] As regards Icus, the island struck no coins during the imperial period, and there are no grounds whatsoever for concluding that it was made independent.[145] The status of Sciathus has occasioned some discussion. From the fact that a dedication made by the island to Septimius Severus is dated by the name of the local archon it has been deduced that the island was granted independence by the emperor.[146] But the force of this argument is decidedly weakened by the fact that in an inscription of the year 116/7 A.D., at a time when that island was certainly subject to Athens, mention is made of an archon of Peparethus.[147] It should, moreover, be noted that Sciathus struck no coins at any time during the imperial period.[148] But while it is true that Peparethus had received its freedom under Commodus and that there are no valid reasons for assuming that Icus and Sciathus were freed by Septimius Severus, there is evidence from coins to show that the latter emperor probably detached the island of Aegina [149] and the city of Crane in Cephallenia from the domain of Athens.[150] However that may be, it seems probable that the biographer of Septimius, when he mentioned the diminution of the privileges of the Athenians by the emperor, was referring to some act on the part of the emperor which in effect restricted the freedom

[143] Peparethus struck coins under Augustus, and again under Commodus. Head, *Hist. Num.*, p. 313; cf. Graindor, *Auguste*, p. 8.

[144] Graindor, *Auguste*, p. 8; Graindor, *Marbres*, p. 60, note 3.

[145] Head, *Hist. Num.*, p. 312; cf. Fredrich, in RE, IX, 991–92; Graindor, *Auguste*, p. 7.

[146] IG, XII, viii, 634 (= SIG, 875); A. Boeckh, in CIG, 2154; C. Fredrich, in AM, XXXI (1906), 106; Hiller von Gaertringen, commentary on SIG, 875. Fredrich (expressing two views) and Bursian (*Geographie von Griechenland*, II, 386, note 5) suggest that the island may have become independent at some time between the reign of Hadrian and that of Septimius Severus.

[147] IG, XII, viii, 645; cf. Graindor, *Auguste*, p. 8; and Graindor, *Marbres*, p. 60, note 3. For the date of this inscrption, see Graindor, *Chronologie*, pp. 116, 124.

[148] Head, *Hist. Num.*, p. 313.

[149] Aegina struck coins during the reign of Septimius Severus. Head, *Hist. Num.*, p. 398. Cf. Graindor, *Auguste*, p. 10.

[150] The city struck coins which bore the image of Julia Domna during the reign of Septimius Severus; see Head, *Hist. Num.*, p. 427; cf. Bürchner, in RE, XI, 205, 214; and Graindor, *Auguste*, p. 10.

of the Athenians in matters of local administration, possibly by the appointment of a *corrector* or some similar official.[151] This supposition is confirmed by an important inscription of the year 195 A.D., or 196 A.D.,[152] in which (1. 6) the empress Julia Domna was honored by the Athenians and assimilated to the cult of Athena Polias in recognition of her intercession with the emperor when an Athenian embassy appeared in Rome to attempt to secure a release from the restrictions which the emperor had imposed upon the city.[153] Probable reconciliation of the Athenians with the emperor is to be seen, also, in the celebration of the festival of the *Severeia* in his honor at Athens beginning in the year 199/200 A.D.[154]

So much for the general trends of the welfare—or woes—of Athens at various times during the first and second centuries A.D. It remains now to consider various questions which are more specifically economic in character. We may begin with commodities which were produced within Attica, some of them for exportation. One of the most important—if not *the* most important—of these commodities was olive oil. Pausanias, when writing of Tithorea in Phocis, states[155] that that place produced the finest quality of oil, but that the largest amounts were produced in Attica and Sicyon. Moreover, the terms of Hadrian's law concerning the sale and exportation of oil, which we have had occasion to consider above in detail, make it quite evident that the Athenian crop commanded a very attractive price on the foreign market. Another product of the Attic countryside, the far-famed honey from Hymettus and from the district of the silver mines,[156] was produced and exported in comparatively moderate amounts. An interesting mosaic of the second century A.D., found in a palace on the Caelian Hill in Rome,

[151] A. von Premerstein, in JOAI, XVI (1913), 249–70, especially 269–70; Graindor, *Marbres*, pp. 60–62 (cf. Graindor, *Auguste*, p. 7).

[152] IG, II–III², 1076; cf. A. von Premerstein, "Athenische Kultehren für Kaiserin Julia Domna," JOAI, XVI (1913), 249–70; Graindor, *Marbres*, pp. 52–62; O. Broneer, in *Hesperia*, IV (1935), 178; Robert, *Études anatoliennes*, p. 14; J. H. Oliver, in *Athenian Studies*, pp. 521–30.

[153] A. von Premerstein, in JOAI, XVI (1913), 269–70; Graindor, *Marbres*, pp. 60–62. For the date of the inscription, see *Marbres*, p. 53.

[154] IG, II–III², 2193, 2196, 2197, 2199, 2201, 2203, 2208, 2222, 2226, 2235, 2237, 3015; cf. Graindor, in *Musée belge*, XXVI (1922), 199–200.

[155] X, xxxii, 19.   [156] See chap. iv, notes 232–36.

shows that the honey was still held in high regard in Italy.[157] The main decoration of the mosaic consists of the portrayal of two boxers; and adjacent to this scene is an inscription, A.MEL|AT.TI| CV, which is interpreted as "Ah! Attic honey." The inscription, taken in conjunction with the main scene, suggests that a pot of Hymettus honey was given to the winner of the boxing match as a prize.[158] Grain was, as ever, produced in quantities insufficient for the needs of the population of Attica. Attic wine was of ordinary quality and did not enjoy an extensive market. Attic quarries, especially those on Pentelicus, continued to produce marble in considerable amounts. Hymettus marble had been introduced into Rome in the first century B.C. and had been employed especially in the ornamentation of wealthy homes in the time of Horace.[159] But there is no evidence to show that more than small amounts of it were exported thither during the first and second centuries A.D.;[160] and even in Attica it had passed out of fashion by the time of Hadrian. On the other hand, the quarries of Pentelicus seem to have been worked extensively. At Athens we find this marble used in public buildings, in most of the extant sculptures of the first and second centuries, and in inscribed stelae.[161] That it was employed in fairly large amounts in Greek cities of the mainland outside of Attica may be deduced from the use Herodes Atticus made of it in reconstructing the stadium at Delphi[162] and in the statues of Demeter and Cora in the Temple of Demeter at Olympia.[163] Moreover, Plutarch tells[164] of seeing at Athens columns of Pentelic marble that had been completely finished preparatory to shipment to Rome to be used by Domitian in his restoration of the Temple of Jupiter Capitolinus. But there is no evidence to show that any con-

[157] CIL, VI, 33975; cf. M. Blake, in *Memoirs of the American Academy in Rome*, XIII (1936), 166.

[158] A. W. Van Buren, *Ancient Rome as Revealed by Recent Excavations* (London, 1936), pp. 121–23; cf. M. Blake, p. 166 (see note 157, above).

[159] *Carm.* II, xviii, 3–5.

[160] Bruzza, pp. 106–204, especially p. 166, Nos. 291, 292, lists only one block each of Hymettus and Pentelic stone among the inscribed blocks of Greek marble found in Rome.

[161] It was used in the reconstruction of the Panathenaic Stadium by Herodes Atticus (Pausanias, I, xix, 6; Philostratus, *Vit. soph.* 550), in the Olympieum, and in Hadrian's Gate (Judeich, *Topographie*, pp. 382–83).

[162] Pausanias, X, xxxii, 1.   [163] Pausanias, VI, xxi, 2.   [164] *Publ.* xv.

siderable amount of this marble was exported to Rome.[165] The ownership of the Attic quarries is not altogether certain, and it may be
that they, like most Greek quarries,[166] were imperial property.
However, the only evidence to this effect (and it is very slight!)
is to be found in an inscription on a block of Hymettus marble
which was imported into Rome[167]—*Eu]tyches ex rat(ione)* ....
prob.....—where *ex ratione* and *prob(ante)*, or *prob(atore)*, en-
courage the belief that the Hymettus quarries belonged to the emperors. In any event, the rather widely held view that Herodes
Atticus owned the quarries on Pentelicus[168] is not susceptible of
proof, for it is based upon a passage in Pausanias[169] which states
merely that the greater part of the Pentelic quarries was used up in
the reconstruction of the Panathenaic Stadium at Athens by
Herodes, and upon the altogether uncertain deduction that the
cognomen of Cla. Hier. Atticus (whose name appears on a block of
Pentelic marble which was imported into Rome) must have been
derived from his master, who was, we are asked to believe, Herodes
Atticus.[170]

Athenian sculptors did not suffer from lack of commissions during
the first and second centuries A.D. Curiously, no statues made by
Athenian artists between the time of Tiberius and that of Trajan
have been found in Italy.[171] But if their work was not valued in
Italy at that time—which is by no means certain, for the chance of
discovery may be responsible for its absence there—the same may
not be said for the Greek cities of the mainland outside of Attica.
A number of statues made by Athenians have been found at Olympia.[172] Moreover, aside from statues sent to other parts of

[165] See note 160, above.

[166] O. Hirschfeld, *Die kaiserliche Verwaltungsbeamten* (2d ed.; Berlin, 1905), p.
149, note 3; Larsen, "Roman Greece," p. 462.

[167] Bruzza, No. 292; Dubois, *Étude*, pp. 101–2.

[168] Bruzza, p. 166; Dubois, *Étude*, pp. 99–100; Fiehn, in RE, Zweite Reihe, III,
2258.   [169] I, xix, 6.

[170] Bruzza, p. 166, No. 291. Graindor, *Hérode*, p. 182, note 2, aptly points out
that if the quarries had belonged to Herodes' family, they would have been confiscated along with the rest of the lands of Hipparchus.

[171] See the table of signed works of Athenian sculptors of this period, along with
the place of discovery, given by Graindor, *Tibère*, p. 174.

[172] Dionysius son of Apollonius, of Athens, made a statue of Agrippina the
Younger which seems to have been set up in the Metroum at Olympia; see G. Treu,

Greece,[173] works of art were exported to Asia Minor during the first century A.D., for Philostratus tells us[174] that Apollonius of Tyana, upon planning a voyage to Egypt, went to the Piraeus and attempted, unsuccessfully, to secure passage on a ship which was on the point of sailing to Ionia with a cargo of statues, some made of

---

in *Olympia*, III, 256; W. Dittenberger, in *Olympia*, V. No. 646; Loewy, *Inschriften*, No. 331. Eleusinius of Athens made a statue of a woman member of a noble Elean family which seems to have been set up in the Heraeum at Olympia; see G. Treu. in *Olympia*, III, 253–54, 258; W. Dittenberger, in *Olympia*, V, No. 645; Loewy, *Inschriften*, No. 335. Also in the Heraeum was a statue of a noble Elean woman made by Aulus Sext(i)us Eraton, of Athens; see G. Treu, in *Olympia*, III, 252–53; W. Dittenberger, in *Olympia*, V, No. 648; Loewy, *Inschriften*, No. 334. A third statue of a noble Elean woman, which was also set up in the Heraeum, was made by Eros, an Athenian sculptor; see G. Treu, in *Olympia*, III, 253–54, 258; W. Dittenberger, in *Olympia*, V, No. 647; Loewy, *Inschriften*, No. 333. Two Athenian sculptors, Hegias and Philathenaeus, executed a statue of Claudius which was probably set up in the Metroum at Olympia; see G. Treu, in *Olympia*, III, 244–45; W. Dittenberger, in *Olympia*, V, No. 642; Loewy *Inschriften*, No. 332. For the Olympia statues, see also Lippold, *Kopien*, p. 210. Inasmuch as the artists' signatures were inscribed on the statues, rather than on the bases, it seems reasonable to suppose that the figures were actually made at Athens (Lippold, *Kopien*, pp. 62, 68). Indeed, most of the imperial portraits that were set up in Greece seem to have been made at Athens. Cf. M. Stuart, "How Were Imperial Portraits Distributed?" *AJA*, XLIII (1939), 601–17, especially 610–12, 615–16. R. Carpenter, in *AJA*, XXXV (1931), 249–61, has argued that the Hermes at Olympia, far from being an original statue made by Praxiteles, was probably made by an Athenian sculptor either of the Julio-Claudian period or of the time of Hadrian. Carpenter's view was influenced by C. Blümel, *Griechische Bildhauerarbeit* (Berlin and Leipzig, 1927; JDAI, Ergänzungsheft XI), pp. 37–48. G. M. A. Richter, in *AJA*, XXXV (1931), 277–90, and V. Müller, in *AJA*, XXXV (1931), 291–95, dispute this theory.

[173] A statue at Sparta was made by Apollonius (?) of Athens; see M. N. Tod and A. J. B. Wace, *A Catalogue of the Sparta Museum* (Oxford, 1906), p. 101 and p. 171, No. 363; Loewy, *Inschriften*, No. 336; C. Robert, in RE, II, 162, No. 124; cf. Graindor, *Tibère*, pp. 176–77. Loewy's (*Inschriften*, No. 337) identification of the sculptor of the statue of Ariston at Chersonesus with Cephisodotus of Athens is not to be accepted, for neither the ethnic nor the name of the sculptor is preserved. Cf. Graindor, *Tibère*, p. 185. The imperial portraits found at Corinth were of Pentelic marble and were probably made at Athens; see E. H. Swift, in *AJA*, XXV (1921), 142; cf. Lippold, *Kopien*, pp. 62, 68. The portrait of Claudius at Delphi (SIG, 801A) was probably made at Athens; cf. M. Stuart, in *AJA*, XLIII (1939). 610–11. The life-sized Pentelic marble head of Memnon (?), found at Loukou in Cynouria, was probably the product of an Athenian workman. See the citations in note 323, below.

[174] *Vit. Apoll.* V, 20. It need not be supposed that the entire cargo was made up of works of art.

gold and ivory, others of gold and marble. Direct evidence that Athenian works of art were being exported in the second century A.D. as well is to be seen in the discovery, in the eastern part of the large harbor of the Piraeus, near the ancient Emporium, of over three hundred sculptured marbles, both statues and reliefs.[175] The sculptures were of the Neo-Attic style, many of them copies, made in the second century A.D., of archaic, fifth, and fourth century works of art.[176] However, it seems quite likely that by no means all of these works were made in Athens, for the marble is not Attic. The most probable explanations of this phenomenon would seem to be, first, that Athenian sculptors imported some marble for use in their studios, and second, that groups of artists who maintained studios in Greek towns outside of Attica used Athens as a sort of clearinghouse for transporting their products to Italy.[177] It seems very likely, however, that Athens was the leading center of Neo-Attic work. It is, likewise, probable that statues commanded a higher price when made by a sculptor who worked at Athens; this would explain the presence at Athens of many sculptors who would otherwise have migrated to more prosperous communities. At any rate, in the time of Hadrian Athens regained much of the prestige it had formerly enjoyed in the world of art.[178] Sculptors at Athens worked in the medium of bronze as well as of marble during the first two centuries of our era,[179] and in the time of Hadrian the practice of making colossal chryselephantine statues was taken up anew.[180] It was especially in the field of portraiture that Greece in

[175] AJA, XXXV (1931), 91; H. Schrader, in *Gnomon*, VII (1931), 165–67, in *Sitzungsberichte der preussischen Akademie der Wissenschaften zu Berlin*, philosophisch-historische Klasse, 1931, pp. 185–92, and in *Wiener Blätter für Freunde der Antike*, VIII (1931), 26–29.

[176] The practice of copying ancient statues at this time is satirized by Lucian, *Jup. trag.* 33, where it is said that the statue of Hermes Agoraeus was covered with pitch from daily casting by the sculptors.   [177] See chap. iv, including note 211.

[178] Cf. J. M. C. Toynbee, *The Hadrianic School* (Cambridge, 1934), p. 26. For an excellent account of Athenian sculpture at this time, see Graindor, *Hadrien*, pp. 253–84.

[179] Lucian, *Philops.* 20, mentions a certain Demetrias of Alopece, who was a maker of bronze statues. For a bronze statue made in Attica at some time between the reign of Tiberius and that of Trajan, see Graindor, *Tibère*, pp. 173, 185–86; cf. AM, XII (1887), 286, No. 202.

[180] Note the colossal chryselephantine statue of Zeus in the Olympieum. Pausanias, I, xviii, 6.

general, and Athens in particular, was proficient during the second century.[181] Attic sculptors also excelled in the making of sarcophagi, which they exported to many widely separated parts of the world— to Italy, Gaul, Spain, Malta, Cyrene, Syria, Asia Minor, South Russia, and, possibly, Tripolis.[182] More humble workers of stone were busied with making sculptured tombstones which were employed in especially large numbers at Athens during the time of Hadrian and the Antonines.[183] And we may believe that the Athenian art industry—it was, in large part, but an industry engaged in making copies of famous works of art for foreign customers—continued to flourish as late as the end of the second and the beginning of the third centuries, for it seems very probable that Athenian statues were imported into Leptis Magna to adorn the buildings erected there in the time of Septimius Severus.[184]

Our information concerning other commodities produced at

[181] A. Hekler, *Greek and Roman Portraits* (New York, 1912), p. XXXVII. For a number of statues in armor produced at Athens by Athenian workmen, see A. Hekler, "Beiträge zur Geschichte der antiken Panzerstatuen," JOAI, XIX–XX (1919), 219–27. A statue of the same type has recently been found in the Agora at Athens; see T. L. Shear, in *Hesperia*, II (1933), 178–83; T. L. Shear, in AJA, XXXVI (1932), 383, 385. Pausanias, I, xviii, 6, mentions two statues of Hadrian in Egyptian stone (basalt or porphyry) that were set up in front of the Olympieum. We have no way of determining whether they were made by Egyptian or Athenian artists. Cf. Graindor, *Hadrien*, p. 259; Lippold, *Kopien*, p. 145.

[182] G. Rodenwaldt, in JDAI, XLV (1930), 184–86; M. Gütschow, *Das Museum der Prätextat-Katakombe* (Vatican City, 1938; Atti della Pontificia Accademia Romana di Archeologia, 3d series, Memorie, IV, ii), pp. 142–49, No. 16, and especially p. 143, note 1; G. Calza, in *Notizie degli scavi di antichità*, 1931, pp. 517–24, where Calza calls his newly discovered sarcophagus Asiatic (but it is shown to be Attic by Miss Gütschow, p. 148); F. Matz, in *Archäologische Zeitung*, XXX (1873), 11. It should be noted that the material of Miss Gütschow's sarcophagus No. 16 seems to have been imported into Attica from Euboea. The Attic sarcophagi were made during the second and third centuries A.D. but are no more closely dated. The Syrian example (from the Mausoleum of Tell Barak, near Caesarea) seems to date from the beginning of the third century A.D.; see C. Watzinger, *Denkmäler Palästinas*, II (Leipzig, 1933–35), 102.

[183] Mühsam, *Die attischen Grabreliefs*, p. 56.

[184] F. Cumont, in CRAI, 1925, p. 164. For Neo-Attic sculptures found in Africa, see chap. iii, note 299, above. Graindor, *Hadrien*, p. 253, note 1, suggests that the archaizing Athena found in the Odeum at Cornith was imported from Athens and set up at the time of the reconstruction of that building by Herodes Atticus. But Broneer, *The Odeum*, pp. 117–23, insists that the statue was made in the early part of the third century A.D. and was set up at the time of the reconstruction of the Odeum in 235 A.D.

Athens is comparatively scanty, but the little that is known of them indicates that they played a relatively unimportant part in the economy of Attica. It seems likely that, just as in the time of Augustus,[185] a number of books were produced for the use of teachers and students in Athenian schools; a few books, possibly, were produced for the export trade. Attic shoes seem to have gained in favor toward the end of the second century, for Clement of Alexandria (fl. c.200 A.D.) shows such familiarity with them that we may deduce that they were imported into Alexandria.[186] Attic woolen cloth and pottery are mentioned in Plutarch's essay *Concerning Hearing*.[187] The man who insists upon the use of the Attic style of speech rather than upon the subject matter, Plutarch argues, is much like the man who refuses an antidote that is not mixed in an Attic pot, or who will not put on a coat in winter unless it is made of Attic wool. No more may be deduced from these words than that some woolen cloth and some pottery were produced in Attica in Plutarch's times. But we learn from archaeological discoveries that, as far as pottery is concerned, little beyond the most ordinary wares was produced. However, despite the fact that much pottery was imported, the so-called Type XX lamp, which was produced at Athens, met the local demand throughout the first century B.C. without competition from foreign makes.[188]

[185] See chap. iv, including note 221. It should be noted that Philostratus, *Vit. soph.* 603, states that the sophist Proclus of Naucratis, who settled at Athens toward the end of the second century A.D., received regular supplies of books and various other articles from Alexandria. It is not necessary to follow W. C. Wright, in her Loeb Library edition of Philostratus and Eunapius, p. 260, note 1, in concluding from this statement that the book trade had deserted Athens for Alexandria.

[186] Clement of Alexandria, *Paed.* II, xi, 116.

[187] Plutarch, *Mor.* ii, 42D. We are perhaps justified in concluding from this passage that the well-known clay from Cape Colias was still employed in making Attic pottery. For the clay from Cape Colias, see also Athenaeus, XI, 482b; Stephanus Byzantius, *s.v.* Κωλιάδος κεραμῆες. For the location of Cape Colias, see J. Day, in AJA, XXXVI (1932), 1–11.

[188] Broneer, *Lamps*, pp. 70–73. Cf. F. Miltner, in *Gnomon*, VIII (1932), 489 (review of Broneer, *Lamps*); H. A. Thompson, in *Hesperia*, II (1933), 203–4. The revenue derived by Athens from its foreign dependencies was very slight. See chap. iv, including notes 242–70. Pausanias, VIII, xxxiii, is guilty of exaggeration when he states that Delos had no inhabitants except for the guards sent by the Athenians to watch over the sanctuary of Apollo. Nevertheless, from the economic point of view the island was of little importance during the empire. See Roussel, DCA, pp. 336–40. The southern part of the island of Scyrus, the part adjoining the

With the profits derived from the exportation of this comparatively modest list of products, and with the revenues derived from students and tourists, the Athenians faced the problem of paying for a respectably large amount of imported commodities, some of which were essential in everyday life, others for the maintenance of local industries. The commodity which the Athenians found it most necessary to import in large amounts was, as ever, grain, which was brought for the most part from South Russia, from Asia Minor, and from Egypt.[189] The organization maintained by the state to assure an adequate supply of this necessity of life had been revamped at the time of Augustus, when a special treasury was formed and placed under the supervision of the hoplite general.[190] But we have reasons for believing that the funds in this treasury were often insufficient to provide an adequate supply of grain. It is difficult to explain otherwise the endowment created by Hadrian to

---

modern port of Tri-Bouki, was prosperous during the empire, for the Romans worked the quarries which were located there; see Strabo, IX, 437; Pliny, NH XXXI, ii, 29; XXXVI, xvi, 130; Eustathius, *Ad Dionys. perieg.* 521; Graindor, *Skyros*, pp. 12, 16. However, the quarries formed part of the imperial domain, and for that reason the working of them, which continued as late as the time of Valens (364–78 A.D.), brought little profit to the Athenians. Cf. Dubois, *Étude*, pp. 129–30; Graindor, *Skyros*, pp. 16–17; Bruzza, pp. 152–53, No. 238. Bruzza's No. 237, which he attributes to Scyrus, belongs rather to Carystus. Cf. Dubois, *Étude*, p. 130. For the other products of Scyrus, see chap. iv, including notes 258–61.

[189] Rostovtzeff, *Roman Empire*, p. 148. Possibly some of Athens' grain supply came from Egypt. Certainly the entire Egyptian crop was not taken by Rome, for, at some time during the first half of the second century A.D., some of it was imported into Sparta. See A. M. Woodward, in BSA, XXVI (1923–24, 1924–25), p. 163, A10, ll. 1–2, and pp. 179–80. Note may also be taken of the importation of grain from Egypt by Tralles (J. R. S. Sterrett, in *Papers of the American School of Classical Studies at Athens*, I [1882–83], 108–9, No. 10) and by Ephesus (*Forschungen in Ephesos* [Vienna, 1906–37], III, 106, No. 16).

[190] See chap. iv, including notes 272–79. Perhaps an additional arrangement for regulating the food supply of the city is to be deduced from an inscription of the end of the first or the beginning of the second century A.D. in which there is recorded the dedication of a statue—by the Areopagus, by the Boule of 600, and by the Demos—to a certain individual who was ἐπιμελητὴς τῆς κατὰ τὴν πόλιν ἀγορᾶς. Underneath the dedication two loaves of bread were sculptured on the stone (IG, II–III², 3545). Graindor (in BCH, XXXVIII [1914], 413, No. 21; cf. *Tibère*, pp. 81–82) has reasonably suggested that this magistrate performed duties like those of the aediles in connection with the *cura annona* at Rome, and more specifically that—under the direction of the *agoranomi*—he had oversight of the quality and the weight of bread sold in the Agora.

provide for yearly distributions of grain.[191] Moreover, we are explicitly informed by Philostratus[192] that a cargo of grain arrived from Thessaly at a moment when there was no money in the treasury, and that Lollianus of Ephesus, the sophist, who was hoplite general at the time, collected sufficient money from his students to pay for it and recompensed them by remitting the fees which he charged for his lectures. Famine, high prices, and, at times, riots ensued when the state was unable to purchase grain. Thus, on one occasion, when a riot broke out in the quarter of the bread-sellers, and a mob of Athenians was about to stone Lollianus, he was saved, Philostratus tells us,[193] by the Cynic philosopher Pancrates, who came forward and diverted the people by saying that Lollianus sold words, not bread. Even in more ordinary times, when there was no deficiency in the available supply, distributions of grain were made to the poor, favored occasions being festivals and the entry into office of a new magistrate.[194]

In the realm of industrial products we find that the Athenian potter produced only the most ordinary wares, and that the finer wares were, almost invariably, imported.[195] Arretine ware, which had been so highly favored in the time of Augustus, continued to be imported as late as the reign of Vespasian,[196] but in smaller amounts;

---

[191] Dio Cassius, LXIX, xvi, 2.   [192] *Vit. soph.* 526.

[193] *Ibid.*, 526. It is possible, also, that the disturbance in front of the house of the general Ammonius mentioned by Plutarch, *Quaest. conv.* II, vi, 1, arose from a similar cause; but this is uncertain. Cf. Graindor, *Tibère*, pp. 137–38.

[194] In the capacity of archon, which office he held toward the end of the first century A.D., Ti. Claudius Callicrates of Tricorynthus distributed a medimnus of grain and 15 drachmas to each citizen. See BCH, XIX (1895), 113 (= IG, II–III². 3546); cf. Graindor, *Chronologie*, pp. 12, 92–93.

[195] Cf. F. O. Waagé, in *Hesperia*, II (1933), 304.

[196] The following wares, with name of potter, provenance, and date, have been found at Athens (the page references are, unless indicated otherwise, to J. H. Iliffe, "Sigillata Wares in the Near East," QDAP, VI [1936], 4–53. See the review of this article, by F. O. Waagé, in AJA, XLIII [1939], 539–43). Arretine ware: Acatus, Arretine (?), Tiberian (?), p. 26; C. Amurius, Tiberian (?), p. 27 (cf. H. Comfort, in JAOS, LVIII [1938], 49; this article will henceforth, in this note, be referred to as Comfort-JAOS); P. Claudius, first century A.D., p. 30; Crom . . . ., Tiberian or later (?), p. 31 (cf. Comfort-JAOS, p. 55); L. Gellius, Tiberio-Claudian, p. 35; C. Meri, first century A.D., p. 52 (cf. Comfort-JAOS, p. 55); P. Clodius Proclus, Claudian, p. 44 (cf. Comfort-JAOS, p. 49); Zoilus, Augusto-Tiberian, p. 53. Gaulish and South Gaulish: Avitus, Gaulish (?), first century A.D., p. 29 (cf. Comfort-JAOS, p. 48); Iulius, South Gaulish, Claudio-Flavian, p. 36; Marcus,

and various *terra sigillata* wares of similar character, which are known under the names of "Tschandarli," "Pergamene," and "Samian," were brought from Asia Minor and the East.[197] Terracotta figurines were imported from Italy during roughly the first half of the first century A.D. and, possibly, from Asia Minor.[198] And beginning with the time of Trajan, Type XXVII lamps were imported from Corinth.[199] To such an extent had the Athenian potter lost his initiative that, beginning with the period of the Antonines, he was unable to do better than make imitations of this lamp.[200] Were more known of the history of ceramics at Athens in the first and second centuries A.D., we should probably find that Athens was more dependent upon the industries of Asia Minor and other eastern regions than the indications set forth above suggest. For building materials, although there was a plentiful supply of marble in Attica, marble was imported from Carystus, Thasus, Phrygia, and Libya for the adornment of buildings erected by Hadrian; and for the

South Gaulish, Flavian, p. 39; (?) Cosius and Vrappus, La Graufesenque, Nero-Vespasian, p. 50 (read L. URB[ani] by Comfort-JAOS, p. 59). Arretine and South Gaulish: C. Crestus, Claudius-Vespasian, p. 31. Additional wares at Athens—they are not dated—are listed by J. H. Iliffe, in QDAP, VI (1936), 4–53, and by H. Comfort, in JAOS, LVIII (1938), 30–60. See also chap. iv, notes 286, 288.

[197] The "Pergamene" ware found in the Agora at Athens is dated for the most part between 100 B.C. and 100 A.D. See F. O. Waagé, in *Hesperia*, II (1933), 286. The "Tschandarli" ware from the Agora is dated between the time of Tiberius and the early years of the second century A.D.; *ibid.*, p. 290. "Samian" ware from the Agora is dated in the first and second centuries A.D.; *ibid.*, p. 292. J. H. Iliffe, in QDAP, VI (1936), 38, lists a "Samian" vase of the first century A.D. which is stamped with the name ΚΟΙΡΑΝΟΣ. For an "eastern" vase of the first century A.D. (?), see p. 35 of Iliffe's article. Eastern wares from the Ceramicus are discussed by A. Oxé, in AM, LII (1927), 222–23, who dates them between the late Hellenistic period and the middle of the first century A.D. For eastern *sigillata* wares, see also chap. iv, note 288.

[198] For imported terra-cotta figurines of "early Roman" date found in the Agora at Athens, see D. Burr, in *Hesperia*, II (1933), 190–91. The execution of one figurine suggests Pompeian work, that of another suggests the work of Smyrna, while other figurines seem to have been imported, although their provenance may not, at present, be determined.

[199] Broneer, *Lamps*, pp. 26, 93–94, 111; H. A. Thompson, in *Hesperia*, II (1933), 204–6, 213.

[200] See the citations in the preceding note. The name of one of the makers of Type XXVII lamps at Athens was Preimos, a name which appears at Corinth at an earlier date. It has been suggested that the Corinthian factory had a branch at Athens, or, possibly, that there were two contemporary factories of the same name (Broneer, *Lamps*, pp. 111–12).

same purpose small amounts of Egyptian stone (basalt or porphyry) and of alabaster were also brought into Attica.[201] Materials had to be imported, also, for the only important industry which continued to thrive at Athens—that of making art products. Gold and ivory, copper and tin, all of which had to be imported, were required in large amounts by workers in this trade;[202] and copper and tin were, of course, essential in the minting of the bronze coinage which the Athenians issued between the time of Augustus and that of Gallienus.[203] For the use of the makers of books it was necessary to import papyrus from Egypt. Finally, for the luxury trade, aromatics and unguents of various kinds were brought from the Orient, in large part by way of Alexandria.[204]

An idea of the extent of the foreign trade of Athens and of the identity of the merchants in whose hands this trade was concentrated may be gained from a consideration of the names of foreigners preserved in the large number of sepulchral inscriptions which has been found in and near the city and the Piraeus.[205] Thrace is represented by 12 names, Macedonia by 5, and Epirus by 4. From northern Greece we find 20 names, of which 3 or 4 are from Thes-

[201] Note may be taken of four statues of Hadrian which were set up in front of the Olympieum; two were in Egyptian stone, and the remaining two in Thasian (Pausanias, I, xviii, 6). One hundred columns of Phrygian marble were employed in the Library of Hadrian, and a like number of columns of Libyan marble in the gymnasium which he built (Pausanias, I, xix, 6). Alabaster was employed in the ornamentation of the Library of Hadrian (Pausanias, I, xviii, 6). Marble from Carystus was employed in the building of the same structure (Graindor, *Hadrien*, p. 232).

[202] Gold, ivory, and other materials required by makers of objects of art were exported in large amounts by Alexandria (Leider, *Der Handel von Alexandria*, p. 30).

[203] J. P. Shear, "The Athenian Imperial Coinage," *Hesperia*, V (1936), 285–332.

[204] During the period of the Roman Empire the products of the South and the East came to Alexandria in larger amounts than before. Only a limited number of the more important modern works on the subject may be cited here: M. Rostovtzeff, "Zur Geschichte des Ost- und Südhandels im ptolemäisch-römischen Aegypten," *Archiv für Papyrusforschung*, IV (1908), 298–315; cf. V (1909), 181; E. H. Warmington, *The Commerce between the Roman Empire and India* (Cambridge, 1928), pp. 6–144; Kortenbeutel, *Ägyptischer Süd- und Osthandel*; Leider, *Der Handel von Alexandria*, p. 30. See also the bibliography given by Heichelheim, *Wirtschaftsgeschichte*, II, 1144, note 19. I have been unable to use M. Chwostow's history of Eastern trade in Greco-Roman Egypt published at Kazan, 1907.

[205] The numbers in the text have been collected from the sepulchral inscriptions published in IG, III and in SEG, I–III. I have been unable to consult Kirchner's new edition: see chap. iii, note 185.

saly, 1 or 2 from Aetolia, 1 from Opuntian Locris, and 12 from Boeotia; of the latter, 5 are from Plataea, 4 from Tanagra, 2 from Thebes, and 1 from Orchomenus. The Peloponnesus is represented by 19, of which 6 are from Corinth, 4 from Argos, and 2 from Sicyon; only 1 name from Patrae is to be noted. The islands of the Aegean are in general not well represented; but Carystus in Euboea, with 13 names, is noteworthy. We find from Bithynia, the Pontus, and the Propontis, 128 names, of which 90 are from Heraclea, 13 from Amisus, 11 from Sinope, 9 from Nicomedia, and 5 from Abydus. The names of 469 individuals from the remaining districts of Asia Minor are preserved. Mysia is represented by 13 names, of which 5 are from Pergamum and 5 from Adramyttium. A single name from Aeolis may be observed, that of an inhabitant of Myrina. Ionia is represented by 349 names, of which 342 are from Miletus, 3 from Smyrna, and 2 from Ephesus. From Lydia there are 14 names, among which we may note 9 from Sardis and 2 from Tralles. From Phrygia 37 names are preserved, among which are 23 from Laodicea and 11 from Apamea. From Caria and Pamphylia we find 4 names each, from Pisidia 5, from Cappadocia 1. Of Galatians 31 names are preserved, of which 30 are from Ancyra. From Cilicia we find 15 names, of which 14 are from Tarsus. Cyprus is represented by 6 names, Crete by 3, Rhodes and Cos by 1 each. From Syria we find 133 names, of which 118 are from Antioch,[206] 6 from Sidon, 4 from Tyre, and 9 from Palestine (Aradus, Ascalon, Damascus, Gadara, Iopes, and Samaria being represented).[207] From beyond Jordan we find 2 Gerasenes and 1 Ammanite. From Armenia 4 names are to be noted, along with 1 each from Babylon, Chaldaea, Edessa, and Ichnaea. Alexandria is represented by 23 names, and Libya and Cyrene by 1 each. From South Russia, and from the eastern and western coasts of the Euxine, we find 1 each from Cholcis, Tyranis,

---

[206] It is possible that some of the names assigned to Antioch on the Orontes really belong to another city of the same name, such as Antioch in Pisidia or Antioch on the Maeander. However, only one name is definitely indicated among the inscriptions as being from the city last mentioned.

[207] The evidence for a fair-sized colony of Jews at Athens is conclusive. Thus Luke tells us in Acts, xvii, 17, that Paul spoke to the Jews of Athens in their synagogue. Jewish sepulchral inscriptions appear in IG, III, 3545–47. Cf. E. Schürer, *Geschichte des jüdischen Volkes* (4th ed.; Leipzig, 1901–9), I, 391, note 72, and p. 724, note 61. Resident Jews in Attica are attested by Philo (*Leg. ad Caium*, 36).

Istrus, and Callatis, and 1 Bosporan, 1 Sarmatian, and 1 Maeotian. From the West 11 "Romans" and 4 other Italians are to be noted. While some transients are undoubtedly included in this list,[208] the fact that the larger part of the names on the tombstones were those of individuals who formed colonies more or less permanently established at Athens is made evident by various instances of intermarriage between men and women of cities other than Athens.[209]

It is instructive to make, for the sake of comparison, a selection of the number of foreigners from various districts which appear in the Attic sepulchral inscriptions of imperial date and to set them down alongside the corresponding numbers from the period between 403 B.C. and the time of Augustus.[210]

Place of Origin[a]	403 B.C. to Augustus	Imperial Period
Northern Greece	115	20
Boeotia	61	12
Thebes	33	2
Peloponnesus	50	19
Corinth	18	6
Sicyon	13	2
Carystus in Euboea	6	13
Bithynia, Pontus, Propontis	183	128
Heraclea Pontica	96	90
Sinope	24	11
Asia Minor[b]	125	469
Miletus	48	342
Ephesus	15	2
Ancyra	8	30
Syria	65 +	133
Antioch	39	118
Alexandria	7	23
Italy	14	15

[a] The figures for regions include the figures for cities in those regions.

[b] Except Bithynia, Pontus, and the Propontis.

---

[208] For example, some may have been students or tourists.

[209] See, for example, IG, III, 2239, 2329, 2389, 2413, 2427, 2464, 2620, 2671, 2734, 2871, 2891. For instances of marriage between Athenian men and foreign women and between Athenian women and foreign men, see IG, III, 2140–2201.

[210] For the numbers between 403 B.C. and the time of Augustus, see chap. iii, including notes 185–91. It is to be observed that names from the fourth century B.C. (when the number of foreigners at Athens was very large) are included in the figures set forth in the text above, and one must allow for this fact in making comparisons with the numbers from the imperial period.

One is struck at once by the severe decline in the number of Greeks from mainland cities other than Athens.[211] Especial note should be taken of the number of Italians; but here caution must be exercised. From inscriptional sources other than tombstones the colony of resident "Romans" at Athens during the Hellenistic period is definitely known to have been large.[212] But during the empire there is no additional evidence to supplement the testimony of the sepulchral inscriptions. We must, therefore, conclude that the Italian colony declined greatly in importance after the time of Augustus. This fact is, however, no occasion for surprise, for during the course of the first century A.D. the trade of Italy experienced a decided decline, owing largely to the development of competitive industries and agriculture in the provinces.[213] At Athens the evidence of importation of the products of Italy disappears not long after the middle of the century, and thenceforth the needs of the local market were to be supplied from the East. Thus it is that large groups of natives of Heraclea Pontica and of Antioch on the Orontes, and smaller groups of natives of Alexandria and of various cities of Asia Minor appear in the Athenian sepulchral inscriptions. The Pontic merchants in Attica imported not only grain, but also those commodities which had bulked large in the trade of their native district for some centuries.[214] From Alexandria, the second

[211] Note the following coins of imperial date which had been found in the Agora at Athens by 1935: 2 from Thessaly, 2 from Thessalonica, 1 from Corcyra, 10 from Corinth, 1 from Tenea, 3 from the Argolid, 2 from Sicyon, 4 from Patrae, and 1 from Elis. Cf. J. P. Shear, in *Hesperia*, V (1936), 130.

[212] See chap. iii, including notes 173–79. It is probable that most of the "Romans" listed in the sepulchral inscriptions in IG, III are not to be dated later than the time of Augustus.

[213] Rostovtzeff, *Roman Empire*, pp. 163–65; J. Keil, in CAH, XII, 236–42; Frank, "Rome and Italy of the Empire," p. 297; Heichelheim, *Wirtschaftsgeschichte*, I, 695. Exportation of sigillate wares from the West to the East ceased about the middle of the first century A.D. See H. Comfort, in JAOS, LVIII (1938), 33. For the disappearance of the *negotiatores* from the East in the course of the first and second centuries A.D., see Hatzfeld, *Trafiquants*, pp. 189–92. Those who remained in the Balkan peninsula as late as the second century A.D. maintained residences in Macedonia and in the Peloponnese.

[214] See the citations in chap. i, note 114; Broughton, "Roman Asia Minor," pp. 877–78. So many natives of the Pontus and of Thrace came to Athens that Philostratus, *Vit. soph.* 553, was able to have a speaker say that the pure Attic speech could no longer be learned in Athens.

most important city of the empire and an important center of trade in articles brought from Asia as well as from Africa, grain, papyrus, materials used in the production of objects of art, and industrial products of various kinds were imported, in addition to unguents, perfumes, spices, and various other products of the Orient destined for the luxury trade.[215] In Syria were centered the trade routes which have provided an important avenue of intercourse between East and West throughout so many centuries.[216] It was the products borne on these far-flung trade routes that the merchants of Antioch, the third most important city in the empire, carried to the cities of the Mediterranean world. At first glance the number of names of natives of Asia Minor which appear on the tombstones seems, in general, to have increased greatly since the Hellenistic period.[217] But this increase is attributable in very large

[215] See the citations in note 204, above. Three Alexandrian coins of Roman date had been found in the Agora at Athens by 1935; cf. J. P. Shear, in *Hesperia*, V (1936), 131. Also found in the Agora by 1935 were eleven coins of the imperial mint at Alexandria, which are dated between the time of Gallienus and the middle of the fifth century A.D.; *ibid.*, pp. 133–47. Philostratus, *Vit. soph.* 603, tells us that Proclus of Naucratis, the sophist who came to Athens to live, frequently imported from Egypt supplies of incense, ivory, myrrh, papyrus, books, and various other articles of similar nature and sold them, at no profit (?), to dealers in the city. Glass was, probably, among the industrial products imported into Athens from Alexandria. For the Alexandrian glass industry, see Kisa, *Glas*, I, 76–78. There is no evidence of glass working at Athens before Christian times. Then only one worker is attested. See IG, III, 3436; cf. Trowbridge, *Philological Studies in Ancient Glass*, pp. 41, 114.

[216] For the trade routes of Syria, see Charlesworth, *Trade Routes*, Chapter III; Heichelheim, "Roman Syria," pp. 198–200; Schaal, *Vom Tauschhandel zum Welthandel*, pp. 157–64; Rostovtzeff, *Caravan Cities*, especially pp. 1–36; Grant, *The Syrian Desert*, pp. 33–78. Seventy-four coins from the imperial mint at Antioch which date between the time of Gallienus and the middle of the fifth century A.D. had been found in the Agora at Athens by 1935. See J. P. Shear, in *Hesperia*, V (1936), 133–47.

[217] Athens appears on the alliance coins of Smyrna in the time of Marcus Aurelius and of Commodus. L. Weber, "Die Homoniemünzen des phrygischen Hierapolis," *Journal international d'archéologie numismatique*, XIV (1912), 65–122, especially p. 112. In Weber's catalogue (pp. 109–14) the only cities outside of Asia Minor to appear on alliance coins of cities of Asia Minor are Byzantium, Perinthus, Athens, Delphi, and Alexandria. Possibly reasons other than commercial were responsible for the names of Athens and Delphi. Only five coins that were struck by cities of Asia Minor under the empire had been found in the Agora and classified as of 1935: 1 from Alexandria Troas, 1 from Parium, 1 from Elea, and 2 from Chios. Cf. J. P. Shear, in *Hesperia*, V (1936), 131. Broughton, "Roman Asia Minor," p. 873, seems

part to the extraordinary increase in the number of Milesians. It is interesting to observe, in this connection, the number of Milesians and of Athenians registered among the Athenian ephebes in three separate periods between the reign of Domitian and that of Trajan.

Date (A.D.)	Athenians	Milesians	Source
			(In IG, II–III²)
84/5–92/3	80	151	1996
112/3	21	79	2024
116/7	4	48	2026

While some of these Milesians may have come to Athens from their native city especially for the purpose of enrolling in the ephebia, and others may have been sons of a sizable colony of resident Milesians at Athens,[218] it is impossible to account for the large registration merely by referring to these two sources. But there are reasons for believing that the term "Milesian" in these inscriptions may include foreigners other than Milesians. In the first place, the word ἐπένγραφοι, which is the usual heading for the list of foreign ephebes,[219] is not employed; instead we find the heading given as Μειλήσιοι. In the second place, two ephebes, who, to judge from their names, must be Romans, are listed among the Μειλήσιοι.[220] It would seem, therefore, that in those years when Milesians were preponderant in the contingent of foreign ephebes all foreigners were listed under the heading Μειλήσιοι.[221] In any event, the sepulchral inscriptions make it evident that the colony of Milesians at Athens was very large. The reason for their coming to Athens is difficult to determine. It is true that the economy of Miletus had experienced a severe decline beginning with the period of the Flavian emperors.[222] But what had Milesians to gain by migrating to Athens?[223]

---

to have included almost all coins from Asia Minor, irrespective of date. However, 378 coins of the imperial mints in Asia, dating between the time of Gallienus and the fifth century A.D., had been found in the Agora at Athens by 1935. Cf. J. P. Shear, in *Hesperia*, V (1936), 131–47.

[218] W. Dittenberger, *De ephebis Atticis* (Göttingen, 1863), p. 81, contended that all these ephebes came from a very large Milesian colony established at Athens.

[219] Cf. Graindor, in *Musée belge*, XXVI (1922), 225–27.

[220] IG, II–III², 1996, l. 95 (Pomponius Clarus), and 2024, l. 42 (Claudius Capito). Cf. Graindor, *Tibère*, p. 88.

[221] See Thalheim, in RE, V, 2739–40, followed by Reinmuth, *The Foreigners in the Athenian Ephebia*, pp. 46–48; see also Graindor, *Tibère*, p. 88.

[222] Broughton, "Roman Asia Minor," p. 755.

[223] It is possible that some were encouraged to come to Athens by relatives al-

Economic conditions can hardly be said to have been favorable there. The suggestion has been made that they were laborers who were interested, perhaps, in finding small plots of land on which to make their homes.[224] This may have been true for many, but certainly not for all of them; it will certainly not explain the enrollment of numerous Milesians in the ephebia. Conditions at Athens had not changed so greatly that sons of laborers were admitted into that institution.

The question immediately prompts itself: To whom did the foreign traders sell their wares and commodities—especially the luxuries from the Orient? Certainly the number of Athenians who were sufficiently well to do to purchase them was comparatively small. The answer is probably fourfold. First, the wealthy visitors and students who thronged Athens in numbers, along with a few Athenians, formed part of the clientele of the traders.[225] Second, many imported commodities were employed in the adornment of the city by Hadrian and Herodes Atticus. Third, the making of objects of art, the only important industry that survived at Athens, required regular suppies of ivory, copper, tin, and precious metals. Fourth, many of the traders who settled at Athens probably sold their wares in other parts of Greece but preferred to maintain their residence at Athens because the city offered more opportunities for pleasant living than could be found in other Greek cities. In any event, whatever the answers to the question may be,

---

ready settled there. A sizable colony of Milesians is attested for the Hellenistic period.

[224] U. Wilamowitz von Moellendorf, in *Göttingische gelehrte Anzeigen*, CLXXVI (1914), 99; cf. F. Hiller von Gaertringen, in RE, XV, 1616; Röhlig, *Der Handel von Milet*, p. 45. One of the Milesians who resided in Athens is represented on a sepulchral stele which was found at Laurium (Graindor, *Marbres*, pp. 9–12; Graindor, *Hadrien*, pp. 280–81). He was a cattle merchant or, perhaps, one of the βοῶναι, whose duty it was to purchase cattle for sacrifices. Cf. P. Stengel, *Die griechische Kultusaltertümer* (3rd ed.; Munich, 1920), p. 50.

[225] Undoubtedly some Athenians earned a livelihood by acting in the capacity of guides for tourists. For the local *periegetae* in Greece, see Bischoff, "Perieget," RE, XIX, 726. The fact that Proclus of Naucratis owned two houses in Athens, one in the Piraeus, and one in Eleusis—the ones outside the city nicely located to take advantage of opportunities for trade—suggests, despite Philostratus' statement (*Vit. soph.* 603) that he sold the wares which he imported from Egypt at no profit, that the sophist was also a merchant who catered to the luxury trade. It was probably not mere piety that prompted his acquisition of a house at Eleusis.

the foreign trade of the city was sufficiently large to maintain at least a moderate degree of prosperity in the Piraeus. Pausanias tells of seeing ship sheds and two markets there.[226] And from two inscriptions which record dedications in honor of members of the family of Herodes Atticus, one in honor of his wife, Regilla, the other in honor of his eldest son, Bradua, we may deduce that the harbor town was by no means a deserted place.[227] One of these inscriptions records the erection, by the businessmen who resided in the Piraeus, of a statue of Regilla which had been voted by the Areopagus.[228] Somewhat later in the century the citizens of the Piraeus, banding themselves together in an informal group [οἱ τὸν Πειραιᾶ κατοικοῦντες πολῖται], dedicated a statue of Bradua in recognition of gifts which he had bestowed upon them.[229]

Some notice must be taken of the type of labor employed at Athens during the first and second centuries A.D. Unfortunately for the purposes of the present enquiry, the Greeks did not follow the common Roman practice of representing on their tombstones the deceased in the pursuit of their daily occupations.[230] Nevertheless, in the few instances where the former occupations of the deceased are specified in Athenian sepulchral inscriptions we have evidence that the normal Greek practice of specialization, which may be observed in the classical and Hellenistic periods, was continued in the imperial period.[231] Thus, the following occupations may be cited: trainer,[232] rhetorician or teacher of eloquence,[233] teacher of

[226] I, i, 3.

[227] Lucian, *Navig.* i, 9, mentions the great excitement occasioned in the Piraeus when an Egyptian grain ship put in there. This is not to be taken as evidence that few ships came into the harbor. The excitement was probably caused by the large size of the ship, which may have been a vessel in the service of the imperial *annona*, bound for Rome. Cf. Gurlitt, *Über Pausanias*, pp. 198–99. For the date and bearing of IG, II–III², 1035, which is usually assigned to the second century A.D., see chap. iv, including notes 152–66.

[228] IG, II–III², 3607. [229] *Ibid.*, 3978; cf. Graindor, *Hérode*, p. 103.

[230] For the Roman practice, see H. Gummerus, "Darstellungen aus dem Handwerk auf römischen Grab- und Votivsteinen," JDAI, XXVIII (1913), 63–226. On p. 66 Gummerus comments upon the scarcity of Attic examples. Cf. Graindor, *Marbres*, p. 12, note 2. A stele of an actor is published in JHS, XXIII (1903), 358–59, Pl. XIII.

[231] For specialization of work throughout the empire during the imperial period, see Heichelheim, *Wirtschaftsgeschichte*, II, 1154.

[232] IG, III, 1434: ἀλείπτης παίδων Καίσαρος. He was an imperial freedman.

[233] *Ibid.*, 1438: ῥήτωρ.

gymnastics,[234] philosopher,[235] doctor,[236] collector of the 5 percent tax on the freeing of slaves,[237] soldier,[238] businessman,[239] peda-gogue,[240] baker,[241] vineyard worker,[242] farm laborer,[243] dealer in salt,[244] nurse,[245] and midwife.[246] As regards slave labor, although our in-formation from literary and epigraphical sources is very scanty, we are probably justified in concluding that it was not extensively employed. Throughout Greece, in the imperial period, the number of slaves seems to have varied in proportion to the development of economic life in the various districts;[247] and inasmuch as industry at Athens had experienced a severe decline, we do not expect to find many slaves there. Probably a few worked in the capacity of sculptor's assistant, or in the ceramic trade; others were em-ployed in work on the land. That slaves—and freedmen as well— were employed in farming, such as the production of olive oil, is shown by Hadrian's oil law, where it is provided that the owners of olive groves must submit to the magistrate who is empowered to deal with the sale of oil a written statement giving the name of the slave or freedman who produced the oil that was harvested from the land in question.[248] Moreover, a few wealthy men, like Herodes Atticus,[249] owned numerous slaves and, in addition, had

[234] *Ibid.*, 1440: παιδοτρίβης.   [235] *Ibid.*, 1441.   [236] *Ibid.*, 1445.

[237] *Ibid.*, 1446 (= ILS, 1867): εἰκοστῆς ἐλευθερίας οἰκονόμος. The inscription is the epitaph of an imperial collector of the tax. Larsen ("Roman Greece," p. 456) expresses the opinion that the bureau was not located at Athens.

[238] IG. III, 1448.   [239] *Ibid.*, 1449: πραγματευτής.   [240] *Ibid.*, 1451.

[241] *Ibid.*, 1452, 1453.   [242] *Ibid.*, 1454: ἀμπελουργός.

[243] *Ibid.*, 1455: γεωργός.   [244] *Ibid.*, 1456: ἀλοπ(ώ)λις.   [245] *Ibid.*, 1457, 1458.

[246] *Ibid.*, 3453: ἰατρίνη. This stone is not included in the collection of material made by Graindor, *Hadrien*, p. 281, note 3. See also Conze, *Die attischen Grab-reliefs*, IV, No. 1914: stele of Hermione, the μεωτική.

[247] Westermann, "Sklaverei," cols. 1024–25. Plutarch, *De lib. ed.* 6–7, mentions the employment in Greece of slaves in the following capacities: teachers, workers on the land, business agents, bankers, and domestic servants.

[248] IG, II–III², 1100, ll. 15–18.

[249] Philostratus, *Vit. soph.* 549. From two inscriptions of the end of the second or the beginning of the third century A.D. (I.G, II–III², 1365, 1366) we learn that Xanthus of Lycia, slave of C. Orbius, established a shrine of Men Tyrannus in the neighborhood of Sunium. Kirchner, in his comments on the inscription, follows H. von Prott and L. Ziehen, *Leges Graecorum sacrae e titulis collectae* (Leipzig, 1896–1906), II, i, 150, in assuming that the slave had been placed at work in the mines at Laurium. But this is manifestly impossible, unless exploitation of the mines for lead continued until c.200 A.D. See. chap. iv, including notes 224–31.

numerous freedmen in their services. But we must conclude that slaves formed only a very inconsiderable part of the laboring population of Athens.

Let us now turn to a very important inscription (IG, II–III², 2776), the interpretation of which is rendered highly problematical by the fragmentary condition in which it exists.[250] The document—we shall call it for convenience "No. 2776"—can be dated in the time of Hadrian;[251] it contains a list of parcels of property and amounts of money registered as follows. There is given first the name of a man or woman—or, in some instances, names of two or more individuals—in the nominative case. In second place is the name of a plot of ground in the genitive case. The third notation is a definition of the location of the plot of ground in question. The fourth, and final, notation is a sum of money reckoned in denarii, drachmas, and fractions of drachmas as small as $\frac{1}{12}$. The denarius is equivalent in value to the old drachma, while the drachma has become the equivalent of the old obol.[252] When several properties are indicated as belonging to the same owner or owners, the grand total is given along with the symbol $\nearrow\!\!\setminus$.[253] No introductory heading of No. 2776 exists, and there may never have been one. For this reason the general nature of the document may be deduced only from various phenomena which are to be observed in connection with the names, the properties, and the sums of money mentioned in it. The highest sum certainly listed is 2,687½ denarii,[254] the lowest 208 denarii. Of the 89 separate sums only 17 are above 1,000 denarii; 7 are 100 denarii or less, 6 are between 200 and 300 denarii,

[250] IG, II–III², 2776, edited by J. Kirchner, and IG, III, 61, edited by W. Dittenberger. Cf. Roberts and Gardner, *Greek Epigraphy*, Part II, No. 96, pp. 252–55. For discussions of the inscription, see T. Mommsen, "Athenische Stiftungsurkunde," *Hermes*, V (1871), 129–37; B. Keil, in *Hermes*, XXIX (1894), 271; Graindor, *Hadrien*, pp. 184–91; and the review of the last-cited book by C. B. Welles, in *AJA*, XXXIX (1935), 423–25, especially p. 424.

[251] From the names of various individuals listed in the inscription Dittenberger, in his commentary on IG, III, 61, was able to determine the proper date.

[252] For the various denominations of coinage cited in the inscription, see T. Mommsen, in *Hermes*, V (1871), 134–37; Head, *Hist. Num.*, pp. 390–91.

[253] The symbol $\nearrow\!\!\setminus$, often encountered in papyri, is to be expanded into ($\gamma i\gamma\nu o\nu\tau a\iota$) $\dot{o}\mu(o\hat{v})$. Cf. A. Wilhelm, in *Anzeiger wiener Akademie*, 1924, p. 136.

[254] It should be stated that two higher amounts are restored (3462½; 3505), but their authenticity is questionable.

12 between 301 and 400, 7 between 401 and 500, 6 between 501 and 600, 5 between 601 and 700, 9 between 701 and 800, 2 between 801 and 900, 4 between 901 and 1,000, 3 between 1,001 and 1,100, 3 between 1,101 and 1,200, 2 between 1,201 and 1,300, 1 between 1,400 and 1,500, 2 between 1,501 and 1,600, 1 between 1,601 and 1,700, 1 between 1,701 and 1,800, 1 between 1,900 and 2,000, 2 between 2,200 and 2,300. Because of the proportionately large number (25) of properties to which sums under 400 denarii are assigned, it might be argued that the largest sums mentioned in the inscription are too high for rent or interest payments, while the smallest sums are too low to represent capital value.[255] But the manifest invalidity of part of this argument appears at once if account is taken of the sales list from Tenos, which is dated in the third century B.C.[256] In this inscription, where sales prices of lands and houses vary between 60 (old) drachmas and 8,000 drachmas, 13 of the 42 sums listed are 400 drachmas or lower. But serious difficulties will be encountered in any attempt to evaluate the properties mentioned in No. 2776. First, we have very little knowledge concerning land values in ancient Greece.[257] Prices are often given in our sources, but only infrequently are the extent and more than the general nature of the property indicated. Second, the extent of the properties listed in No. 2776 is in no case indicated. Some of the plots, such as, for example, the gardens, were undoubtedly small; and other plots may have been comparatively small fields rather than farms. Third, we have no satisfactory knowledge concerning the real value of money at Athens during the imperial period. The fractional sums in the inscription have been cited as proof that the purchasing power of money was very high during the second century A.D.[258] But it is to be observed that the smallest fraction em-

[255] Cf. T. Mommsen, in *Hermes*, V (1871), 131.

[256] IG, XII, v, 872.   [257] Cf. Jardé, *Céréales*, p. 149.

[258] Graindor, *Hadrien*, pp. 188–89. To bolster his contention that the purchasing power of money was high at Athens in the time of Hadrian, Graindor cites (*Hadrien*, p. 184) a passage from Lucian, *Dial. mer.* vi, 1, following the reading of K. Mras, *Kleine Texte für Vorlesungen und Übungen*, Heft 160³ (Bonn, 1930); cf. Mras, "Das Existenzminimum im alten Athen," *Charisteria Alois Rzach* (Reichenberg, 1930), pp. 148–49. The dramatic date of the dialogue goes back to the early years of the New Comedy, a period when Athens was very prosperous. Lucian puts in the mouth of a mother words to the effect that, after the death of her husband, who was a blacksmith, she had sold his hammer, tongs, and anvil for two minas,

ployed is $\frac{1}{2}$ (new) obol, which equals $\frac{1}{72}$ denarius or $\frac{1}{12}$ (old) obol, and that similar small fractions were employed in the accounts of the Temple administrators at Delos, where the χαλκοῦς was equated with $\frac{1}{12}$ (old) obol.[259] Moreover, an even smaller coin, the κόλλυβος, the exact value of which is not known, was employed at Athens as early as the second half of the fifth century B.C.[260] However, such small fractions were employed in connection with landed property for the first time in No. 2776. But the employment of these fractions does not support the contention that the real value of money was high unless it can, at the same time, be established that the sums set forth in these fractional figures were capital sums. Actually, the prevalence of these small fractional figures in the inscription suggests that the amounts represent percentages of some larger amount. This conjecture receives support from the frequent occurrence of sums concluded with the following figures, which are here set forth in two series for the sake of emphasizing their relation to larger amounts.[261] Note first the series $12\frac{1}{2}$, 25, $37\frac{1}{2}$, 50, $62\frac{1}{2}$, 75, and $87\frac{1}{2}$; then the series $6\frac{1}{4}$, $18\frac{3}{4}$, $31\frac{1}{4}$, $43\frac{3}{4}$, $56\frac{1}{4}$, $68\frac{3}{4}$, $81\frac{1}{4}$, and $93\frac{3}{4}$. In each of these series the arithmetical progression is by eighths of 100, and when they are multiplied by 4, 8, 12, 16, 20, 24, or other multiples of 4, the individual sums are resolved into even numbers. On the basis of these phenomena

---

and that on this amount she and her daughter had subsisted for seven months. Graindor maintains that this would have been manifestly impossible in the very prosperous fourth century B.C. and that, therefore, Lucian attributed to that period conditions that existed in his own time. We may observe, however, that very recently Heichelheim, *Schwankungen*, pp. 98–101, has calculated that in 329/8 B.C. the living cost for a single adult ranged between $93\frac{1}{2}$–$138\frac{1}{2}$ drachmas per year; and in 282 B.C. it was about 140 drachmas per year. In the latter year, it has been calculated (by Larsen, "Roman Greece," p. 413), a family of four could live for one year on 362 drachmas. On this basis a family of two could have lived very readily on 200 drachmas for seven months.

[259] This is the observation of Larsen, "Roman Greece," p. 490.

[260] A series of small bronze coins of this denomination was first identified by J. Svoronos, in *Journal international d'archéologie numismatique*, XIV (1912), 123–29, 155. Inasmuch as they are mentioned in Aristophanes, *Pax*, 1200, such coins must have been employed before 421 B.C., at which time the comedy was produced. Cf. K. Regling, "Kollybos," RE, XI, 1099-1100.

[261] More than one third of the sums listed in the inscription are of the fractional character observed in the two series of figures listed in the text. More than two thirds were concluded with the figures, both fractional and round, set forth in those series.

Theodor Mommsen assumed[262] that the individual sums listed in No. 2776 represented amounts on which 8 percent interest was to be paid. But this assumption is not at all likely. Even if one should grant that a specified round sum of money was desired through some settlement of the amounts mentioned in the inscription, it would not follow that more than one third of the sums were intentionally given the fractional character noted above so as to produce a grand total of interest payments in a round number. It is, on the other hand, most probable that the sums in No. 2776 represent 25 percent, $12\frac{1}{2}$ percent, $8\frac{1}{3}$ percent, $6\frac{1}{4}$ percent, 5 percent, or $4\frac{1}{6}$ percent of larger sums. On the basis of these percentages the capital values of the properties listed in the inscription would amount to the sums (given in denarii) set forth in the Table. As we have already observed, we know nothing concerning the extent of the plots involved, and little concerning the real value of money at Athens in the time of Hadrian or the value of Athenian land in general. Is it possible, then, to deduce from these statistics the probable capital values of the properties listed in the inscription? The only legitimate procedure seems to be to compare the various sums with the values of Attic properties as they are attested by literary sources and inscriptions. These sources, it may be stated, range in date between the fourth and the second centuries B.C. Whatever the true percentages of capital values represented by the sums listed in No. 2776, the statistics seem to show that the owners of many of the properties were moderately prosperous or even well-to-do individuals. The fact that this inference is altogether probable is borne out by three considerations. First, the prosperous condition of numerous owners is shown by their possession of Roman citizenship, as manifested in their *nomina*. In this connection the following *nomina* may be cited: Aelius (1), Arrius (3), Claudius (12), Flavius (12), Julius (2), Junius (4), Ventidius (1), Vibullius (1), and Vipsanius (1). Second, there appears among the owners the name of at least one Athenian archon, Ti. Claudius Lysiades, archon at some time near 138 A.D.;[263] Ly-

---

[262] In *Hermes*, V (1871), 131–33.

[263] Graindor, *Hadrien*, p. 91, note 1; cf. *Chronologie*, pp. 135–37. In his edition of the inscription Dittenberger restored (IG, III, 61B, II, 37) the name of Φ[ουλ]ούιος Μητ[ροδῶρος?], who was archon at some time between 98/9 A.D. and 109/10 A.D.

TABLE OF HYPOTHETICAL VALUES[a] OF PROPERTIES REPRESENTED IN IG, II–III^2, 2776

SUMS GIVEN	NO. OF SUMS	TOTAL VALUE OF PROPERTY IF SUMS GIVEN REPRESENT PERCENTAGES OF CAPITAL VALUE					
		25%	12½%	8⅓%	6¼%	5%	4⅙%
-100	7	-400	-800	-1,200	-1,600	-2,000	-2,400
200-300	6	800-1,200	1,600-2,400	2,400-3,600	3,200-4,800	4,000-6,000	4,800-7,200
301-400	12	1,204-1,600	2,408-3,200	3,612-4,800	4,816-6,400	6,020-8,000	7,224-9,600
401-500	7	1,604-2,000	3,208-4,000	4,812-6,000	6,416-8,000	8,020-10,000	9,624-12,000
501-600	6	2,004-2,400	4,008-4,800	6,012-7,200	8,016-9,600	10,020-12,000	12,024-14,400
601-700	5	2,404-2,800	4,808-5,600	7,212-8,400	9,616-11,200	12,020-14,000	14,424-16,800
701-800	9	2,804-3,200	5,608-6,400	8,412-9,600	11,216-12,800	14,020-16,000	16,824-19,200
801-900	2	3,204-3,600	6,408-7,200	9,612-10,800	12,816-14,400	16,020-18,000	19,224-21,600
901-1,000	4	3,604-4,000	7,208-8,000	10,812-12,000	14,416-16,000	18,020-20,000	21,624-24,000
1,001-1,100	3	4,004-4,400	8,008-8,800	12,012-13,200	16,016-17,600	20,020-22,000	24,024-26,400
1,101-1,200	3	4,404-4,800	8,808-9,600	13,212-14,400	17,616-19,200	22,020-24,000	26,424-28,800
1,201-1,300	2	4,804-5,200	9,608-10,400	14,412-15,600	19,216-20,800	24,020-26,000	28,824-31,200
1,400-1,500	1	5,600-6,000	11,200-12,000	16,800-18,000	22,400-24,000	28,000-30,000	33,600-36,000
1,501-1,600	2	6,004-6,400	12,008-12,800	18,012-19,200	24,016-25,600	30,020-32,000	36,024-38,400
1,601-1,700	1	6,404-6,800	12,808-13,600	19,212-20,400	25,616-27,200	32,020-34,000	38,424-40,800
1,701-1,800	1	6,804-7,200	13,608-14,400	20,412-21,600	27,216-28,800	34,020-36,000	40,824-43,200
1,900-2,000	1	7,600-8,000	15,200-16,000	22,800-24,000	30,400-32,000	38,000-40,000	45,600-48,000
2,200-2,300	2	8,800-9,200	17,600-18,400	26,400-27,600	35,200-36,800	44,000-46,000	52,800-55,200
2,687½	1	10,700	21,400	32,100	43,000	53,750	64,200

[a] All values are in denarii.

siades was a member of one of the most prominent Athenian families of the second century A.D.[264] Third, several individuals who are named in the inscription could not have owned the various properties listed under their names had they not been at least moderately prosperous or well to do.[265] But let us now see how the figures given in the Table compare with the known values of Athenian lands in earlier times. The following prices may be observed in Attic mortgage inscriptions assigned to dates between the fourth and the second centuries B.C.[266]

Provenance of Inscription	Type of Property	Value	Source
1. Ceratea (deme of Cephale [?])	Land, house	1 talent, 2,000 dr.	IG, II–III², 2659
2. Amarouseion (deme of Athmonon)	Land	1 talent	2670
3. Near Mt. Hymettus	Land	1 talent	2713
4. Spata	Land, house	1 talent	2699
5. Plain of Thria	Land, house	4,500 dr.	2662
6. Spata	Land, house	3,000 dr.	2660
7. Spata	Land, house	2,700+ dr.	2679
8. Icaria	Land, house	1,500 dr.	AJA, 1888, p. 425, No. 3
9. Decelea	Land	1,200 dr.	IG, II–III², 2719
10. Athens (near Callirrhoe)	Land, house	1,130 dr.	2685
11. Near Mt. Hymettus	Land	1,050 dr.	2681
12. Marcopoulo	Land	1,000 dr.	2712
13. Athens	Land, house	300 dr.	2684
14. Chasani (deme of Halimus)	Land, house	200 dr.	2686
15. Piraeus	Land	150 dr.	2704

While most of the higher prices are for a house in addition to land, it will be observed that Nos. 2 and 3 are landed property in entirety.[267] Furthermore, we must observe that, in view of the

---

Cf. Graindor, *Tibère*, p. 190 and *Chronologie*, pp. 110–14. But Kirchner now restores (IG, II–III², 2776, l. 193) Φ[λα]ούιος Μητ . . . . . One may also observe the names of the following *prytaneis* who are listed in the inscription: Flavius Philotimus and Flavius Dorotheus (l.69); P. Aelius Attalus (l.42); Claudius Callistomachus (l. 48). Flavius Dorotheus also held the office of hoplite general. Cf. IG, II–III², 3605.

[264] Graindor, *Hadrien*, p. 135; see notes 339–42, below.

[265] See below, including notes 310–11.

[266] A collection of these inscriptions, together with a detailed treatment of the legal questions involved, has been made by Dareste, Haussoulier, and Reinach, *Recueil*, I, viii, 107–42. Additional examples are to be found in IG, II–III².

[267] The properties listed in No. 2776 seem to have consisted entirely of land.

very substantial security that was required, the true value of the
mortgaged properties will probably be approximated if we multi-
ply all these sums by two.[268] The mortgage inscriptions, therefore,
attest the existence of undivided landed properties worth as much
as 16,000 drachmas. If we turn now to the Attic orators, we may
note the following values of undivided landed properties:[269]

Property	Value	Source
Estate of Phaenippus in the Mesogeia	52 talents	Demosthenes, *Phaen.* 1040, 1045
Land at Thria	2½ talents	Isaeus, XI, 42
Land at Eleusis	2 talents	XI, 41
Landed property	100 minas	Demosthenes, *Contr. Steph.* 28
Land at Athmonon	75 minas	Isaeus, VI, 33
Landed property	70 minas	II, 34
Land at Phlya	1 talent	VIII, 35
Land at Prospalta	3,000 drachmas	XI, 44
Land at Alopece	2,000 drachmas	Aeschines, *Contr. Tim.* 97
Land at Oenoe	500 drachmas	Isaeus, XI, 44

The estate of Phaenippus was, however, exceptional in the history
of Athenian landed property. In any event, it is evident that well-
to-do individuals often owned undivided properties worth sums
ranging between 6,000 drachmas and 15,000 drachmas, or even
more. But these are values of landed properties in the fourth century B.C. By the end of the third century B.C. the value of land
seems to have declined sharply.[270] Moreover, the extent to which
agriculture recovered, in the imperial period, from the depression
which settled upon it in Hellenistic times is not known.[271] We cannot, therefore, be certain concerning the extent of undivided plots
of land at Athens in the time of Hadrian. The most that can be said
is that a comparison of the values set forth in the Table, based on
No. 2776, with the values observed in the mortgage inscriptions
and in the writings of the Attic orators would seem to indicate

[268] See Guiraud, *Propriété foncière*, p. 392.
[269] All items except the first were assembled by Guiraud, *Propriété foncière*,
p. 393. The value of the first is given as estimated by Jardé, *Céréales*, pp. 158–59.
Inasmuch as the estate of Aristophanes, mentioned by Lysias, XIX, 29 and 42,
probably consisted of lands situated in more than one locality—although Lysias
does not specifically make this assertion—the lands owned by him have not been
included in the list set forth in the text.
[270] Heichelheim, *Schwankungen*, pp. 82–83; Larsen, "Roman Greece," pp. 402–7.
[271] In any event, cultivation of cereals and of olive oil was now profitable.

that the sums listed in No. 2776 represent 12½ percent, 25 percent, or, possibly 8⅓ percent of larger amounts, and that they were probably loans secured by landed property. Any smaller percentage would presuppose the holding in one locality of considerably larger parcels of land than is otherwise attested in our sources. If loans were actually made at the rate of 12½ percent or 8⅓ percent of the values of the properties in question, it is quite probable that No. 2776 records a list of mortgage payments which were employed in support of an alimentation project. The essential feature of these projects was the provision made for a yearly income to be used to aid families in rearing free-born children.[272] In some instances this yearly income was made available through a gift of some private citizen,[273] in other instances through interest payments on mortgages which the state took on landed property.[274] Indeed, Theodor Mommsen interpreted the inscription as the record of an *obligatio praediorum*.[275] However, two arguments have been advanced in opposition to his thesis.[276]

[272] For the *alimenta* in general, see A. M. Ashley, "The 'Alimenta' of Nerva and His Successors," *English Historical Review*, XXXVI (1921), 5–16; J. Carcopino, in REA, XXIII (1921), 287–303; De Ruggiero, *Diz. ep.*, I, 408–10; R. P. Longden, in CAH, XI, 210–11; T. Mommsen, "Die italische Bodentheilung und die Alimentartafeln," *Hermes*, XIX (1884), 393–416 (reprinted in his *Gesammelte Schriften*, V [Berlin, 1908], 123–45); Frank, "Rome and Italy of the Empire," pp. 65–67.

[273] Such as, for example, Pliny's private endowment. See Pliny, *Epist.* VII, xviii; cf. De Ruggiero, *Diz. ep.*, I, 408; Frank, "Rome and Italy of the Empire," p. 106.

[274] For the procedure followed in Trajan's alimentation projects, see the Tabula Ligurum Baebianorum (CIL, IX, 1455) and the Tabula Veleiatium (CIL, XI, 1147). For the latter, see F. G. de Pachtere, *La Table hypothécaire de Veleia: Étude sur la propriété foncière dans l'Apennin de Plaisance* (Paris, 1920; Bibliothèque de l'École des Hautes Études, Fasc. 228); see also J. Carcopino's review of this monograph, in REA, XXIII (1921), 287–303. If the amounts loaned were actually 8⅓ percent or 12½ percent of the value of the lands, then the transactions indicated in No. 2776 would conform quite well to the practice followed at Veleia, where loans were made at first on the basis of 10 percent of the value of the farms, and later on the basis of 8 $\frac{1}{20}$ percent. Cf. De Pachtere's monograph, p. 101.

[275] In *Hermes*, V (1871), 130–33. For Hadrian's interest in the *alimenta*, see Spartianus, *Vit. Hadr.* vii, 8; cf. Frank, "Rome and Italy of the Empire," p. 70.

[276] By Graindor, *Hadrien*, p. 187. Graindor also argued that the document could not have been an *obligatio praediorum* because the rate of interest (8 percent) to be paid according to Mommsen's assumption (in *Hermes*, V [1870], 132) was higher than that charged in the definitely identified *alimenta*. However, as we have seen, there is no evidence for asserting that the transaction detailed in the Athenian inscription involved a payment of 8 percent interest.

First, the form of No. 2776 differs considerably from that of known alimentation deeds, all of which are written in Latin. In No. 2776 the name of the owner, or of the owners, of the property is given in the nominative case, which is followed by the genitive of the name of the property, and then by a sum of money. For example (ll. 69–72):

Φλ Δωρόθεος Φλ Φιλότειμος Φλ Λολ- ✕ χπϛ<
λία Φλ Μεγίστη κήπου πρὸς τῆ
'Αχαρνικῆ πύλη προσαγορευομένου Κειονίου

Of course, the question arises, does the genitive in which the name of the property is given mean that the sum specified has been paid on the property in question or is owed on account? On the other hand, in the Ligurian alimentation deed the name of the owner is given in the ablative, which is followed by the name of the property in the genitive, by the name of the pagus where it is located in the ablative, by the name of the owners of neighboring properties in the ablative, and finally, in order, by the estimated value of the property, by the amount received by the owner, and by the amount of interest to be paid semiannually or, possibly, annually. For example (CIL, IX, 1455, III, ll.39–40):

Turselio Pudente fund(i) Caerelliani pag(o) Mefla-   HS LXXV
no adf(ine) Rubrio aest (imatorum) HS L̅ in HS I̅I̅I̅

Moreover, the nature of the register is described in the introductory heading of the inscription.

Second, a few of the properties mentioned in the Athenian inscription are defined in too vague a fashion to be adequate for an *obligatio praediorum*. Thus, we find fractional properties such as: θριωσίῳ πρὸς τῷ Μύρμηκι καὶ ἄλλου χωρ(ίου) μέρους τρίτου [ll. 62–63]; Κλ Με[νε]χάρηα μερῶν τεσσάρων [ll. 91–92]; Κλ Δεκο-[μος(?)——]οω μέρους ἕκτου [ll. 92–93].

The first argument is not necessarily decisive. While the forms in which imperial *alimenta* were recorded might be expected to bear some resemblance to each other, one may not be certain how close that resemblance should be. As regards the significance of the genitive case, that will be explained only when the introductory heading of the inscription is found or when the general nature of the document has been determined. The second argument is not valid. Several instances of joint tenants, or tenants in common, are to be noted in No. 2776. It may, therefore, be assumed that in those cases where fractional parts of property are listed only one of the co-tenants has participated in the financial transaction which the inscription records. It will be observed that these properties are located by deme and by the name of the owner, and, although such descriptions may be somewhat vague, it must be remembered that many deeds of conveyance, even in our own times, leave something to be desired in the way of clarity. In conclusion, one may rightly state, I believe, that a good case may be made for considering No. 2776 the record of an *obligatio praediorum*.[277] But the proof is by no means decisive. Graindor's alternative interpretation, that No. 2776 records a number of mortgages which provide security for loans received from the ἀργυροταμίαι, would be acceptable were it not for the difficulty of explaining why so many well-to-do— and even some prominent—Athenian citizens are found among the mortgagors. This phenomenon is best explained by construing the inscription as the record of an alimentation project.

Whatever the proper interpretation of No. 2776, there is much important information concerning Attic agriculture and the Attic countryside to be gleaned from it.[278] Various types of land and crops are mentioned in the inscription: a field kept as a garden,[279] valley land,[280] pasture land with forests and thickets,[281] a garden of the formal type,[282] a gourd or cucumber patch,[283] woodland,[284] tree-

---

[277] Graindor, *Hadrien*, p. 189. For such transactions, see notes 272–74, above. However, Graindor prefers (*Hadrien*, pp. 184–85, 188–89) to see in the inscription a record of sales similar to that preserved in the well-known inscription from Tenos (IG, XII, v, 872). The first editor of the inscription, Eustratiadis (in *Eph. nova*, 1870, p. 415), preferred to see in it a land register like those from Astypalaea (IG, XII, iii, 180) and from Thera (IG, XII, iii, 343–49).

[278] See the interesting comments of Graindor, *Hadrien*, pp. 190–91. E. Curtius, "Zur Topographie von Attica," *Archäologische Zeitung*, XXIX (1872), 3–7, must be used with caution. See also Curtius, *Stadtgeschichte*, pp. 278–79.

[279] ἀγρόκηπος, l. 145.   [280] βῆσσα, l. 117.

[281] ἐσχατία, l. 52. For the interpretation of this word, see Jardé, *Céréales*, p. 93. In their translation of the sales inscription from Tenos (IG, XII, v, 872) Dareste, Haussoulier, and Reinach, *Recueil*, I, 67, render the word as "dépendances" and interpret it (p. 102) as "des domaines ou métairies, isolés, ordinairement enclos de murs."

[282] κῆπος, l. 70.   [283] σικύα, l. 146.   [284] ὕλη, l. 201.

less land,[285] ordinary farm land,[286] a parcel with mulberry trees,[287] other parcels with peach trees,[288] and a parcel which had formerly belonged to an association of vineyard owners.[289] In other passages[290] we find what seem to be references either to walnut trees, or possibly, if we follow the suggestion of Graindor,[291] to the lands of Hipparchus which had been confiscated, and later sold, by the Fiscus. Many of the plots were located in the most fertile regions of Attica: in the Mesogeia,[292] in the district of Oropus[293] (now under the control of the Athenians), in the Thriasian plain,[294] and in the plain of Acharnae.[295] A garden—apparently a formal garden—was located near the Acharnian Gate.[296] Other plots were located, in addition to the deme name, by means of unofficial, but widely understood, place names.[297] Some fields were located along the Cephisus,[298] another near Hymettus.[299] Additional parcels are indirectly located by the fact that they were formerly lands which had belonged to demes, but which had been acquired by private individuals.[300] Not only were deme lands sold, but lands that had

---

[285] ψειλόν, l. 13.

[286] χωρίον, passim. In ll. 108–9 there are two listings of πέτρας Παιανιοῖ. Reference is here probably made to lands abutting on the rocky terrain of the eastern slopes of Hymettus.

[287] συκάμεινον, ll. 55–56.   [288] Περσικά, l. 91; Περσικῶν, ll. 91, 113.

[289] ἀμπελουργῶν, l. 55; cf. Graindor, Hadrien, pp. 83–84.

[290] βασιλικῶν, ll. 202, 203, 209.

[291] Hadrien, p. 191. The contrast between τὰ τῶν ἰδιωτῶν χω[ρία] and ἐκ τῶν αὐτοῦ χωρίων in IG, III, 55 (omitted in IG, II–III²) suggests to Graindor (in REG, XXXI [1918], 228 and 232) the existence in Attica of something akin to the βασιλικὴ γῆ of Egypt. For the latter, see U. Wilcken, Grundzüge und Chrestomathie der Papyruskunde (Leipzig and Berlin, 1912), I, i, 303, 304, and 310.

[292] Lines 24, 45, 47, 66–67, 204.

[293] Lines 13, 103, 151, 152, 181, 211.   [294] Lines 62, 196, 197.

[295] Line 101. In Lucian, Icaromen. 18, Menippus is represented as much amused at men who take pride, among other things, in owning all the land of Oenoe or a thousand plethra at Acharnae. While allowance must be made for the hyperbole, it is still permissible to take this passage as probable evidence that there were a number of individuals in Attica with large holdings of land.

[296] κήπου πρὸς τῇ Ἀχαρνικῇ πύλῃ προσαγορευομένου Κειονίου, ll. 70–72.

[297] [πρ]ὸ[ς τῷ] Αἰθ[ίο]πι = Phlya, l. 10; πρὸς τῷ Τρι[κε]φ[ά]λῳ = Erchia, l. 82; πρὸς τῷ Περσικῶνι = Phyle, l. 91; πρὸς τῷ Μύρμηκι = Thria, ll. 62–63; πρὸς τῷ ἐμβόλῳ = Acharnae, ll. 101–2; πρὸς τῷ Ἀνδροφόνῳ Κώνῳ = Ionidae, ll. 50–51; cf. Graindor, Hadrien, pp. 190–91.   [298] Lines 86, 167.   [299] Lines 58–59.

[300] This seems to be indicated by the genitive of various deme names, where an extraordinary apocope of final ν has taken place: Αἰθαλιδῶ, l. 12; Ἰωνιδῶ,

formerly belonged to the Amphiaraum[301] and to the Metroum in Oropus were acquired by private individuals.[302] Properties were also located by reference, in addition to deme names' to special farm buildings,[303] to cattle stalls,[304] to an inn and an adjacent pottery shop,[305] to watch posts at Aphidna,[306] and to a contrivance with a release mechanism of some sort.[307]

Another interesting phenomenon to be noted in connection with No. 2776 is the number of women listed as owners of land. Out of fifty-two names, twenty-one are those of women, and most of these, as their *gentilicia* show, possessed Roman citizenship. Some of them were sole owners of property, as, for example, Arria Athenion (ll. 11–19) with eight properties,[308] Julia Antiocha (ll. 115–19) with four or more, Claudia Damoclea (ll. 85–87) with two or three, Claudia Tertulla (ll. 96–98) with four, and Junia Euploia (ll. 187–90) with three or more. A number of other women were sole owners of single parcels. In several instances women appear as joint owners

---

ll. 16, 26, 50, 119; Εἰφιστιαδῶ, l. 17; Εἰρ[εσιδῶ], l. 194; Λακκιαδῶ, ll. 31–32, 187–88. Cf. Graindor, *Hadrien*, p. 191. For the right of the deme to sell its lands, see Schoeffer, in RE, V, 13.

[301] ψειλοῦ 'Αμφιαράου, l. 13.   [302] χωρ[ίον] Μητρώου ἐν 'Ωρωπῷ, l. 103.

[303] Note πύργος, l. 115; πυργίδιον, ll. 15, 24, 117–18; τετραπύργια, l. 118; πυραμίς, l. 16. The latter may, however, be a proper name, as suggested in the new Liddell and Scott. πύργοι in the territory of Pergamum were partly fortified, partly agricultural villas belonging to the Persian landlords (M. Rostovtzeff, in *Anatolian Studies* [Ramsay], p. 374). Similar buildings are also attested for the neighborhood of Carthage. See Appian, *Pun.* 101 (cf. 68); T. R. S. Broughton, *The Romanization of Africa Proconsularis* (Baltimore, 1929), pp. 62–64. The πύργος in which Herodes Atticus resided when he appeared before Marcus Aurelius at Sirmium in Pannonia (Philostratus, *Vit. soph.* 560) must also have been a secure place of refuge. In Egypt, Palestine, and Arabia πύργοι seem to have been agricultural buildings attached to villas. See F. Preisigke, in *Hermes*, LIV (1919), 423–28 (Egypt); E. Meyer, in *Hermes*, LV (1920), 100–102 (Palestine); A. Alt, in *Hermes*, LV (1920), 334–36 (Arabia); J. Hasebroek, in *Hermes*, LVII (1922), 621–23 (Arabia). The τετραπύργια also seems to have been a fortified villa. See Plutarch, *Eum.* viii; cf. Rostovtzeff, *Studien*, pp. 253–54. Ruins of such a structure near Metropolis in Lydia are described by J. Keil and A. von Premerstein, "Bericht über eine dritte Reise in Lydien," *Denkschriften der kaiserliche Akademie der Wissenschaften in Wien*, philosophisch-historische Klasse, LVII (1914), 102. The Attic πύργοι and τετραπύργια must have been of the strictly agricultural type, for there would seem to have been no necessity for places of refuge.

[304] βαῦλοι (for βόαυλοι), l. 207.

[305] Lines 200–1.   [306] φρουρίων, l. 96.   [307] σχαστηριῶν, ll. 52–53.

[308] A total of 6,968¾ is set down opposite the name of Arria Athenion.

with men who were, apparently, their brothers or husbands. In each of these instances a single parcel is involved. Flavia Lollia and Flavia Megiste are joint owners with Flavius Dorotheus and Flavius Philotimus (ll. 69–72); Junia Euploia and Junia Philippa with Junius Diomideus (ll. 184–86); and [Arria Sym]pherousa and Arria Do[- - -] with Arrius Ap[- - -] (ll. 39–41). Moreover, inasmuch as their names appear without the name of a κύριος or *tutor*, all the women must have possessed full property rights,[309] irrespective of their possession of, or lack of, Roman citizenship.

Finally, one may deduce from No. 2776 a few important details concerning the concentration of landed properties in the hands of wealthy owners and the method by which large estates were formed. A number of individuals are listed as owners of properties in different demes—in some instances in widely separated demes. Arria Athenion (ll. 11–19) owned eight parcels, to which a total of 6,968$\frac{3}{4}$ denarii is assigned. Of these parcels one is located in each of the following demes: Aethalidae, Gargettus, Ionidae, Eiphistiadae, and Colonus; one at Oropus, and two in demes whose names have not been preserved. Claudius Pannychus is listed (ll. 50–56) as owning five properties, to which a total of 5,687$\frac{1}{2}$ denarii is assigned. Of these properties one is located near Corydallus, one at a place designated by the name 'Ωρεαδῶ (l. 53), and one in each of the following demes: Ionidae, Bate, and Athmonon. Flavia Phila is listed (ll. 60–64) as owner of three properties, to which a total of 1,125 denarii is assigned. Of these properties two were located at Lamptrae and one at Thria. Vibullius Pempteides of Marathon (ll. 107–10) owned three parcels, to which a total of 2,146$\frac{7}{8}$ denarii is assigned. Two of these properties were located at Paeania, and one at Phlya. Philargyrion is listed (ll. 152–57) as owner of seven properties, one of which was located at Oropus, and six in demes whose names have not been preserved. A total of 2,510$\frac{7}{8}$ denarii is assigned to these properties. F[la]vius Metro[- - -] is listed (ll. 193–204) as owner of twelve properties, to which a total of 15,750 denarii is assigned. Of these properties two were located at Thria, one in the Mesogeia, and one in each of the following demes: Oe, Eiresidae,

---

[309] Cf. Graindor, *Hadrien*, p. 190. For the guardianship of women under Roman law, see Cuq, *Manuel*, pp. 220–22.

Alopece, Lamptrae, and Acharnae; four were located in demes whose names have not been preserved. At the end of the extant portion of No. 2776 a total of 3,750 denarii is assigned to a group of properties, but neither the name of the owner nor the locations of the properties has been preserved. If, as we have assumed above, the sums listed in the inscription are to be construed as loans of $8\frac{1}{3}$ percent, $12\frac{1}{2}$ percent, or 25 percent of the value of the various properties, the total value of each of these groups of properties will amount to the following sums (reckoned in denarii):

LINES OF INSCRIPTION	PROPRIETOR	SUM GIVEN (*in denarii*)	TOTAL VALUE OF PROPERTY IN DENARII IF LOANS ARE AT:		
			25%	$12\frac{1}{2}$%	$8\frac{1}{3}$%
11–19	Arria Athenion	6,968¾	27,875	55,750	83,625
50–56	Claudius Pannychus	5,687½	22,750	45,500	67,250
60–64	Flavia Phila	1,125	4,500	9,000	13,500
107–10	Vibullius Pempteides	2,146⅞	8,587½	17,175	25,766½
152–57	Philargyrion	2,510⅝	10,042½	20,085	30,127½
193–204	F[la]vius Metro[- - -]	15,750	63,000	126,000	189,000
End	Anonymous	3,750	15,000	30,000	45,000

When these sums are compared with the valuations of estates of the fourth century B.C.[310] it appears that, if loans were made at the rate of 25 percent of the value of the properties, Attic estates of the second century A.D. must have been somewhat larger than they were in the fourth century B.C.; and if loans were made at the rate of $12\frac{1}{2}$ percent or $8\frac{1}{3}$ percent, Athenian lands in the time of Hadrian must have belonged in even larger amounts to wealthy holders.[311] This conclusion would conform well with the general character of the imperial period at Athens as it is shown in this chapter. But the picture must not be overdrawn. Concentration of Athenian landed properties in the hands of the wealthy had begun long before the time of Hadrian. With the breaking up of the landed properties of the old-established γένη in the sixth century B.C., land came more and more to be held in comparatively small plots, with the result that by the fourth century B.C. large estates were exceptional.[312] However, a movement in the opposite direction set

[310] For the values of fourth-century estates, see above, including notes 266, 269.

[311] Some allowance must be made for a change in real value of money between the fourth century B.C. and the second century A.D.

[312] E. Ciccotti, *Le Déclin de l'esclavage antique*, p. 120 (French trans. G. Platon; Paris, 1910); Guiraud, *Propriété foncière*, pp. 391–94.

in at that time. The small holders became involved in financial difficulties; mortgages were incurred and foreclosed, with the wealthy becoming owners of numerous small farms.[313] The formation of comparatively large holdings in landed properties took place at a rapid rate.[314] The following accumulations of land in different demes, held in each instance by a single owner, may be cited:[315] (1) at Eleusis and Thria,[316] (2) at Oenoe and Prospalta,[317] and (3) at Amphitrope, Sphettus, Alopece, and Cephisia.[318] In the fourth century B.C., then, individual properties were often not grouped together—and No. 2776 shows that land was held in a similar fashion in the second century A.D. But, in the meantime, the process of elimination and concentration continued. By the time of Hadrian the wealthy must have held a larger share of Athenian lands than ever before. In the fourth century large estates did not consist of contiguous lands, but rather of numerous small parcels located at different places.[319] And this is equally true in the time of the empire. The Athenian inscription under discussion confirms the thesis that never were large estates like the latifundia of Italy formed in Attica.[320]

An interesting confirmation—if further confirmation be desired—of the contention that in the second century A.D. landed estates of the wealthy usually comprised properties somewhat removed from each other may be found in the location of properties which are known to have belonged to Herodes Atticus. In a passage in his *Lives of the Sophists*[321] Philostratus informs us that Herodes lived in Cephisia and in Marathon, the demes of Attica which he loved best. Fortunately, a clue concerning the location of Herodes' properties in these demes, as well as in other parts of Attica and of Greece, may be gained, again from Philostratus, who tells us that Herodes erected about his estates statues of his three foster sons in the attitudes of "hunting, having hunted, and about to hunt,"[322] with in-

[313] E. Ciccotti, *Le Déclin de l'esclavage antique*, pp. 114–15; Heichelheim, *Wirtschaftsgeschichte*, I, 388–89.   [314] Cf. Jardé, *Céréales*, p. 119.

[315] Cf. B. Haussoulier, *La Vie municipale en Attique* (Paris, 1884), p. 67.

[316] Isaeus, XI, 41 and 42.   [317] Isaeus, XI, 44.

[318] Aeschines, *Contr. Tim.* 97–99.

[319] The statement was made by Jardé, *Céréales*, p. 121.

[320] Cf. Jardé, *Céréales*, pp. 121–22.   [321] *Vit. soph.* 562.

[322] *Vit. soph.* 558–59: εἰκόνας γοῦν ἀνετίθει σφῶν θηρώντων καὶ τεθηρακότων καὶ θηρασόντων κτλ.

scriptions calling down curses upon the head of anyone who disturbed them. By chance, a number of herms, now headless, but inscribed with similar execrations, have been found, and it is from the places where they were found that the location of some of Herodes' properties may be deduced.[323] Six of the herms have been found at Cephisia, one at Souli (near Marathon), one at Bei (about two kilometers south of Marathon), one at Ninoi (about two kilometers west of Marathon), one at Masi (in northern Attica), one at Varnava (in northern Attica), one at Loukou (in Cynouria), one at Tragounera (in Euboea), while one is of unknown provenance. In addition to the holdings indicated by these herms Herodes owned a group of houses, formerly the property of his father, near the Theater of Dionysus at Athens,[324] a property at Corinth,[325] a property known as the Triopium, on the Appian Way near Rome,[326] and a property in Egypt which had formerly belonged to Claudia Athenais, his daughter.[327]

That substantial amounts of Attic land were held by the wealthy

[323] For detailed citations of the publications of these herms, see Graindor, *Hérode*, p. 115, note 1; in BCH, XXXVIII (1914), 358. A marble head of Memnon, one of the three τρόφιμοι of Herodes, now in the Berlin Museum, was found at Loukou; it probably formed part of one of the herms set up on Herodes' estate there. See H. Schrader, "Ueber den Marmorkopf eines Negers in den königlichen Museen," *Berlin Winckelmannsprogramm*, LX (1900); Graindor, in BCH, XXXIX (1915), 402–12; Graindor, *Hérode*, p. 115; R. Kekule von Stradonitz, *Die griechische Skulptur* (3d ed., B. Schroeder; Berlin, 1922), p. 369; Dickins, *Hellenistic Sculpture*, p. 28; G. H. Beardsley, *The Negro in Greek and Roman Civilization: a Study of the Ethiopian Type* (Baltimore, 1929), pp. 132–33. Additional literature is cited by Graindor, *Hérode*, p. 115, note 2, and by Mrs. Beardsley.

[324] Philostratus, *Vit. soph.* 547.

[325] A herm of Herodes, found at Corinth, bears the inscription Ἡρώδης ἐνθάδε περιεπάτει (A. Philadelpheus, in BCH, XLIV [1920], 170–80).

[326] IG, XIV, 1390–91; IGRR, I, 193–95; CIL, VI, 1342; cf. Graindor, *Hérode*, pp. 94–100, 214–18. J. Weiss, in RE, Zweite Reihe, VII, 176–77. The property originally belonged to Regilla and after her death was dedicated to her by Herodes; it was dedicated under the name of the Triopium.

[327] The οὐσία Προφητιανή of Claudia Athenais, located in the Hermupolites, is mentioned in P. Strassburg, 78 (127/8 A.D.); cf. 74 (126 A.D.). After her death, at some time before 160 A.D. (Philostratus, *Vit. soph.* 557–58; cf. Graindor, *Hérode*, pp. 101, 106), the property probably came to Herodes. This property is not cited by Graindor (*Hérode*, p. 115, note 1) in his list of Herodes' holdings. An additional property is to be added to this list if we accept the suggestion of H. Diptmar, in *Blätter für bayerische Gymnasialschulen*, XXIII (1897), 660 and note 7, that Regilla owned property at Canusium in Italy.

is not at all surprising, for from other sources we learn of the existence at Athens of an oligarchy of wealthy and noble families.[328] The class consciousness of these families is made evident by the great stress which they laid upon genealogies.[329] They took pride in tracing their ancestry back to famous Athenians of the classical period and, in extreme cases, even to the gods, while some were content with an ancestor among the mythical heroes or with an ancient Athenian king.[330] To cite a few examples, one family traced its ancestry back nineteen generations to Themistocles, another to Pericles, and another to Pericles, Conon, and Alexander the Great.[331] Most of the important liturgical offices at Athens in the period of the empire were held by members of these families. Indeed, a disproportionately large number of archons was selected from among the members of a very limited number of families. Among the archons during the period of the empire the members of three families appear most often, the family of Herodes Atticus, that of Leonides of Melite, and that of Diocles of Phalerum.[332]

[328] Cf. Graindor, *Hérode*, p. 1; Graindor, *Tibère*, pp. 145–46; Graindor, *Hadrien*, pp. 132–35. Prominent among these families were some which exercised a practical monopoly over the priesthoods at Eleusis. The exalted station of these priests is shown by the fact that special seats were reserved for them in the Theater of Dionysus (IG, II–III², 5028, 5044, 5053; cf. Graindor, *Hadrien*, p. 132). See also the genealogy of the family of T. Flavius Alcibiades, an important family whose members held priesthoods at Eleusis (Graindor, *Hadrien*, p. 134; cf. G. Hirschfeld, in *Hermes*, VII [1873], 52–61; W. Dittenberger's commentary on IG, III, 656). Another important family which held priesthoods at Eleusis was that of Ti. Claudius Lysiades, a descendant of Leonides of Melite. For the genealogy of this family, see Graindor, in BCH, XXXVIII (1914), 428; cf. Graindor, *Hadrien*, pp. 133, 135.

[329] Cf. Hertzberg, *Geschichte Griechenlands*, II, 374–75. Descent by the female line as well as by the male was emphasized. See W. Dittenberger, in *Hermes*, XX (1885), 6; cf. Graindor, *Tibère*, p. 145.

[330] Cf. Graindor, *Hérode*, p. 1.

[331] IG, II–III², 3610, 3546, and 3679, respectively.

[332] Other instances of members of the same family holding the archonship may be cited: T. Flavius Leosthenes (I), archon before 112 A.D. (Graindor, *Chronologie*, pp. 106–7); his son T. Flavius Alcibiades (III), archon in 122/3 A.D. (*ibid.*, p. 116); the son of the preceding, Flavius Alcibiades (IV), archon in 142/3 A.D.; *ibid.*, pp. 144–47, where the name is given as T. Flavius Alcibiades (II). For the stemma of the family, along with citations of the liturgies performed by them, see Graindor, *Hadrien*, p. 134. Two brothers held the archonship in the time of Augustus (Graindor, *Chronologie*, Nos. 3 and 14). Another pair of brothers held the office in the latter half of the second century A.D. (*ibid.*, Nos. 148 and 156).

The following members of Herodes' family[333] held the archonship:

1. Polycharmus, four generations removed from Herodes by direct descent—between 9/8 B.C. and 22/3 A.D.[334]
2. L. Vibullius Hipparchus, Herodes' uncle through his marriage into the family of Vibullius Rufus—117/8 A.D.[335]
3. Herodes Atticus—126/7 A.D.[336]
4. P. Aelius Vibullius Rufus, cousin (?) of Herodes—155/6 A.D.[337]
5. Ti. Claudius Bradua Atticus, Herodes' son—between 186/7 A.D. and 191/2 A.D.[338]

The following members of the family of Leonides of Melite[339] held the archonship:

1. Leonides, son of Leonides—13/2 B.C.[340]
2. Ti. Claudius Lysiades (II), four generations removed, by direct descent, from Leonides—during the reign of Hadrian[341]
3. Ti. Claudius Demostratus, brother of Lysiades (II)—toward the beginning of the reign of Antonius Pius
4. Aelius Praxagoras (II), fifth generation removed, by direct descent, from Leonides (I)—157/8 A.D.
5. Claudius Philippus, son of Ti. Claudius Demostratus—between 187/8 A.D. and 200 A.D.[342]

The following members of the family of Diocles of Phalerum[343] appear in the list of archons:

1. Diocles—114/5 A.D.
2. Aelius Alexandrus (I), son of Diocles—under Hadrian

---

[333] For the stemma of the family see Graindor, *Hérode*, pp. 4, 8, 29; cf. BCH, XXXVIII (1914), 439.

[334] Graindor, *Chronologie*, pp. 64–65.

[335] Graindor, *Chronologie*, pp. 116–24; Graindor, *Hérode*, p. 29.

[336] Graindor, *Chronologie*, pp. 127–29.

[337] Graindor, *Chronologie*, pp. 156–58; Graindor, *Hérode*, p. 29.

[338] Graindor, *Chronologie*, pp. 201–2.

[339] For the stemma of the family, see Graindor, in BCH, XXXVIII (1914), 429; J. Kirchner, commentary on IG, II–III², 3609. The ancestry of this family may be traced back to certain individuals who were active at Delos in the island's most prosperous period. See chap. iv, including note 359.

[340] Dinsmoor, *Archons*, pp. 282–84, 287.

[341] Graindor, *Chronologie*, pp. 135–37. Ti. Claudius Leonides (III), brother of Lysiades (II), did not hold the archonship as suggested in BCH, XXXVIII (1914), 429.

[342] For the last three, see Graindor, *Chronologie*, pp. 140–41, 160, and 211, respectively.

[343] For the stemma of the family, see Graindor, *Chronologie*, p. 155, note 1; for the individuals, pp. 115, 132, 153–58, 161–62, 184–85, 225–27.

3. Aelius Ardys, grandson of Diocles—150/1 A.D.
4. Aelius Callicrates, grandson of Diocles—151/2 A.D. (?)
5. P. Aelius Alexandrus (II), grandson of Diocles—154/5 A.D.
6. Aelius Gelos (II), grandson of Diocles—163/4 A.D. or later
7. P. Pompeius (or Pomponius) Hegias (I), great-grandson of Diocles and cousin of the individuals listed under 3, 4, 5, and 6—c.178/9 A.D.
8. P. Pompeius (or Pomponius) Hegias (II), son of the individual listed under 7—beginning of the third century A.D.
The individuals listed under 3, 4, 5, and 6 were brothers.

Let it be remembered that only the *archon eponymus* and the *archon basileus* were eligible to become members of the Areopagus and that the Areopagus was the most powerful political assemblage at Athens in Roman times.[344] If, then, as Keil has suggested,[345] the number of Areopagites was ordinarily about twenty-five, it becomes evident that the ruling power reposed in the hands of a very few families. A similar tendency is to be observed in the tenure of the office of hoplite general, where again the incumbents came from among the members of a comparatively few families. But the manifestation of this tendency takes a form differing from that observed in the instance of the archonship, for there was no limitation on the number of times that an individual might hold the generalship. It will suffice to cite two instances of repeated tenure of the office.[346] Aeolion son of Antipatrus, of Phlya, held the office seven times during the first century A.D.[347] Ti. Claudius Novius was holding the office for the eighth time in 61 A.D.[348]

The extreme frequency with which members of these families held the most important offices is to be explained only on economic grounds.[349] Since Hellenistic times the Athenians had expected of their magistrates substantial contributions toward various public services,[350] and in the Roman period the tradition persisted. Thus, one officeholder records in an inscription the facts that he had held the office of archon at the cost of a distribution of one medimnus of grain and fifteen drachmas to each citizen, and that during his

[344] Keil, *Areopag*, pp. 84–86.   [345] *Ibid.*, pp. 89–91.
[346] A list of individuals who held the office more than once has been compiled by Graindor, in BCH, XXXVIII (1914), 404, note 1; cf. Graindor, *Tibère*, pp. 75–79.
[347] IG, II–III², 3182, 3539.
[348] *Ibid.*, 1990. For the career of this important man, see Graindor, *Tibère*, pp. 141–43.
[349] Cf. Keil, *Areopag*, p. 89.   [350] Ferguson, in *Klio*, IV (1904), 7, note 1.

tenure of the office of γραμματεὺς βουλῆς καὶ δήμου he had given two denarii to each citizen.[351] Obviously only a comparatively small number of Athenians could meet the contributions required of officeholders, and it is for this reason that we find, over and over again, the members of a few families holding the chief offices of state. A further substantiation of the economic explanation of the tenure of offices is to be deduced from two additional phenomena. First, a number of distinguished foreigners were granted Athenian citizenship and elected to the archonship. The following instances may be cited:

1. Cotys, a Thracian prince—between 1 A.D. and 10 A.D.[352]
2. Lacon, one of the Euryclids of Sparta—between 9/8 B.C. and 13/4 A.D.[353]
3. Rhoemetalces νεώτερος, king of Thrace—36/7 A.D.[354]
4. The emperor Domitian—c.84/5 A.D.[355]
5. Q. Trebellius Rufus, a native of Toulouse—between 85/6 A.D. and 94/5 A.D.[356]
6. C. Julius Antiochus Epiphanes Philopappus, son of the deposed ruler of Commagene in Syria—c.87/8 A.D.[357]
7. P. Aelius Hadrianus, before his accession as emperor—112/3 A.D.[358]

It was certainly not out of pure sentiment that these individuals were invested with the highest office in the city. In most instances the bestowal of the office was probably made in recognition of substantial gifts received from the beneficiary of the honor. Moreover, it was a welcome relief to the depleted ranks of the wealthy to find an outsider to take over, on occasion, the costly burden of the archonship. Second, "anarchy" occurred six times at Athens during the period of the empire, the first instance in 82/3 A.D. or 83/4 A.D., and the latest at about the beginning of the third century A.D.[359] Prior to the time of Augustus the lack of an archon in any year was ordinarily occasioned by some disturbance of a po-

---

[351] IG, II–III², 3546; cf. Keil, *Areopag.* p. 87. It should be borne in mind that the drachma here listed is the new drachma, worth one old obol or one sixth of a denarius.

[352] Graindor, *Chronologie*, pp. 52–54; cf. Graindor, *Auguste*, pp. 88–89.

[353] Graindor, *Chronologie*, pp. 59–62; cf. Graindor, *Auguste*, pp. 90–92.

[354] Graindor, *Chronologie*, pp. 69–70; cf. Graindor, *Tibère*, pp. 48–49.

[355] Graindor, *Chronologie*, pp. 93–95; cf. Graindor, *Tibère*, pp. 18–19.

[356] Graindor, *Chronologie*, pp. 100–102; cf. Graindor, *Tibère*, p. 144; Jullian, *Histoire de la Gaule*, IV, 426, note 5.

[357] Graindor, *Chronologie*, pp. 95–100; Graindor, *Tibère*, pp. 51–52.

[358] Graindor, *Hadrien*, pp. 25–29; Graindor, *Chronologie*, pp. 116–22.

[359] Graindor. *Chronologie*, pp. 291–98, Nos. 64, 68, 127, 130, 143, and 161.

litical nature. But for the period of the empire this explanation does not hold. "Anarchy" in that period must, then, be explained on the ground that, since the number of citizens sufficiently wealthy to meet the burdens of the office was very small, and since the office could not be held more than once by the same person, in some years no individual could be found to assume the archonship.[360]

It will be instructive to consider in somewhat greater detail the most important family of Roman Athens, that of the millionaire sophist Herodes Atticus. On his father's side the sophist traced his ancestry back to the Aeacids;[361] and, as Philostratus informs us,[362] he also claimed descent from Miltiades and Cimon. The pride he took in these ancestors is to be seen in the name of Herodes' daughter Elpinice—a very uncommon name in Attica.[363] The earlier Elpinice, who was the daughter of Miltiades and sister of Cimon, married that Callias who was the richest citizen of Periclean Athens, and it is remotely possible that the origin of the wealth of the later Elpinice's father, Herodes, is to be traced back to that time.[364] However that may be, members of the family had attained to considerable prominence at Athens by the middle of the first century B.C. Herodes (II), six generations directly removed from Herodes Atticus, was archon in 60/59 B.C.[365] and his son Eucles (V) held the same office probably in 46/5 B.C.;[366] both played prominent parts in connection with the building of the Market of Caesar and Augustus.[367] Beginning with Hipparchus, the grandfather of

[360] Graindor, *Chronologie*, pp. 11–12; Graindor, *Tibère*, p. 73. If Graindor's chronological arrangement of the archons is correct, severe economic difficulties at Athens may be indicated for the years between 82 A.D. and 92 A.D. In his list of archons (*Chronologie*, pp. 291–300, especially 295) note the following series: No. 64—"anarchy," 82/3 A.D. or 83/4 A.D.; No. 65—Domitian, c.84/5 A.D.; No. 66—C. Julius Antiochus Philopappus, c.87/8 A.D.; No. 67—Q. Trebellius Rufus, c.90/1 A.D.; No. 68—"anarchy," c.91/2 A.D. During this decade, therefore, no Athenian is known to have held the office of archon; the three known incumbents were of foreign extraction.

[361] Philostratus, *Vit. soph.* 545–46.

[362] *Ibid.*, 546–47. The relationship is to be attributed to intermarriage, for Herodes, Miltiades, and Cimon were not members of the same tribe. Cf. Graindor, *Hérode*, p. 2.

[363] PA, Nos. 4677, 4678.   [364] Graindor, *Hérode*, p. 3.

[365] Dinsmoor, *Archons*, pp. 280–82. For the stemma of the family, see Graindor, *Hérode*, pp. 4, 8, 29.   [366] Dinsmoor, *Archons*, pp. 280, 281, 284, 285.

[367] See chap. iv, including notes 101, 126.

Herodes, the family attained very great prominence.[368] Hipparchus'
fortune was so large that it attracted great attention even at Rome,
where he was reputed to possess one hundred million sesterces.[369]
However, his wealth and position may have brought about his un-
doing, for in 92/3 A.D., when Domitian exiled or executed a large
number of wealthy men,[370] Hipparchus seems to have been accused
of attempting to form at Athens an extraconstitutional regime like
that of the Euryclids at Sparta; his lands were confiscated by the
Fiscus, and he was himself probably put to death or exiled.[371]
Since confiscation of his lands was occasioned by the emperor's desire for money, it would seem that they were sold soon thereafter
to private individuals.[372] At any rate, they were certainly in private
hands by the time of Hadrian, for in that emperor's oil law we find
special privileges being granted "the owners of the lands of Hipparchus which were sold by the Fiscus."[373]

Although he had lost his father's fortune, Ti. Claudius Atticus
Herodes, Hipparchus' son, "was not overlooked by fortune," to
cite the words of Philostratus,[374] from whose *Lives of the Sophists* the
following account is taken.[375] In one of the houses which he had
acquired near the Theater of Dionysus at Athens Atticus found an

[368] Graindor, *Hérode*, p. 11. For Hipparchus, see *ibid.*, pp. 11–17; Groag, in RE,
III, 2725, No. 179; K. Münscher, in RE, VIII, 923.

[369] Suetonius, *Vesp.* xiii; cf. Groag, in RE, III, 2725, No. 179.

[370] Eusebius, *Chron.* Year of Abraham 2109; cf. Stein, in RE, VI, 2576.

[371] Philostratus, *Vit. soph.* 547. For the interpretation of ἐπὶ τυρραννικαῖς αἰτίαις,
see Graindor, *Hérode*, pp. 12–14, 17.

[372] *Ibid.*, pp. 15–16; Graindor, in REG, XXXI (1918), 232. Rostovtzeff (*Studien*,
p. 386; cf. *Roman Empire*, p. 322) maintains that the lands were sold under Trajan
or Hadrian in pursuance of their policy of encouraging the ownership of land by
small holders. Abbott and Johnson, *Municipal Administration*, p. 413, contend
that the lands of Hipparchus remained an imperial estate and were not sold outright. The suggestion of M. P. Charlesworth, in CAH, XI, 29, note 1, that some of
the confiscated lands in Euboea mentioned by Dio Chrysostomus, VII, 12, had
originally belonged to Hipparchus, is not susceptible of proof.

[373] IG, II–III², 1100, ll. 3–5: οἱ τὰ Ἱππάρχου χωρία τὰ ὑπὸ τοῦ φίσκου πραθέντα
κεκτημένοι. Cf. ll. 29–31.

[374] *Vit. soph.* 547.

[375] *Ibid.*, 547–48. Cf. Zonaras, XI, 20 (taken from Philostratus); Libanius, *Or.*
IV, 7 (p. 289, ed. Foerster). Suidas, *s.v.* Ἡρώδης and the Scholiast to Aristeides,
III, 739 (ed. Dindorf) have it that Herodes discovered the treasures. For Atticus,
see PIR, II², p. 173, No. 801; Groag, in RE, III, 2677–78, No. 71; Graindor,
Marbres, pp. 81–86; Graindor, *Hérode*, pp. 19–38; Graindor, *Tibère*, pp. 19–25.

immense treasure. With caution he wrote to the emperor—Nerva—
saying that he had found a treasure in his house and asking what
disposition should be made of it. Nerva replied: "Use what you
have found." Without abandoning his caution, Atticus wrote
again, saying that the amount of the treasure was beyond his
station in life. To this letter the emperor replied: "Then misuse
your windfall, for it is yours." At first blush this account seems
rather fantastic, but upon consideration of the various circumstances attending the burial and the discovery of the treasure, one
is inclined to grant the story greater credence. The following
interpretation would seem to be substantially correct.[376] Having a
premonition of what was to happen, Hipparchus buried what he
could of his fortune with the intention that Atticus should "dis-
cover" it and assert ownership over it at some more auspicious
time. Inasmuch as the disposition of unearthed treasures rested
with the emperor—it was not until the time of Hadrian that the
title to such treasures was vested, without further ado, in the
finder[377]—Atticus would, very naturally, not report his "discovery"
until an emperor less greedy than Domitian had ascended the
throne. Hence, it was only when Nerva came to the throne at Rome
that Atticus ventured to address to the emperor the cautious
messages related by Philostratus. The latter then goes on to say
that, upon his discovery of the treasure, Atticus became powerful.
Moreover, his influence and prestige were enhanced by the fortune
of his wife, Vibullia Alcia, who was, at the same time, his niece
and a member of a very wealthy and prominent family.[378] The

[376] Graindor's interpretation (*Marbres*, pp. 81–86; cf. *Hérode*, pp. 20–24; *Tibère*,
pp. 19–25) is very plausible.

[377] Spartianus, *Vit. Hadr.* xviii, 6; Justinian, *Inst.* II, i, 39. Before the time of
Hadrian the matter rested with the discretion of the emperor. Cf. P. Bonfante,
"La Vera Data di un testo di Calpurnio siculo e il concetto romano del tesoro,"
Mélanges P. Girard (Paris, 1912), I, 123–42.

[378] Cf. Philostratus, *Vit. soph.* 548. Vibullia Alcia was the daughter of Vibullius
Rufus; her mother was Claudia Alcia, sister of Atticus. For the stemma of the
family, see Graindor, *Hérode*, p. 29; PIR², II, chart facing p. 182, where L. Vibullius
Hipparchus is listed as a son of L. Vibullius Rufus and as a nephew of Vibullia
Alcia. Two members of the family were elected to the archonship at Athens: L.
Vibullius Hipparchus, brother of Vibullia Alcia, archon in 117/8 A.D. (Graindor,
Chronologie, pp. 116–24), and his son P. Aelius Vibullius Rufus, archon in 155/6
A.D. (*ibid.*, p. 156). Although he seems not to have held office at Athens, Atticus,
like many wealthy Easterners, enjoyed a distinguished political career at Rome,

extent of his wealth is shown by a number of acts of generosity on his part. His son Herodes, while serving in the capacity of an imperial official—apparently as a *corrector*—in Asia, wrote to the emperor Hadrian with the request that three million drachmas be appropriated to provide an adequate water supply for Alexandria Troas.[379] Hadrian granted the request and appointed Herodes to take charge of the project. When, however, the outlay reached seven million drachmas, instead of the three million which the emperor had granted, various officials in Asia protested to Hadrian, saying that it was scandalous that the tribute from five hundred cities should be squandered upon the water supply of a single city. Thereupon, Hadrian expressed his disapproval to Atticus, who replied that he would give his son all that was spent above three million drachmas, and that his son would, in turn, give it to the city. Moreover, Atticus is known to have bestowed gifts upon other Greek cities, among them Gythium[380] and Megara,[381] and upon the κοινόν of the Greeks at Plataea.[382] Other ways in which he showed his liberality are related to us by Philostratus, who says[383] that Atticus would often sacrifice a hundred oxen to Athena in a single day; that he would feast the Athenian populace at large on the same occasion; and that, at the Dionysia, he used to give wine to all the citizens and to the strangers who attended the festival.

But the most significant proof of Atticus' wealth and of his

---

where he was admitted to the Senate with praetorian rank during the reign of Nerva. See Groag, in RE, III, 2677; L. R. Dean, in AJA, XXIII (1919), 173, No. 16; Graindor, *Hérode*, pp. 25–26; Graindor, *Marbres*, pp. 86–88. The consulship was bestowed upon him twice. See Philostratus, *Vit. soph.* 545; Suidas, *s.v.* Ἡρώδης; *Prolegomena* in Aristeidem, III, 739 (ed. Dindorf); IG, VII, 88; B. Stech, *Senatores Romani qui Fuerint inde a Vespasiano usque ad Traiani exitum* (Leipzig, 1912; *Klio*, Beiheft X), p. 94, No. 1329; p. 103, No. 1523; G. Lully, *De senatorum Romanorum patria* (Rome, 1918), p. 200, No. 1328. He seems also to have been appointed governor of Judea. See Graindor, *Hérode*, pp. 26–27; G. A. Harrer, *Studies in the History of the Roman Province of Syria* (Princeton, 1915), pp. 18–19. We may also observe that the elegance of Atticus' table became a commonplace at Rome (Juvenal, *Sat.* xi, 1).

[379] Philostratus, *Vit. soph.* 548; cf. Graindor, *Hérode*, pp. 32–33. Although the amounts given are not specifically stated as drachmas, they are probably to be construed as such, for it seems to have been Philostratus' regular practice to employ Attic numeration. Cf. *ibid.*, p. 32, note 2.

[380] IG, V, i, 1147; II–III², 3596. [381] IG, VII, 88; Graindor, *Hérode*, p. 34.

[382] IG, VII, 2509; cf. SIG, 854, note 7. [383] Philostratus, *Vit. soph.* 549.

generosity is to be found in his will, by the terms of which he created the most important endowment of ancient times that is known to us.[384] In this will an annual payment of one mina was bequeathed to each citizen of Athens. But the terms of the will were never carried out. Instead, when its provisions were made known, the Athenians agreed to accept a single payment of five minas. Moreover, Philostratus[385] tells us, when they came to the banks to collect the five minas, they were held liable for the debts their fathers and grandfathers owed Herodes' parents, with the result that some received only a small amount, others nothing at all, while still others were held as debtors. In passing, the observation may be made that two facts—that numerous Athenians were in debt to Atticus and that these debts were collected when the Athenians went to the banks to obtain their legacies—indicate very probably that a large portion of Atticus' fortune was invested in the business of banking. But to return to the endowment created by the will, it is apparent that a very large capital sum would have been required to establish such a foundation. The assumption has been made that there were approximately twelve thousand Athenian citizens in the second century A.D.,[386] and that the foundation would, therefore, have been liable for yearly payments totalling twelve thousand minas, a sum which, assuming a return of 5 percent, requires an endowment of twenty-four million drachmas. Although we are not justified in estimating the population of the city at this time so closely,[387] it is, perhaps, admissible to employ some such figure to arrive at a remote approximation of the total sum required to meet the payments for which provision was made in the will. One may wonder why the Athenians agreed to accept the single payment of five minas instead of yearly payments of one mina. Were they in such great need that they were compelled to accept unfavorable terms? Or were they so greedy that desire for money blinded them to the advantages of continued yearly payments? The explanation is to be found, rather, in the technicalities of Roman law.[388] Atticus was a Roman citizen and, as such, could will money or property only to

[384] *Ibid.*, 549; cf. Graindor, *Hérode*, pp. 71–79; Graindor, *Marbres*, pp. 88–91; Laum, *Stiftungen*, Vol. I, p. 143; Vol. II, No. 18.

[385] *Vit. soph.* 549.   [386] Graindor, *Hérode*, pp. 71–72.

[387] See Appendix.   [388] Cf. Graindor, *Hérode*, pp. 72–75.

Roman citizens;[389] only through the instrumentality of a trust could he bestow a legacy upon the numerous Athenians who did not possess Roman citizenship.[390] Moreover, it was only the conscience of the trustee—no law required it—that could compel him to carry out the terms of a will.[391] Consequently, inasmuch as Herodes was undoubtedly the trustee named in Atticus' will, it becomes clear how the Athenians were persuaded to accept an unfavorable settlement.[392] Herodes exerted pressure upon them: they could take a single payment of five minas or nothing at all. Any doubt that may persist as to the validity of this interpretation is dispelled by three additional facts: (1) It was through an agreement made with Herodes that the Athenians accepted a compromise settlement.[393] (2) Philostratus tells[394] us that, because they felt that they had been deprived of their rightful legacy, the Athenians cherished a lasting hatred for Herodes and said that the Panathenaic Stadium was well named, since it was built with money taken away from them. (3) A probable reference to Herodes' failure to carry out the terms of the trust is to be found in a letter addressed to Marcus Aurelius by Fronto,[395] who denounces the sophist as an impious son and one who had no regard for his father's wishes.

The larger portion of Herodes' wealth consisted of the fortunes which he inherited from his father and mother.[396] But Philostratus tells us that his wealth came from various sources and several estates.[397] Although Philostratus does not disclose the identity of

[389] Cf. L. Mitteis, *Reichsrecht und Volksrecht* (Leipzig, 1891), pp. 153–54.

[390] Gaius, *Instit.* II, 285; cf. R. Leonhard, in RE, VI, 2274; Cuq, *Manuel*, p. 792. The names that appear in the ephebic lists provide proof that relatively few Athenians possessed Roman citizenship at this time. Cf. Graindor, *Hérode*, p. 73.

[391] Cf. Gaius, *Inst.* II, 231. For the procedure under a trust, cf. R. Leonhard, in RE, VI, 2272–75.

[392] Herodes' action must have taken place before the time, during the reign of Hadrian, when the practice of making bequests to non-Romans through a trust was prohibited by law. Cf. Gaius, *Inst.* II, 285; Ulpianus, XXV, 6; Cuq, *Manuel*, p. 792, note 2.

[393] Philostratus, *Vit. soph.* 549, states that, according to the agreement, Herodes was relieved of the obligation of making further payments to the Athenians.

[394] *Ibid.*, 549.

[395] Fronto, *Ad Marc. Caes.* iii, 3 (p. 41, ed. Naber); cf. Graindor, *Hérode*, p. 76.

[396] Philostratus, *Vit. soph.* 547, 548.

[397] Philostratus, *Vit. soph.* 547.

these estates, we cannot be far wrong in assuming that one of them
was that of his wife, Regilla, who belonged, in her own right, to a
very distinguished family.[398] It will suffice to state that through her
father, Appius Annius Gallus, she was related to Annia Galeria
Faustina, the wife of Antoninus Pius.[399] The extent of Herodes'
wealth is best shown by the numerous structures which he erected
and gave to various cities of Greece, Asia Minor, and Italy. The
aqueduct at Alexandria Troas and the buildings which he erected
in Athens have already been mentioned. Of the other structures
which were erected through his generosity only the most important
will be cited here.[400] At Delphi he erected the stadium,[401] of which
substantial remains are preserved to the present day, and an
exedra.[402] At Olympia he built an aqueduct[403] with an imposing
façade which took the form of an exedra.[404] At Corinth he thoroughly remodeled the Odeum[405] and, apparently, redecorated the
court which lay in front of the façade of the Fountain of Peirene,
in the lower town.[406] In Italy Herodes built an aqueduct at Canusium,[407] and a building called the Triopium, which was a memorial
to Regilla, on a property located on the Appian Way, near Rome.[408]

[398] For the stemma of the family, see PIR, I², chart facing p. 124; Klebs, in RE,
I, 2289–90.

[399] PIR, I², p. 134, No. 720.

[400] The building activities of Herodes are discussed in detail by Graindor, *Hérode*,
pp. 179–230.

[401] Philostratus, *Vit. soph.* 551; Pausanias, X, xxxii, 1; cf. F. Poulsen, *Delphi*
(London, 1920), p. 54; Graindor, *Hérode*, pp. 188–91.

[402] SIG, 860.   [403] Philostratus, *Vit. soph.* 551.

[404] *Olympia*, II, 134–39; V, 615–39; Gardiner, *Olympia*, pp. 173, 294–99; Graindor,
Hérode, pp. 191–200.

[405] Broneer, *The Odeum*, pp. 1–2. The Odeum was originally built in the latter
part of the first century A.D. (O. Broneer, in AJA, XXXII [1928], 462), and
Herodes was responsible for the reconstruction of it at about 175 A.D. Philostratus,
Vit. soph. 551, merely states that Herodes built it for the Corinthians.

[406] Rhys Carpenter, *Ancient Corinth: a Guide to the Excavations* (2d ed.; Macon,
France, 1933), pp. 38–39; R. B. Richardson, in AJA, IV (1900), 236–37; B. Powell,
in AJA, VII (1903), 43–45. Herodes also erected a group of chryselephantine
statues in the Temple of Poseidon on the Isthmus of Corinth (Philostratus, *Vit.
soph.* 551; Pausanias, II, i, 7).

[407] Philostratus, *Vit. soph.* 551. It is possible that Herodes built an aqueduct at
Ephesus, but the evidence is very uncertain. Cf. Graindor, *Hérode*, p. 201.

[408] IGRR, I, 193–95; IG, XIV, 1390–91; CIL, VI, 1342; cf. Graindor, *Hérode*,
pp. 94–100, 214–18; J. Weiss, in RE, Zweite Reihe, VII, 176–77.

Moreover, from Philostratus' statement[409] that Herodes bestowed
a number of gifts upon the cities of Euboea, the Peloponnesus, and
Boeotia, we are justified in deducing that Herodes erected various
other structures which have not been preserved and which are not
now attested by any specific evidence. But the most cherished
ambition of the wealthy sophist—to dig a canal through the Isthmus
of Corinth[410]—was never realized. Nevertheless, so extensive were
his gifts that one of his modern biographers has been able to conclude,[411] with good reason, that with his private means Herodes
erected almost as many and as expensive buildings as Augustus
had with funds that belonged to the state.

It appears, therefore, that a number of wealthy families resided
at Athens in the first two centuries of our era; and of these families
that of Herodes Atticus was by far the wealthiest. Some of the
other families we have taken note of, while undoubtedly well to
do, might not have been considered wealthy in any part of the empire other than a poor country like Greece. However that may be,
it is the life of these wealthy families that is most often described
in our sources. Aside from the instances of wealth and extravagant
expenditures we have already noted, two additional accounts may
be mentioned. First, the sophist Proclus, who came to Athens from
Naucratis in the latter part of the second century A.D., was sufficiently wealthy to own four houses—two in Athens, and one each
at Eleusis and the Piraeus.[412] Moreover, his son—undoubtedly like
other young dandies of the time—spent money with reckless
abandon. Philostratus tells us that he squandered his father's

---

[409] *Vit. soph.* 551.   [410] *Ibid.*, 551–52.

[411] Graindor, *Hérode*, p. 230. At Athens Herodes held the office of agoranomus
and that of archon. And, like many wealthy individuals who lived in the eastern
provinces of the empire, he enjoyed a distinguished political career at Rome,
where he held the offices of quaestor, of praetor, of *corrector*, and of consul (*ibid.*,
pp. 55–70). Two tales concerning extravagant expenditures on the part of Herodes
also throw indirect light on the immensity of his fortune. He was said to have paid
the sophist Polemo of Laodicea 250,000 drachmas for his lectures (Philostratus, *Vit.
soph.* 538). Philostratus also tells us (*Vit. soph.* 574) that Herodes was so pleased
with what seemed to be spontaneous praise from the lips of Alexander of Seleucia
in Cilicia that he gave him ten pack animals, ten horses, ten cupbearers, ten short-
hand writers, twenty talents of gold, a very large amount of silver, and two lisping
children from Collytus.

[412] Philostratus, *Vit. soph.* 603.

fortune in breeding fighting cocks, quails, dogs, puppies, and
horses; and that the father, instead of upbraiding his son, actually
joined him in his prodigalities. Second, the birthday party given
for his daughter by a certain Scambonides, described in one of
Alciphron's epistles,[413] may be taken as representative of the social
life of the wealthier families of the city. Present among the guests
was a large number of the wealthiest and most illustrious citizens
of Athens, along with a contingent of intellectuals consisting of
philosophers of the Stoic, the Peripatetic, the Epicurean, the
Pythagorean, and the Cynic schools. Entertainment was provided
by dancing girls, singers, performers on the cithara and the lyre,
actors of the mime, and parasites. But such brilliant social gather-
ings were only for the wealthy few. Along with these individuals we
may, perhaps, reckon a very limited middle class; however, by far
the largest part of the population consisted of the very poor. Not
only do the bread riots and the distributions of grain which we have
noted above point in this direction, but other familiar indications
of a poverty-stricken proletariat are to be observed in the gladia-
torial combats (which aroused the disgust of Dio Chrysostomus[414]
and of Apollonius of Tyana[415] and provoked a lively protest from
the philosopher Demonax[416]) and in the *venationes* which were
held on occasion in the Stadium.[417] It is certainly not without good
reason that Lucian[418] makes one of his characters say that the
Athenians had for long had philosophy and poverty for foster
brothers, and that they looked askance at any man, citizen or
foreigner, who, encouraging luxurious living, thereby spoiled the
simple life. We should accept Lucian's portrayal of the lot of most
of the Athenians, but we should not go on to assume (following a
distinguished scholar of our own times[419]) that, because they con-

---

[413] III, 19 (55), ed. Schepers. The appearance of the name of one character whose
historicity is undoubted—Pancrates the Cynic—is probably sufficient proof, even
in default of identification of other characters with historical persons, that Alciphron's epistle is a comparatively realistic portrayal of such a party as the one
he describes. Cf. Graindor, *Hadrien*, p. 196.

[414] XXXI, 121.   [415] Philostratus, *Vit. Apoll.* IV, xxii.   [416] Lucian, *Dem.* 57.

[417] A *venatio* was presented in the Panathenaic Stadium by Hadrian (Spartianus,
Vit. Hadr. xix, 2–3). *Naumachiae* were presented in the Theater of Dionysus in
the third century A.D. See Bulle, *Untersuchungen*, p. 80.

[418] *Nigr.* 12–13; cf. 14.   [419] J. Keil, in CAH, XI, 560.

centrated on intellectual interests, the Athenians lacked the "push-fulness necessary for business enterprise." A superficial reading of Philostratus' *Lives of the Sophists* and of Eunapius' *Lives of the Philosophers and Sophists* will provide convincing proof that philosophy was actually a thriving trade.[420] But it was, unfortunately, not the citizens of Athens who made the most of the trade! However, the difficulties of the city are to be attributed to a number of other factors, some of which we have already had occasion to observe. Among these factors are poverty of natural resources (with the consequent difficulty in paying for imported commodities), loss of empire, and the shifting of trade routes. But another factor, which became very acute during the period of the Roman Empire, is to be seen in the gross maldistribution of wealth. The estates of the wealthy—especially such enormous estates as those of Hipparchus and of Herodes—must have been accumulated through an unscrupulous exploitation of the poor; and, once these large accumulations were made, the initiative of the mass of Athenians was thoroughly stifled. Perhaps the most forceful indication of this state of society is to be seen in the contrast between the immense wealth of Herodes on the one hand and the debts owed him by the Athenians on the other. The question naturally arises: In what properties and forms of business enterprise were the fortunes of the wealthy invested? Part of the answer we have already seen—a large part was absorbed in landed properties worked and managed by freedmen and slaves, as well as by freeborn laborers. On the other hand, their available cash resources were probably invested in usury, a business in which Athens, if we may believe Plutarch,[421] was surpassed—in mainland Greece—by Corinth

---

[420] It is to be noted that various sophists, some of whom taught at Athens, attained to senatorial rank at Rome. Cf. A. Stein, *Der römische Ritterstand* (Munich, 1927; Münchener Beiträge zur Papyrusforschung und antiken Rechtsgeschichte, X), pp. 239–41.

[421] *Mor.* 831A. We have already seen that the fortune of the family of Herodes Atticus was founded, at least in part, on the banking business. See my discussion above, including notes 384–86. IG, II–III², 2776, may not be cited as evidence of 8 percent interest being charged at Athens. See my discussion above, including note 262. The 12 percent interest payment in IG, II–III², 1104, is not to be cited as evidence for the rate of interest normally charged at Athens, for the percentage mentioned there was to apply to a penalty payment in case of default by a public

and Patrae only. It is, of course, possible—but we have no proof of it—that the wealthy controlled the only industry of importance to survive at Athens under the empire, that of the making of objects of art for exportation to foreign districts. It is true that at various times during the first two centuries of our era the city received splendid gifts from the emperors, from wealthy foreigners, and from wealthy citizens; that many festivals were added to the religious calendar, and that these festivals were occasions for distribution of grain; and that there were great celebrations on the occasions of the visits of the emperor Hadrian. There is, therefore, justification for asserting, as Graindor did,[422] that life at Athens, particularly in the second century A.D., was one continuous festival. But it must not be forgotten that luxurious buildings, pageantry and display, and doles were but the thinnest of veneers for a poverty which lay close beneath the resplendent surface.

---

official. See my discussion above, including notes 93–95. The normal rate of interest in other parts of the Greek world seems to have varied between 6 percent and 9 percent (Billeter, *Geschichte des Zinsfusses*, pp. 103–9).

[422] *Hadrien*, pp. 181–82.

CHAPTER VI

THIRD CENTURY A.D.

THE LITTLE that is known from literary sources concerning the history of Athens in the third century A.D. does not enable us to tie up the city's destiny with that of the remainder of the empire, and although a more considerable body of information is forthcoming from epigraphical sources, the part that is apposite to considerations of an economic character is relatively insignificant. It is, therefore, impossible to determine the extent to which Athens was affected by the political and monetary anarchy from which the Roman world at large was suffering during this century.[1] We may be certain, of course, that the city did not escape unscathed—no community could have remained unaffected by the crisis. However, the very scanty indirect evidence at our disposal tends to show that during the latter third of the century—following the invasion of the Heruli in 267 A.D.—the economic life of the city fell to a very low ebb. It is, therefore, convenient to divide our consideration of the economic life of the city into two sub-periods—that between 200 A.D. and 267 A.D., and that between 267 A.D. and the end of the century.

If building activity alone were taken as the gauge of the economic well-being of Athens, one would have to conclude that the city fared very badly during the first sixty-seven years of the third century. Not only were no public buildings of importance erected, but the construction even of monuments of lesser importance seems to have been undertaken only with great infrequency. A priest of "Zeus in the Palladium"—who was a member of the γένος of the Bouzygae—erected at his own expense a new statue of Pallas in

---

[1] Rostovtzeff, *Roman Empire*, pp. 416–48. For the inflation of the currency, see Heichelheim, *Wirtschaftsgeschichte*, I, 685–86.

the Palladium on the Acropolis.[2] Another Athenian met the expense of work on a φρούριον on the Acropolis.[3] And in 253 A.D., or possibly in 262 A.D., the Athenians, becoming apprehensive at the time of the barbarian invasion of northern Greece and the siege of Thessalonica, repaired the walls of the city.[4] From neither literary nor archaeological sources do we have evidence of further additions to the city's monuments or of restoration of its buildings.[5] It must, however, be borne in mind that, with the exception of Herodes Atticus, few Athenians bestowed buildings upon the city during the first two centuries A.D. It would seem, therefore, that the great decline in building activity in the third century should be taken not as proof of the presence of fewer men of wealth, but rather as an indication that there were fewer foreigners interested in, or able to make gifts to, the city.

Although imperial favor was lacking in the period that elapsed between the rule of the Antonines and the accession of the emperor Constantine, the university had been established on so firm a basis that it continued in a relatively flourishing condition for some fifty years after the death of Marcus Aurelius.[6] Students continued to come to Athens in numbers, and the list of the teachers of the period who are named in the pages of Philostratus' *Lives of the Sophists* is far from unimposing. The city's drawing power as an educational center at this time is further attested by the number of foreigners—scarcely smaller than in the latter years of the preceding century—who became members of the Athenian ephebia. The registration—both of foreigners and of Athenians—in various years during the third century was as follows:

[2] IG, II–III², 3177.

[3] *Ibid.*, 3193.

[4] It is most often assumed that this work was carried out in 253 A.D. See Zosimus, I, xxix, 2–3; Zonaras, XII, 23; George Syncellus, 381C; cf. Judeich, *Topographie*, p. 104, note 5; A. von Premerstein, in *Zeitschrift für deutsches Altertum und deutsche Litteratur*, LX (1923), 79. Larsen, "Roman Greece," p. 494, favors the date of 262 A.D. which is given by *Vit. Gall.* v–vi. The repair of the fortifications was accomplished without imperial aid. See p. 79 in Premerstein's article.

[5] Possibly, however, the remodeling of the Clepsydra, which took place before the building of the so-called Valerian Wall, was undertaken before 267 A.D. See T. L. Shear, in *Hesperia*, VII (1938), 334–35.

[6] Walden, *Universities*, pp. 99–100.

Date (A.D.)	Athenians	Foreigners	Source
c.200	61	32	IG, II–III², 2199
c.200	70	61	2191
Early 3d cent.	34+		Hesperia, IV (1935), 186–88 [f]
c.200	76	27	IG, II–III², 2193
Before 212	60[a]	31+	2207
c.212/3	57+	38+	2208
217/8	65[b]		2221
226/7–234/5	92+	44+	2235
230–235	78+	5+	2237
238/9–243/4	229[c]		2239
243/4 or a little later	229[d]		2243
262/3 or 266/7	313[e]	52	2245

[a] Estimate. [b] Estimate. [c] Includes *mellepheboi* (see Appendix, including note 28).
[d] Estimate; includes *mellepheboi*. [e] Includes *mellepheboi*.
[f] Cf. *Hesperia*, II (1933), 411.

Indeed, the vitality of the ephebic institution at this time is especially noteworthy. Not only is it to be observed that the number of Athenian ephebes continued at approximately the same level as in the latter half of the second century, but it is striking in particular that at no other time in their history was the number of ephebic festivals greater than during the years between 200 A.D. and 267 A.D.[7] Moreover, other important festivals, such as the Dionysia and the Panathenaea, continued to be celebrated.[8] That the Athenian festivals were of more than local importance is shown by the fact that traveling athletes, who made the rounds of the games in various parts of the Greek world, came to Athens to take part in them. Thus, we learn from an inscription of the time of Caracalla,[9] found at Sardis, that the prominent athlete M. Aurelius Demostratus Damas, who was awarded honorary citizenship at Athens, Alexandria, Antinoöpolis, Nicomedia, Tralles, Ephesus, Smyrna, Miletus, Pergamum, Corinth, Argos, Lacedaemon, Delphi, and Elis, and who was accredited with more than one hundred victories

[7] P. Graindor, "Études sur l'éphébie attique sous l'empire," *Musée belge*, XXVI (1922), 165–228, especially 175. In IG, II–III², 2199, which is dated c.200 A.D., the *agonothetae* of the agonistic festivals are listed: Antinoeia (in Athens), Hadrianeia, Antinoeia (in Eleusis), Theseia, Germanikeia, Epinikia, Philadelpheia, Severeia, Antoneia, Commodeia, and Athenaea. Except for the Theseia— in which the ephebes actually took part—all these are ephebic festivals.

[8] For the Dionysia of c.220 A.D., see Philostratus, *Vit. Apoll.*, IV, 21.

[9] W. H. Buckler and D. M. Robinson, *Sardis* (Leyden, 1932; Publications of the American Society for the Excavation of Sardis, VII), Part I, No. 79A, l. 10.

in athletic contests, won ten victories in Athenian games, three in the Panhellenia, and one in the Hadrianeia, along with an unspecified number of victories in the Panathenaea and the Olympieia. Undoubtedly numerous visitors were attracted to these games, and from them various Athenians derived a limited amount of income. But by far the largest number of visitors came to attend the Mysteries, which were restored to something of their former brilliance in the early years of the century.[10] It is precisely the early years of the century—the time when he was writing—to which Philostratus refers when he writes[11] that at the time of the Mysteries there was no city in Greece more populous than Athens.

Concerning the commodities produced at Athens in the third century for sale on the local and the foreign markets we have very little information. It is probable—although we have no specific evidence from the third century—that Athenian farmers continued to produce, partly for the local market and partly for exportation, relatively large amounts of oil. Attic honey seems also to have retained at least a part of its foreign market, for there is evidence that it was being imported into Egypt at this time.[12] In the realm of industry we find continued activity of Athenian workers in the years of the third century preceding the reign of Gallienus. Athenian sculptors apparently retained some of their market of former times; and those workers who produced sarcophagi kept the markets they had enjoyed in the latter part of the second century.[13] Less ac-

[10] IG, II–III², 1078. Gallienus was greatly interested in the cults of Attica, and seems to have been initiated into the Mysteries at Eleusis. See *Vit. Gall.* xi, 3; cf. Graindor, *Marbres*, p. 80; A. von Domaszewski, "Beiträge zur Kaisergeschichte," *Philolologus*, LXV (1906), 351–52; A. von Domaszewski, *Geschichte der römischen Kaiser* (Leipzig, 1909), II, 306. Out of a very fragmentary inscription (AE, 1895. p. 103, No. 17), which does not appear in IG II–III², Graindor, *Marbres*, pp. 75–80, evolves the hypothesis that Gallienus strove to imitate Hadrian by reforming the constitution of Athens and especially by attempting to provide an adequate and reasonably priced food supply for pilgrims attending the Mysteries. More specifically, Graindor believes that Gallienus, like Hadrian, attempted to bring about the transfer of the center of the fish sellers' trade from the Piraeus to Eleusis. The evidence is, however, much too scanty to support such definite conclusions.

[11] *Vit. Apoll.* IV, 17.

[12] The use of Attic honey is prescribed in a magical formula of the third century A.D. (P. Lond. 121).

[13] Copies of works of art of an earlier age were still made. For the sarcophagi, see the citations in chap. v, note 182.

complished workers of stone made sculptured tombstones; but the use of these declined in the course of the century.[14] The Athenian lamp-making industry became suddenly very prosperous in the third century.[15] Throughout the second century Athens had imported most of its lamps from Corinth, where most of the lamps then used in Greece were produced. Toward the end of that century Athenian potters began to imitate the Type XXVII lamp, which had been developed by Corinthian workers; and in the following century the Athenian industry grew to such an extent that it began to export lamps in number to Corinth and other parts of Greece, and in smaller amounts to Sicily, South Russia, and Egypt.[16] Mention may also be made of the Athenian shoemaker's trade, which had developed to such an extent that its products were being exported to Alexandria by the beginning of the third century.[17]

When notice is taken of imported products, it will be found that all good pottery was of foreign make, as hitherto during the Roman period.[18] Other imported commodities were incense, ivory, myrrh, papyrus, and books, which were brought from Egypt.[19] Beyond this, direct evidence is lacking. But we may be sure that, as in centuries past, the Athenians found it necessary to import substantial amounts of grain from foreign lands—perhaps from Asia Minor, Egypt, and South Russia.[20]

[14] Mühsam, *Die attischen Grabreliefs*, pp. 56–57.

[15] K. Kübler, in AM, LIII (1928), 181; Broneer, *Lamps*, pp. 26, 111–14; cf. H. A. Thompson, in *Hesperia*, II (1933), 206.

[16] See the citations in the preceding note.

[17] From the manner in which Clement of Alexandria (fl. c.200 A.D.) mentions (*Paed.* II, xi, 116) Attic and Sicyonian shoes it is permissible to deduce that they were being imported into Alexandria.

[18] F. O. Waagé, in *Hesperia*, II (1933), 304. Waagé reports (*ibid.*, pp. 302–3) the finding, in the Agora, of Group A Roman ware which was imported from Italy, from Asia Minor, or from some part of Greece other than Athens; he reports, also, the finding in the Agora of some Group B Roman ware which, possibly, was imported before 300 A.D. Cf. H. Comfort, in RE, Supplementband VII, 1305. A third-century terra-cotta figurine of a type found in Cyprus and in Italy, but which is made of clay from Asia Minor, has been found in the Agora; see D. Burr, in *Hesperia*, II (1933), 191. It is probable that numerous additional examples of imported wares will have been identified when definitive publications of the ceramic wares have been completed.   [19] Philostratus, *Vit. soph.* 603.

[20] Note may be taken of two very fragmentary inscriptions of the early years of the third century (IG, II–III², 1118, 1119) which seem to contain the provisions of laws (or imperial edicts?) regulating the sale and price of grain.

Trade probably continued to attract foreign merchants to the city, but the number residing there must have been much smaller than in the second century. The Piraeus was not yet devoid of commercial activity. At about the beginning of the third century Proclus of Naucratis, a sophist who was at the same time interested in trade, owned a house in the port town and imported various commodities from Egypt.[21] Another indication of activity at the Piraeus is to be found in an inscription of the third century which sets forth a list of the *orgeones*, priests, and priestesses of Euporia Thea Belela.[22] Moreover, it is very probable that the harbor was still used by the Romans as a naval station.[23]

Just as in the second century, the members of a relatively small number—perhaps even smaller than in the preceding century—of wealthy families continued to hold the chief offices of state, and it is a reasonable assumption that a proportionately large amount of the wealth of Attica was held by them. But we have very little specific information concerning their economic condition. It will, therefore, suffice to take brief notice of only a few individual members of these families. First to be mentioned is M. Ulpius Eubiotus Leurus, archon at Athens at some time around the middle of the third century;[24] his gift to the city of two hundred and fifty thousand drachmas, in addition to grain, at the time of "the great famine"[25] may be taken as an indication that he was probably one of the wealthiest Athenians of his time. Another individual who is worthy of mention is [Flavius Asclepia]des, herald of the Areopagus, whose will, made at some time between 238/9 A.D. and 243/4 A.D., created an endowment that provided, for each member of the Areopagus, a month's entertainment at the end of the year and a banquet on his birthday.[26] Finally, mention may be made of P. Herennius Dexippus the historian, member of an illustrious family,[27] incum-

---

[21] Philostratus, *Vit. soph.* 603.

[22] IG, II–III², 2361; cf. Graindor, *Album*, p. 63, No. 93.

[23] For the evidence concerning Roman soldiers and sailors at the Piraeus, see chap. iv, note 188.　　[24] Graindor, *Chronologie*, No. 203, pp. 283–84.

[25] IG, II–III², 3697; cf. 3698–3700.

[26] IG, II–III², 2773; Graindor, *Album*, p. 68, No. 101; cf. Laum, *Stiftungen*, Vol. II, No. 17. For the date of his archonship, see Graindor, *Chronologie*, p. 252, No. 179.

[27] For the stemma of the family, see J. Kirchner's commentary on IG, II–III², 3665; cf. Graindor, in BCH, LI (1927), 282.

bent of a hereditary priesthood and of the offices of *archon eponymus* (c.252/3 A.D.), *archon basileus*, herald of the Areopagus, *agonothetes* of the great Panathenaea, and panegyriarch; he was, also, leader of the Athenian forces against the Heruli in 267 A.D.[28]

The following conclusions concerning the economic condition of Attica during the first sixty-seven years of the third century may be drawn from the very scanty evidence which we have surveyed. First, the continued registration of relatively large numbers of ephebes and the flourishing condition of the ephebic festivals would indicate that prosperity had not declined greatly since the latter years of the second century; and the fact that the university continued to attract large numbers of students would point in the same direction. Second, there is no reason to assume a decline in agriculture. Indeed, it may be assumed that, just as in the second century, the wealth of the most prosperous inhabitants was founded on landed property. Third, Athenian industry seems to have retained the very modest prosperity which it had enjoyed in the second century, for whatever decline in revenues was suffered by the makers of objects of art was probably balanced by the increased profits of the lamp makers, who had found foreign outlets for their products. Fourth, although numerous foreign visitors were still attracted to the city, no longer did foreigners—or, for that matter, citizens—lavish upon the city gifts such as those which had made possible the erection of public buildings in the second century; and, in consequence, Attic economic life in general was deprived of the stimulus it had formerly enjoyed from such expenditures. A final observation may be made—that no satisfactory conclusion concerning the prosperity of Attica may be drawn from estimates of the population in the third century.[29]

In 267 A.D., during the reign of Gallienus, Athens was captured by a band of Heruli who came from the north, by way of the sea.[30]

---

[28] IG, II–III², 2931, 3198, 3667–71; cf. Graindor, *Chronologie*, pp. 263–66, No. 183; Schwartz, in RE, V, 288.

[29] This problem is discussed in detail in the Appendix.

[30] George Syncellus, 382D; *Vit. Gall.* xiii, 8–9; Zonaras, XII, 26; Zosimus, I, xxxix, 1; Dexippus in Jacoby, *Fragmente*, No. 100, frag. 28 (cf. FHG, III, 680, frag. 21). Cf. Hertzberg, *Geschichte Griechenlands*, III, 170–79; Wachsmuth, *Die Stadt Athen*, I, 707–9; A. von Premerstein, in *Zeitschrift für deutsches Altertum und deutsche Litteratur*, L (1923), 77–79; O. Fiebiger and L. Schmidt, in *Denkschriften*

The historian Dexippus, whom we have had occasion to notice above, hastily assembled a band of two thousand citizens and, ultimately, with the aid of what seems to have been a part of the imperial fleet, expelled the barbarians from the city. It is useless to follow certain nineteenth-century historians in speculating on a possible exhilarating effect upon the Athenians and other Greeks from their efforts in driving the invaders out;[31] the most that can be said is that the Athenians still possessed sufficient vitality to rise to the occasion, but that this vitality was unable to stave off the serious decline in economic life that oppressed the country during the remainder of the century. The invaders left a large part of the city in ruins[32]—the regions of the Agora[33] and the Dipylon[34] were thoroughly destroyed—and very little, if anything, was done to repair the damage or to erect new buildings in place of those that had been destroyed.[35] The building of the so-called Valerian Wall

---

der kaiserliche Akademie der Wissenschaften in Wien, philosophisch-historische Klasse, LX (1917), commentary on No. 287.

[31] G. Finlay, *Greece under the Romans* (Everyman's Library edition), p. 108, advances the hypothesis that as a result of the barbarian invasions the number of slaves declined so greatly (they were either killed or carried away as plunder) that wages of free laborers rose. Going further, he assumes that the wealthy found their property threatened by the poor. His general conclusion is that the devastation wrought upon the country by the Goths and the havoc occasioned by the great plague brought about a great improvement in the condition of the Greeks. As Hertzberg, *Geschichte Griechenlands*, III, 194–95, insists, Finlay's argument is entirely conjectural. Nevertheless, Hertzberg believes that the invigoration of the Greeks that ensued as a result of the expulsion of the Goths actually did bring about relatively prosperous conditions in Greece in the fourth century A.D.

[32] The doubts expressed by Wachsmuth, *Die Stadt Athen*, I, 707–8, and Judeich, *Topographie*, p. 104, that many of the city's monuments were destroyed by the Heruli are shown by recent excavations to be groundless.

[33] See, for example, H. A. Thompson, in *Hesperia*, VI (1937), 76–77; T. L. Shear, in *Hesperia*, V (1936), 6. It is not feasible to cite every apposite reference that may be found in the reports of the excavators.

[34] For the destruction of the Pompeum by the Heruli, see K. Kübler, in AM, LIII (1928), 182.

[35] A large water basin was built just below the Clepsydra at c.275 A.D. T. L. Shear, in *Hesperia*, VII (1938), 332–35. The reconstruction of the stage of the Theater of Dionysus by the archon Phaedrus is sometimes assigned to the third century (Dörpfeld and Reisch, *Das griechische Theater*, p. 94; Fiechter, *Dionysostheater*, p. 82). Other scholars are less certain, assigning the work to the third *or* the fourth century. See Bieber, *Denkmäler*, p. 19; Judeich, *Topographie*, p. 105. But Dinsmoor, in AJA, XIV (1910), 481–83, has shown that the materials used in

at c.276/7 A.D.[36] is certainly not to be taken as evidence of renewed vitality, but rather of the opposite: this hastily erected
rampart enclosed a narrowly restricted area north of the Acropolis,[37] rather than anything like the city of the years preceding
267 A.D. But it would be a matter for great surprise if Athens had
been able to escape from the consequences of the chaos that pervaded the empire in the second half of the century—a chaos result-
ing from the exhaustion of the imperial treasury by the military
campaigns on all the borders of the realm and from the disastrous
inflationary policy pursued by the emperors. Salaries hitherto paid
to professors out of the Fiscus were discontinued at this time, and
the university entered upon the leanest years it had thus far experienced.[38] Fewer students came to the city, and the number of
teachers declined; in consequence, the city was deprived of the
rather considerable profit it had formerly derived from its student
population. Also attributable to the decline in prosperity (as well
as to the rise of Christianity) was the rapid decline and disappearance of the ephebia. Although an attempt was made to continue
the institution after the invasion of the Heruli, the effort seems to
have met with no success; the latest evidence of its existence is to
be found in a recently discovered inscription of the latter part of
the century, some few years after 267 A.D.[39] Moreover, like all
other local coinages in the empire,[40] that of Athens was discontinued at the time of Gallienus.[41] Athenian makers of objects of art
lost their markets; no ornamented Attic grave stelae are dated later

---

the work could not have been built into the stage before the time of the construction of the so-called Beulé Gate. The latter structure was erected in the fourth
century A.D.—probably in the latter part of the century. For the date, see Judeich,
Topographie, p. 105; Graindor, in BCH, XXXVIII (1914), 272–95. The stage of
Phaedrus is assigned to the fourth century A.D. by Bulle, Untersuchungen, p. 16.
The archonship of Phaedrus is assigned to the end of the fourth or the beginning
of the fifth century by Graindor, Chronologie, pp. 269–71.

[36] For the date, see Dinsmoor, in Hesperia, IX (1940), 52; cf. T. L. Shear, in
Hesperia, IV (1935), 332–34; VII (1938), 332–33; VIII (1939), 218.

[37] Cf. Judeich, Topographie, p. 165.

[38] Walden, Universities, p. 105.

[39] The inscription is published by J. H. Oliver, in Hesperia, II (1933), 505–11.

[40] Mattingly, Roman Coins, pp. 212–13.

[41] J. P. Shear, "Athenian Imperial Coinage," Hesperia, V (1936), 285–332,
especially 327.

than Gallienus;[42] the production of sculptured sarcophagi was discontinued during the course of the century.[43] For a brighter side to the picture very little is to be said. Athenian potters continued to enjoy an export market for their lamps.[44] And possibly Athenian festivals retained enough importance to attract, now and then, competing athletes from foreign districts. The evidence that bears on this point is all too slight, but we may at least take passing notice of an athlete who, as we learn from a papyrus of 298 A.D.,[45] was granted honorary citizenship at Athens and at Oxyrhynchus in recognition of his victories in the games.

The Athenians attempted to maintain the outward forms of their political institutions after 267 A.D.—but it appears that they met with some difficulty, for soon after the expulsion of the Heruli there is attested the first instance of repeated tenure of the archonship under the empire.[46] From this fact we are probably justified in deducing that the number of wealthy citizens able to sustain the financial burdens associated with the tenure of the important magistracies had declined under the impact of adverse economic conditions. Although the Roman world began to recover from extreme depression and anarchy when Diocletian came to the throne, the revival experienced by Athens—if, indeed, the city recovered at all—must have been extremely modest.

[42] Mühsam, *Die attischen Grabreliefs*, p. 57.

[43] G. Rodenwaldt, in JDAI, XLV (1930), 186; and the citations in chap. v, note 182.

[44] K. Kübler, in AM, LIII (1928), 181; Broneer, *Lamps*, pp. 111–14. It is to be observed that potters' ovens were erected over the ruins of the Pompeum after the destruction of that building by the Heruli. Cf. A. Brueckner, in AM, LVI (1931), 6–7.

[45] P. Ox. 1643.

[46] The name of this archon was T. Flavius Mondo. His repeated tenure of the archonship is attested by an inscription published by J. H. Oliver, in *Hesperia*, II (1933), 505–11. Mondo seems to have been a member of a distinguished Boeotian family which moved to Athens in the third century A.D.

CHAPTER VII

AFTERMATH: FOURTH AND FIFTH CENTURIES

FROM contemporary writings a few interesting—and illuminating—comments that throw light on the economic condition of Athens in the fourth and fifth centuries A.D. have come down to us. First to be mentioned is the so-called *Expositio totius mundi et gentium,* which is an account of the climate, commerce, general productivity, and other aspects of various parts of the world; it was first written in Greek by an Egyptian trader in the second half of the fourth century A.D., and afterwards, at a much later date, translated into a crude Latin version, in which it is now extant.[1] The apposite portion of this account runs as follows:

... After Thessaly there is the land of Achaea (Greece and Laconia), which abounds in learning, but in other respects is not self-sufficient, for it is a small and mountainous province and can not produce as much grain as Thessaly. But it yields a small amount of oil and the Attic honey, and it is to be praised rather for the renown of its philosophy and rhetoric: in other respects not so much. It has these fine cities: Corinth and Athens. Corinth, a city with much commerce, has an outstanding building in its amphitheater, but Athens has learning and ancient traditions and something worthy of mention in the citadel, where it is wonderful to see the wars of men of old celebrated by the many statues.[2]

That Greece—Athens in particular—suffered from a shortage of

[1] The latest edition (with commentary) of this account is by G. Lumbroso, in Atti della reale Accademia dei Lincei, classe di scienze morali, storiche e filologiche, serie quinta, VI (1898), 124–68. Other editions are by C. Müller, *Geographi Graeci minores* (Paris, 1861), II, 513–28, and by A. Riese, *Geographi Latini minores* (Heilbronn, 1878), pp. 104–26. Cf. M. Schanz, C. Hosius, and G. Krüger, *Geschichte der römischen Litteratur* (2d ed.; Leipzig, 1920), IV, ii, 125–27. P. Vinogradoff, in *Cambridge Medieval History,* I, 548, maintains that the *Expositio* was translated into Latin in the time of Constantius, soon after 345 A.D.

[2] Lines 283–92 in Lumbroso's edition (see the preceding note); section 52 in Müller's edition (see the preceding note). The translation is my own.

grain is but a continuation of a theme which, as we have often had occasion to observe, ran through Athenian history from very early times. And lest it be thought that in some almost miraculous fashion conditions had changed by the fourth century A.D., we may devote passing attention to evidence which corroborates the account of the Egyptian trader. The emperor Constantine, Julian informs us,[3] made yearly distributions of grain at Athens and filled the office of general, the function of which—under the empire—was mainly to oversee the city's grain supply.[4] At a slightly later date Prohaeresius was summoned to Gaul by the emperor Constans and made such a fine impression that upon the eve of his return to Athens he was allowed to request any gift he wished. Thereupon he asked the emperor to provide for the yearly cost of the grain supply of Athens by giving the city several large tribute-paying islands. The request was granted, and at the same time the sophist was appointed to the office of general.[5] But the problem of the city's grain supply became, in the fourth century, even more serious than it had been in former years, for, as Eunapius informs us,[6] while Byzantium had in former times furnished Athens with a regular supply of grain, beginning with the time of Constantine, the city, now the imperial capital Constantinople, could hardly secure an adequate supply for itself, let alone export any surplus to the Athenians. Indeed, sources of supply that had been, before that time, available to the Athenians—Asia, Syria, Phoenicia, and Egypt—were henceforth monopolized by Constantinople.[7] To return to the *Expositio*, the commerce of Athens is depicted as non-existent, but the continuing reputation of the university is asserted. We shall have more to say on these subjects later. Of the oil mentioned in the *Expositio*, we are probably justified in assuming that a certain amount was produced in Attica.

The reputation of Attic honey is attested by another writer, whose accounts agree well with that of the *Expositio*—with the

---

[3] Or. I, 8c; cf. Graindor, *Album*, pp. 73–74.

[4] Actually, Julian says that the emperor held the office of στρατοπεδάρχης at Athens. However, this official is to be identified as the general. For the function of the latter at Athens under the empire, see chap. iv, including notes 273–78.

[5] Eunapius, 492. The office is designated στρατοπεδάρχης, as in the case of the emperor Julian. See the preceding note.

[6] 492.   [7] Cf. Leider, *Der Handel von Alexandria*, pp. 68–69.

important exception of his estimate of the Athenian schools. In a letter to his brother Euoptius, Bishop Synesius of Cyrene,[8] who flourished c.400 A.D., wrote as follows:

I hope that I may profit as much as you desire from my residence at Athens. It seems to me that I have already grown more than a palm and a finger's length in wisdom, and I can give you at once a proof of the progress I have made. Well, it is from Anagyrus that I am writing to you; and I have visited Sphettus, Thria, Cephisia, and Phalerum. But may the accursed ship-captain perish who brought me here! Athens has no longer anything sublime except the country's famous names. Just as in the case of a victim burnt in the sacrificial fire, there remains nothing but the skin to help us to reconstruct a creature which was once alive—so ever since philosophy left these precincts, there is nothing for the tourist to admire except the Academy, the Lyceum, and, by Zeus, the Decorated Porch which has given its name to the philosophy of Chrysippus. This is no longer Decorated, for the proconsul has taken away the panels on which Polygnotus of Thasos had displayed his skill.

To-day Egypt has received and cherishes the fruitful wisdom of Hypatia. Athens was aforetime the dwelling-place of the wise: to-day the bee-keepers alone bring it honour. Such is the case of that pair of sophists in Plutarch who draw the young people to the lecture room—not by the fame of their eloquence, but by pots of honey from Hymettus.[9]

And in another letter, also written to his brother, the bishop has the following to say:

A great number of people, either private individuals or priests, by moulding dreams, which they call revelations, seem likely to do me harm when I am awake, if I do not happen with all speed to visit sacred Athens. Whenever, then, you happen to meet a skipper sailing for the Piraeus, write to me, as it is there that I shall receive my letters. I shall gain not only this by my voyage to Athens—an escape from my present evils, but also a relief from doing reverence to the learning of those who come back from Athens. They differ in no wise from us ordinary mortals. They do not understand Aristotle and Plato better than we, and nevertheless they go about among us as demi-gods among mules, because they have seen the Academy, the Lyceum, and the Poecile where Zeno gave his lectures on philosophy. However,

---

[8] For good up-to-date accounts of Synesius, see O. Bardenhewer, *Geschichte der altkirchlichen Literatur* (Freiburg i. B., 1924), IV, 21–22, 101–22; FitzGerald, *Letters of Synesius*, pp. 11–73; Geffcken, *Der Ausgang des griechisch-römischen Heidentums*, pp. 215–21; cf. Von Campenhausen, in RE, Zweite Reihe, IV, 1362–65; G. Grützmacher, *Synesios von Kyrene: ein Charakterbild aus dem Untergang des Hellentums* (Leipzig, 1913); W. S. Crawford, *Synesius the Hellene* (London, 1901); Catholic University of Patristic Studies, LXIII, 1940.

[9] *Epist.* cxxxvi. The translation is that of FitzGerald, *Letters of Synesius*. For the Greek texts of the letters, see R. Hercher, *Epistolographi Graeci* (Paris, 1873), IV, 638–739; J. P. Migne, *Patrologia Graeca*, LXVI. For the chronology of the letters, see O. Seeck, in *Philologus*, LII (1893), 442–83.

the Poecile no longer deserves its name, for the proconsul has taken away all the pictures, and has thus humiliated these men's pretensions to learning.[10]

Both Synesius and the author of the *Expositio*, it will be observed, pay tribute to the monuments of Athens. These monuments, of course, attest the former glory of Athens, rather than a vigorous economic life at the time the accounts were written, for after the time of Herodes Atticus few buildings of consequence were erected in the city.[11] It remains to explain the discrepancies between the

[10] *Epist.* liv. The rendering is that of FitzGerald, *Letters of Synesius.*

[11] Building activity at various dates throughout the fourth and fifth centuries A.D. may be briefly noted as follows: (1) Transformation of the precinct of Hephaestus under Christian auspices, probably in the fourth century (D. B. Thompson, in *Hesperia*, VI [1937], 401). (2) Partial reconstruction of the long narrow stoa located to the south of the so-called South Stoa in the Agora, in the fourth century (T. L. Shear, in *Hesperia*, VI [1937], 358). (3) Possibly a number of lecture halls built for students in the philosophical schools, at about the middle of the fourth century (Judeich, *Topographie*, p. 105; cf. A. von Premerstein, in JOAI, XV [1912], 30–32). But it may be that these structures should be identified with the buildings which Cervonius, proconsul of Achaea, erected for the benefit of the students at this time; see Himerius, *Or.* IV, i, 9; cf. Judeich, *Topographie*, p. 105; Wachsmuth, *Die Stadt Athen*, I, 711–12. (4) Reëmployment of the foundations of the Odeum in the Agora for a new building, on the northern façade of which were erected the figures which later gave rise to the name of the so-called Stoa of the Giants, in the second half of the fourth century (T. L. Shear, in *Hesperia*, V [1936], 11). (5) Restoration of the neglected quarter of Collytus by Ampelius, proconsul of Achaea, in the latter half of the fourth century (Photius, *Bibl.* cod. 243, p. 375b 8). (6) Probable reconstruction (revealed by excavations) of the city wall near the Pnyx, in the time of Julian (361–63 A.D.) (H. A. Thompson, in *Hesperia*, V [1936], 200. This emperor was reputed to have done much for the Greeks in the way of erecting buildings and repairing fortifications; see Mamertinus, *Grat. act. Jul.* 9; cf. Wachsmuth, *Die Stadt Athen*, I, 712–13). (7) Building of the so-called Beulé Gate, in the latter half of the fourth century (see chap. vi, note 35). (8) Reconstruction of the stage of the Theater of Dionysus by the archon Phaedrus, in the latter half of the fourth century (see chap. vi, note 35). (9) Erection of a large building east of Theseum Hill and northwest of the Odeum, in the section of the Agora labeled II by the excavators, at the very end of the fourth or in the fifth century (T. L. Shear, in *Hesperia*, IV [1935], 315–17). (10) Reconstruction of the Bouleuterion, in the late fourth or in the fifth century (H. A. Thompson, in *Hesperia*, VI [1937], 171–72). (11) Erection of two buildings—one of them large, with a peristyle court, and not a private house—on the lower slopes of the Areopagus, at the end of the fourth or the beginning of the fifth century (T. L. Shear, in *Hesperia*, VIII [1939], 214, 216; however, see H. A. Thompson, *The Tholos of Athens and its Predecessors*, pp. 121–26, who maintains that the house with the peristyle court does not antedate 500 A.D.). (12) Erection of a large and elaborate Roman bath over the eastern end of the stoa in the Agora to which the excavators have given the name of South

two accounts of the university. The fortune of the Athenian schools had fallen to a low ebb at the end of the third century,[12] but a striking revival came in the time of Constantine,[13] who reinstituted several measures and originated various others to improve the lot of the professors and their families.[14] From that time up to the invasion of the Goths in 396 A.D. the university at Athens occupied the foremost position among the higher schools of the empire.[15] Famous teachers and students later to become famous—we find their names in the pages of Eunapius' *Lives of the Sophists:* Julian the Sophist, Prohaeresius, Himerius, Themistius, Libanius, and others—came from widely separated parts of the empire. But, even in the course of this splendid period, signs of impending decline were not wanting. The emperor Constantine, although by no means unfavorably disposed toward Athens, had removed many works of art from the city and from Greece at large to adorn his new capital.[16] Moreover, Eunapius tells us that Libanius, influenced by the fear that he might be held in low esteem if he continued to live in a small town like Athens, took up permanent residence at Constantinople.[17] However seriously the life of the university may have been affected by the devastation wrought by the Goths in 396 A.D., more serious setbacks came with the establishment of Christianity as the state religion at the end of the fourth century, and with the completion of the final stages of the organization of the university at Constantinople in 425 A.D.[18] Thus, by the beginning of the fifth century, the resplendence of the Athenian university had passed beyond recall. It is this period of decline that Synesius describes in his letters. But in spite of the jealousy which apparently existed between the Athenian and the Alexandrian

---

Stoa, c.400 A.D. (T. L. Shear, in *Hesperia*, IV [1935], 360–62; A. W. Parsons, in *Hesperia*, V [1936], 90). (13) Erection, on the foundations of a stoa originally built north of the Hephaesteum in the first century B.C., of a new building with concrete walls, at some time after the third century A.D. (T. L. Shear, in *Hesperia*, VI [1937], 339). (14) Reconstruction of the Tholos, at the beginning of the fourth century A.D. (H. A. Thompson, *The Tholos of Athens and its Predecessors*, p. 136).

[12] Walden, *Universities*, p. 105.   [13] *Ibid.*, pp. 106–7.

[14] *Cod. Theod.* XIII, iii, 1; *Cod. Jus.* X, 53.

[15] Vasiliev, *Byzantine Empire*, I, 125.

[16] Wachsmuth, *Die Stadt Athen*, I, 714, note 3; Hertzberg, *Geschichte Griechenlands*, III, 260, 269.   [17] 495.

[18] Vasiliev, *Byzantine Empire*, I, 125–26; Walden, *Universities*, pp. 108, 122.

schools[19] (Synesius was a devotee of the latter) there emerge through the bishop's prejudiced statements various indications— more especially in the passage in which reference is made to "sacred Athens"—of the esteem in which the university at Athens was still held.

In another letter, written to his brother when both were in Cyrene, Synesius gives us a fleeting glimpse of one Athenian trade which enjoyed at least moderate prosperity—to the extent of having a foreign market:

They say that a fellow who sells boots has come from Athens. It is the same person, I think, from whom you bought for me last year some lacing shoes. Now, according to my information, he has extended the area of his trade; he has robes in the Attic style, he has light summer clothes which will become you, and mantles such as I like for the summer season. Before he sells these goods, or at least the finest of them, invite the stranger here, for you must remember that the first purchaser will choose the best of everything, without troubling himself about those who come to buy after him, and buy for me three or four of these mantles. In any case whatever you pay, I will repay you many times over.[20]

So much for the literary evidence concerning the economic life of Athens in the fourth and fifth centuries A.D. The archaeological evidence at our disposal supplements, and partially corroborates, this picture of an Athens dependent to a great extent upon importation from foreign quarters. Throughout the fourth century a special type of pottery with stamped ornamentation, now known as Group B ware, was imported from Egypt.[21] Possibly during the first half-of that century pottery now known as Group A ware may have been imported from a district not yet adequately identified—from Italy, from Asia Minor, or from some other part of Greece.[22] From c.350 A.D. through the fifth century A.D.—and possibly longer still—pottery now known as Group C ware was im-

[19] Cf. FitzGerald, *Letters of Synesius*, pp. 125–26.

[20] *Epist.* lii. The rendering in the text is that of FitzGerald, *Letters of Synesius*. A reflection of the renown of Attic shoes is to be seen in Synesius' *Eulogy of Baldness*, where (*Calv. Enc.* section 13, in J. P. Migne, *Patrologia Graeca*, LXVI, 1192) the strong man is said to have leaped more precisely on his bald head than on a pair of Attic slippers. For Attic shoes in Egypt c.200 A.D., see chap. vi, including note 17.

[21] F. O. Waagé, in *Hesperia*, II (1933), 302–3; K. Kübler, in AM, LVI (1931), 80–81; cf. H. Comfort, in RE, Supplementband VII, 1305.

[22] F. O. Waagé, in *Hesperia*, II (1933), 302; cf. H. Comfort, in RE, Supplementband VII, 1305.

ported from Egypt.[23] The list of imported wares is concluded with
the finer examples of Type XXXI lamps, which were brought,
probably from Egypt, in the course of the fifth century.[24] No
wares of any appreciable merit were produced in Athens in Roman
times.[25] Local industry devoted its energies to producing the
cheaper, everyday wares, and to copying some of the finer imported wares.[26] However, we know that some of these wares—
both ordinary local wares and the imitation wares—found somewhat of an export market, for throughout the fourth and the fifth
centuries the Athenian lamp maker enjoyed a near monopoly of
the Corinthian market.[27] Beyond this we have no evidence concerning the condition of Athenian industry in the fourth and fifth
centuries.[28] Mention should, perhaps, be made of the fact that, in
the fifth century, an abortive attempt was made to reopen the
mines at Laurium.[29] Had this attempt succeeded, the story of
Athens might have been greatly changed, for one of the main

[23] F. O. Waagé, in *Hesperia*, II (1933), 303–4; cf. H. Comfort, in RE, Supplementband VII, 1305.

[24] H. A. Thompson, in *Hesperia*, II (1933), 210–12.

[25] F. O. Waagé, in *Hesperia*, II (1933), 304.

[26] The finer examples of Type XXXI lamps were imported; thereupon they were
imitated by local Athenian craftsmen. See H. A. Thompson, in *Hesperia*, II (1933),
211.

[27] Broneer, *Lamps*, p. 27. Lamps of Types XXVIII, XXIX group 2, and XXXI,
all apparently manufactured at Athens, were imported into Corinth (*ibid.*, 113–14).
For Type XXVIII lamps at Athens, see H. A. Thompson, in *Hesperia*, II (1933),
209. Some Type XXXI lamps, as we have observed, were brought to Athens from
Egypt, but it was apparently the Athenian imitations of this type (cf. preceding
note) that were imported into Corinth.

[28] It is probably not permissible to deduce the existence of any considerable
amount of production of glass at Athens at this time from the Jewish or Christian
sepulchral inscription of the glassworker Euphrasius. See IG, III, 3436; cf. Trowbridge, *Philological Studies in Ancient Glass*, pp. 114, 133.

[29] Davies, *Roman Mines*, p. 251; Ardaillon, *Mines du Laurium*, p. 165; Cordella,
Le Laurium, pp. 22–23, 32–33. The finding of fifth-century coins in the mining area
is mentioned by Ardaillon, p. 165. Cordella, pp. 32–33, states that *fourth-century*
[sic] coins were found at Ergastiria (Argastirakia). At this place there is a Byzantine
church, and, apparently, the last active center of metallurgical working was
located there (*Cordella*, pp. 22–23). Davies, p. 251, states that a certain Greek of
Cythnos gave him a "late-empire" lamp from a mine near Sunium (cf. *Man*, 1931,
p. 6), and informed him that Byzantine lamps and medieval coins had been found
there. For very slight indications of metalworking (not all necessarily of classical
date) in other parts of Attica, see Davies, pp. 251–52.

factors—in addition to loss of empire and shifting channels of trade—that made the decline of the city almost inevitable was its extreme poverty in natural resources.

From the meager evidence cited above, and from the fact that new buildings were erected in the Agora region after the middle of the fourth century,[30] one is probably justified in maintaining that during the second half of that century Athens regained some measure of the prosperity which it had enjoyed in the first sixty-five years of the preceding century. In 396 A.D. the city may have suffered somewhat at the hands of the Goths,[31] and the fact that a water mill could be built in the Agora soon after the middle of the fifth century[32] evidences the precipitous decline in the years following 400 A.D. Less than a century later, in 529 A.D., when the Athenian schools of philosophy were closed in pursuance of the terms of Justinian's edict,[33] the last stay of Athenian prosperity disappeared.

It is to be observed that, beginning with the time of Constantine, the main current of Athenian trade followed the trade routes which ran north and south through the eastern part of the Mediterranean, while relations with the West were enjoyed only infrequently.[34]

[30] Cf. *Hesperia*, V (1936), 6 (by T. L. Shear), 90 (by A. W. Parsons), and *passim*.

[31] The miraculous delivery of the city described by Zosimus (V, 5; cf. Hertzberg, *Geschichte Griechenlands*, III, 391–93; Wachsmuth, *Die Stadt Athen*, I, 715–16) is not to be accepted. The evidence (from the excavations in the Agora) of any destruction in the city at this time is not clear. Cf. T. L. Shear, in *Hesperia*, V (1936), 11. In the course of the same invasion Eleusis was destroyed by the Goths, and the celebration of the Mysteries came to an end (Eunapius, 476; cf. Hertzberg, *Geschichte Griechenlands*, III, 394–95). The Athenians were thereupon deprived of another source of income—the expenditures of the visitors during the celebration of the Mysteries—which they had enjoyed in centuries past.

[32] Cf. A. W. Parsons, in *Hesperia*, V (1936), 70–90, especially 87–90.

[33] Geffcken, *Der Ausgang des griechisch-römischen Heidentums*, p. 214; Vasiliev, *Byzantine Empire*, I, 226; Walden, *Universities*, pp. 126–27.

[34] On the basis of a hoard of coins of Constantinian date which was found in Attica, A. R. Bellinger, in *AJA*, XXXII (1928), 496–501, has maintained that in the time of Constantine Athens enjoyed trade relations firstly with cities in the region of the Propontis, secondly (but to a considerably smaller extent) with Thessalonica, and thirdly (but of a comparatively slight volume) with Antioch and Alexandria, while business with Rome and the West was practically nonexistent. (The hoard from which these deductions were made contained the following coins from the mints here indicated: Nicomedia—28, Cyzicus—26, Constantinople—19, Heraclea—13, Thessalonica—11, Alexandria—4, Antioch—4, Rome—1. Thirty-three coins were not identified as to mint.) Bellinger went on to compare the Attic

Under these circumstances it is no occasion for surprise to observe the displacement of classical forms of art by various oriental motifs.[35] But we encroach on the story of the Byzantine period, and to the historian of that period must be left the task of recounting—in greater detail than the meager sketch essayed in the preceding pages—the economic history of Athens in the years that followed the close of the third century A.D.

---

hoard with an Egyptian hoard of Constantinian date (published by J. G. Milne, in *Journal international d'archéologie numismatique*, XVI [1914], 1–27) and with the coins found at Corinth in the excavations of 1925. He came to the conclusion that, either Athens was no longer located on the main routes from Corinth to Egypt (Alexandria) and from Corinth to Constantinople, or the route across the Isthmus of Corinth had been abandoned. Bellinger's conclusions are now supported by the coins which have been found in large numbers in the Agora at Athens. These coins show, moreover, that the same conditions continued throughout the fourth and the fifth centuries. Space is not available here to set down a detailed statement of the mints from which the Agora coins came, but they may be readily observed in the publication of J. P. Shear, "Analytical Table of Coins," *Hesperia*, V (1936), 123–50, especially pp. 133–46. The coins classified in this article were, it is to be observed, those which had been identified and catalogued by July 1, 1935. However, note must be taken of the fact that, while the coins found at Athens suggest that trade with Egypt was on a comparatively small scale, archaeological discoveries seem to indicate that the Athenians were rather good customers of the Egyptians during the fourth and fifth centuries A.D. Explanation of this apparent discrepancy is probably to be found in the fact that after 324 A.D. the government forbade the removal from the country of more than a very limited amount of currency. See Mattingly, *Roman Coins*, p. 257. The small number of coins at Athens from the mint at Alexandria is not, therefore, to be taken as proof of infrequent trade relations between Athens and Egypt.

[35] Cf. D. B. Thompson, in *Hesperia*, II (1933), 191–92, 194; K. Kübler, in AM, LVI (1931), 79–86.

APPENDIX

EVIDENCE ON THE POPULATION OF ATHENS

A. W. GOMME begins his excellent treatise entitled *The Population of Athens in the Fifth and Fourth Centuries B. C.* with a statement to the effect that, despite the importance of the subject and our highly unsatisfactory knowledge concerning it, we are tempted—because of the extreme paucity of satisfactory evidence—to refrain from any attempt to solve the problem of population in ancient times. It is with complete recognition of the fact that the evidence for determining the population of Athens during the period with which this monograph is concerned is even more meager that the following pages are written. Moreover, because of the fact— so adequately demonstrated by Gomme (p. 40, note 4)—that by the third century B.C. families had for a long time lived outside their demes of registration, no attempt will be made to determine the apportionment of population, as to residence, among the various demes. And since the evidence is lacking altogether, no attempt will be made to estimate the number of resident foreigners and slaves.

The latest period for which we have comparatively definite and satisfactory evidence concerning the population of Athens is that of Demetrius of Phalerum, during whose ascendancy at Athens (317–307 B.C.) a census of all the male inhabitants of Attica was taken.[1] Among those registered were 21,000 Athenian citizens, all of them, apparently, men of military age. It is to be observed that this counting was made in one of the most prosperous periods of the city's history, but after a considerable decline in population had ensued owing to the attraction of Athenians to lands opened up in the East by the conquests of Alexander and to various other causes.[2] Subsequent to this census there is very little direct literary or epigraphical testimony concerning the number of inhabitants who resided in Attica. An inscription[3] which is probably to be dated in the time of Augustus records the number of votes cast by members of the Ecclesia—3,461 affirmative, 155 negative—in approving a measure which had come before them, but the relationship of these numbers to the entire citizen population cannot be determined. Finally, statements that may be related to the population of Attica at the time at which they were written are to be found in the works of two authors of the third century A.D. Inasmuch, however, as that century requires consideration apart from other periods,

[1] Ctesicles in Athenaeus, VI, 272c; cf. Ferguson, *Athens*, p. 54; Beloch, *Griechische Geschichte*, III, ii, 405; Beloch, *Bevölkerung*, pp. 4–5, 57–60, 84; Gomme, *Population*, pp. 18–19.

[2] Cf. Gomme, *Population*, p. 19.

[3] IG, II–III², 1035, especially l. 3. For the date, see chap. iv, including notes 152–66. On the basis of the numbers given in this inscription Keil estimates (*Areopag*, p. 88, note 135) that there must have been at least 5,000 citizens at Athens in the second century A.D. Observe the date which he accepts for the inscription.

analysis of these statements may, for the moment, be postponed. But passing notice should be taken of two accounts of the population not of Attica, but of Greece as a whole. Writing in the first half of the second century B.C., the historian Polybius asserted[4] that owing to the prevalence of a low birth rate and a general decrease of population the cities of Greece had become deserted and that even the land had ceased to be productive. We have already had occasion to observe that whatever the condition of the remainder of Greece may have been the historian's sweeping assertion is by no means a correct description of the conditions that obtained at Athens. The second portrayal to be observed is a statement which Plutarch places in the mouth of a character (a certain Ammonius) in one of his dialogues.[5] Ammonius is made to say that in the time when he was speaking—about the end of the first century A.D.—Greece had become so depopulated as a result of former wars and civil strife that only with difficulty could it assemble 3,000 men, the number which Megara alone had formerly sent to Plataea. This statement must, however, be construed as a rhetorical exaggeration of the type that we meet most frequently in the literary accounts that deal with Greece in the imperial period.[6] If the statement is taken to mean that no more than 3,000 men who were fit for military service could be found in all of Greece, no proof at all is required to demonstrate its absurdity.[7] If, on the other hand, Ammonius (i.e., Plutarch) meant to say that all Greece could furnish only 3,000 hoplites—3,000 men who could meet the property qualification of former days—he must still be charged with exaggeration.[8] But this latter description would undoubtedly come nearer the truth, for throughout the period of Roman domination wealth was gradually being concentrated in the hands of fewer and fewer individuals, with the result that the number of citizens able to meet the hoplite census was much smaller than it had been at the time of the Persian Wars.[9] In any event, this portrayal of conditions in Greece possesses no value for the determination of the population of Athens in the first and second centuries A.D.

Direct testimony concerning the number of inhabitants of Attica during the period of Roman domination is, therefore, all but nonexistent. Hence it is not surprising that some of the current estimates of population during this period—or portions of the period—are no more than conjectures based upon general historical considerations. With these conjectures we need not linger. Other estimates are scarcely more felicitous, for they are based upon very inadequate indirect evidence. But no other evidence is available. The most highly favored method of calculation has been that which utilizes the numbers of Athenians recorded in the ephebic lists.[10] But in 1927 Graindor conceived the idea of attempting to deduce the number of Athenian citizens in the time of Augustus from the number of γεννῆται listed in an inscription of the Augustan period which sets forth the names of heads of families—with one exception, in line 22—who belonged to the γένος of the Amy-

[4] XXXVI, xvii.   [5] De defectu orac. 8.

[6] See chap. iv, including notes 1–20.

[7] However, Dessau, Geschichte der römischen Kaiserzeit, II, ii, 549, note 2, is inclined to take Plutarch's statement at its face value.

[8] As suggested by Hertzberg, Geschichte Griechenlands, II, 190–93; cf. Mommsen, Provinces, I, 268, note 1; Larsen, "Roman Greece," pp. 481–82.

[9] Cf. Hertzberg, Geschichte Griechenlands, II, 192–93; Larsen, "Roman Greece," pp. 481–82.   [10] For example, Beloch, Bevölkerung, pp. 70–72, 74.

nandridae.[11] In this inscription[12] the names of 62 individuals are registered, each according to the phyle to which he belonged. The inscription is, however, fragmentary, the names from only three phylae being completely preserved, while those from three other phylae are lacking entirely. But if one takes the average number of names, nine, from the three phylae whose names are completely preserved, and assumes that each of the missing phylae was represented by a like number, it may be assumed that the complete list originally contained 89 (62 + 27) names. If, then, the approximately 70 γένη which are known to have existed in Attica[13] survived in the time of Augustus, one may reckon a population consisting of approximately 6,000 (actually 6,230) individuals who were heads of wealthy families. And this number, Graindor has surmised,[14] must be doubled to arrive at the total number of citizens (at least 12,000 over eighteen years of age). In support of this estimate Graindor refers[15] to the (approximately) 130 ephebes who are registered in the only extant ephebic list of Augustan date.[16]

What may be said concerning these two methods of estimating the population of Attica during the period of Roman domination? Let us consider first the utilization of lists of γεννῆται in this connection. One of the most obvious deficiencies of this method is to be seen in the fact that there are no other satisfactory lists of γεννῆται with which the results obtained for the Augustan period may be checked.[17] A second difficulty is made evident by the fact that, by the beginning of the empire, an individual might belong to more than one γένος.[18] A third—and very important—difficulty is that we possess no evidence whatsoever to justify the assumption that there were still 70 γένη at Athens in the time of Augustus. And, finally, it must be recognized that even granting the determination by Graindor's method of the approximate number of heads of families *with means* there is no evidence to enable us to determine the proportion of well-to-do citizens to the entire citizen population. The relative proportion of well to do and poor must have varied considerably at different times throughout the period of Roman domination, owing to fluctuations of prosperity as well as to the progressive concentration of wealth and the progressive decline of economic vitality. We must conclude that this method is of limited validity; that it may be employed only in conjunction with general historical considerations, and then only to arrive at an estimate of relative population and prosperity during a specific period of the city's history.

[11] Graindor, *Auguste*, pp. 98–99.   [12] IG, II–III², 2338.

[13] C. Lecrivain, in Daremberg-Saglio, II, 859–60.

[14] Graindor, *Hérode*, p. 72, follows this procedure in estimating the population of Attica in the second century A.D., at the time of Herodes Atticus. Although he took this position subsequent to the writing of *Auguste*, pp. 98–99, the reasoning that underlies both statements would indicate that the passages taken together may be considered a complete statement of Graindor's viewpoint. Beloch, *Bevölkerung*, p. 74, assumed that in the second century B.C. the proportion of "propertied" citizens (i.e., those who possessed 2,000 dr.; cf. *ibid.*, p. 70) to "non-propertied" citizens stood at 3:5 or 3:6.   [15] *Auguste*, p. 98.   [16] IG, II–III², 1963.

[17] Two additional lists are extant, one of 161/2 A.D. (*ibid.*, 2339), the other of c.200 A.D. (*ibid.*, 2340), but both are so fragmentary as to render deductions unwarranted.

[18] B. D. Meritt, in *Hesperia*, IX (1940), 94; cf. W. S. Ferguson, in *Hesperia*, VII (1938), 50–51.

What, then, are we to conclude concerning the validity of utilizing the ephebic lists in the determination of the population of Attica during the period with which we are concerned? In the first place, it is important to bear in mind the fact that participation in the ephebic training was changed from a compulsory to a voluntary basis at the end of the fourth century B.C.[19] As a result of this change only those sons were enrolled in the ephebic system whose parents were wealthy or well-to-do citizens, not only able to pay, but also interested in paying, for the training. And even if it be assumed that the sons of all the wealthy participated, it would be impossible, as we have noted above, to determine the relative proportion of these youths to the entire body of Athenian youths. In the second place, after enrollment in the ephebia had been placed upon a voluntary basis, there remained no longer a set age for entering upon the training. Various instances of brothers[20]—certainly all of them were not twin brothers!—enrolled in the same year have been observed in the lists, and it may be that even youths of sixteen were admitted.[21] It is, therefore, absolutely impossible to utilize actuarial computations in determining the proportion of enrolled ephebes to the total population.[22] Third, utilization of data contained in the lists is rendered difficult by the fact that many of them have been preserved in a fragmentary condition, with the result that resort must be taken to estimates of the number of names each originally contained. It becomes readily apparent, therefore, that the population of Attica during the period of Roman domination may not be deduced from the ephebic lists. But the lists are not altogether without value. In utilizing them it will not be valid procedure to draw deductions from the lists of individual years, for in various years crises of a nature unknown to us and certain unexplainable causes seem to have occasioned a reduction in registration. But, if the numbers of ephebes over a period of, say, twenty-five or fifty years be averaged, it may reasonably be concluded that the registration reflects very roughly the prosperity, or lack of prosperity that the city enjoyed during that period. Let us, therefore, set down the ephebic registration between the beginning of the third century B.C. and the end of the second century A.D., and in pursuance of the principle just enunciated, determine the extent to which the indications of prosperity (or lack of prosperity) shown by the numbers of ephebes agree with the deductions that may be drawn from general historical considerations.[23]

[19] Ferguson, *Athens*, pp. 127–28; P. Girard, in Daremberg-Saglio, II, 624; Thalheim, in RE, V, 2738.

[20] U. Köhler, in AM, IV (1879), 333; Thalheim, in RE, V, 2738; P. Girard, in Daremberg-Saglio, II, 624; Graindor, *Chronologie*, p. 17.

[21] A sixteen-year-old boy is represented as an ephebe on duty at the Piraeus in Terence, *Eun.* 290, 693, 824; cf. P. Østbye, *Die Schrift vom Staat der Athener und die attische Ephebie* (Christiana, 1893), p. 30; C. A. Forbes, *Greek Physical Education* (New York, 1929), pp. 152–53.

[22] Possibly a mean age of eighteen for entrance into the ephebia may be assumed. Cf. Graindor, *Chronologie*, p. 18.

[23] I have followed Dinsmoor, *Archon List*, in dating the lists between 267/6 B.C. and 102/1 B.C., and Dinsmoor, *Archons*, in dating those between 98/7 B.C. and 38/7 B.C. In dating the lists between 13/2 B.C. and 190–200 A.D. I have followed Graindor, *Chronologie*, *Album*, *Tibère*, and *Hadrien*—except for one year (c.110), where I have followed J. Kirchner's dating in IG, II–III².

Date	No. of Ephebes	Source
B.C. Early 3d cent.	34[b]	*Hesperia*, IV (1935), 186–88 [i]
267/6	30–40	IG, II–III², 665
248/7	29[c]	681
244/3	23	766
237/6	c.31	787
216/5	c.50 (?)	794 [j]
172/1	56 (?)	*Hesperia*, III (1934), 14–18, No. 17
138/7	58+	FDD, III, ii, 23; SIG, 696D
128/7	107	IG, II–III², 1960; FDD, III, ii, 24[k]
123/2	c.120	1006
119/8	124	1008
117/6	162	1009
107/6	116	1011
106/5	97	FDD, III, ii, 25; SIG, 711F
102/1	102	IG, II–III², 1028
98/7	66+	FDD, III, ii, 26; SIG, 728F, G
90–80 (?)	3[d]	IG, II–III², 1031
80/79	105	1039
c.40	37+	1961
38/7	52 or 53	1043
13/2	130[e]	1963
A.D. 45/6	102 [f]	1969, 1970
41/54	96[g]	1973
84/5–92/3	94	1996
c.100/1	60	2017
c.100/1 and before 111/2	52	2018
c.110[a]	120	2020
112/3	21	2024
116/7	4	2026
142/3	54	2044
145/6	106	2052, 2055
150/1	70	2065
155/6	79+	2050
157/8	133[h]	2067
158/9	106+	2068
164/5	143+	2085
166/7	95	2086
167/8	26 or 27	2094
172/3	80	2097
175/6–177/8	106	2103
181/2–191/2	60–65 (?)	2119
186/7–191/2	76+	2113
192/3	85	2130
190–200	94	2128

[a] According to Kirchner.   [b] Incomplete.   [c] Incomplete.   [d] Fragmentary.
[e] Estimate: 65 in 6 tribes.   [f] Estimate.   [g] Estimate.   [h] Incomplete.   [i] Cf.
Hesperia, II (1933), 411.   [j] Cf. *Harvard Studies in Classical Philology*, XLVIII
(1937), 109.   [k] Cf. *Hesperia*, IV (1935), 71–81.

The following deductions seem to be justified:

1. The ephebic lists would indicate that the third century B.C. was a period of depression; and this deduction is confirmed by general historical considerations.

2. Inasmuch as only one ephebic list of the first half of the second century B.C. is preserved, no conclusion is justified. But, on the basis of general historical considerations, we have seen that this was a period of reviving prosperity.

3. The ephebic lists, supported by general historical considerations, indicate a period of remarkable prosperity beginning at the middle of the second century B.C. and continuing to the time of Sulla. Some confidence seems to have remained even a few years later than Sulla. Note the surprisingly large ephebic registration in 80/79 B.C.

4. The ephebic lists, supported by general historical considerations, indicate a remarkable revival of prosperity in the time of Augustus and a continuation of this prosperity (not supported by general historical considerations) at a somewhat lower level throughout the remainder of the first century A.D. Graindor's view (based on a deduction from the list of γεννῆται) that Athens was comparatively well populated in the time of Augustus is to be accepted, but no estimate of the population is admissible.

5. The ephebic lists, supported by general historical considerations, indicate an increase in prosperity beginning during the reign of Trajan and continuing, with minor fluctuations, throughout the reign of Marcus Aurelius.

6. The ephebic lists, supported by general historical considerations, indicate a moderate decline in prosperity beginning soon after 180 A.D. and continuing to the end of the second century A.D.

It appears, then, that the registration of Athenian ephebes in various years may be taken as rough indications of the degree of prosperity enjoyed by the city; but that greater weight may be attached to their testimony if other evidence is adduced in their support.

Inasmuch as it has recently been held that "the inscriptions show that population and prosperity increased up to the sack of Athens by the Heruli in 267,"[24] it has seemed best to segregate consideration of the question of the population of Athens in the third century A.D. We have already observed[25] that general historical considerations indicate a continuance, with only a slight decline, during the first sixty-seven years of the third century of the prosperity which the city enjoyed during the latter years of the second century. Moreover, the ephebic lists, if interpreted in accordance with the general principles enunciated above, support this conclusion. The Athenians registered in the third-century lists number as follows:[26]

Date (A.D.)	No. of Ephebes	Source (in IG, II–III²)
c.200	70	2191
c.200	76	2193
c.200	61	2199
Beginning of 3d cent. before 212	60c	2207

[24] Larsen, "Roman Greece," p. 492.   [25] See chap. vi.

[26] In dating the lists I have followed Graindor, Chronologie and Album—except for two years in which I adhere to J. Kirchner's dating in IG, II–III².

Date (A.D.)	No. of Ephebes	Source
c.212/3	57+	2208
217/8 or soon after[a]	65[d]	2221
226/7–234/5	92+	2235
230–235[b]	78+	2237
238/9–243/4	229[e]	2239
243/4 or a little later	229[f]	2243
262/3 or 266/7	313[g]	2245

[a] According to Kirchner.   [b] *Ibid.*   [c] Estimate.   [d] Estimate: 42 in 8 tribes.
[e] Includes *mellepheboi.*   [f] Estimate; includes *mellepheboi.*   [g] Includes *mellepheboi.*

Careful note should be taken of the fact that the registration of Athenians in the last three lists includes not only ephebes, but also οἱ περὶ τοῦ Διογενείου, who seem to have been the *mellepheboi.*[27] The latter were young boys who, at about the age of fifteen, as we learn from Censorinus,[28] began to prepare themselves for enrollment in the ephebia. It is very questionable, therefore, whether the registration of boys of normal ephebic age in the last three lists exceeded that of the lists dated in earlier years of the third century. Consequently, even if the ephebic lists were used—as they should not be used—to arrive at an estimate of population, one would find no indication of an increase in population during the third century.

From the fact that the membership of the Boule was increased from 500 to 750 in the third century one might be tempted to conclude that the population of the city had increased. However, the change is first attested, it is to be noted, by an inscription of c.270 A.D.,[29] after the invasion of the Heruli, at a time when general historical considerations indicate a great decline in the city's prosperity. One may, therefore, ask—and with good reason—whether the new arrangement was necessarily inspired by a change in the number of Athenian citizens. It is obvious that not every change in the membership of the Boule is of significance as an indication of a change in population.[30] Certainly no one would seriously contend that the lowering of the membership of this body from 600 to 500 in the time of Hadrian should be construed as indicating a decline in the population of Attica.[31] It is Graindor's belief that the enlargement in membership was brought about by Gallienus in the last years of his reign, and that the emperor was motivated merely by a desire to reform the constitution of Athens, following the precedent set by Hadrian.[32] This deduction is, however, entirely hypothetical.[33] It is much more likely that the very great increase in membership during the third century, at the very time when chaos pervaded the entire Roman world and economic vitality was approaching its lowest ebb, was occasioned by extraordinary influences then at work within Attica. And we need not look far to ascertain one of the causes— perhaps the most important—which was responsible for the change. During this century it became increasingly more difficult to find citizens who were financially

[27] Graindor, in *Musée belge*, XXVI (1922), 225–28.
[28] *De die nat.* 15.   [29] IG, II–III², 3669.
[30] In the time of Cleisthenes and later, under Demetrius Poliorcetes, the change was occasioned by an increase in the number of tribes. Cf. W. Dittenberger, in *Hermes*, IX (1874), 397, note 1; A. Wilhelm, in JOAI, III (1900), 197.
[31] Graindor, *Hadrien*, pp. 19, 83–85.
[32] Graindor, *Marbres*, p. 78.   [33] See chap. vi, note 10.

able, as well as qualified, to hold public office. About a quarter of a century after the enlargement of the Boule we find—the first attested instance under the empire —the archonship being held twice by the same man.[34] Obviously, the restriction upon repeated tenure of the office had been removed. Likewise, it seems reasonable to suppose that the restriction upon membership in the Boule was also relaxed[35] and that, at the same time, the membership was increased in order to counteract, to some degree, concentration of legislative authority in the hands of a more limited number of *bouleutae* whose tenure would extend beyond two years.

Some account must be taken of two statements in the writings of third-century authors to determine whether the approximate population of Attica may be deduced from them. From the writings of the historian Dexippus[36] we learn that the force with which he harried the Heruli in 267 A.D. consisted of 2,000 men. The second statement, which appears in the writings of Porphyry of Tyre,[37] who resided at Athens in the middle of the third century,[38] is, closely paraphrased, to the effect that if it should be found that 3,000 men resided at Athens, we would say that they were few in number; but if 300 should reside in a country village, we would say they were numerous—and yet the number of men at Athens would be many times greater. As regards the first of these statements, it may be assumed that the force commanded by Dexippus consisted of men between the ages of eighteen and fifty-nine. But the fact that this body of men was hastily assembled makes it apparent that not all male residents of Attica between these ages were included. Consequently, the relationship of Dexippus' 2,000 men to the entire population of Attica (or of Athens alone) may not be calculated with the aid of actuarial statistics. Likewise, the figure contained in Porphyry's statement is difficult—indeed, impossible—to interpret. The distinctly hypothetical nature of the statement makes it highly improbable that the philosopher was even pretending to set forth an approximation of the city's population. (It is to be borne in mind that he is speaking of the city alone, not of Attica as a whole.) But if it be insisted that the statement represents a reasonably close estimate, how are we to interpret ἄνθρωποι? It is impossible to think that the word includes all inhabitants, men, women, and children, citizens and foreigners alike. It is also unthinkable that it includes all Athenian men, women, and children, because 3,000 individuals (children included) could not have accounted for the economic activity that is attested for the first

[34] See the inscription recently found in the Agora and published by J. H. Oliver, in *Hesperia*, II (1933), 505–11.

[35] U. Kahrstedt, *Untersuchungen zur Magistratur in Athen* (Stuttgart, 1936), pp. 135–37, maintains that in the sixth century B.C. there could have been no regulation prohibiting an individual from serving for more than two years in the Boule. In the third century A.D. a return to the earlier practice may well have been made. In any event, the change seems to have been a temporary expedient, for we find the Boule consisting of 300 members in the fourth century A.D. Cf. IG, II–III², 3716, 4222.

[36] Dexippus in Jacoby, *Fragmente*, No. 100, frag. 28 (cf. FHG, III, 680, frag. 21).

[37] *In categ.* p. 109, ll. 17–21 (ed. A. Busse): ἐν μὲν γὰρ ταῖς 'Αθήναις εἰ τύχοι τρισχιλίων ὄντων ἀνθρώπων φαμὲν ὀλίγους εἶναι, ἐν δὲ τῇ κώμῃ κἂν ὦσιν τριακόσιοι, λέγομεν πολλοί εἰσιν, καίτοι πολλαπλασίων ὄντων 'Αθήναζε.

[38] W. von Christ and W. Schmid, *Geschichte der griechischen Litteratur* (6th ed., by O. Stählin, Munich, 1912–24), II, ii, 853.

sixty-seven years of the third century by archaeological discoveries.[39] It becomes apparent, therefore, that neither the statement of Dexippus nor that of Porphyry may be utilized in computing the population of Attica during the third century A.D.

Whatever conclusions are to be formed concerning the population of Attica during the period of Roman domination must be of a very general nature. The following assertions may be ventured. Following the conquest of the East by Alexander, Athens, along with the remainder of Greece, experienced a decline in population which probably continued throughout the third century B.C. With reviving prosperity in the second century B.C. came a moderate increase, brought about largely by the rearing of larger families. During the troubled years between 86 B.C. and the accession of Augustus a moderate reaction set in, to be reversed at the end of the civil wars. Throughout the first and the second centuries A.D. the population probably remained comparatively stable, with a slight recession in the first sixty-seven years of the third century. The great decline in prosperity that followed the invasion of the Heruli may have been accompanied—the evidence is very insecure —by a severe decline in population.

[39] See chap. vi. Even if Porphyry's 3,000 ἄνθρωποι be construed as men above the age of eighteen—not a very likely interpretation—the total population of the city would not have amounted to more than 12,000. See the assemblage of actuarial statistics and the discussion by Gomme, *Population*, pp. 75–79. If a like number be allowed for the countryside, the total population would amount to 24,000.

BIBLIOGRAPHY

No ATTEMPT has been made to give a complete bibliography of the subject treated in this book. The following citations are set down for the convenience of the reader and for the purpose of relieving the notes of the encumbrance of frequent repetition of bibliographical data.

Abbott, F. F., and A. C. Johnson. Municipal Administration in the Roman Empire. Princeton, 1926.

Anatolian Studies Presented to William Hepburn Buckler. Manchester, 1939. Publications of the University of Manchester, No. CCLXV.

Anatolian Studies Presented to Sir William Mitchell Ramsay. Manchester, 1923.

Ardaillon, E. Les Mines du Laurium dans l'antiquité. Paris, 1892. Bibliothèque des Écoles françaises d'Athènes et de Rome, LXXVII.

Arnim, H. von. Leben und Werke des Dio von Prusa. Berlin, 1898.

Athenian Studies Presented to William Scott Ferguson. Cambridge, Mass., 1940. Harvard Studies in Classical Philology, Supplementary Volume I.

Aymard, A. Les Premiers Rapports de Rome et de la Confédération achaienne (198–189 avant J.-C.). Bordeaux, 1938.

Beazley, J. D., and B. Ashmole. Greek Sculpture and Painting. Cambridge, 1932.

Beloch, K. J. Die Bevölkerung der griechisch-römischen Welt. Leipzig, 1886.

——— Griechische Geschichte. 2d ed., 1912–27. Volumes I–II, Strassburg; III–IV, Berlin and Leipzig.

Bieber, M. Die Denkmäler zum Theaterwesen im Altertum. Berlin and Leipzig, 1920.

——— The History of the Greek and Roman Theater. Princeton, 1939.

Billeter, G. Geschichte des Zinsfusses im griechisch-römischen Altertum bis auf Justinian. Leipzig, 1898.

Boethius, A. Die Pythaïs: Studien zur Geschichte der Verbindungen zwischen Athen und Delphi. Uppsala, 1918. Dissertation.

Broneer, O. The Odeum. Cambridge, Mass., 1932. Corinth: Results of Excavations Conducted by the American School of Classical Studies at Athens, Volume X.

——— Terracotta Lamps. Cambridge, Mass., 1930. Corinth: Results of Excavations Conducted by the American School of Classical Studies at Athens, Volume IV, Part II.

Broughton, T. R. S. "Roman Asia Minor," in An Economic Survey of Ancient Rome, edited by Tenney Frank; IV, 499–916, 936–50. Baltimore, 1938.

Brückner, A. Der Friedhof am Eridanos bei der Hagia Triada zu Athen. Berlin, 1909.

Bruzza, L. "Iscrizioni dei marmi grezzi," Annali dell' Instituto di corrispondenza archeologica, Rome, 1870, pp. 106–204.

Bulle, H. Untersuchungen an griechischen Theatern. Munich, 1928. Abhandlungen der bayerischen Akademie der Wissenschaften, philosophisch-philologisch-historische Klasse, XXXIII.

Bursian, C.   Geographie von Griechenland. Leipzig, 1862–72.

Caley, E. R.   The Composition of Ancient Greek Bronze Coins. Philadelphia, 1939. Memoirs of the American Philosophical Society, XI.

Charlesworth, M. P.   Trade Routes and Commerce of the Roman Empire. 2d ed., Cambridge, 1926.

Clerc, M.   Les Métèques athéniens. Paris, 1893. Bibliothèque des Écoles françaises d'Athènes et de Rome, LXIV.

Colin, G.   Le Culte d'Apollon pythien à Athènes. Paris, 1905.

Collignon, M.   Histoire de la sculpture grecque. Paris, 1892–97.

Conze, A.   Die attischen Grabreliefs, herausgegeben im Auftrage der kaiserlichen Akademie der Wissenschaften zu Wien. Berlin, 1893–1922.

Cordella, A.   Le Laurium. Marseilles, 1871.

Courby, F.   Les Vases grecs à reliefs. Paris, 1922. Bibliothèque des Écoles françaises d'Athènes et de Rome, CXXV.

Cuq, E.   Manuel des institutions juridiques des Romains. 2d ed., Paris, 1928.

Curtius, E.   Die Stadtgeschichte von Athen. Berlin, 1891.

Curtius, E., and J. A. Kaupert.   Karten von Attika. Berlin, 1904.

Dareste, R., B. Haussoulier, and T. Reinach.   Recueil des inscriptions juridiques grecques. Paris, 1891.

Daux, G.   Delphes au IIe et au Ier siècle depuis l'abaissement de l'Étolie jusqu'à la paix romaine, 191–31 av. J.-C. Paris, 1936. Bibliothèque des Écoles françaises d'Athènes et de Rome, CXL.

Davies, O.   Roman Mines in Europe. Oxford, 1935.

De Ruggiero, E.   Dizionario epigrafico di antichità romane. Rome, 1895–.

Dessau, H.   Geschichte der römischen Kaiserzeit. Berlin, 1924–30.

Deubner, L.   Attische Feste. Berlin, 1932.

Dickins, G.   Hellenistic Sculpture. Oxford, 1920.

Dinsmoor, W. B.   The Athenian Archon List in the Light of Recent Discoveries. New York, 1939.

——— The Archons of Athens in the Hellenistic Age. Cambridge, Mass., 1931.

Dörpfeld, W., and E. Reisch.   Das griechische Theater. Athens, 1896.

Dubois, C.   Étude sur l'administration et l'exploitation des carrières (marbres, porphyre, granit, etc.) dans le monde romain. Paris, 1908.

Durrbach, F.   Choix d'inscriptions de Délos; Textes historiques, Volume I, Fascicles 1–2. Paris, 1921–22.

Ferguson, W. S.   Hellenistic Athens. London, 1911.

——— Athenian Tribal Cycles in the Hellenistic Age. Cambridge, Mass., 1932.

——— "The Priests of Asclepius," University of California Publications in Classical Philology, I (1906), 131–73. Reprinted 1907.

Fiechter, E. R.   Das Dionysos-theater in Athen. Stuttgart, 1935–36. Sächsische Forschungsinstitute in Leipzig. Forschungsinstitut für klassische Philologie und Archäologie. Antike griechische Theaterbauten, Hefte 5–7.

FitzGerald, A.   The Letters of Synesius of Cyrene Translated into English with Introduction and Notes. Oxford, 1926.

Frank, T.   An Economic History of Rome. 2d ed., Baltimore, 1927.

——— ed., An Economic Survey of Ancient Rome. Baltimore, 1933–40.

NOTE: Volume I (1933) contains "Rome and Italy of the Republic" and Volume V (1940) "Rome and Italy of the Empire," both by Tenney Frank.

Frazer, J. G. Pausanias's Description of Greece. 2d ed., London, 1913.

Fuhrmann, H. Philoxenos von Eretria. Göttingen, 1931.

Gardiner, E. N. Greek Athletic Sports and Festivals. London, 1910.

———— Olympia. Oxford, 1925.

Geffcken, J. Der Ausgang des griechisch-römischen Heidentums. Heidelberg, 1920.

Glotz, G. Ancient Greece at Work. London, 1926. Translation from the French Le Travail dans la Grèce ancienne, Paris, 1920.

Gomme, A. W. The Population of Athens in the Fifth and Fourth Centuries B.C. Oxford, 1933. Glasgow University Publications, XXVIII.

Grace, V. "Stamped Amphora Handles Found in 1931–1932," Hesperia, III (1934), 197–310.

Graindor, P. Album d'inscriptions attiques d'époque impériale. 1924. Recueil de travaux publiés par la Faculté de Philosophie et Lettres de l'Université de Gand, LIII–LIV.

———— Athènes sous Auguste. 1927. Recueil de travaux publiés par la Faculté des Lettres de l'Université Égyptienne, I.

———— Chronologie des archontes athéniens sous l'empire. 1922. Mémoires de l'Académie royale de Belgique, Classe des lettres des sciences morales et politiques, deuxième série, VIII.

———— Athènes sous Hadrien. Cairo, 1934.

———— Un Milliardaire antique, Hérode Atticus et sa famille. 1930. Recueil de travaux publiés par la Faculté des Lettres de l'Université Égyptienne, V.

———— Marbres et textes antiques d'époque impériale. 1922. Recueil de travaux publiés par la Faculté de Philosophie et Lettres de l'Université de Gand, L.

———— Histoire de l'île de Skyros jusqu'en 1538. 1906. Bibliothèque de la Faculté de Philosophie et Lettres de l'Université de Liége, XVII.

———— Athènes de Tibère à Trajan. 1931. Recueil de travaux publiés par la Faculté des Lettres de l'Université Égyptienne, VIII.

Grant, C. P. The Syrian Desert. New York, 1938.

Griffith, G. T. The Mercenaries of the Hellenistic World. Cambridge, 1935.

Guiraud, P. La Propriété foncière en Grèce jusqu'à la conquête romaine. Paris 1893.

Gurlitt, W. Über Pausanias. Graz, 1890.

Hatzfeld, J. Les Trafiquants italiens dans l'orient hellénique. Paris, 1919. Bibliothèque des Écoles françaises d'Athènes et de Rome, CXV.

Head, B. V. Historia Numorum. 2d ed., Oxford, 1911.

Heichelheim, F. M. Die auswärtige Bevölkerung im Ptolemäerreich. 1925. Klio, Beiheft XVIII = Neue Folge, Beiheft V.

———— "Roman Syria" in An Economic Survey of Ancient Rome, edited by Tenney Frank; IV, 121–257, 927–29. Baltimore, 1938.

———— Wirtschaftliche Schwankungen der Zeit von Alexander bis Augustus. Jena, 1930. Beiträge zur Erforschung der wirtschaftliche Wechsellagen, Aufschwung, Krise, Stockung. Heft 3.

———— Wirtschaftsgeschichte des Altertums vom Palaiolithikum bis zur Völkerwanderung der Germanen, Slaven, und Araber. Leiden, 1938.

284 BIBLIOGRAPHY

Hermann, K. F. Lehrbuch der griechischen Staatsaltertümer. Sixth edition by
V. Thumser, Freiburg, 1889.
Hertzberg, G. F. Die Geschichte Griechenlands unter der Herrschaft der Römer.
Halle, 1866–75.
Hörmann, H. Die inneren Propylaeen von Eleusis. Berlin, 1932.
Jacoby, F. Die Fragmente der griechischen Historiker. Volumes I–II, Berlin,
1925–30; III, Leyden, 1940.
Jardé, A. Les Céréales dans l'antiquité grecque. Paris, 1925. Bibliothèque des
Écoles françaises d'Athènes et de Rome, CXXX.
Judeich, W. Topographie von Athen. 2d ed., Munich, 1931.
Jullian, C. Histoire de la Gaule. Paris, 1908–26.
Keil, B. Beiträge zur Geschichte des Areopags. 1919. Berichte über die Ver-
handlungen der sächsischen Akademie der Wissenschaften zu Leipzig, philolo-
gisch-historische Klasse, LXXI.
Kisa, A. Das Glas im Altertume. Leipzig, 1908.
Klee, T. Zur Geschichte der gymnischen Agone an griechischen Festen.
Leipzig and Berlin, 1918.
Kolbe, W. Die attischen Archonten. 1908. Abhandlungen der Gesellschaft der
Wissenschaften zu Göttingen, philologisch-historische Klasse, Neue Folge, X.
Kortenbeutel, H. Der ägyptische Süd- und Osthandel in der Politik der Ptolemäer
und römischen Kaiser. Berlin, 1931. Dissertation.
Kuenzi, A. ΕΠΙΔΟΣΙΣ, Sammlung freiwilliger Beiträge zu Zeiten der Not in
Athen. Bern, 1923. Dissertation.
Laidlaw, W. A. A History of Delos. Oxford, 1933.
Lamb, W. Greek and Roman Bronzes. New York, 1929.
Lapalus, E. L'Agora des Italiens. Paris, 1939. Exploration archéologique de
Délos, XIX.
Larsen, J. A. O. "Roman Greece" in An Economic Survey of Ancient Rome,
edited by Tenney Frank; IV, 259–498, 930–35. Baltimore, 1938.
Laum, B. Stiftungen in der griechischen und römischen Antike. Leipzig and
Berlin, 1914.
Lawrence, A. W. Later Greek Sculpture and Its Influence on East and West.
New York, 1927.
Lehmann-Hartleben, K. Die antiken Hafenanlagen des Mittelmeeres. 1923. Klio,
Beiheft XIV.
Leider, E. Der Handel von Alexandria. Hamburg, 1933. Dissertation.
Lewis, N. L'Industrie du papyrus dans l'Égypte gréco-romaine. Paris, 1934.
Dissertation.
Lippold, G. Kopien und Umbildungen griechischer Statuen. Munich, 1923.
Loewy, E. Inschriften griechischer Bildhauer. Leipzig, 1885.
——— Neuattische Kunst. Leipzig, 1922.
Mattingly, H. Roman Coins from the Earliest Times to the Fall of the Western
Empire. London, 1928.
Mattingly, H., and L. Sydenham. The Roman Imperial Coinage. London, 1923–
38.
Mélanges Cagnat. Paris, 1912.
Mélanges Gustave Glotz. Paris, 1932.
Milchhoefer, A. Karten von Attika, Erläutender Text, Hefte VII–VIII. Berlin,
1895.

Minns, E. H.   Scythians and Greeks. Cambridge, 1913.

Mommsen, A.   Feste der Stadt Athen. Leipzig, 1898.

Mommsen, T.   The Provinces of the Roman Empire from Caesar to Diocletian. 2d ed., London, 1909. English translation by W. P. Dickson.

Mühsam, A.   Die attischen Grabreliefs in römischer Zeit auf Grund der Ausgabe der Akademie der Wissenschaften zu Wien: Alexander Conze, "Die attischen Grabreliefs," Band IV, Kunstgeschichtlich bearbeitet. Berlin, 1936. Dissertation.

Müller, C. O.   Geographi Graeci minores. Paris, 1855–61.

Niese, B.   Geschichte der griechischen und makedonischen Staaten. Gotha, 1893–1903.

Noe, S. P.   A Bibliography of Greek Coin Hoards. 2d ed., New York, 1937. Numismatic Notes and Monographs, No. 78.

Olympia: die Ergebnisse der von dem deutschen Reich veranstalteten Ausgrabung, edited by E. Curtius and F. Adler. Berlin, 1890–97.

Ormerod, H. A.   Piracy in the Ancient World. Liverpool and London, 1924.

Pfuhl, E.   Malerei und Zeichnung der Griechen. Munich, 1923.

Picard, C.   La Sculpture antique de Phidias a l'ère byzantine. Paris, 1926.

Pritchett, W. K., and B. D. Meritt.   The Chronology of Hellenistic Athens. Cambridge, Mass., 1940.

Reinmuth, O. W.   The Foreigners in the Athenian Ephebia. Lincoln, 1929. University of Nebraska Studies in Language, Literature, and Criticism, No. 9.

Robert, L.   Études anatoliennes. Paris, 1937. Études orientales publiés par l'Institut français d'Archéologie de Stamboul, V.

Roberts, E. S., and E. A. Gardner.   An Introduction to Greek Epigraphy, Part II, The Inscriptions of Attica. Cambridge, 1905.

Robinson, D. M.   Ancient Sinope. Baltimore, 1906. Dissertation.

Röhlig, J.   Der Handel von Milet. Hamburg, 1933. Dissertation.

Rostovtzeff, M.   Caravan Cities. Oxford, 1932.

——— Iranians and Greeks in South Russia. Oxford, 1921.

——— Studien zur Geschichte des römischen Kolonates. Berlin, 1910. Archiv für Papyrusforschung, Beiheft I.

——— The Social and Economic History of the Hellenistic World. To appear under the imprint of the Oxford University Press, Oxford.

——— The Social and Economic History of the Roman Empire. Oxford, 1926. German edition, Leipzig, 1930. Italian edition, Florence, 1933.

Roussel, P.   Délos, colonie athénienne. Paris, 1916.

Schaal, H.   Vom Tauschhandel zum Welthandel. Leipzig and Berlin, 1931.

Segrè, A.   Metrologia e circolazione monetario degli antichi. Bologna, 1928.

Seltman, C.   Greek Coins. London, 1933.

Sundwall, J.   Untersuchungen über die attischen Münzen des neueren Stiles. Helsingfors. Öfversigt af Finska Vetenskaps-Societetens Förhandlingar, Volume XLIX, 1906–7, No. 9 [referred to as I]; Volume L, 1907–8, No. I [referred to as II].

Svoronos, J. N.   Les Monnaies d'Athènes. Munich, 1923–26.

Tarn, W. W.   Hellenistic Civilization. 2d ed., London, 1930.

Thompson, H. A.   The Tholos of Athens and its Predecessors. 1940. *Hesperia,* Supplement IV.

——— "Two Centuries of Hellenistic Pottery," *Hesperia,* III (1934), 311–480.

Tod, M. N., and A. J. B. Wace. Catalogue of the Sparta Museum. Oxford, 1906.

Trowbridge, M. L. Philological Studies in Ancient Glass. Urbana, 1928. University of Illinois Studies in Language and Literature, XIII.

Vasiliev, A. A. History of the Byzantine Empire. Madison, 1928–29. University of Wisconsin Studies in the Social Sciences and History, Nos. 13–14.

Wachsmuth, C. Die Stadt Athen im Alterthum. Leipzig, 1874–90.

Walden, J. W. H. The Universities of Ancient Greece. New York, 1910.

Westermann, W. L. "Sklaverei," RE, Supplementband VI, cols. 894–1068. 1935.

Wilcken, U. Alexander the Great. London, 1932. English translation by G. C. Richards. German edition, Leipzig, 1931.

Wilhelm, A. Beiträge zur griechischen Inschriftenkunde. Vienna, 1909. Sonderschriften des oesterreichischen archäologischen Instituts.

Ziebarth, E. Beiträge zur Geschichte des Seeraubs und Seehandels im alten Griechenland. Hamburg, 1929.

INDEX

GREEK HISTORY

AN ARNO PRESS COLLECTION

Aeschinis. **Aeschinis Orationes.** E Codicibus Partim Nunc Primum Excussis, Edidit Scholia ex Parte Inedita, Adiecit Ferdinandus Schultz. 1865.

Athenian Studies; Presented to William Scott Ferguson (*Harvard Studies in Classical Philology,* Supplement Vol. I). 1940.

Austin, R[eginald] P. **The Stoichedon Style in Greek Inscriptions.** 1938.

Berve, Helmut. **Das Alexanderreich:** Auf Prosopographischer **Grundlage.** Ersterband: Darstellung; Zweiterband: Prosopoghaphie. 1926. 2 volumes in one.

Croiset, Maurice. **Aristophanes and the Political Parties at Athens.** Translated by James Loeb. 1909.

Day, John. **An Economic History of Athens Under Roman Domination.** 1942.

Demosthenes. **Demosthenes,** Volumina VIII et IX: Scholia Graeca ex Codicibus Aucta et Emendata, ex recensione Gulielmi Dindorfii. 2 volumes. 1851.

Ehrenberg, Victor. **Aspects of the Ancient World:** Essays and Reviews. 1946.

Finley, Moses I. **Studies in Land and Credit in Ancient Athens, 500-200 B.C.:** The Horos Inscriptions. 1952.

Glotz, Gustave. **La Solidarité de la Famille dans le Droit Criminel en Grèce.** 1904.

Graindor, Paul, **Athènes Sous Hadrien.** 1934.

Grosmann, Gustav. **Politische Schlagwörter aus der Zeit des Peloponnesischen Krieges.** 1950.

Henderson, Bernard W. **The Great War Between Athens and Sparta.** 1927.

Herodotus. **Herodotus: The Fourth, Fifth, and Sixth Books.** With Introduction, Notes, Appendices, Indices, Maps by Reginald Walter Macan. 1895. 2 volumes in one.

Herodotus. **Herodotus: The Seventh, Eighth, and Ninth Books.** With Introduction, Text, Apparatus, Commentary, Appendices, Indices, Maps by Reginald Walter Macan. 1908. 3 volumes in two.

Jacoby, Felix. **Apollodors Chronik.** Eine Sammlung der Fragmente (*Philologische Untersuchungen,* Herausgegeben von A. Kiessling und U. v. Wilamowitz-Moellendorff. Sechzehntes Heft). 1902.

Jacoby, Felix. **Atthis:** The Local Chronicles of Ancient Athens. 1949.

Ledl, Artur. **Studien zur Alteren Athenischen Verfassungsgeschichte.** 1914.

Lesky, Albin. **Thalatta:** Der Weg der Griechen Zum Meer. 1947.

Ollier, Francois. **Le Mirage Spartiate.** Etude sur l'idéalisation de Sparte dans l'antiquité Greque de l'origine Jusqu'aux Cyniques and Etude sur l'idéalisation de Sparte dans l'antiquité Greque du Début de l'école Cynique Jusqu'à la Fin de la Cité. 1933/1934. 2 volumes in one.

Ryffel, Heinrich. ΜΕΤΑΒΟΛΗ ΠΟΛΙΤΕΙΩΝ Der Wandel der Staatsverfassungen (*Noctes Romanae.* Forschungen Uber die Kultur der Antike, Herausgegeben von Walter Wili, #2). 1949.

Thucydides. **Scholia in Thucydidem:** Ad Optimos Codices Collata, edidit Carolus Hude. 1927.

Toepffer, Iohannes. **Attische Genealogie.** 1889.

Tscherikower, V. **Die Hellenistischen Städtegründungen von Alexander dem Grossen bis auf die Römerzeit** (*Philologus,* Zeitschrift fur das Klassische Alterum, Herausgegeben von Albert Rehm. Supplementband XIX, Heft 1). 1927.

West, Allen Brown. **The History of the Chalcidic League** (*Bulletin of the University of Wisconsin,* No. 969, History Series, Vol. 4, No. 2). 1918.

Woodhouse, William J. **Aetolia:** Its Geography, Topography, and Antiquities. 1897.

Wüst, Fritz R. **Philipp II. von Makedonien und Griechenland in den Jahren von 346 bis 338** (*Münchener Historische Abhandlungen.* Erste Reihe: Allgemeine und Politische Geschichte, Herausgegeben von H. Günter, A. O. Meyer und K. A. v. Müller. 14, Heft). 1938.